BOYS over FLOWERS

Hana Yori Dango

4

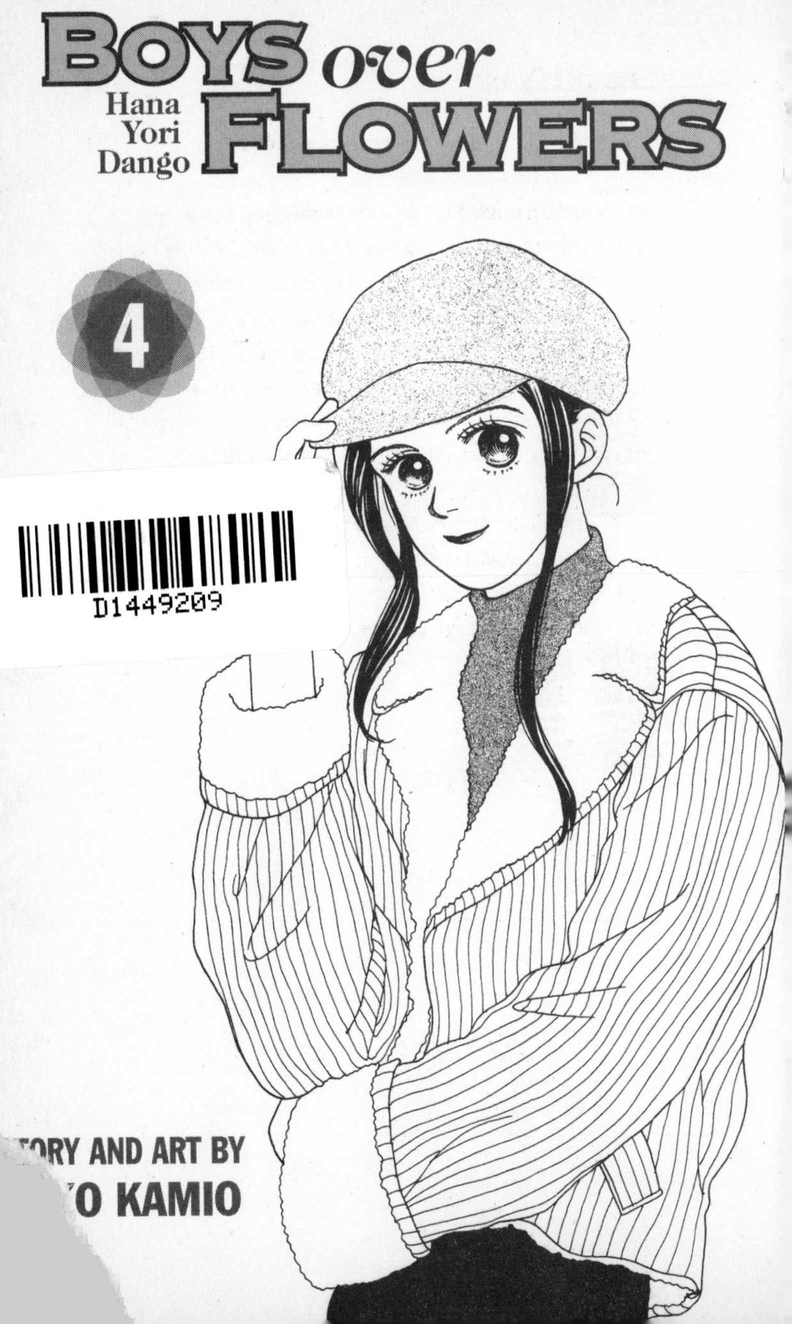

ORY AND ART BY

O KAMIO

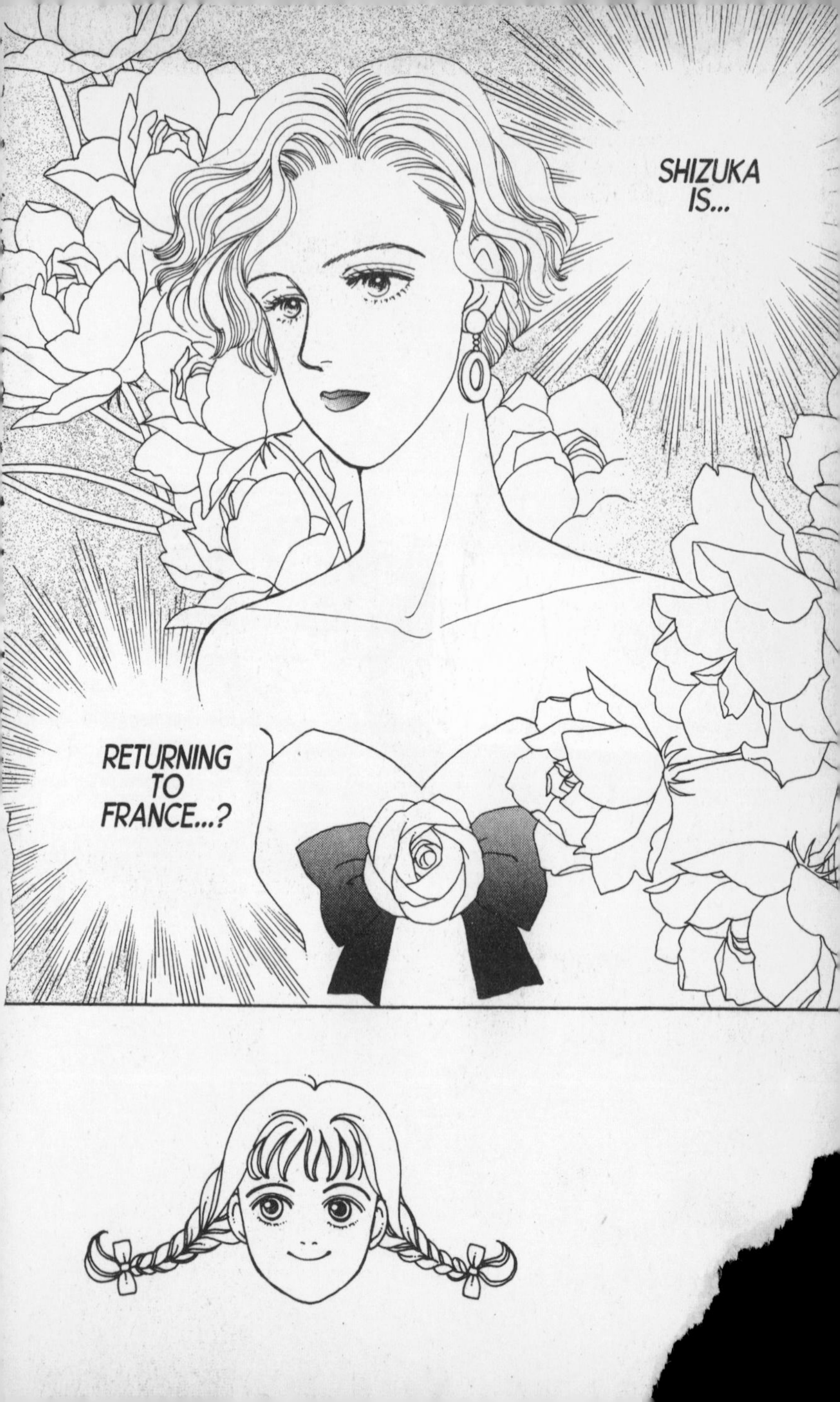
SHIZUKA IS...
RETURNING TO FRANCE...?

Boys over Flowers
Hana Yori Dango
Vol. #4
Shōjo Edition

Story and Art by
Yoko Kamio

English Adaptation by
Gerard Jones

Translator/JN Productions
Touch-up & Lettering/Stephen Dutro
Cover Design/Yuki Ameda
Graphics & Design/Yuki Ameda
Editor/Ian Robertson

Managing Editor/Annette Roman
Editor in Chief/William Flanagan
Production Manager/Noboru Watanabe
Sr. Director of Licensing & Acquisitions/Rika Inouye
Vice President Marketing/Liza Coppola
Sr. Vice President of Editorial/Hyoe Narita
Publisher/Seiji Horibuchi

Printed in Canada.

Published by VIZ, LLC
P.O. Box 77010
San Francisco, CA 94107

Shōjo Edition
10 9 8 7 6 5 4 3 2 1
First printing, January 2004

www.viz.com

store.viz.com

Story thus far

Tsukushi's life at Eitoku seems to get more turbulent all the time.

Tsukushi continues to fight back against the F4 and protect Kazuya, an old friend, who has also been given the infamous "red tag." Rui's old flame, Shizuka, returns from France. It seems almost impossible to compete with this perfect girl. Tsukushi joins Kazuya and his family for summer vacaction at their villa in Atami. Friction erupts between Kazuya and Domyoji after Tsukushi and Domyoji's kiss at the end of volume two. Even more juicy tension develops between Shizuka and Rui, but Tsukasa interrupts. Tsukushi overhears Rui telling Shizuka what he thinks of Tsukushi. Domyoji begins spreading rumors that Tsukushi is in love with him. He soon finds out that she is in love with Rui and he goes on a rampage. His rampage extends to an attack on Tsukushi herself. At her own birthday party Shizuka reveals her plan to forego her inheritance and leave Japan forever. Could this open the door for Tsukushi to be with Rui?!

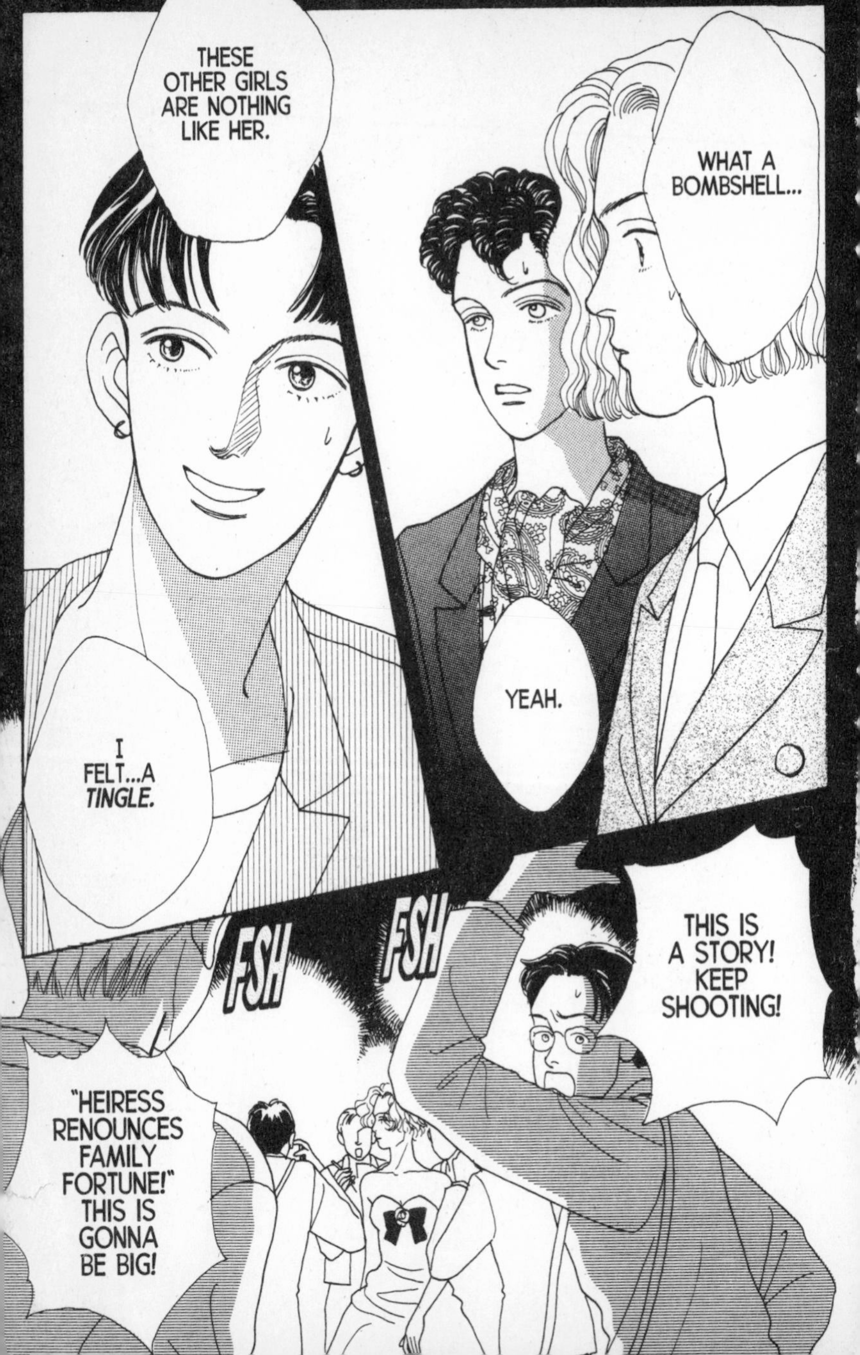
WHAT A BOMBSHELL...
YEAH.
THESE OTHER GIRLS ARE NOTHING LIKE HER.
I FELT...A *TINGLE.*
THIS IS A STORY! KEEP SHOOTING!
FSH
FSH
"HEIRESS RENOUNCES FAMILY FORTUNE!" THIS IS GONNA BE BIG!

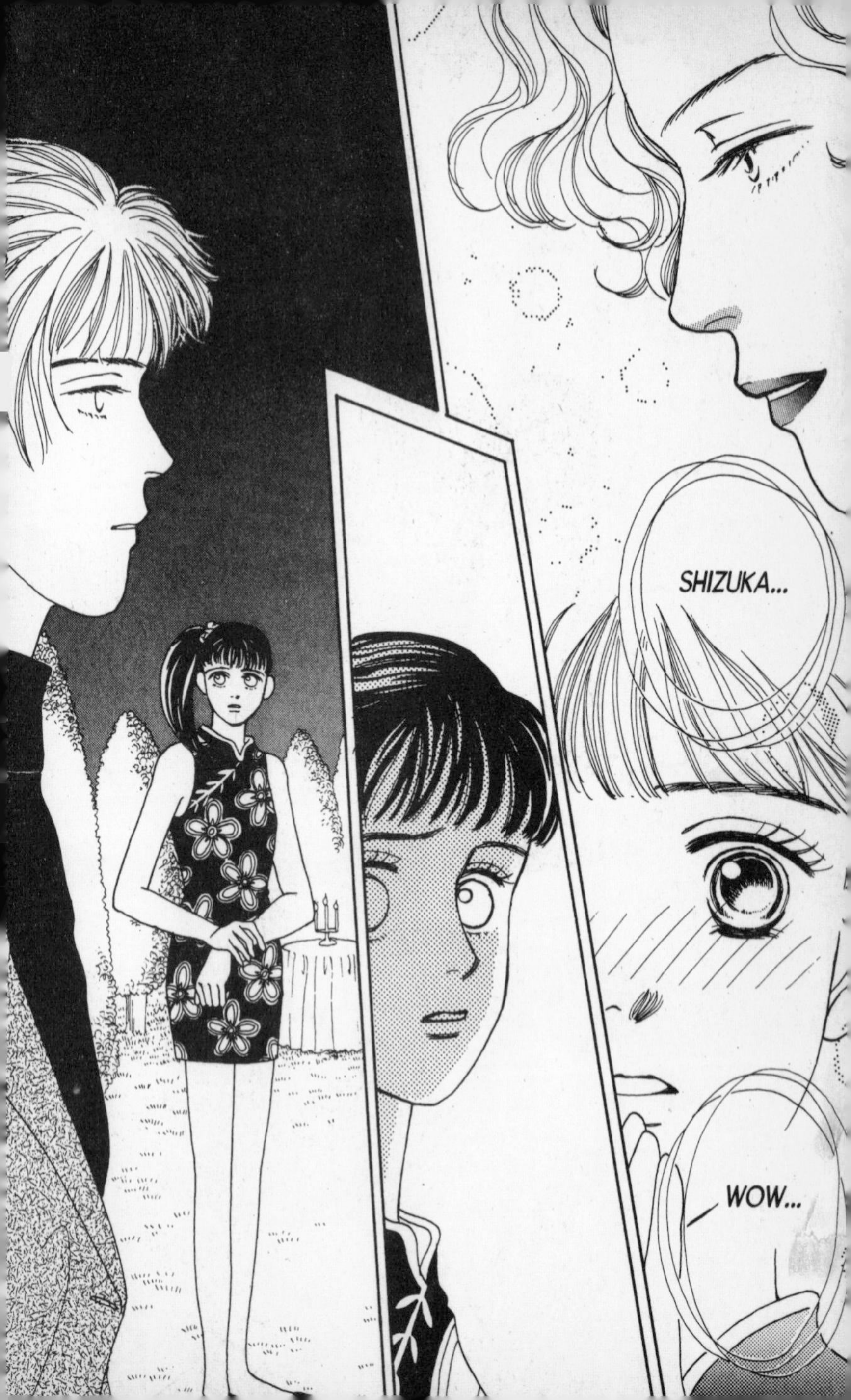
SHIZUKA...
WOW...

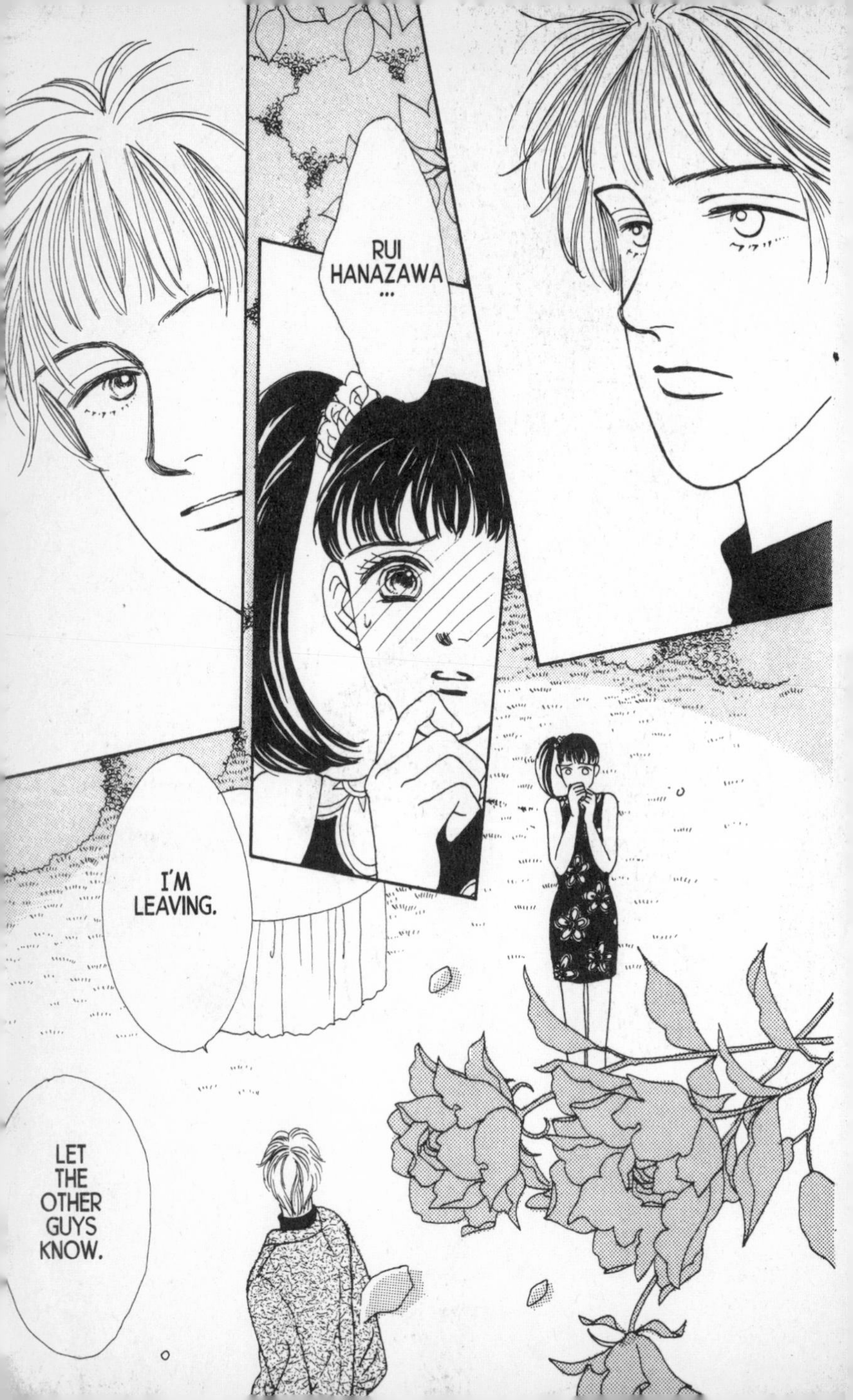
RUI HANAZAWA ...
I'M LEAVING.
LET THE OTHER GUYS KNOW.

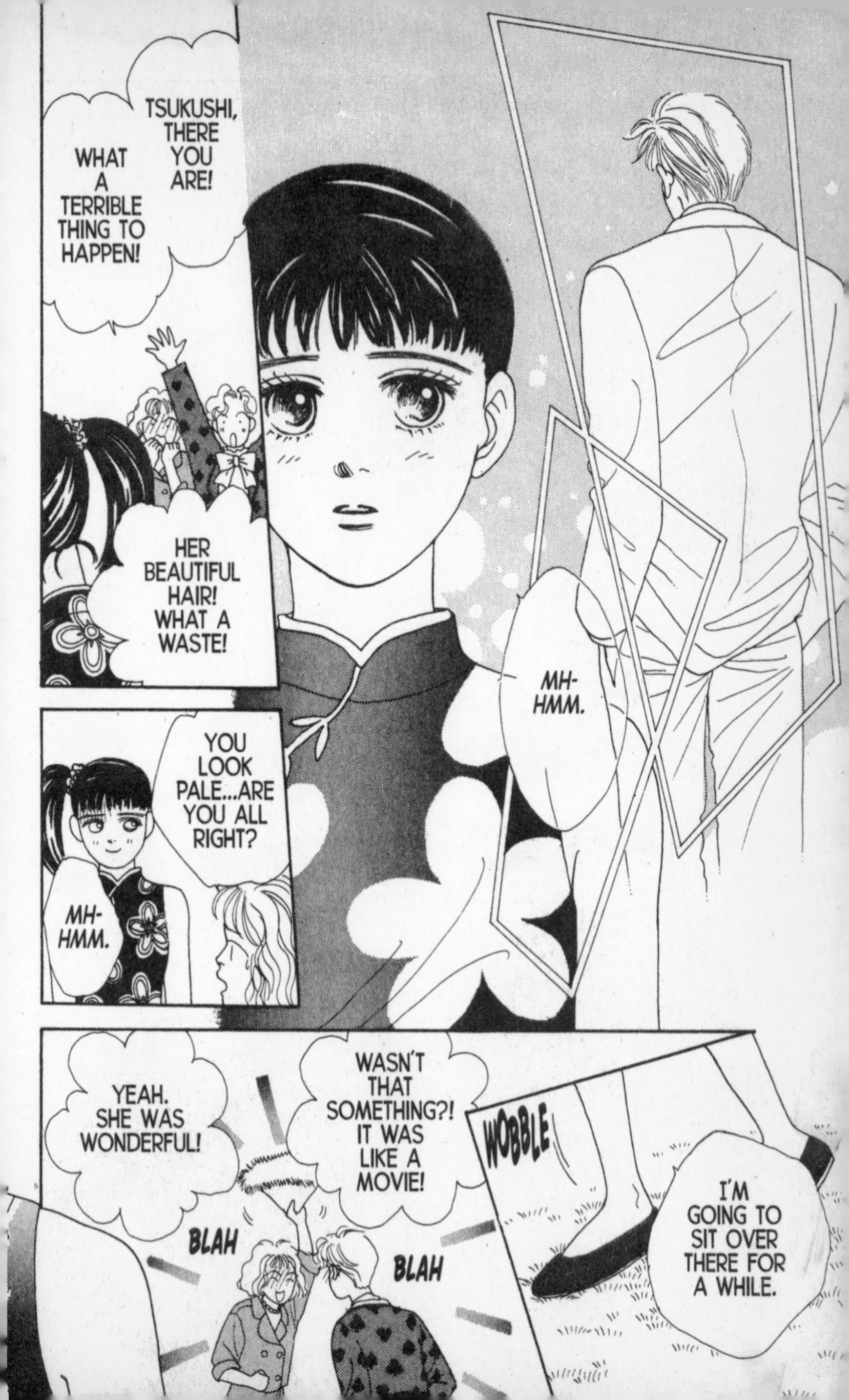
MH-HMM.
TSUKUSHI, THERE YOU ARE!
WHAT A TERRIBLE THING TO HAPPEN!
HER BEAUTIFUL HAIR! WHAT A WASTE!
YOU LOOK PALE...ARE YOU ALL RIGHT?
MH-HMM.
WOBBLE
I'M GOING TO SIT OVER THERE FOR A WHILE.
WASN'T THAT SOMETHING?! IT WAS LIKE A MOVIE!
YEAH. SHE WAS WONDERFUL!
BLAH
BLAH

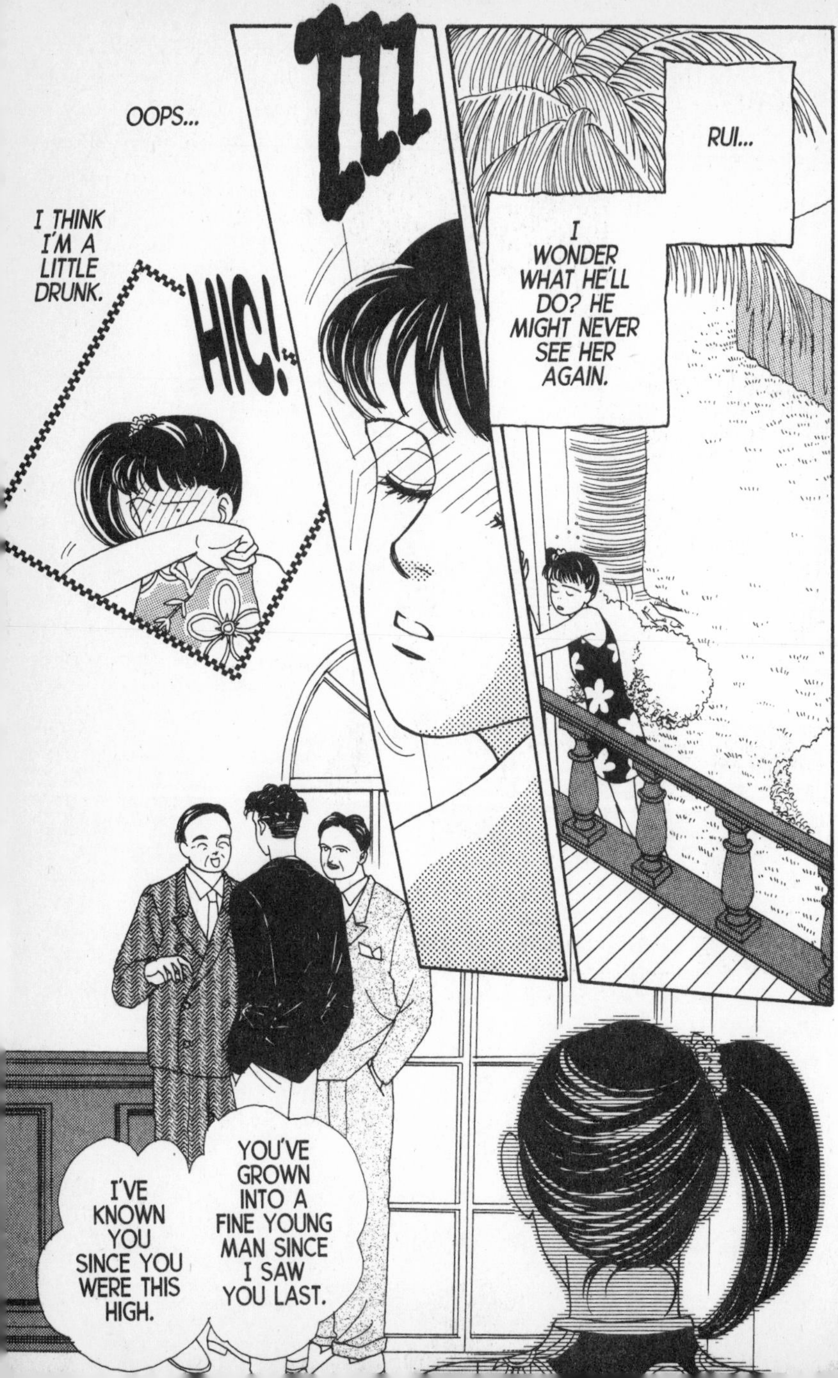
RUI...
I WONDER WHAT HE'LL DO? HE MIGHT NEVER SEE HER AGAIN.
ZZZ
OOPS...
HIC!
I THINK I'M A LITTLE DRUNK.
YOU'VE GROWN INTO A FINE YOUNG MAN SINCE I SAW YOU LAST.
I'VE KNOWN YOU SINCE YOU WERE THIS HIGH.

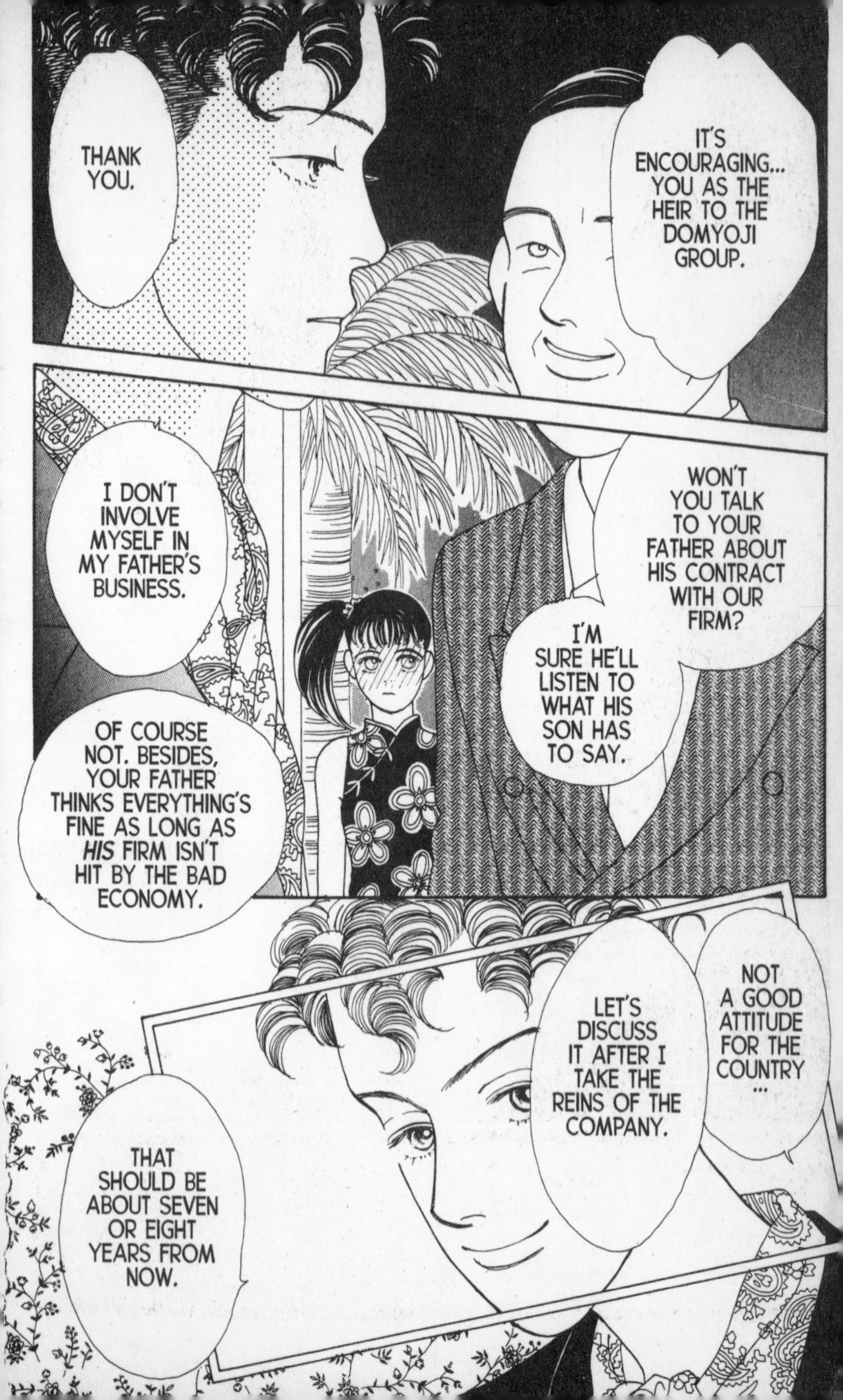
IT'S ENCOURAGING... YOU AS THE HEIR TO THE DOMYOJI GROUP.
THANK YOU.
WON'T YOU TALK TO YOUR FATHER ABOUT HIS CONTRACT WITH OUR FIRM?
I'M SURE HE'LL LISTEN TO WHAT HIS SON HAS TO SAY.
I DON'T INVOLVE MYSELF IN MY FATHER'S BUSINESS.
OF COURSE NOT. BESIDES, YOUR FATHER THINKS EVERYTHING'S FINE AS LONG AS *HIS* FIRM ISN'T HIT BY THE BAD ECONOMY.
NOT A GOOD ATTITUDE FOR THE COUNTRY...
LET'S DISCUSS IT AFTER I TAKE THE REINS OF THE COMPANY.
THAT SHOULD BE ABOUT SEVEN OR EIGHT YEARS FROM NOW.

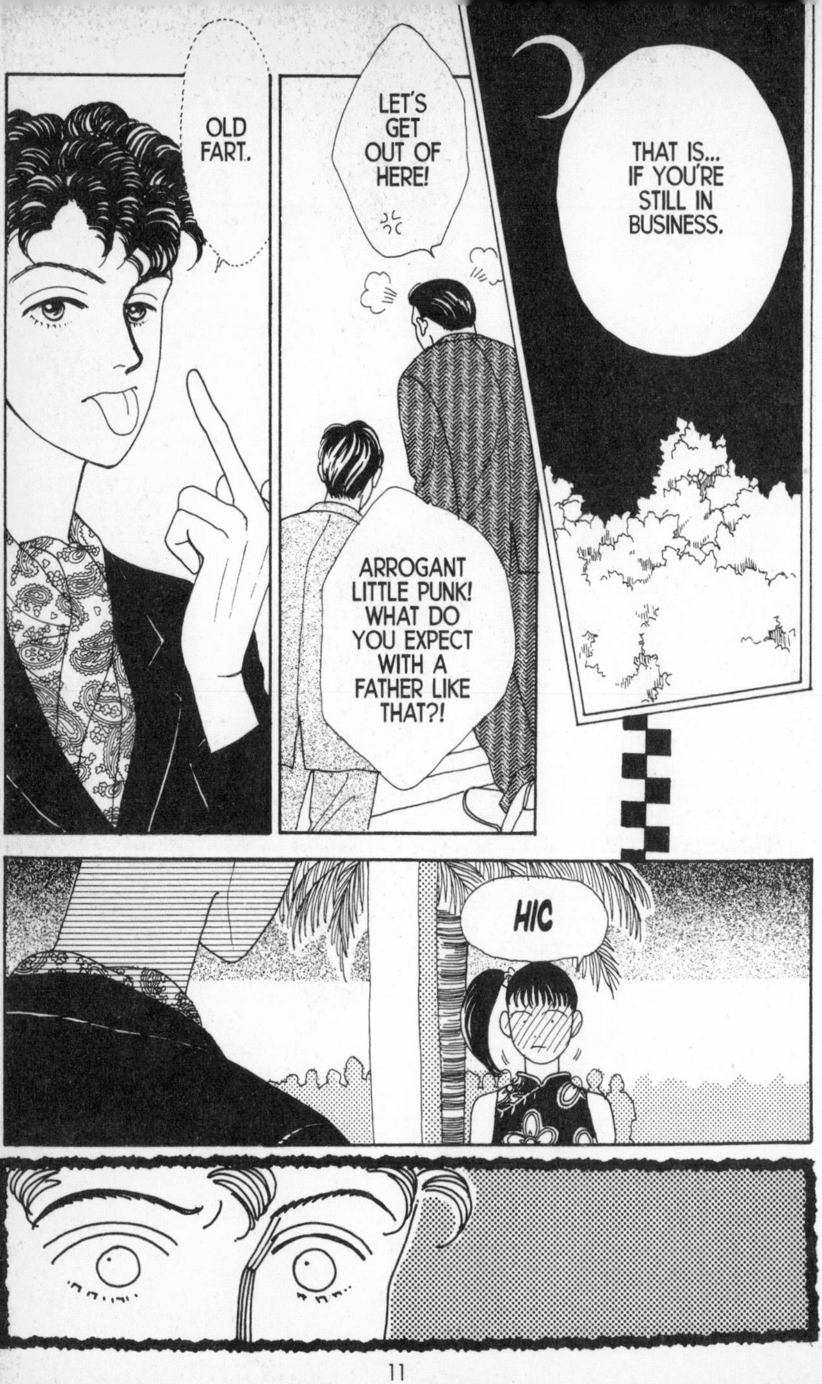
THAT IS... IF YOU'RE STILL IN BUSINESS.
LET'S GET OUT OF HERE!
ARROGANT LITTLE PUNK! WHAT DO YOU EXPECT WITH A FATHER LIKE THAT?!
OLD FART.
HIC

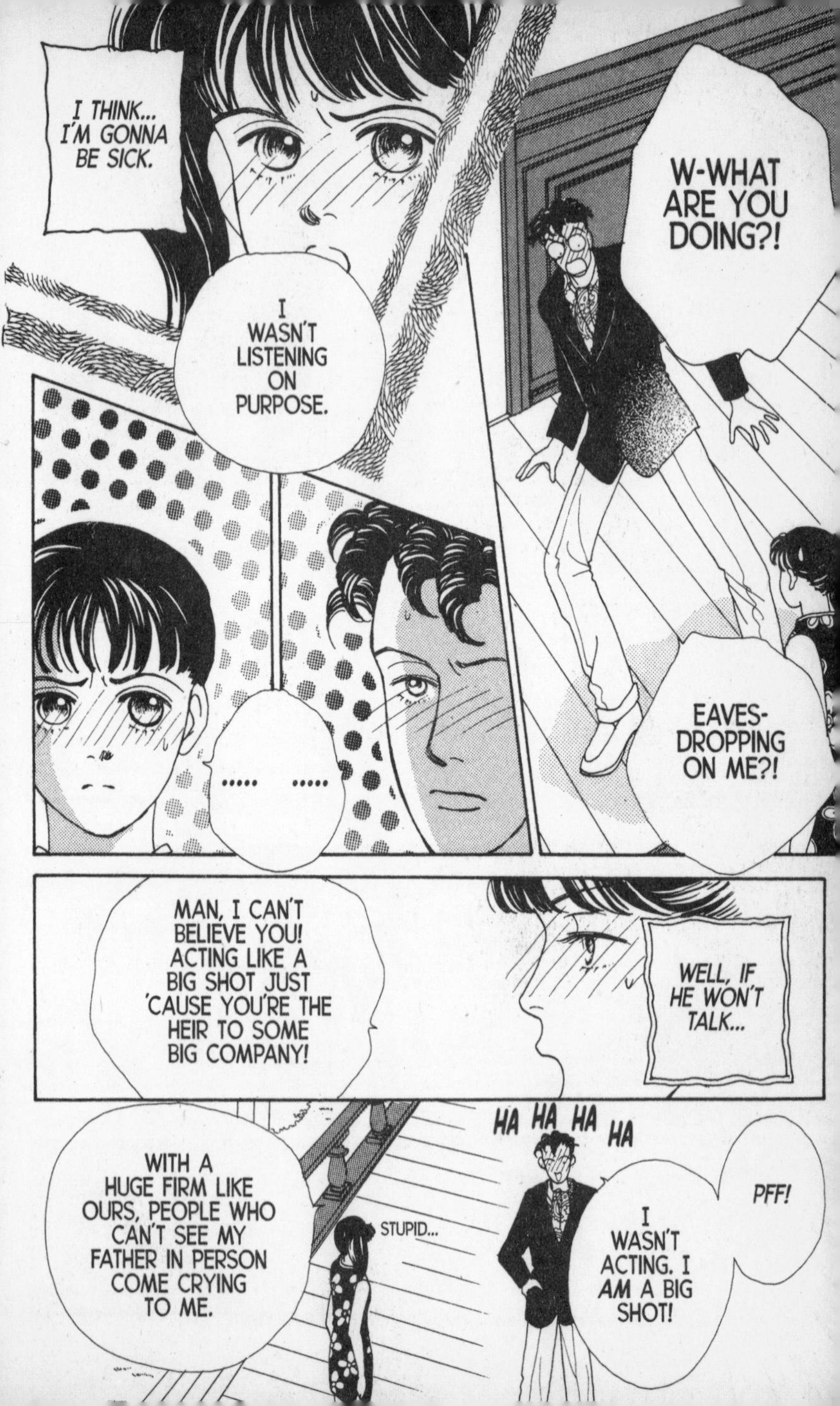
W-WHAT ARE YOU DOING?!
EAVES-DROPPING ON ME?!
I THINK... I'M GONNA BE SICK.
I WASN'T LISTENING ON PURPOSE.
....
WELL, IF HE WON'T TALK...
MAN, I CAN'T BELIEVE YOU! ACTING LIKE A BIG SHOT JUST 'CAUSE YOU'RE THE HEIR TO SOME BIG COMPANY!
PFF!
HA HA HA HA
I WASN'T ACTING. I AM A BIG SHOT!
STUPID...
WITH A HUGE FIRM LIKE OURS, PEOPLE WHO CAN'T SEE MY FATHER IN PERSON COME CRYING TO ME.

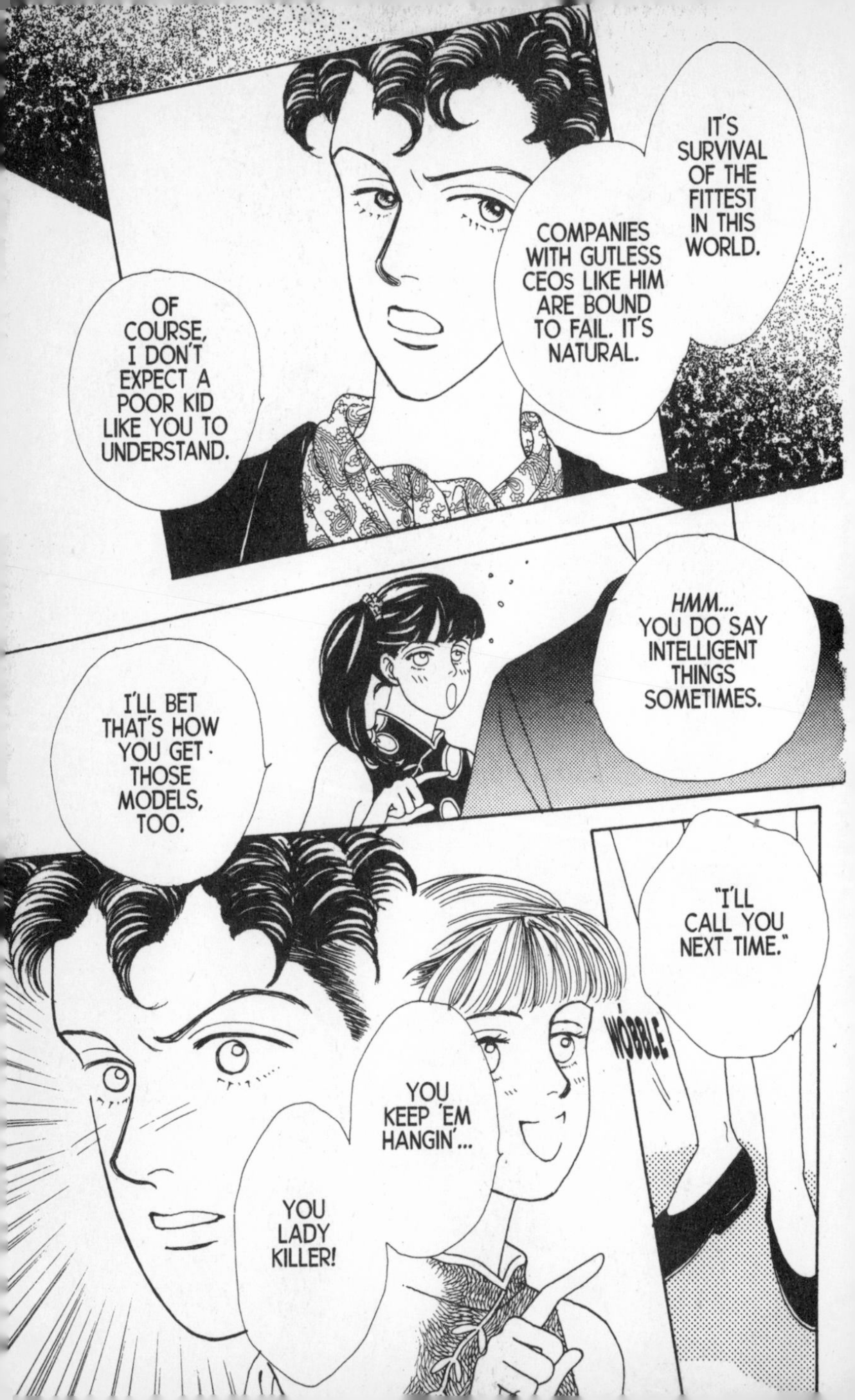
IT'S SURVIVAL OF THE FITTEST IN THIS WORLD.
COMPANIES WITH GUTLESS CEOs LIKE HIM ARE BOUND TO FAIL. IT'S NATURAL.
OF COURSE, I DON'T EXPECT A POOR KID LIKE YOU TO UNDERSTAND.
HMM... YOU DO SAY INTELLIGENT THINGS SOMETIMES.
I'LL BET THAT'S HOW YOU GET THOSE MODELS, TOO.
"I'LL CALL YOU NEXT TIME."
WOBBLE
YOU KEEP 'EM HANGIN'...
YOU LADY KILLER!

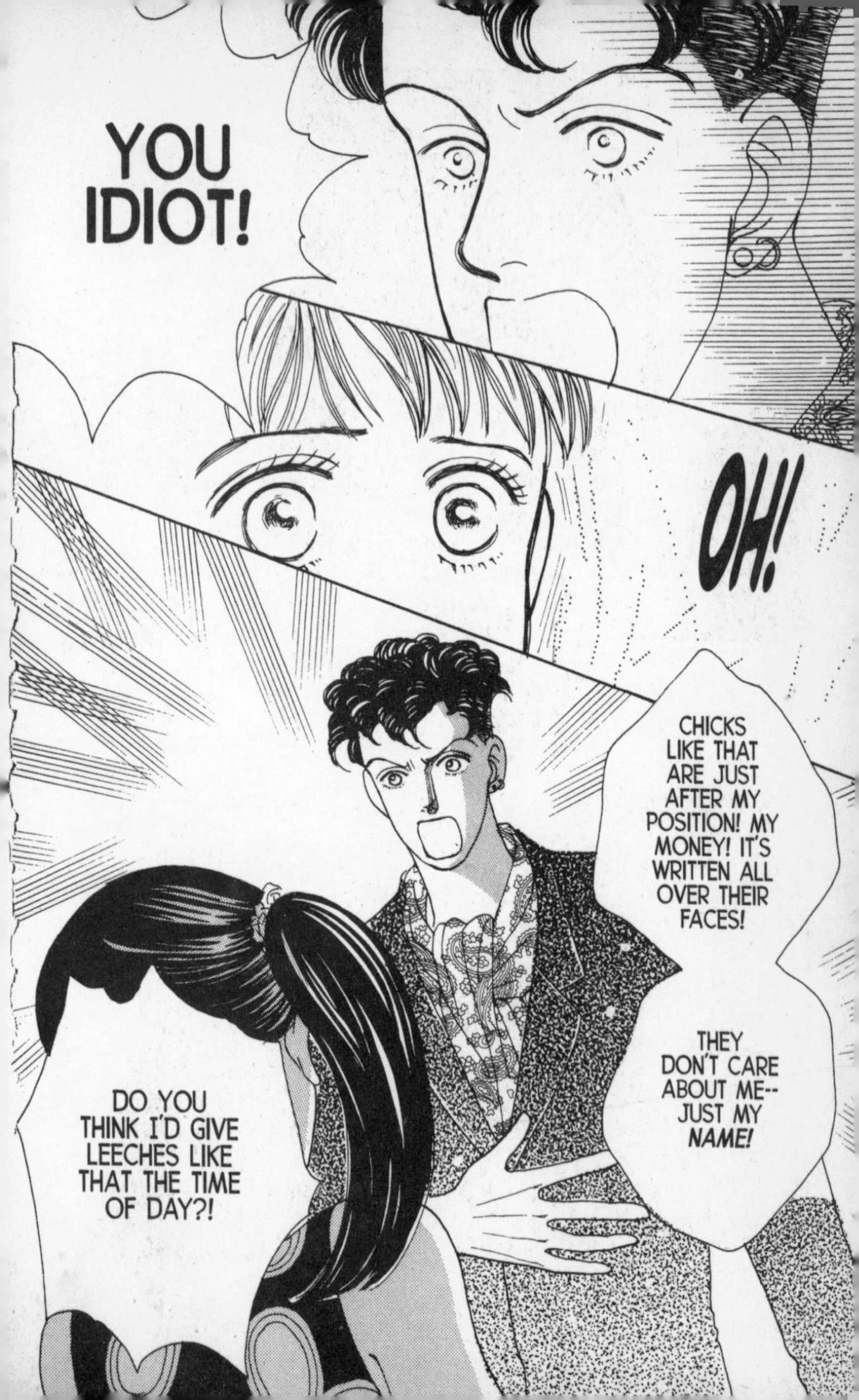
YOU IDIOT!
OH!
CHICKS LIKE THAT ARE JUST AFTER MY POSITION! MY MONEY! IT'S WRITTEN ALL OVER THEIR FACES!
THEY DON'T CARE ABOUT ME-- JUST MY *NAME!*
DO YOU THINK I'D GIVE LEECHES LIKE THAT THE TIME OF DAY?!

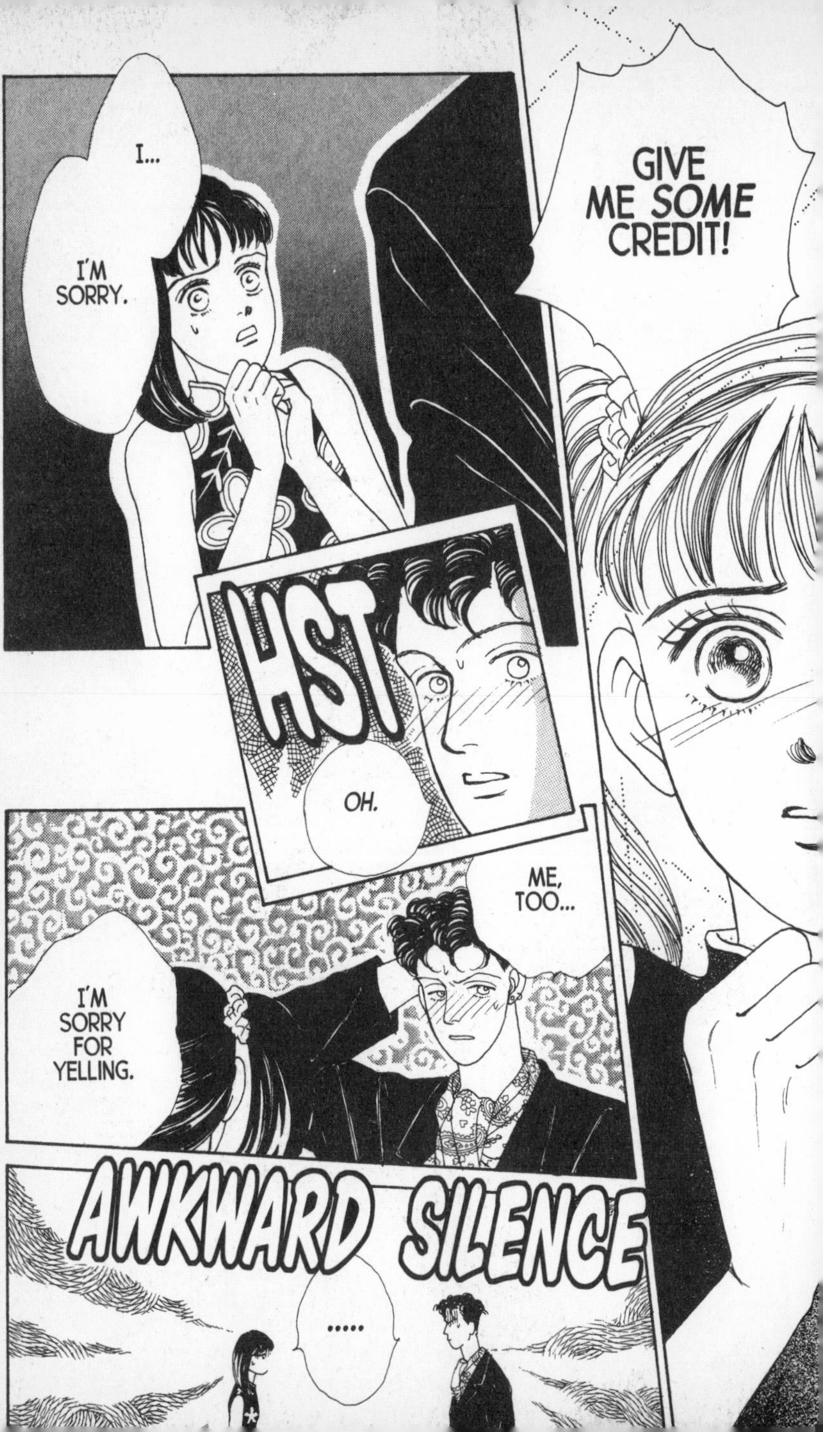
GIVE ME SOME CREDIT!
I...
I'M SORRY.
HST
OH.
ME, TOO...
I'M SORRY FOR YELLING.
AWKWARD SILENCE
.....

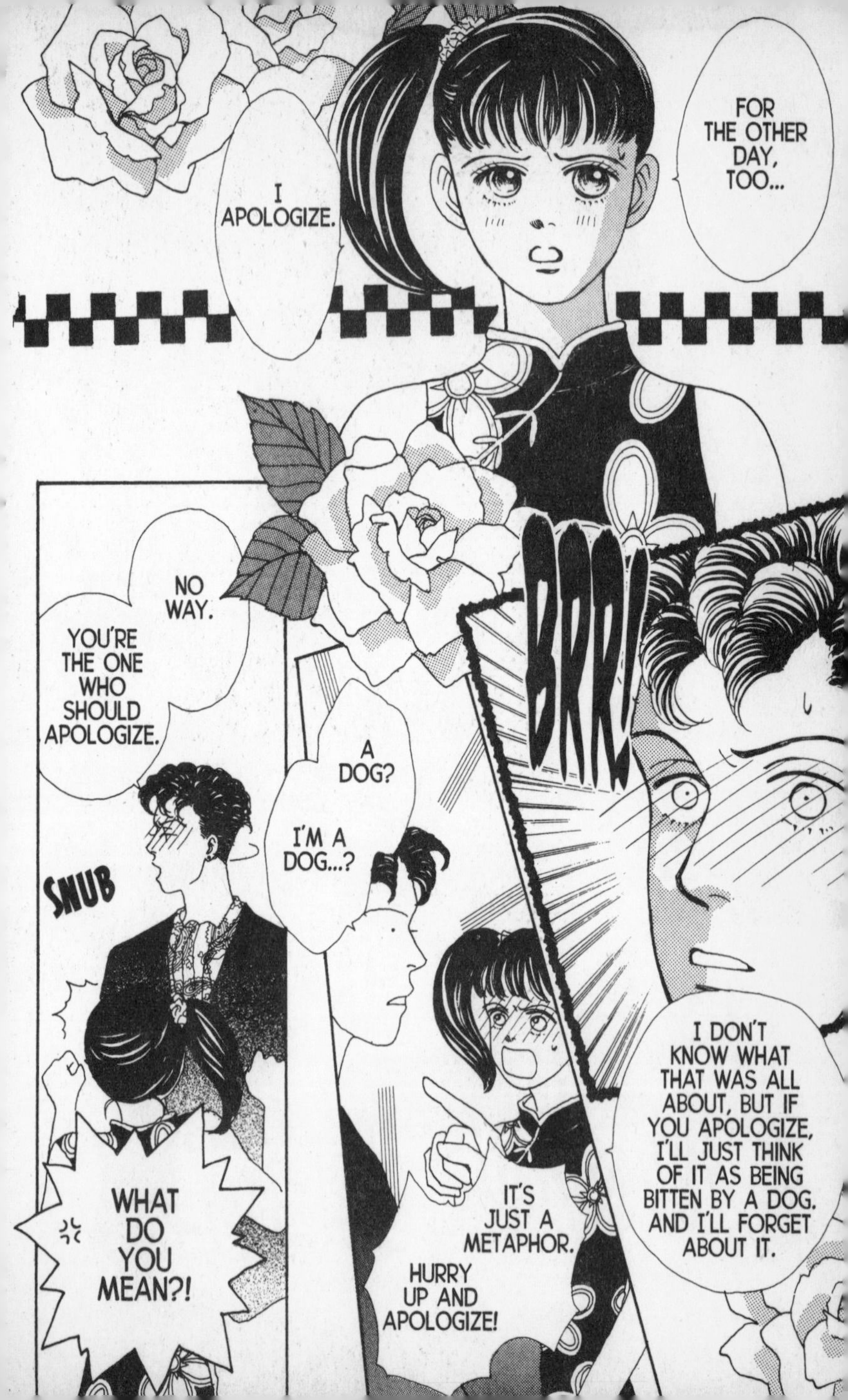
FOR THE OTHER DAY, TOO...
I APOLOGIZE.
BRR!
I DON'T KNOW WHAT THAT WAS ALL ABOUT, BUT IF YOU APOLOGIZE, I'LL JUST THINK OF IT AS BEING BITTEN BY A DOG. AND I'LL FORGET ABOUT IT.
A DOG?
I'M A DOG...?
IT'S JUST A METAPHOR.
HURRY UP AND APOLOGIZE!
NO WAY.
YOU'RE THE ONE WHO SHOULD APOLOGIZE.
SNUB
WHAT DO YOU MEAN?!

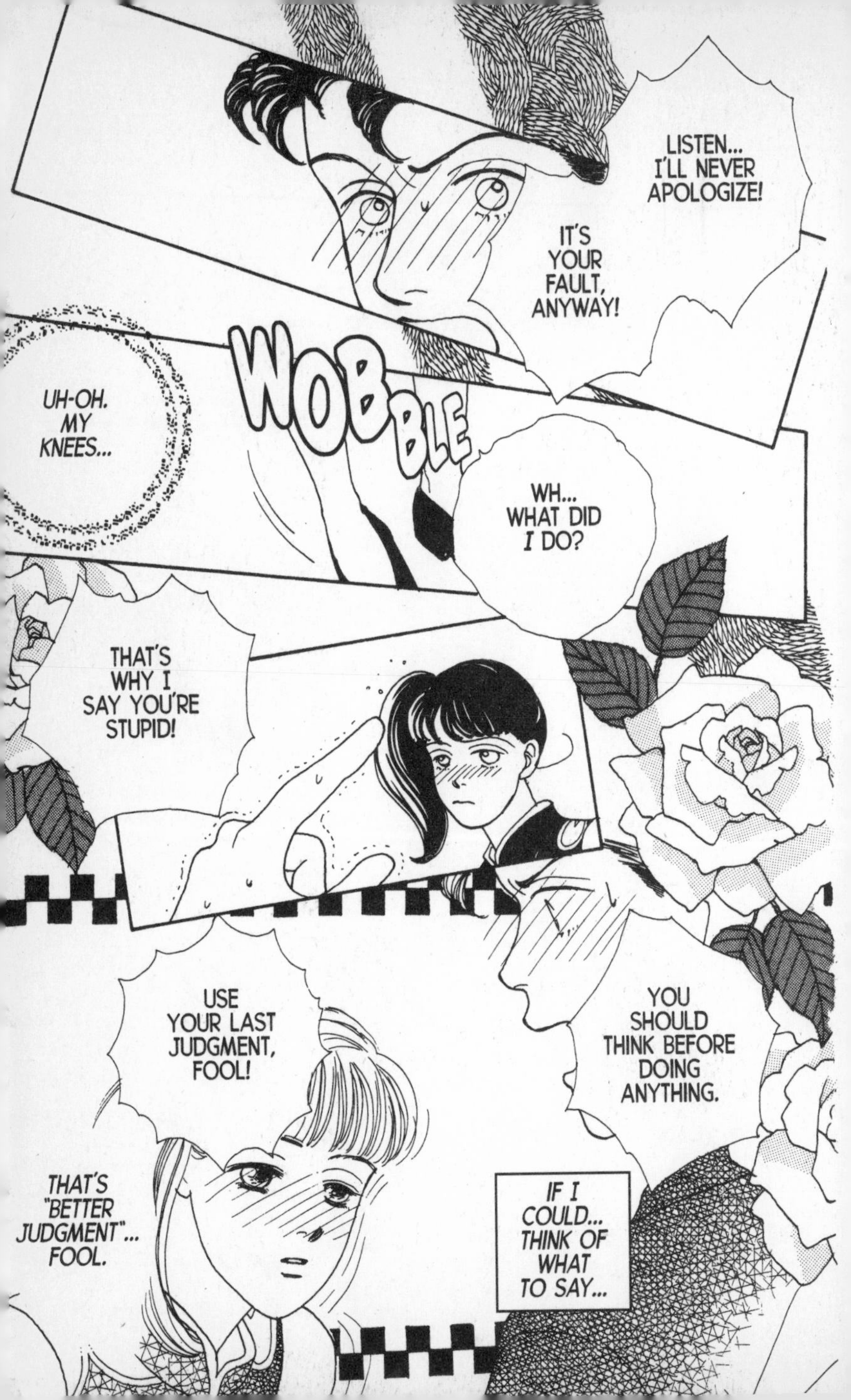
LISTEN... I'LL NEVER APOLOGIZE!
IT'S YOUR FAULT, ANYWAY!
WH... WHAT DID *I* DO?
WOBBLE
UH-OH. MY KNEES...
THAT'S WHY I SAY YOU'RE STUPID!
YOU SHOULD THINK BEFORE DOING ANYTHING.
USE YOUR LAST JUDGMENT, FOOL!
IF I COULD... THINK OF WHAT TO SAY...
THAT'S "BETTER JUDGMENT"... FOOL.

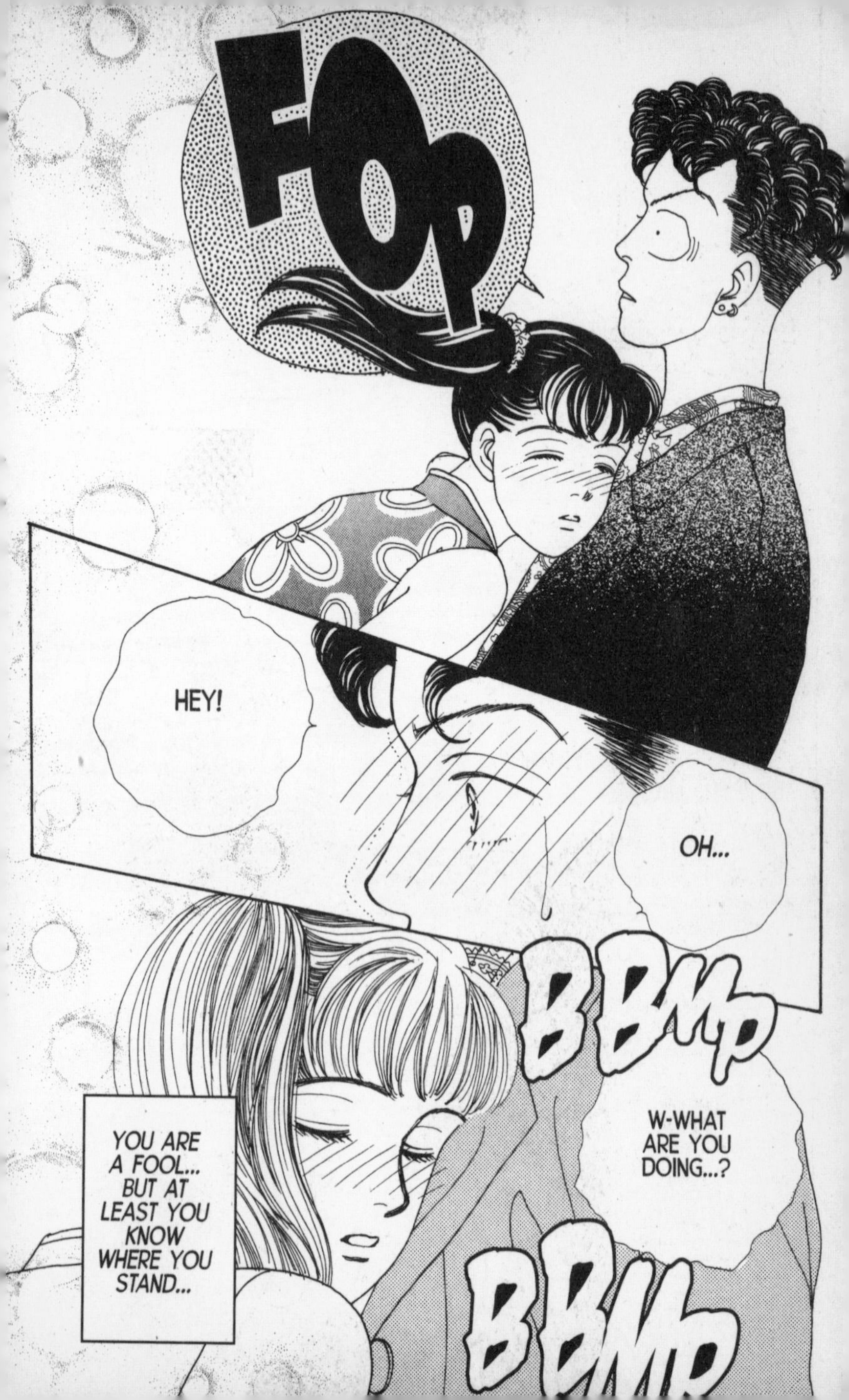
FOP
OH...
HEY!
BBMP
W-WHAT ARE YOU DOING...?
YOU ARE A FOOL... BUT AT LEAST YOU KNOW WHERE YOU STAND...
BBMP

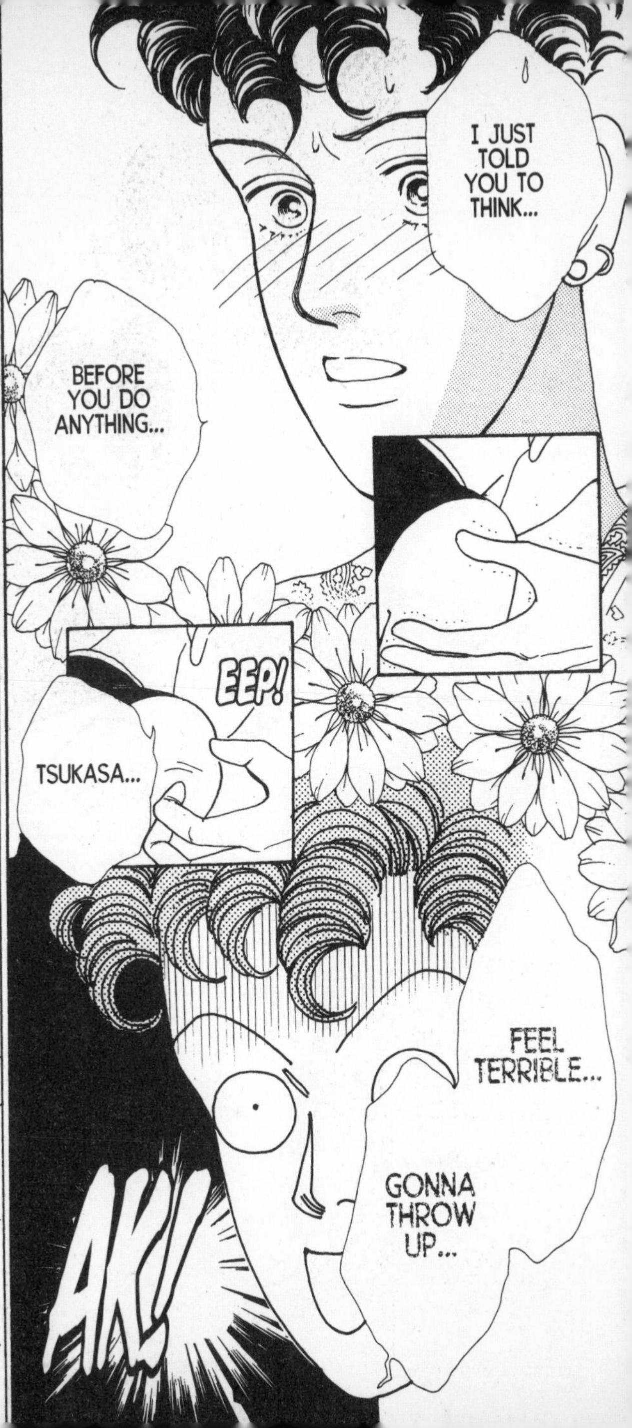
I JUST TOLD YOU TO THINK...
BEFORE YOU DO ANYTHING...
EEP!
TSUKASA...
FEEL TERRIBLE...
GONNA THROW UP...
AK!

Hello, we're in Volume 4 already!

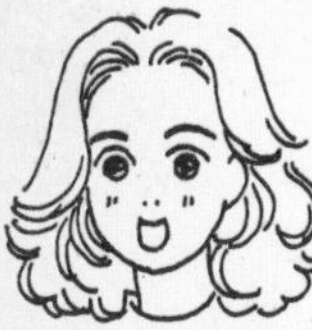

I'd like to thank all you faithful readers.

The other day, I saw some high school girls buying Boys Over Flowers Vol. 3.

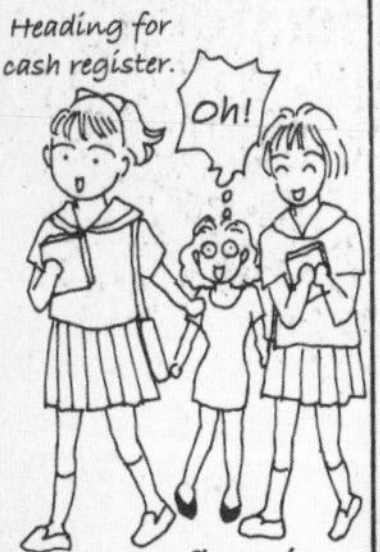
Heading for cash register.
Oh!

It was the first time I'd seen anyone buy my comics...

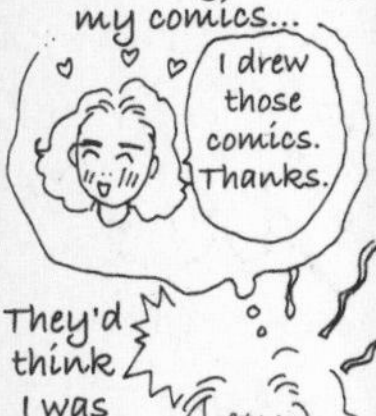
I drew those comics. Thanks.

They'd think I was crazy. What do I say?

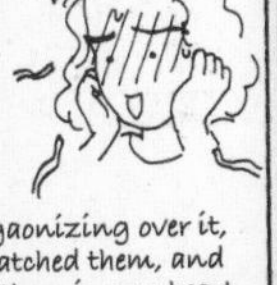

After agaonizing over it, I just watched them, and thanked them in my heart. (Am I a fool?) Thank you to the two girls in the bookshop in the 2nd floor of Milord in Shinjuku.

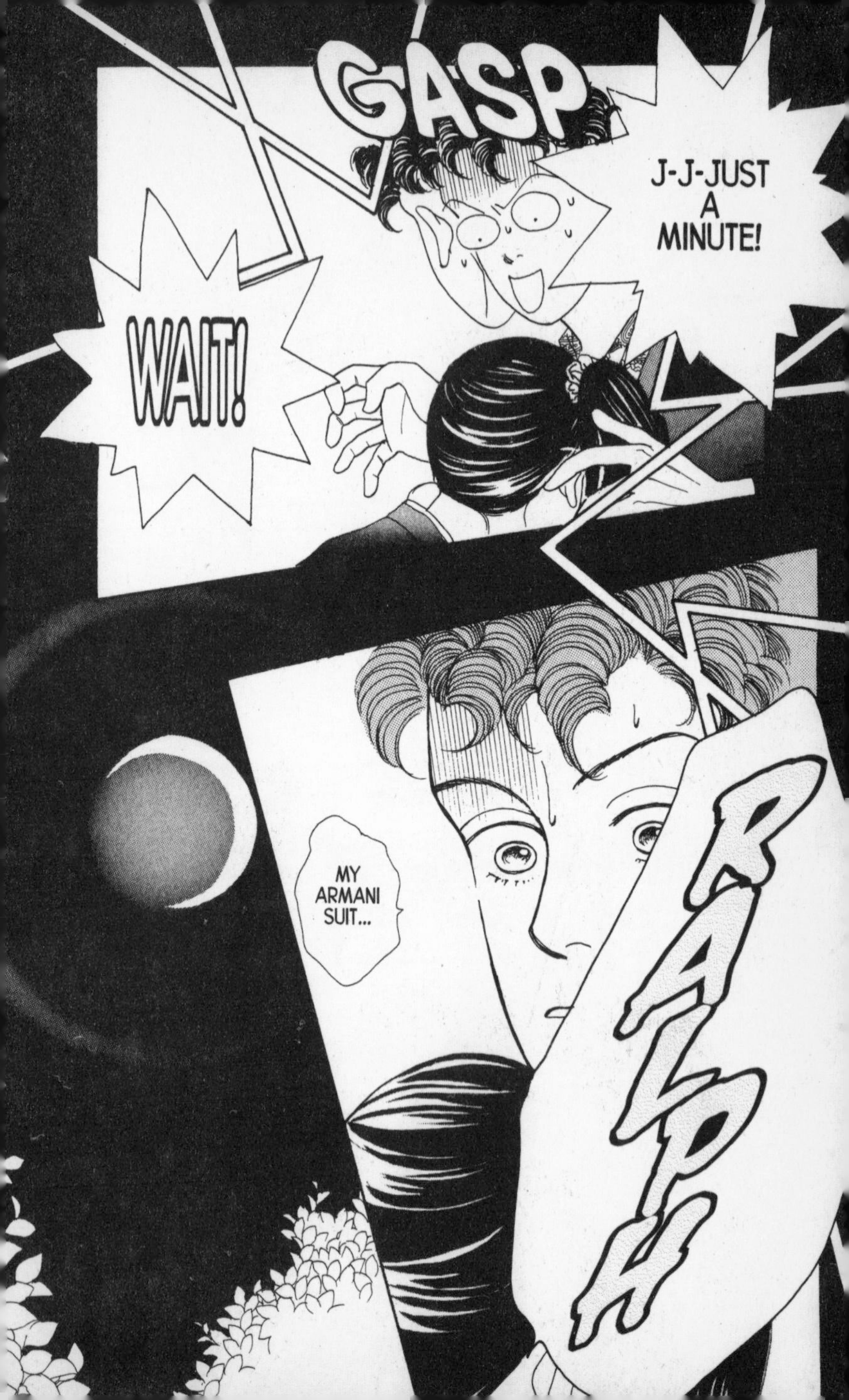
GASP
J-J-JUST A MINUTE!
WAIT!
MY ARMANI SUIT...

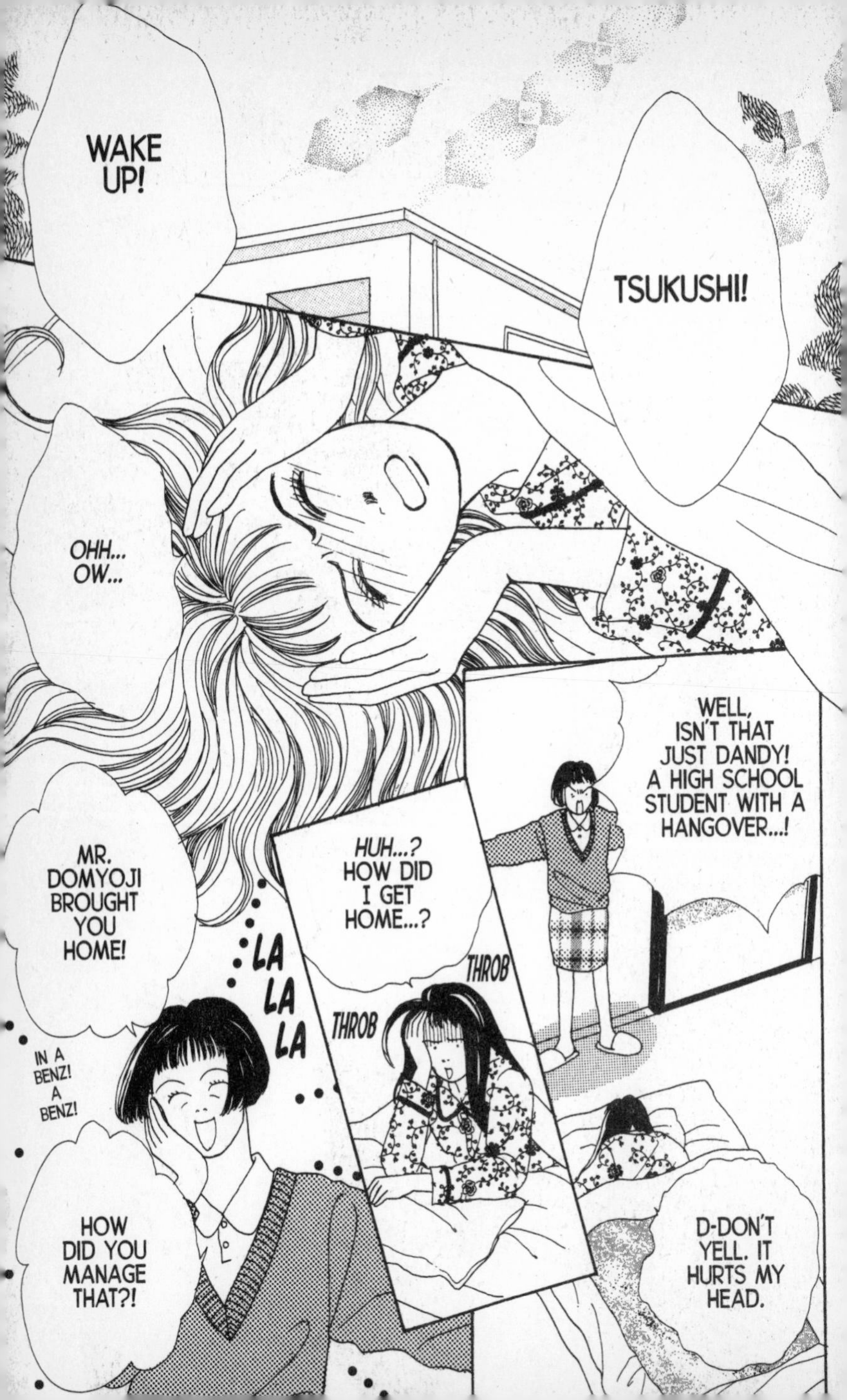
TSUKUSHI!
WAKE UP!
OHH... OW...
WELL, ISN'T THAT JUST DANDY! A HIGH SCHOOL STUDENT WITH A HANGOVER...!
D-DON'T YELL. IT HURTS MY HEAD.
HUH...? HOW DID I GET HOME...?
THROB
THROB
MR. DOMYOJI BROUGHT YOU HOME!
LA LA LA
IN A BENZ! A BENZ!
HOW DID YOU MANAGE THAT?!

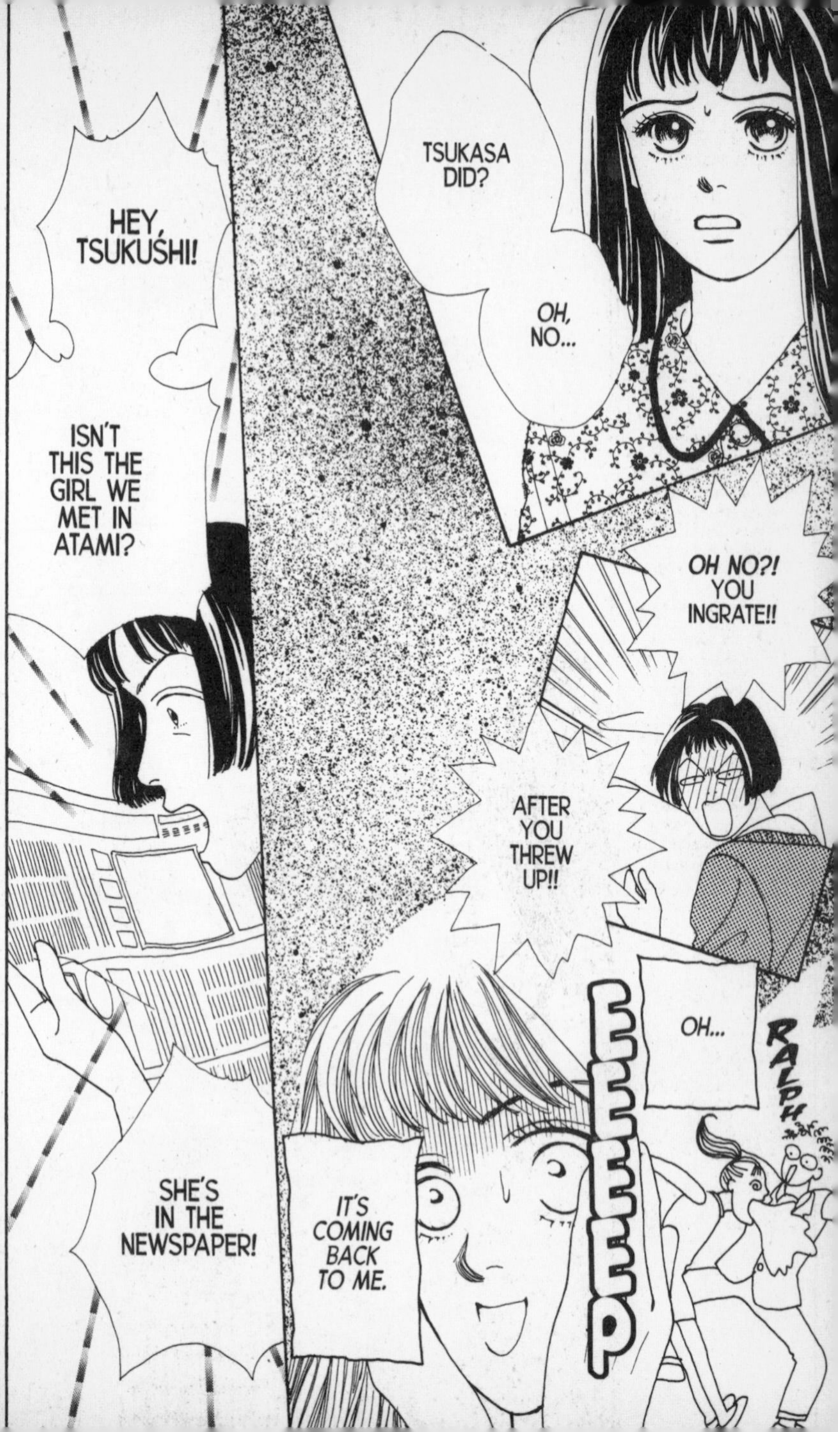
TSUKASA DID?
OH, NO...
OH NO?! YOU INGRATE!!
AFTER YOU THREW UP!!
OH...
RALPH
EEEEP
IT'S COMING BACK TO ME.
HEY, TSUKUSHI!
ISN'T THIS THE GIRL WE MET IN ATAMI?
SHE'S IN THE NEWSPAPER!

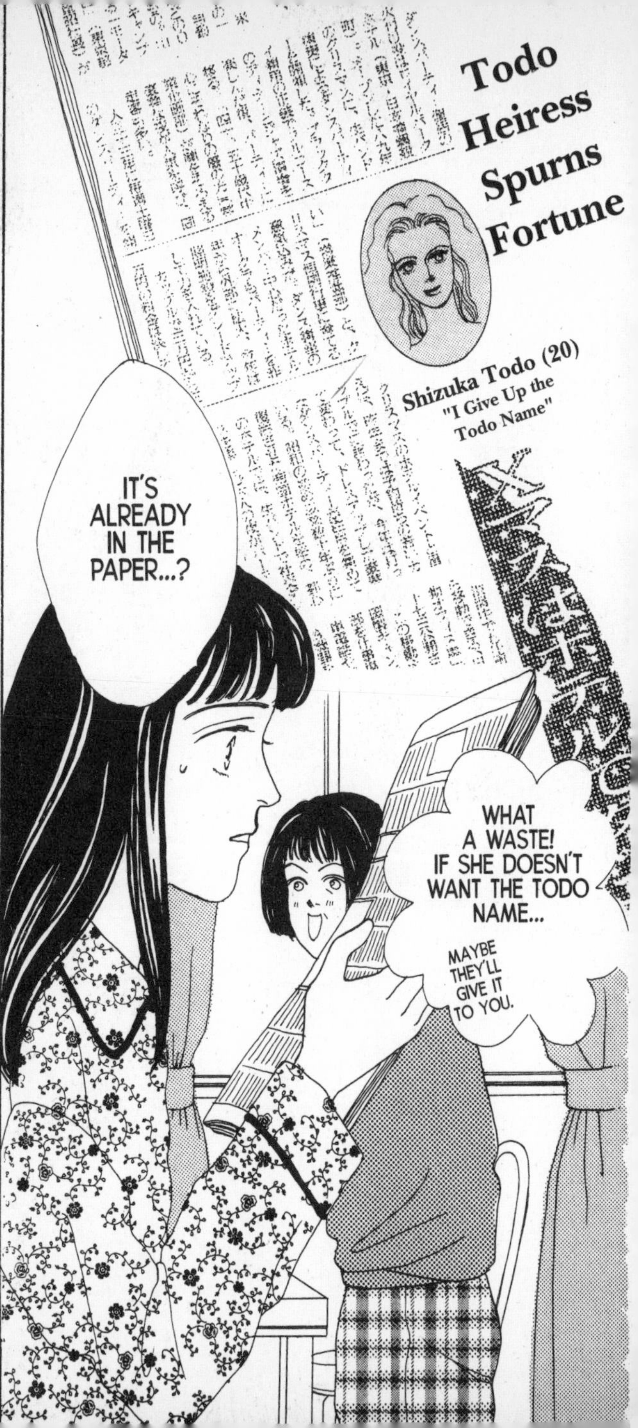
Todo Heiress Spurns Fortune
Shizuka Todo (20)
"I Give Up the Todo Name"
IT'S ALREADY IN THE PAPER...?
WHAT A WASTE! IF SHE DOESN'T WANT THE TODO NAME...
MAYBE THEY'LL GIVE IT TO YOU.

1

"Hana Yori Dango" CD Report

The recording was a massive undertaking, lasting from 11:30AM to 5:30PM. (Due to my work schedule, I could only sit in from 4:00PM.)

This was my first experience, but I have nothing but admiration for the people involved! The voice actors seemed like ordinary people at first glance, but once they started reading their lines, they sparkled. Voice-over actors are great... very professional.

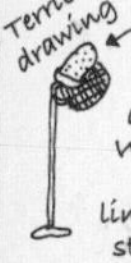
Terrible drawing

There were about three mikes like this standing around the room. When it came time for a character's lines, the actor would stand up and walk over to a mike to read them.

Arriving late, the first thing that caught my eye was...actor Takuya Kimura taking a break in the corridor.

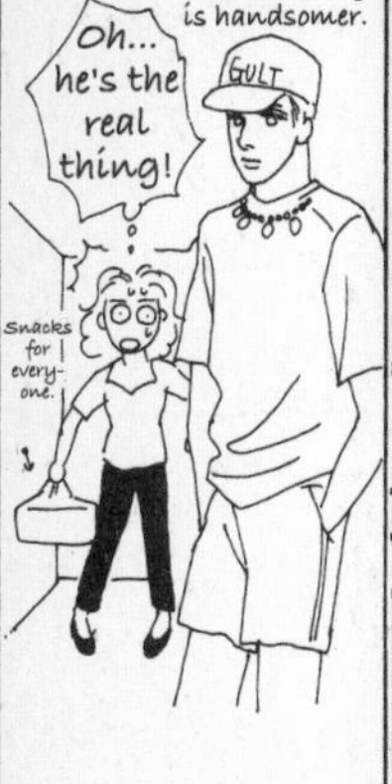
The real thing is handsomer.
Oh... he's the real thing!
GULT
Snacks for every-one.

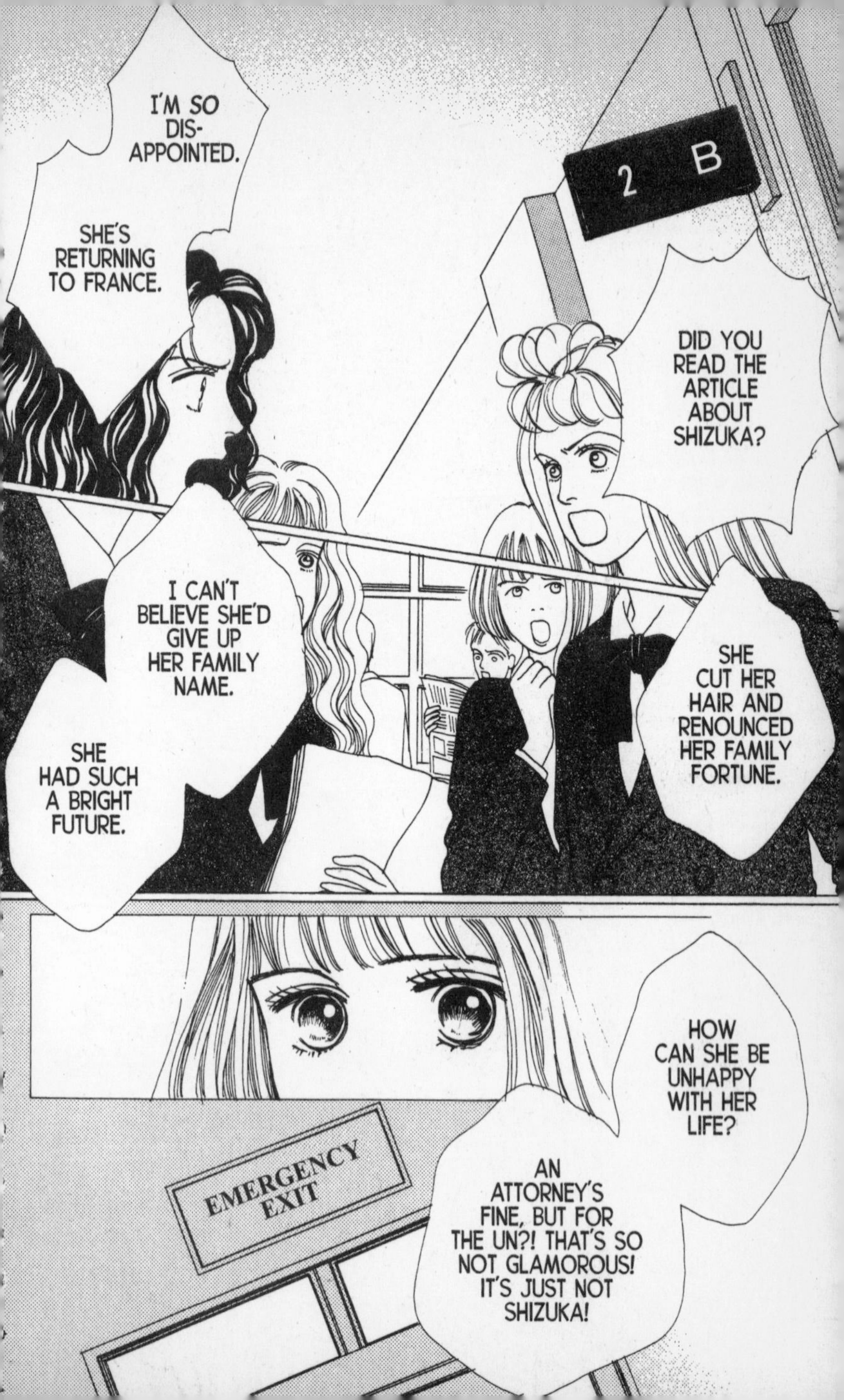

2 B
DID YOU READ THE ARTICLE ABOUT SHIZUKA?
SHE CUT HER HAIR AND RENOUNCED HER FAMILY FORTUNE.
I'M SO DIS-APPOINTED.
SHE'S RETURNING TO FRANCE.
I CAN'T BELIEVE SHE'D GIVE UP HER FAMILY NAME.
SHE HAD SUCH A BRIGHT FUTURE.
HOW CAN SHE BE UNHAPPY WITH HER LIFE?
AN ATTORNEY'S FINE, BUT FOR THE UN?! THAT'S SO NOT GLAMOROUS! IT'S JUST NOT SHIZUKA!
EMERGENCY EXIT

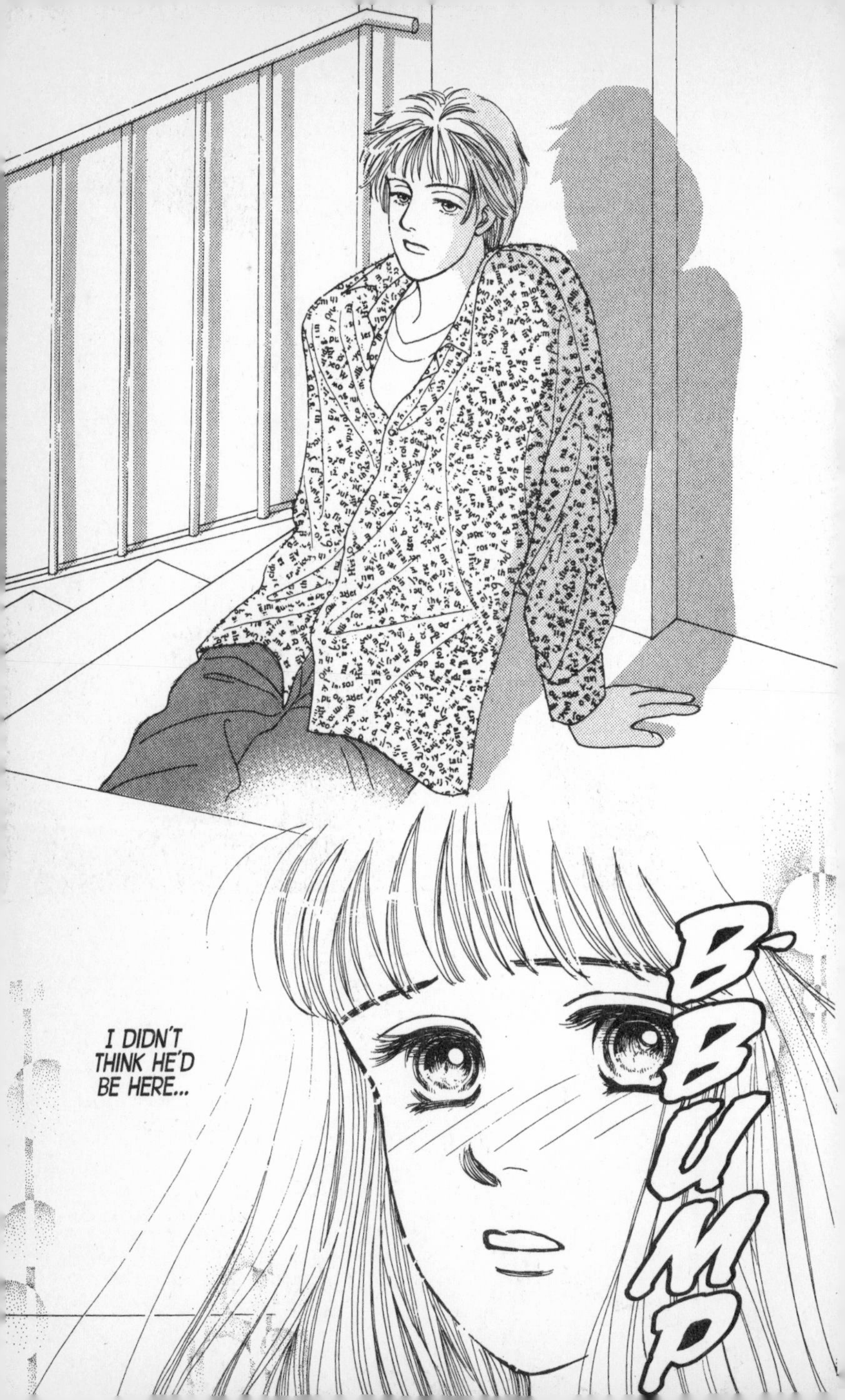
B-BUMP
I DIDN'T THINK HE'D BE HERE...

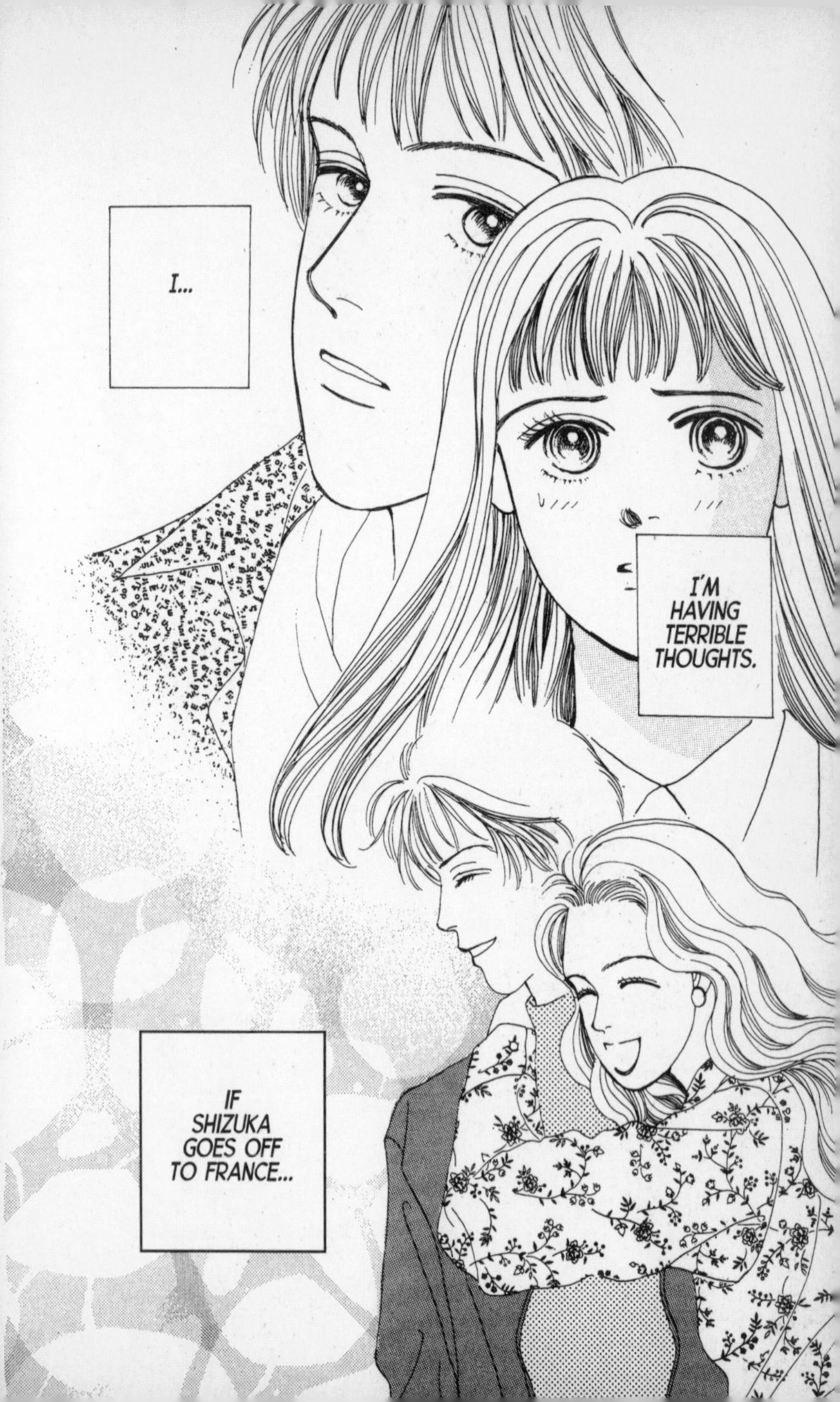
I...
I'M HAVING TERRIBLE THOUGHTS.
IF SHIZUKA GOES OFF TO FRANCE...

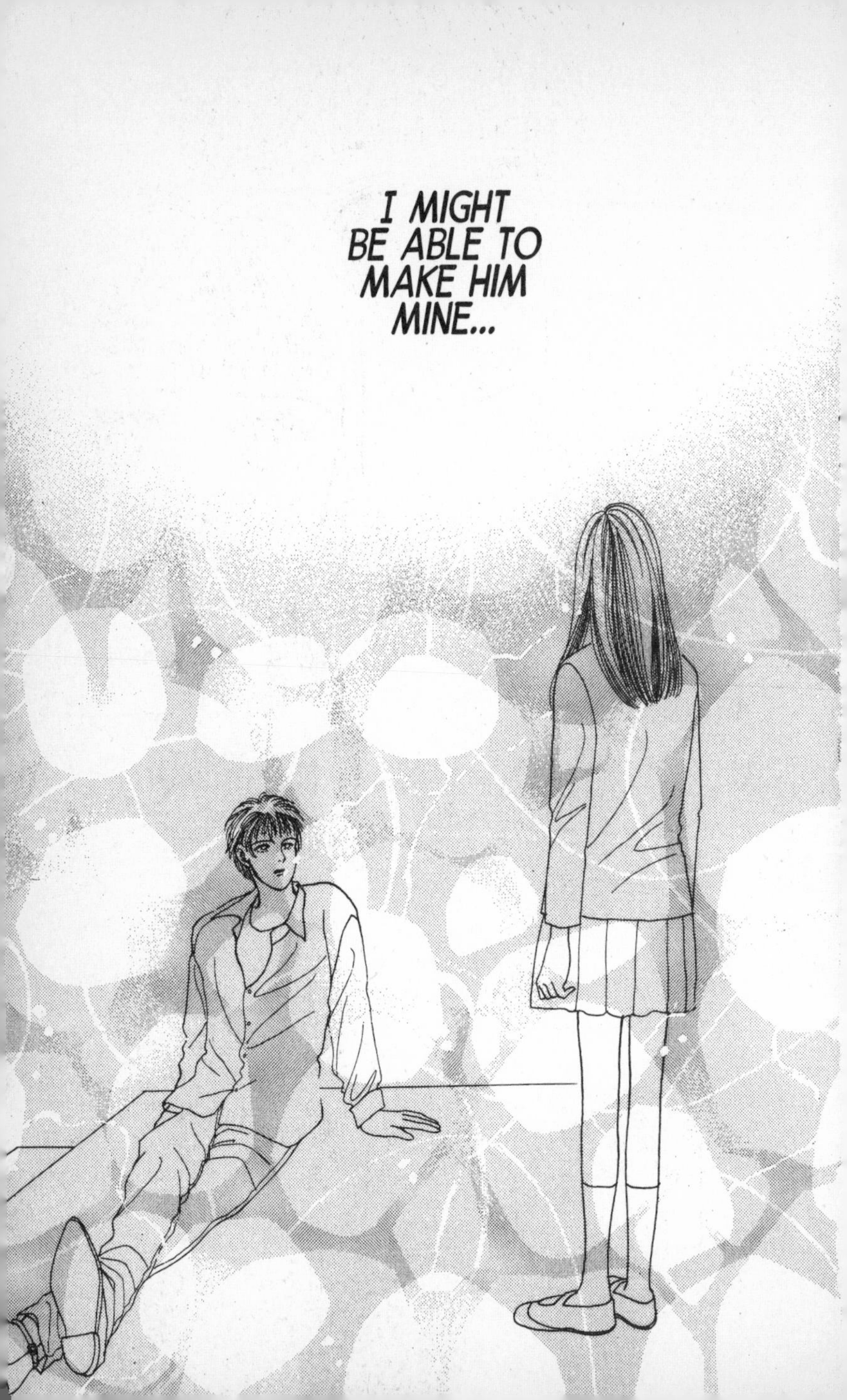
I MIGHT BE ABLE TO MAKE HIM MINE...

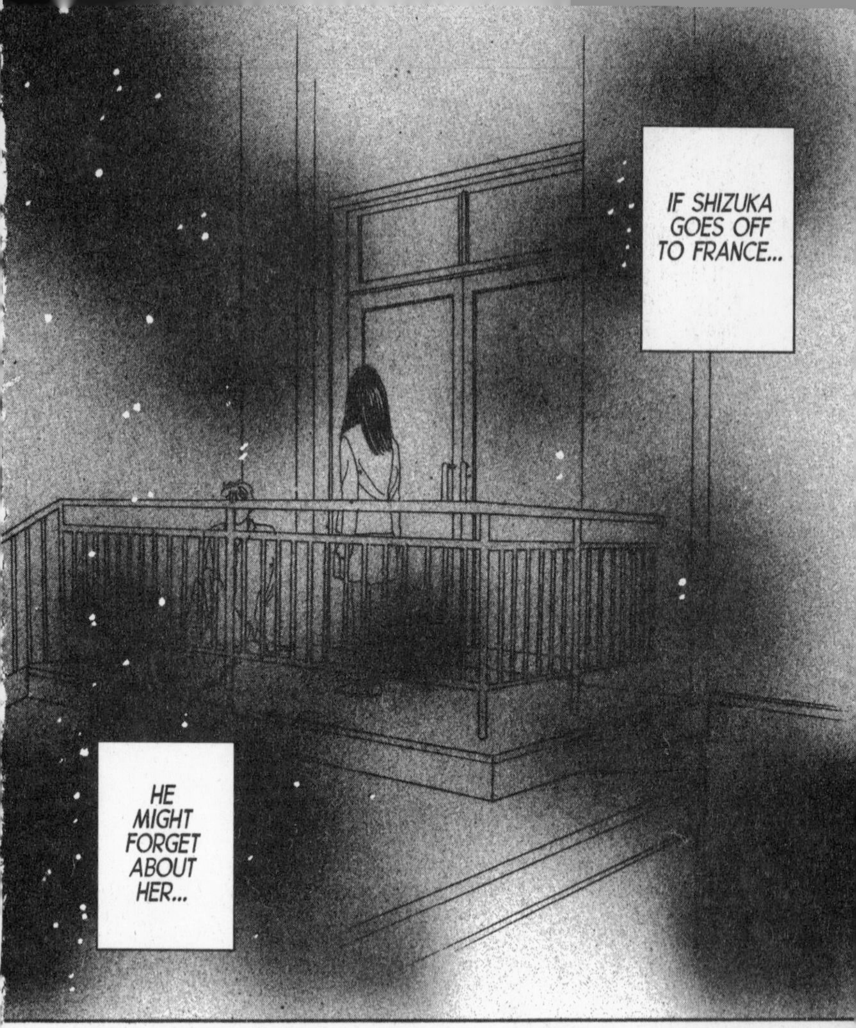
IF SHIZUKA GOES OFF TO FRANCE...
HE MIGHT FORGET ABOUT HER...

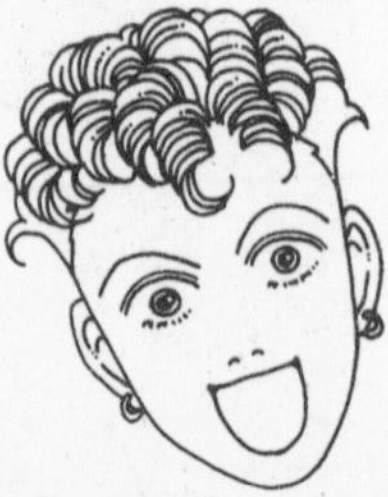

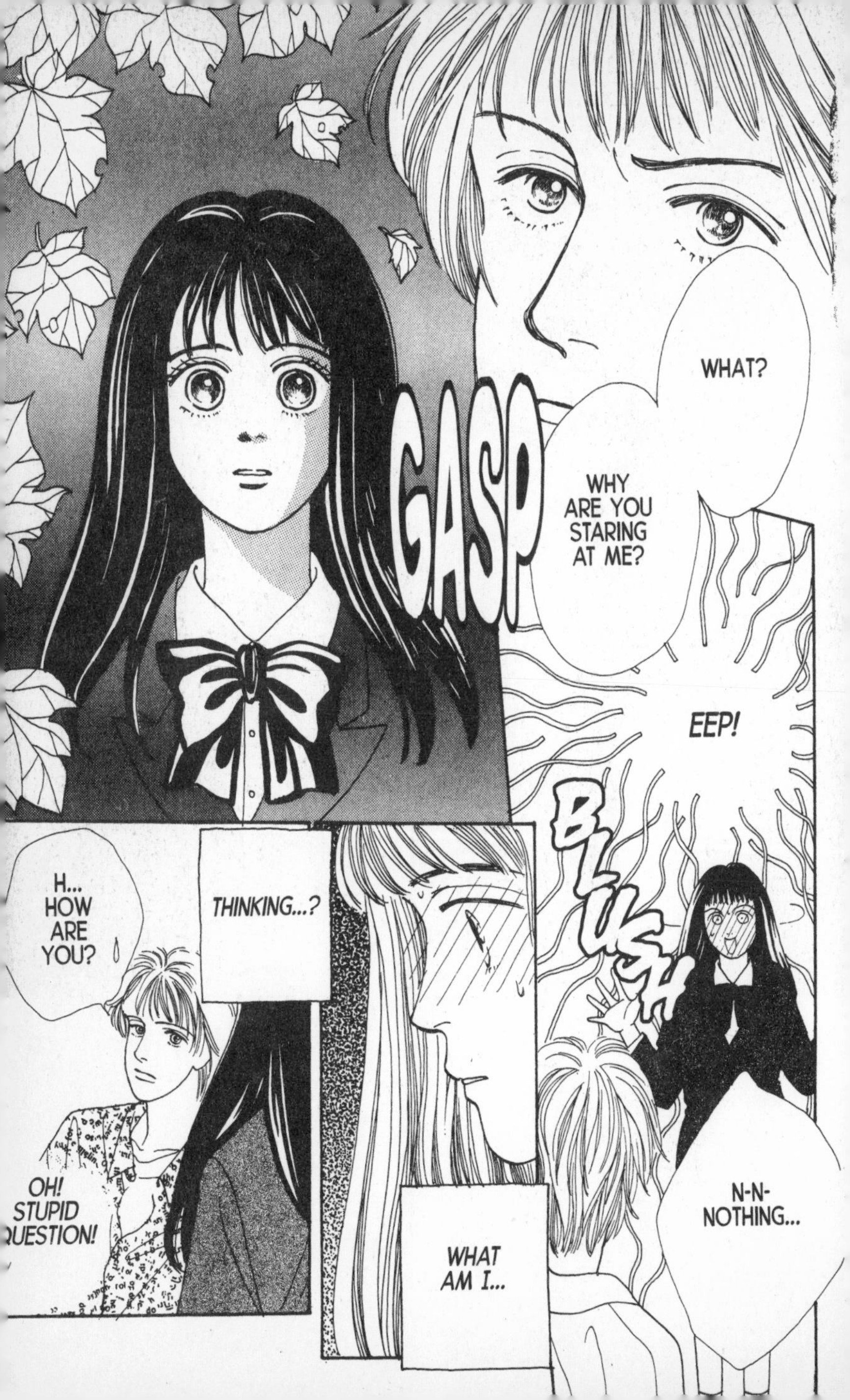
WHAT?
WHY ARE YOU STARING AT ME?
GASP
EEP!
BLUSH
N-N-NOTHING...
WHAT AM I...
THINKING...?
H... HOW ARE YOU?
OH! STUPID QUESTION!

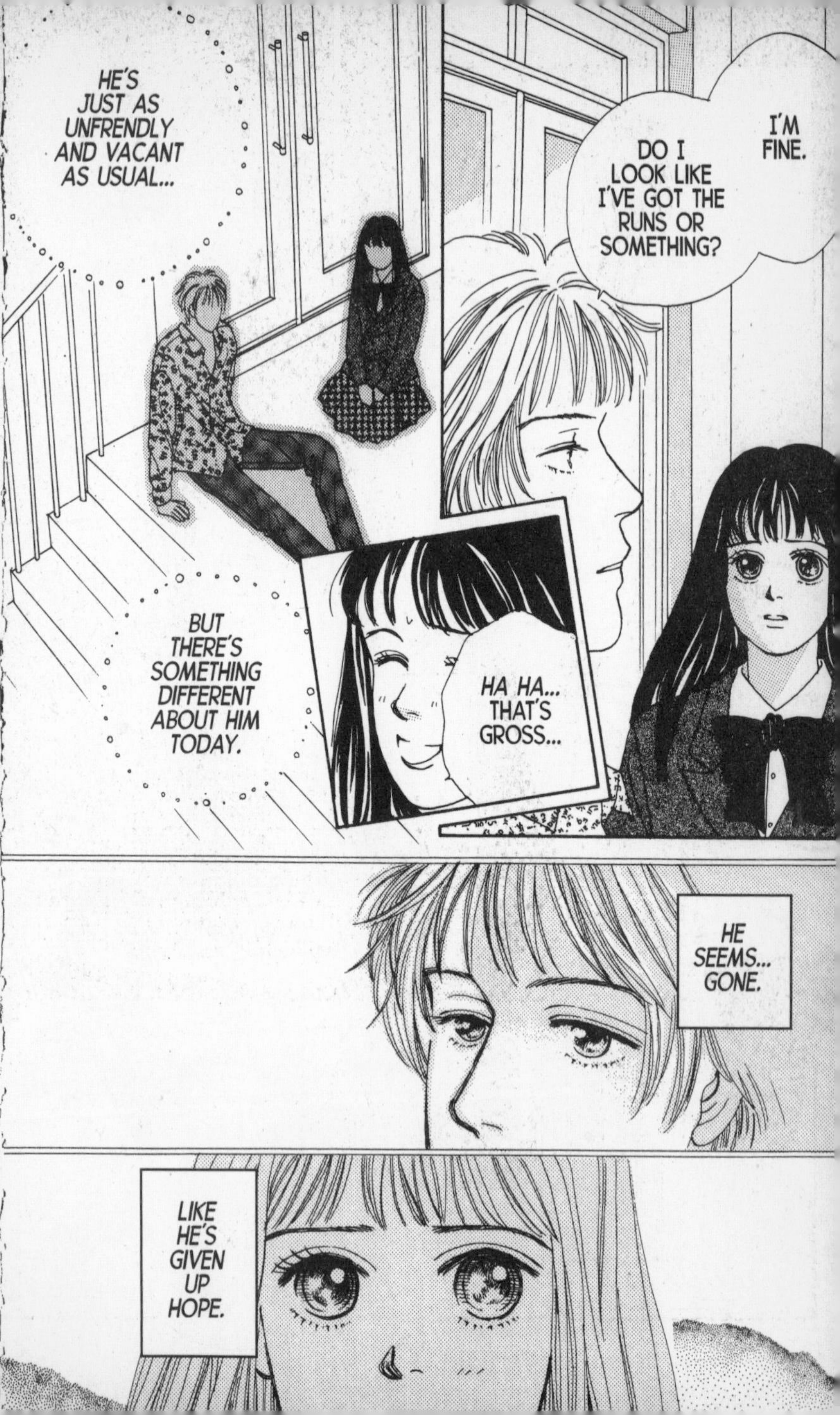
I'M FINE.
DO I LOOK LIKE I'VE GOT THE RUNS OR SOMETHING?
HA HA... THAT'S GROSS...
HE'S JUST AS UNFRENDLY AND VACANT AS USUAL...
BUT THERE'S SOMETHING DIFFERENT ABOUT HIM TODAY.
HE SEEMS... GONE.
LIKE HE'S GIVEN UP HOPE.

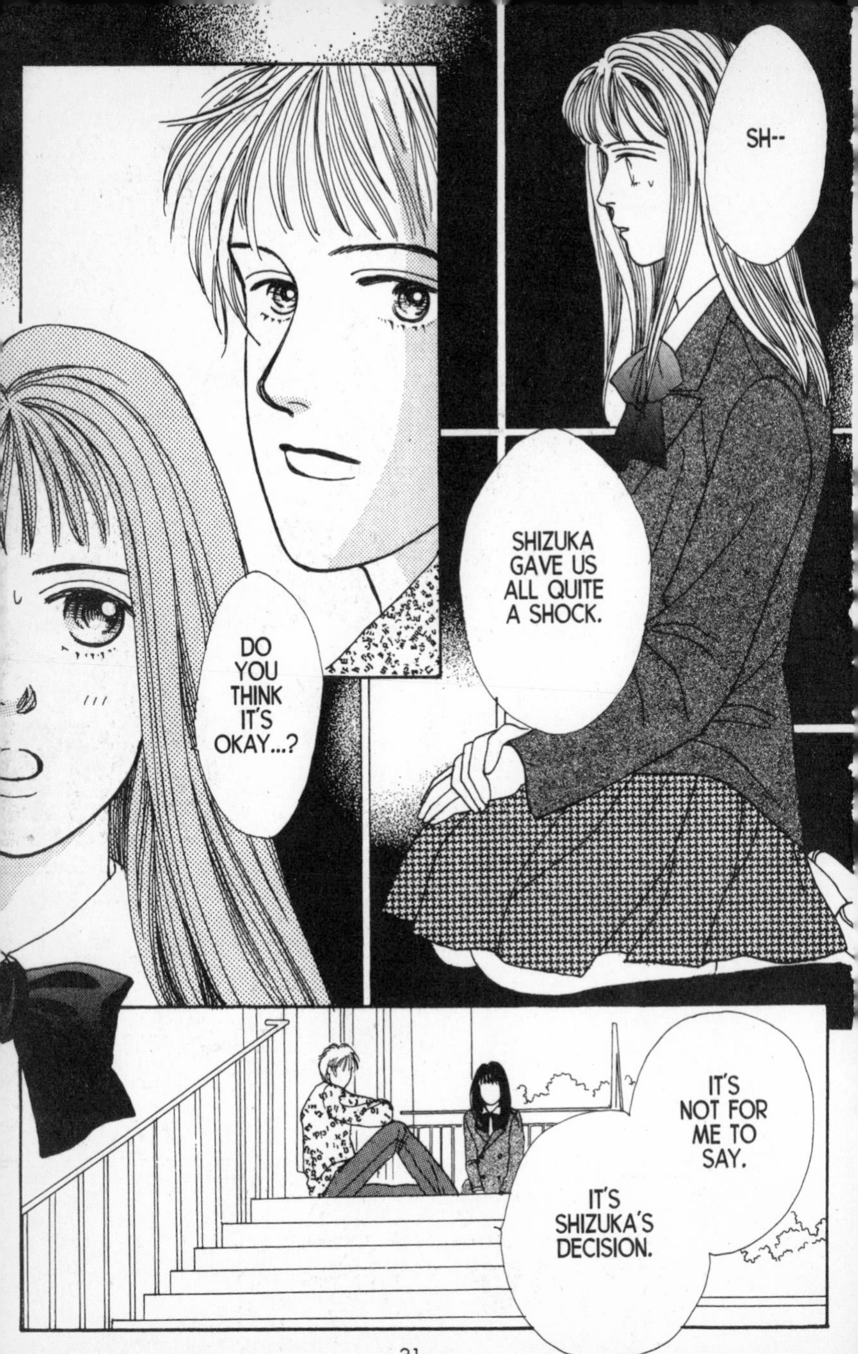
SH--
SHIZUKA GAVE US ALL QUITE A SHOCK.
DO YOU THINK IT'S OKAY...?
IT'S NOT FOR ME TO SAY.
IT'S SHIZUKA'S DECISION.

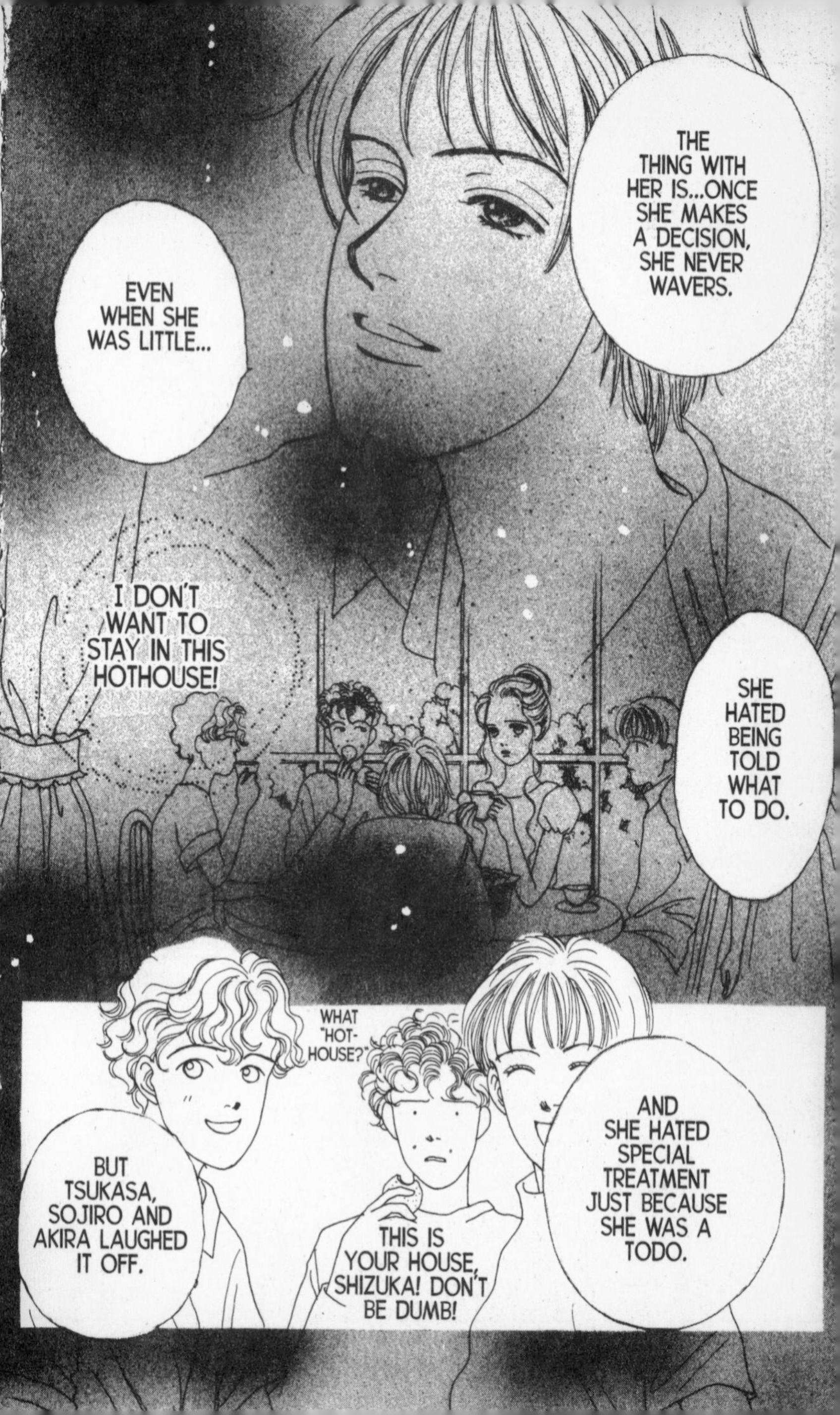
THE THING WITH HER IS...ONCE SHE MAKES A DECISION, SHE NEVER WAVERS.
EVEN WHEN SHE WAS LITTLE...
I DON'T WANT TO STAY IN THIS HOTHOUSE!
SHE HATED BEING TOLD WHAT TO DO.
AND SHE HATED SPECIAL TREATMENT JUST BECAUSE SHE WAS A TODO.
WHAT "HOT-HOUSE?"
THIS IS YOUR HOUSE, SHIZUKA! DON'T BE DUMB!
BUT TSUKASA, SOJIRO AND AKIRA LAUGHED IT OFF.

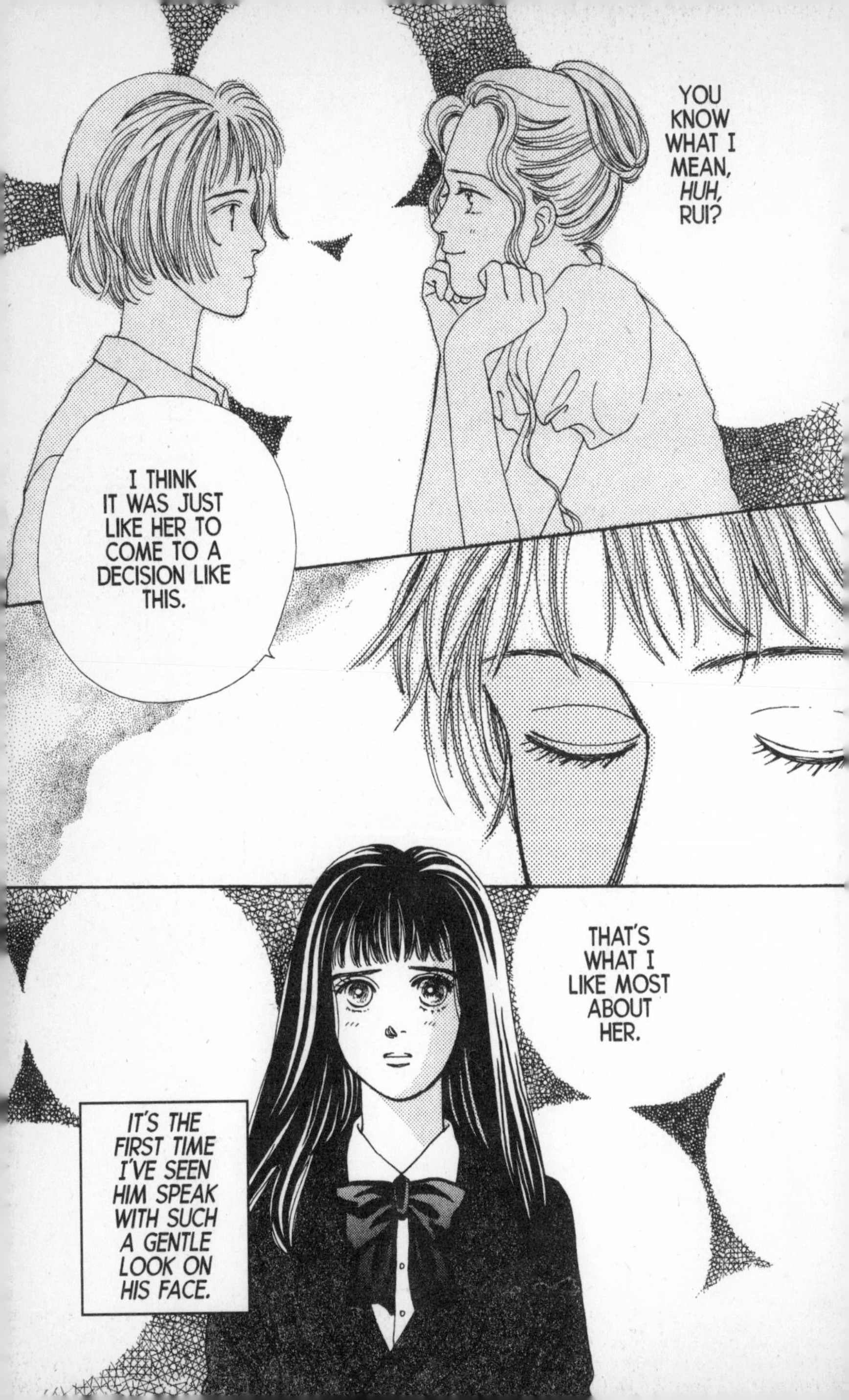
YOU KNOW WHAT I MEAN, *HUH,* RUI?
I THINK IT WAS JUST LIKE HER TO COME TO A DECISION LIKE THIS.
THAT'S WHAT I LIKE MOST ABOUT HER.
IT'S THE FIRST TIME I'VE SEEN HIM SPEAK WITH SUCH A GENTLE LOOK ON HIS FACE.

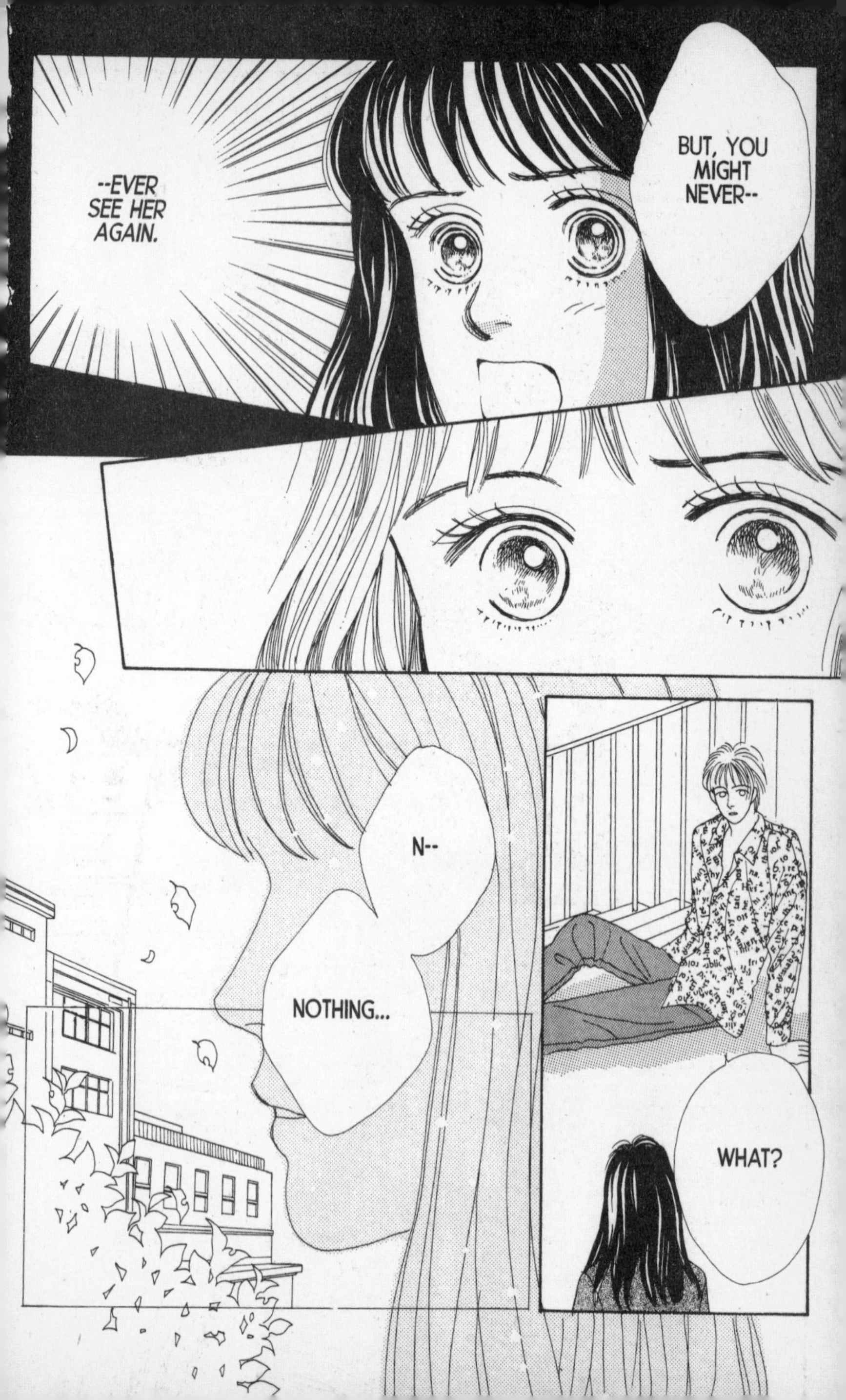
BUT, YOU MIGHT NEVER--
--EVER SEE HER AGAIN.
WHAT?
N--
NOTHING...

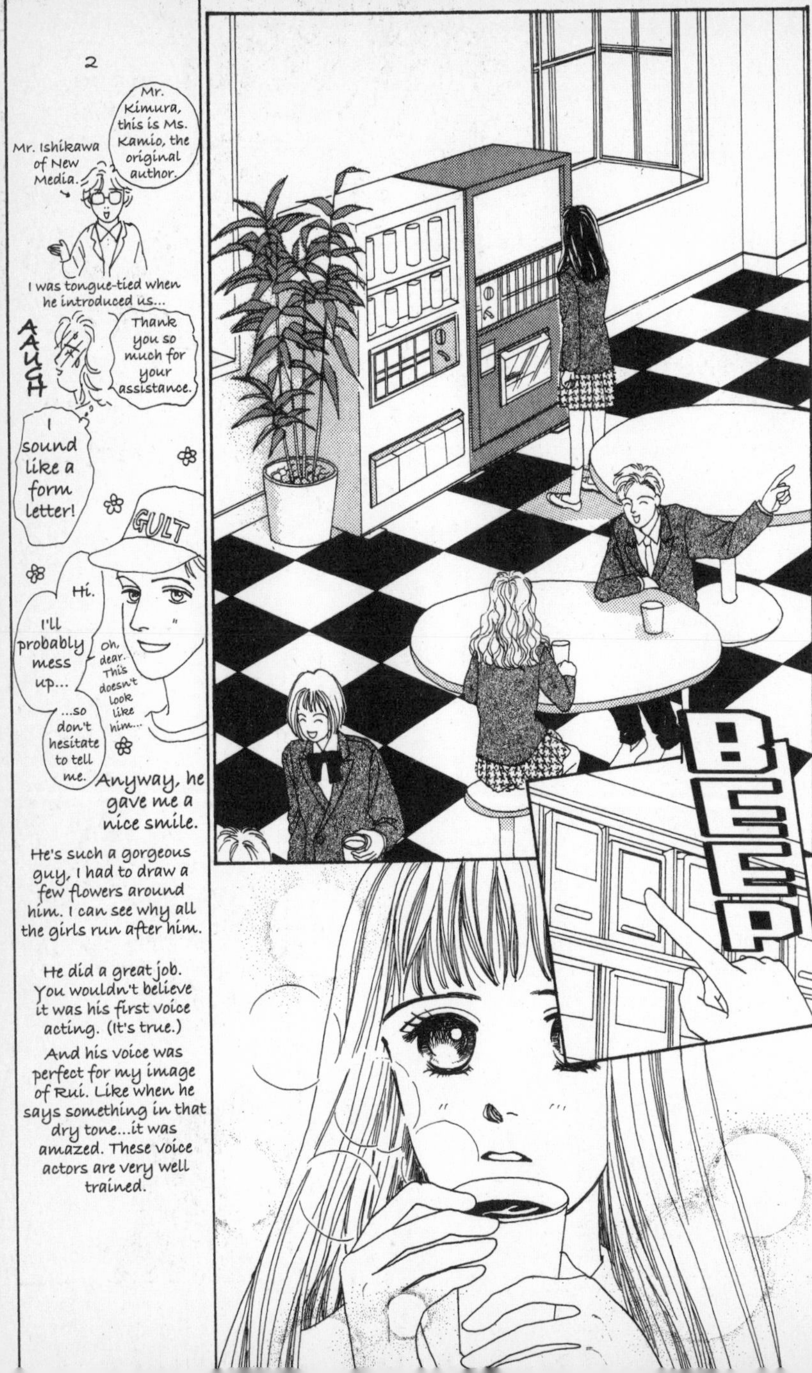
BEEP

2

Mr. Ishikawa of New Media.

Mr. Kimura, this is Ms. Kamio, the original author.

I was tongue-tied when he introduced us...

AAUGH

Thank you so much for your assistance.

I sound like a form letter!

GULT

Hi.

I'll probably mess up...

...so don't hesitate to tell me.

Oh, dear. This doesn't look like him...

Anyway, he gave me a nice smile.

He's such a gorgeous guy, I had to draw a few flowers around him. I can see why all the girls run after him.

He did a great job. You wouldn't believe it was his first voice acting. (It's true.)

And his voice was perfect for my image of Rui. Like when he says something in that dry tone...it was amazed. These voice actors are very well trained.

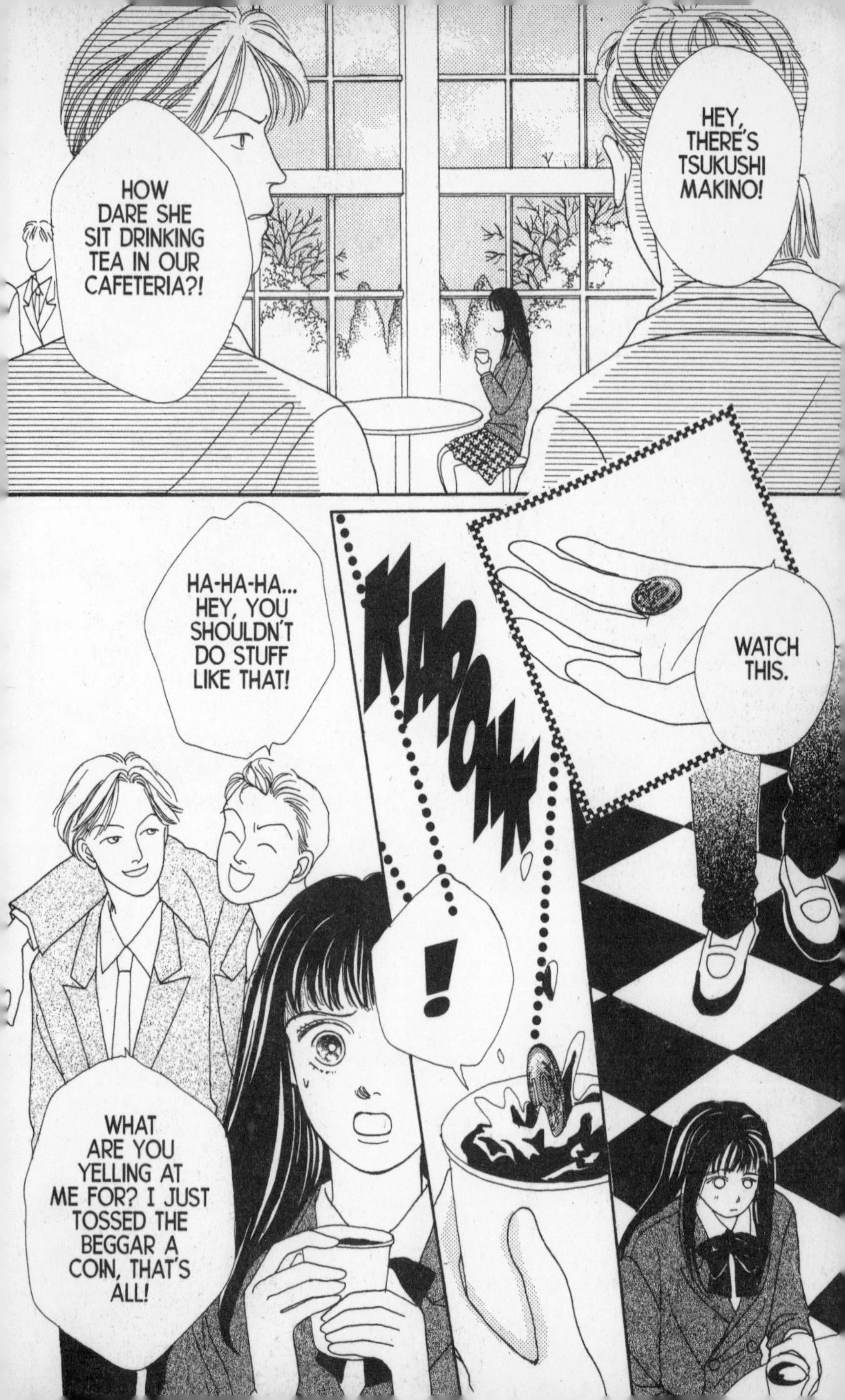
HEY, THERE'S TSUKUSHI MAKINO!
HOW DARE SHE SIT DRINKING TEA IN OUR CAFETERIA?!
WATCH THIS.
KAPONK
HA-HA-HA... HEY, YOU SHOULDN'T DO STUFF LIKE THAT!
!
WHAT ARE YOU YELLING AT ME FOR? I JUST TOSSED THE BEGGAR A COIN, THAT'S ALL!

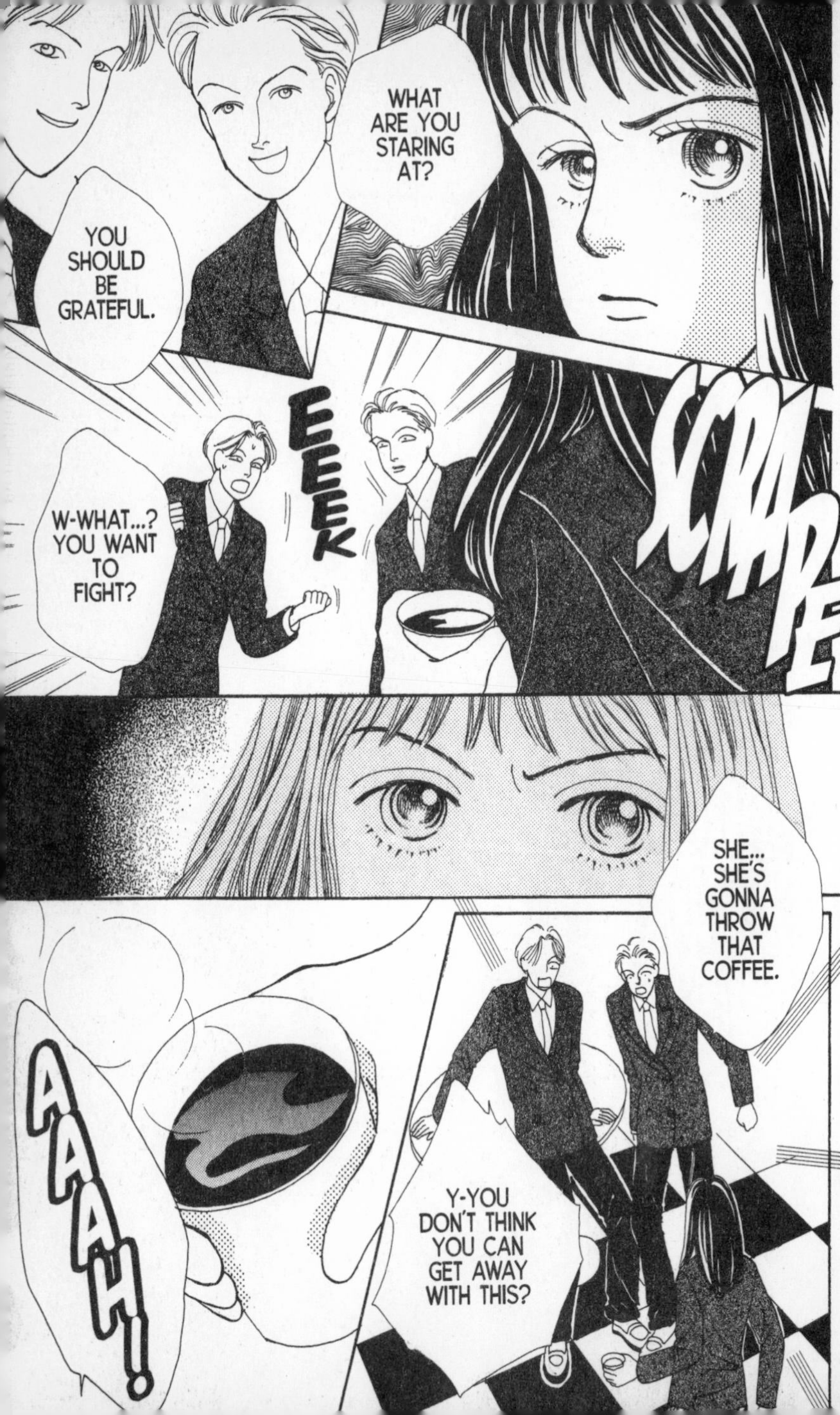
WHAT ARE YOU STARING AT?
YOU SHOULD BE GRATEFUL.
SCRAPE
EEEEK
W-WHAT...? YOU WANT TO FIGHT?
SHE... SHE'S GONNA THROW THAT COFFEE.
Y-YOU DON'T THINK YOU CAN GET AWAY WITH THIS?
AAAAH!

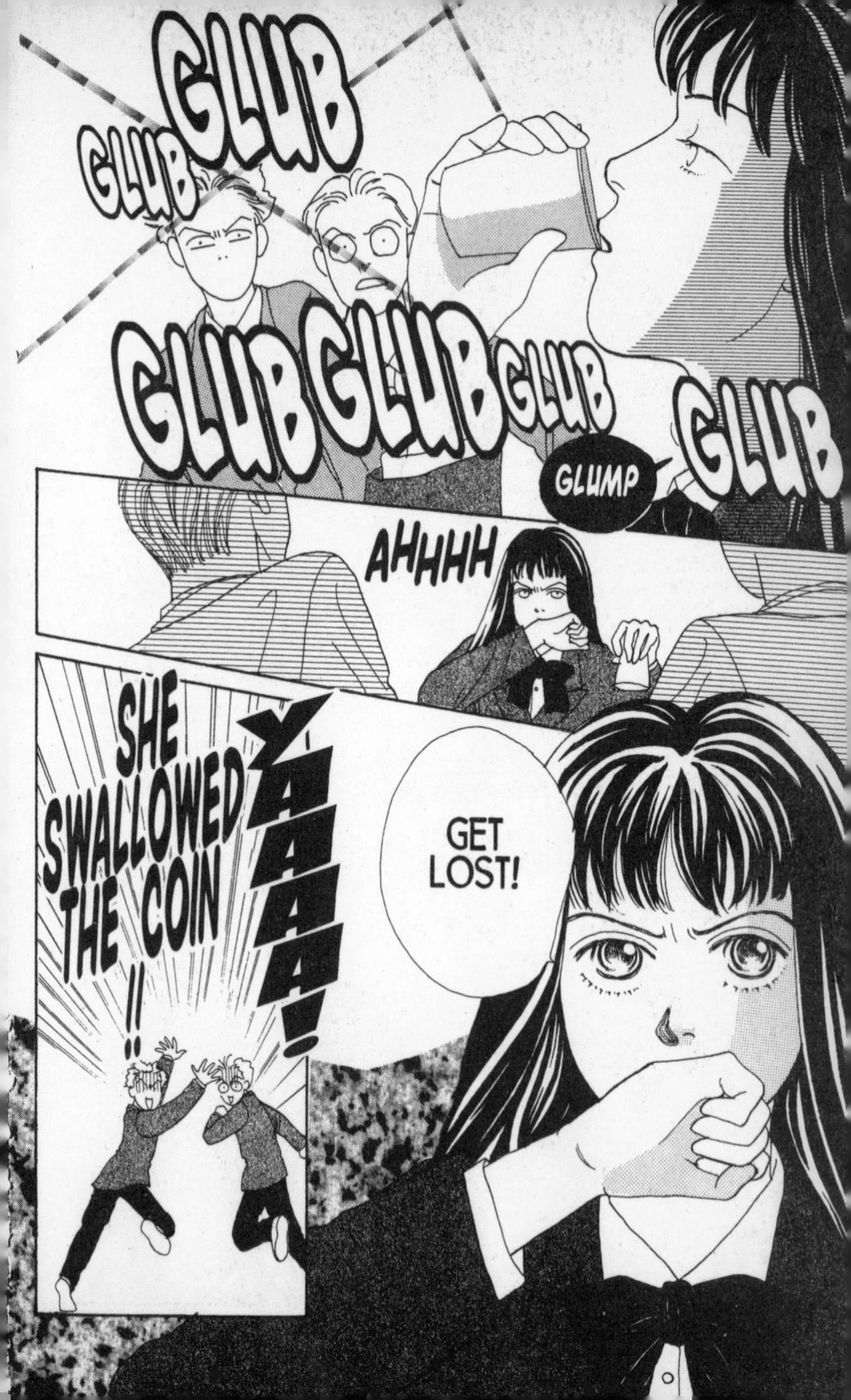
GLUB GLUB
GLUB GLUB GLUB
GLUB
GLUMP
AHHHH
GET LOST!
YAAAA!
SHE SWALLOWED THE COIN !!

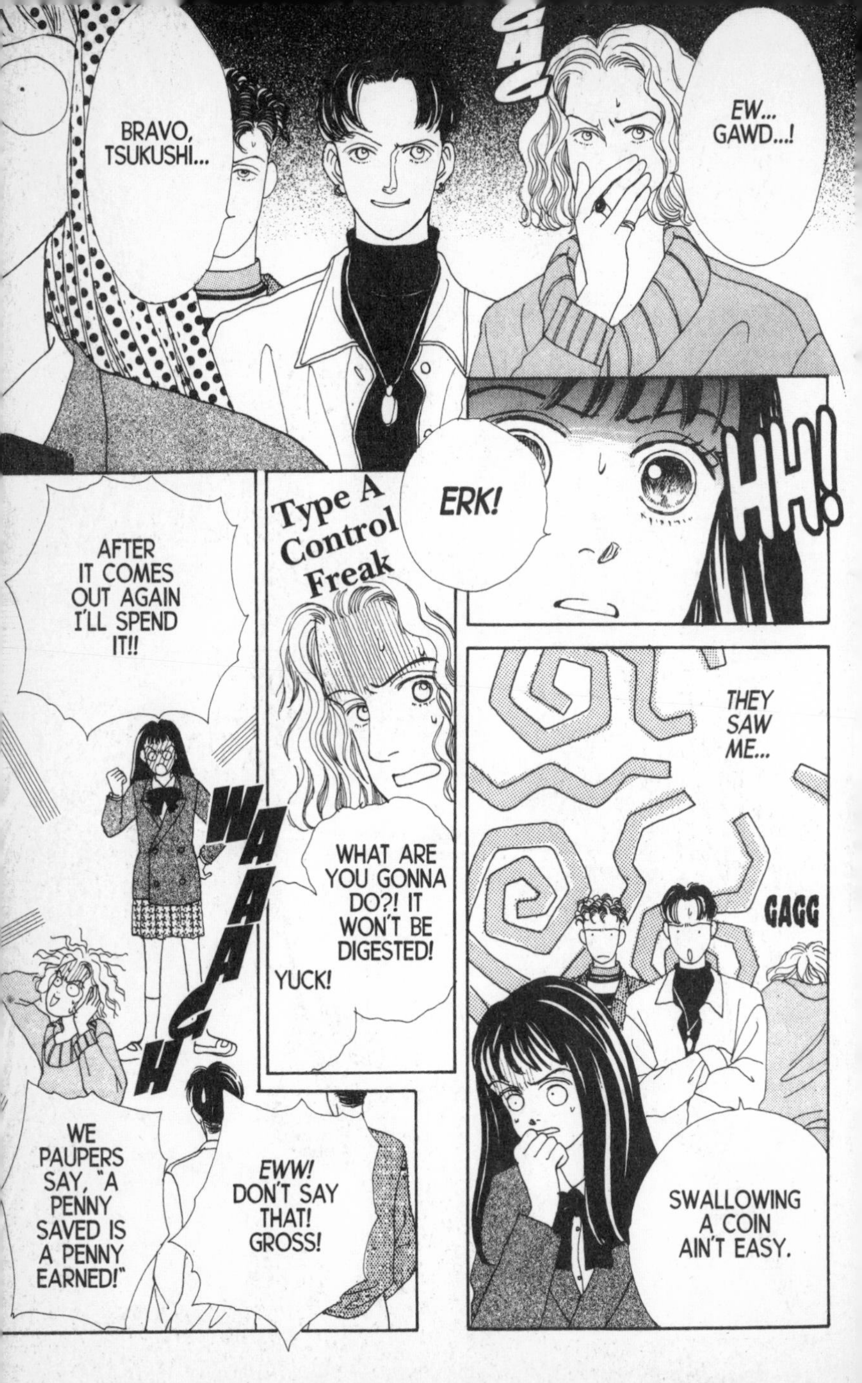
GAG
EW... GAWD...!
BRAVO, TSUKUSHI...
HH!
ERK!
THEY SAW ME...
GAGG
SWALLOWING A COIN AIN'T EASY.
Type A Control Freak
WHAT ARE YOU GONNA DO?! IT WON'T BE DIGESTED!
YUCK!
AFTER IT COMES OUT AGAIN I'LL SPEND IT!!
WAAAAGH
EWW! DON'T SAY THAT! GROSS!
WE PAUPERS SAY, "A PENNY SAVED IS A PENNY EARNED!"

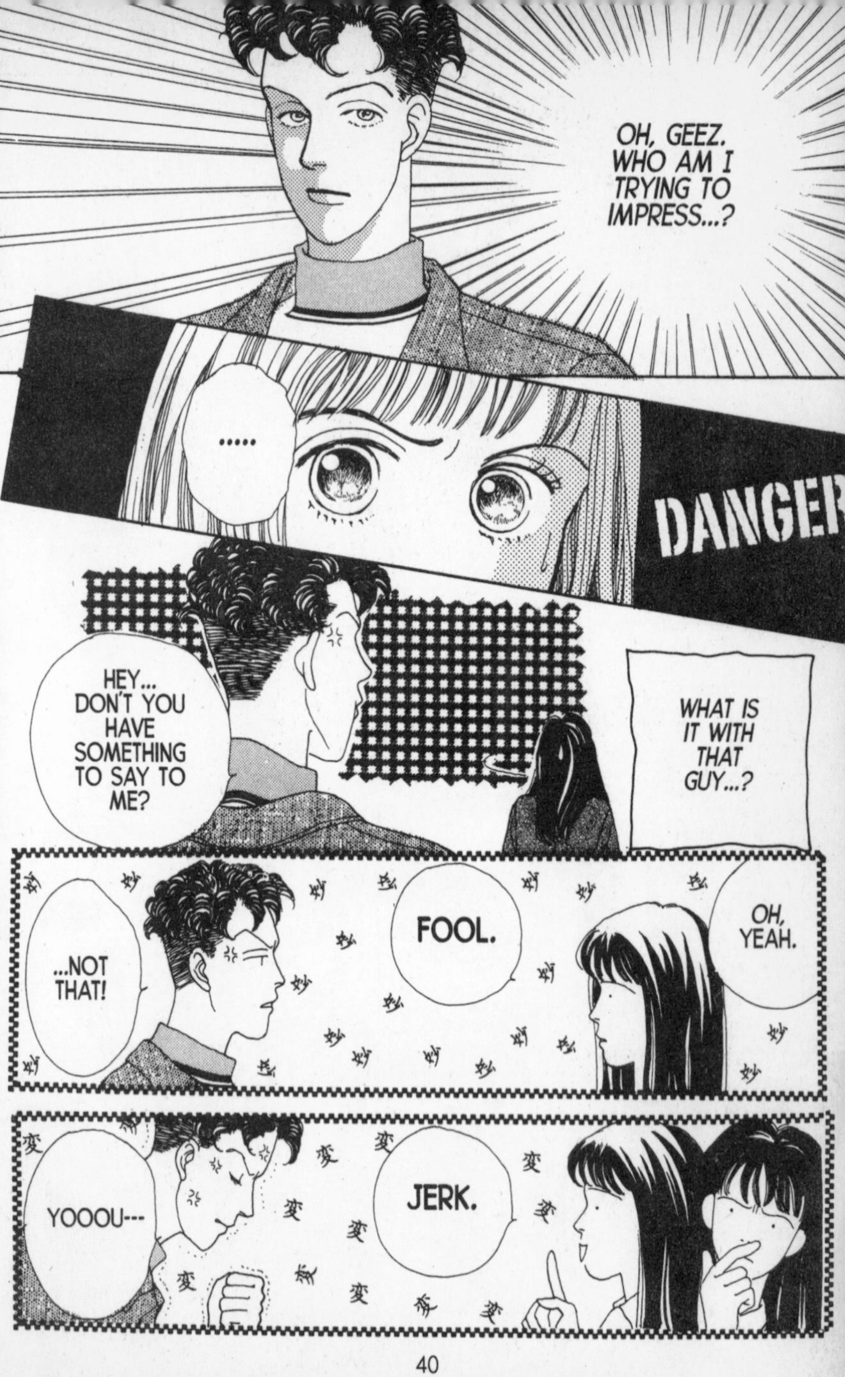
OH, GEEZ. WHO AM I TRYING TO IMPRESS...?
.....
DANGER
WHAT IS IT WITH THAT GUY...?
HEY... DON'T YOU HAVE SOMETHING TO SAY TO ME?
OH, YEAH.
FOOL.
...NOT THAT!
JERK.
YOOOU---

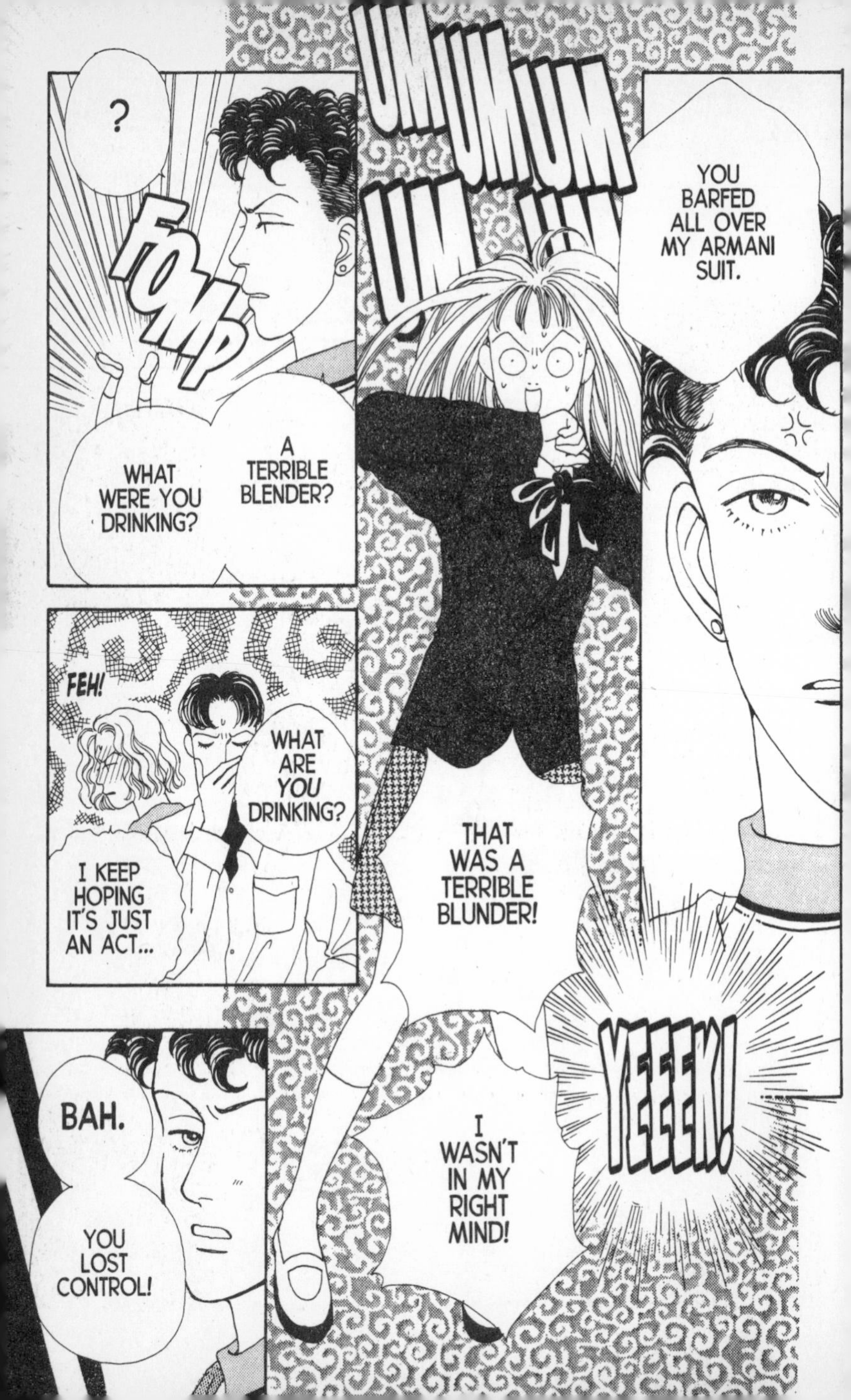

YOU BARFED ALL OVER MY ARMANI SUIT.
UM UM UM UM
THAT WAS A TERRIBLE BLUNDER!
YEEEK!
I WASN'T IN MY RIGHT MIND!
?
FOMP
A TERRIBLE BLENDER?
WHAT WERE YOU DRINKING?
FEH!
WHAT ARE *YOU* DRINKING?
I KEEP HOPING IT'S JUST AN ACT...
BAH.
YOU LOST CONTROL!

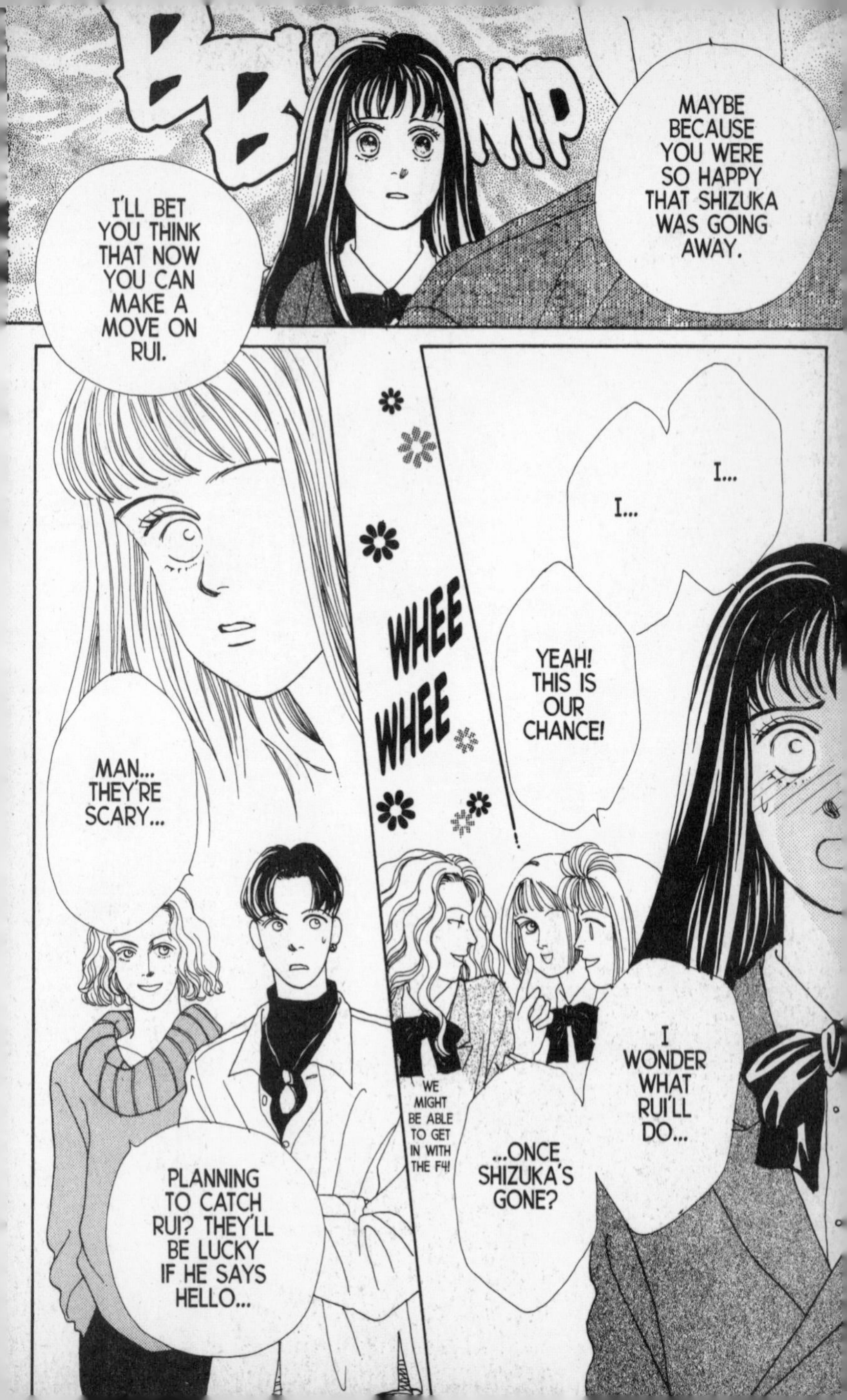
MAYBE BECAUSE YOU WERE SO HAPPY THAT SHIZUKA WAS GOING AWAY.
I'LL BET YOU THINK THAT NOW YOU CAN MAKE A MOVE ON RUI.
I... I...
YEAH! THIS IS OUR CHANCE!
WHEE WHEE
I WONDER WHAT RUI'LL DO...
...ONCE SHIZUKA'S GONE?
WE MIGHT BE ABLE TO GET IN WITH THE F4!
MAN... THEY'RE SCARY...
PLANNING TO CATCH RUI? THEY'LL BE LUCKY IF HE SAYS HELLO...

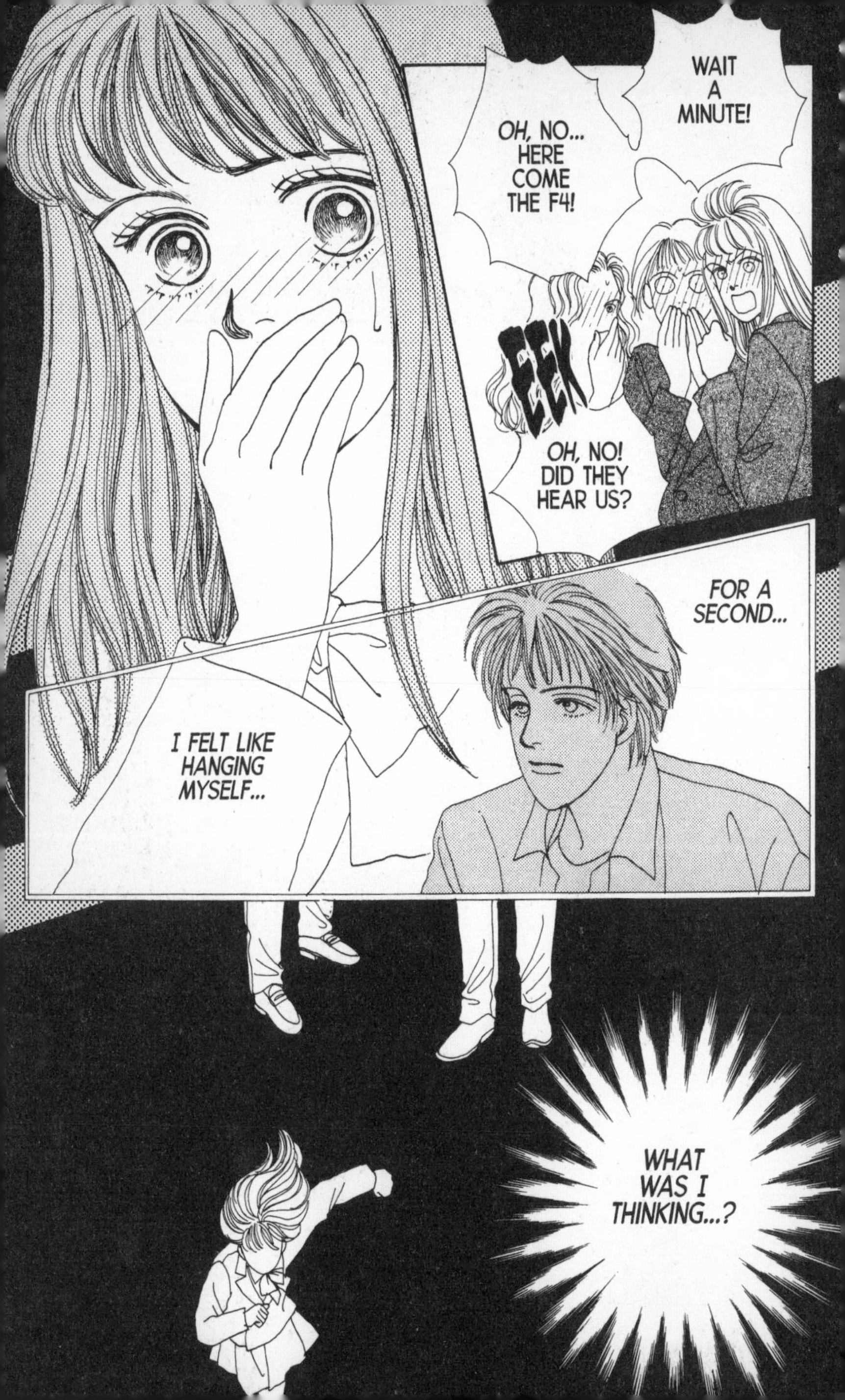
WAIT A MINUTE!
OH, NO... HERE COME THE F4!
EEK
OH, NO! DID THEY HEAR US?
FOR A SECOND...
I FELT LIKE HANGING MYSELF...
WHAT WAS I THINKING...?

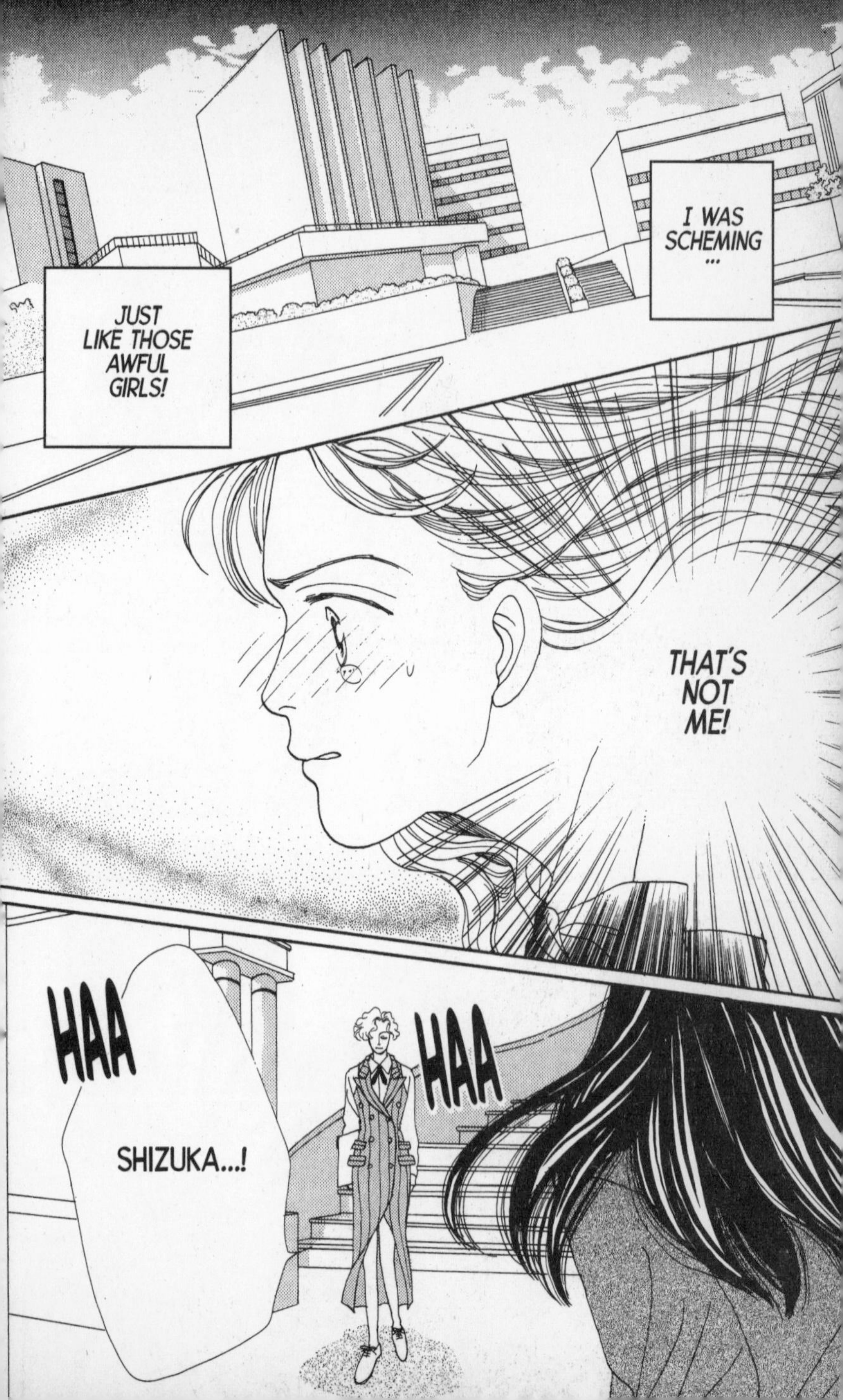
I WAS SCHEMING ...
JUST LIKE THOSE AWFUL GIRLS!
THAT'S NOT ME!
HAA
HAA
SHIZUKA...!

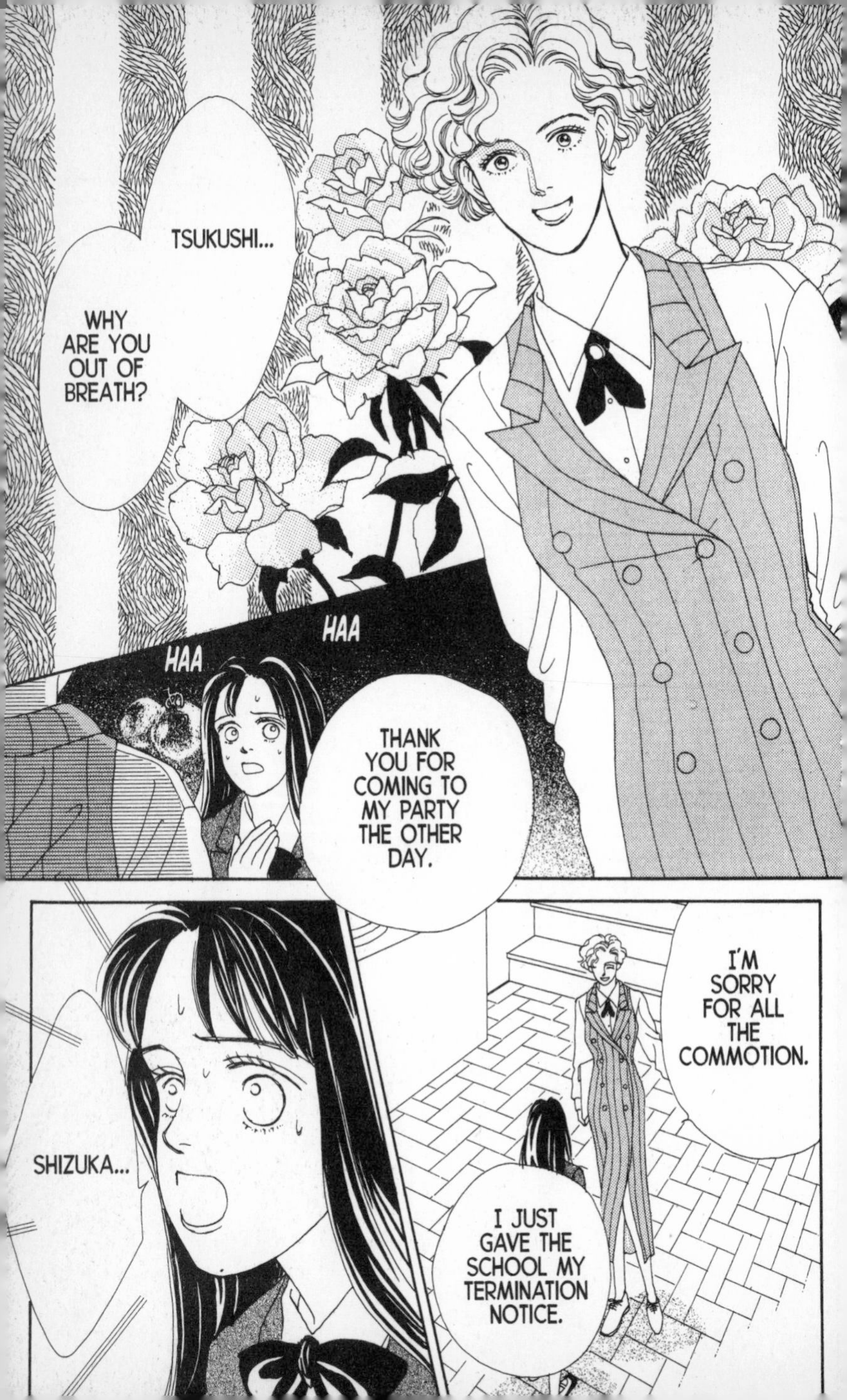
TSUKUSHI...
WHY ARE YOU OUT OF BREATH?
HAA
HAA
THANK YOU FOR COMING TO MY PARTY THE OTHER DAY.
I'M SORRY FOR ALL THE COMMOTION.
I JUST GAVE THE SCHOOL MY TERMINATION NOTICE.
SHIZUKA...

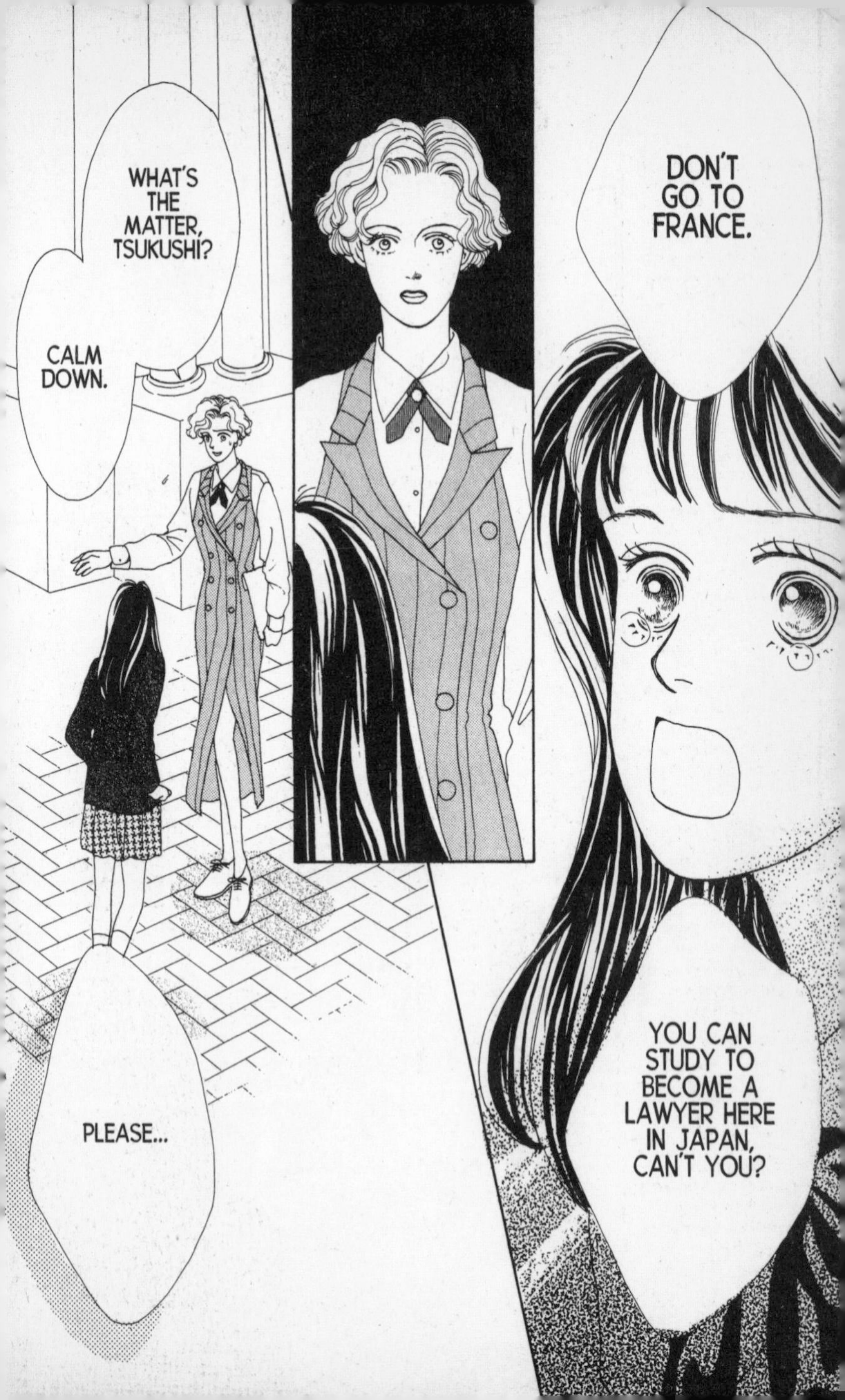
DON'T GO TO FRANCE.
YOU CAN STUDY TO BECOME A LAWYER HERE IN JAPAN, CAN'T YOU?
WHAT'S THE MATTER, TSUKUSHI?
CALM DOWN.
PLEASE...

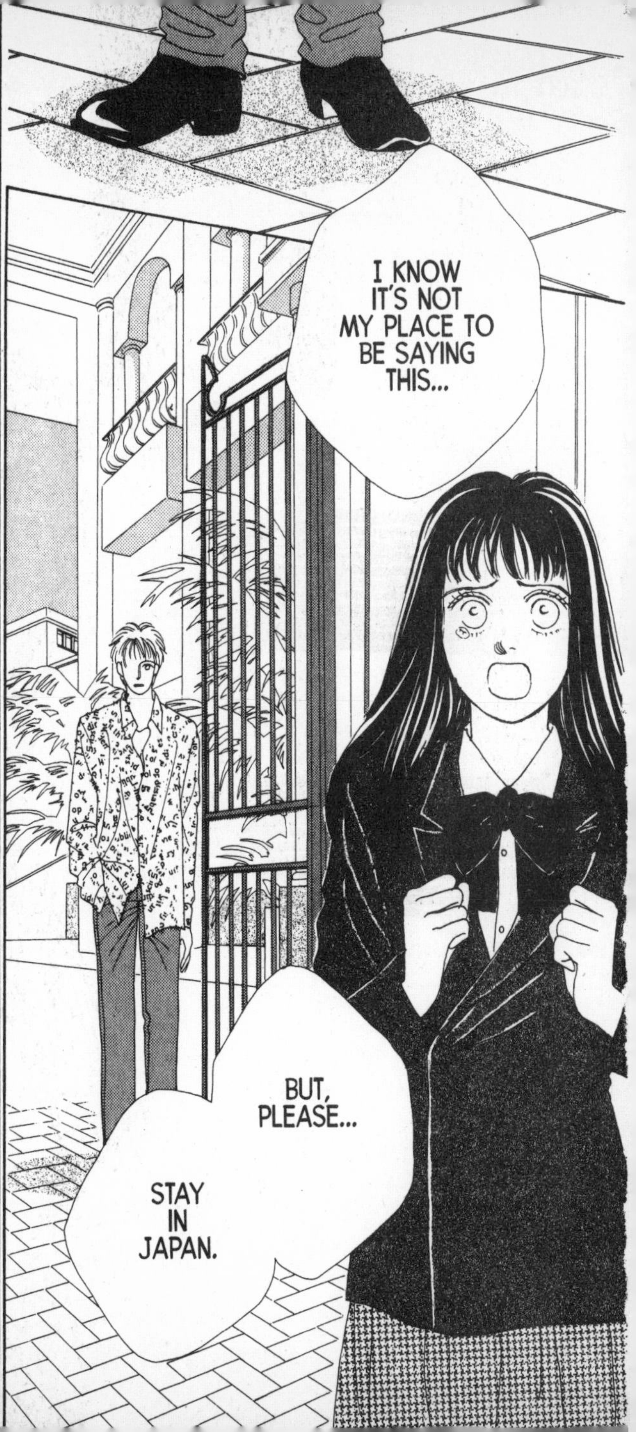
I KNOW IT'S NOT MY PLACE TO BE SAYING THIS...
BUT, PLEASE...
STAY IN JAPAN.

3

Mr. Nishio, who voiced Tsukasa's part, was very good, too. He caught that slightly dopey drawl of Tsukasa's very well. He was dressed all in black, too.

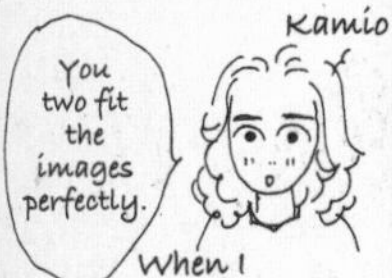
Kamio
You two fit the images perfectly.

When I said that...

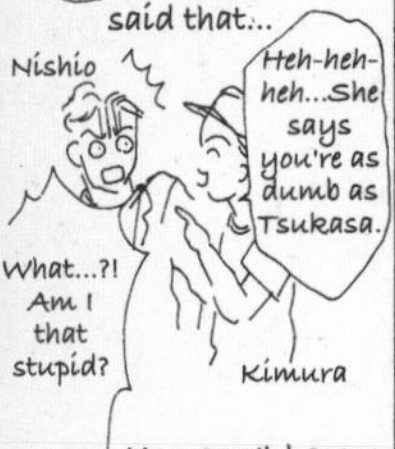
Nishio
Heh-heh-heh...She says you're as dumb as Tsukasa.
What...?! Am I that stupid?
Kimura

He wasn't happy about it.

Tomosa Yokoyama, who voiced Tsukushi's part, was very pretty and slim.

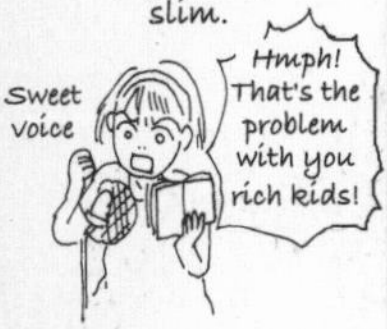
Sweet voice
Hmph! That's the problem with you rich kids!

And the actress who did Shizuka's part was very beautiful.

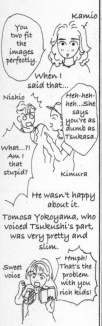

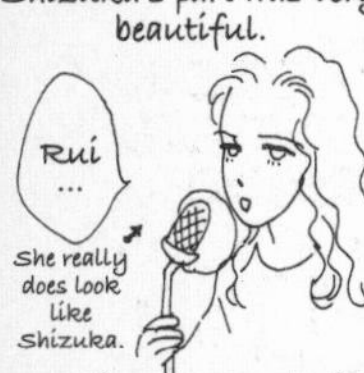
Rui ...
She really does look like Shizuka.

Her voice was wonderful and very sexy. Afterwards, Mr. Kimura said...

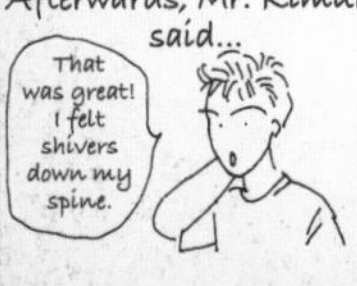
That was great! I felt shivers down my spine.

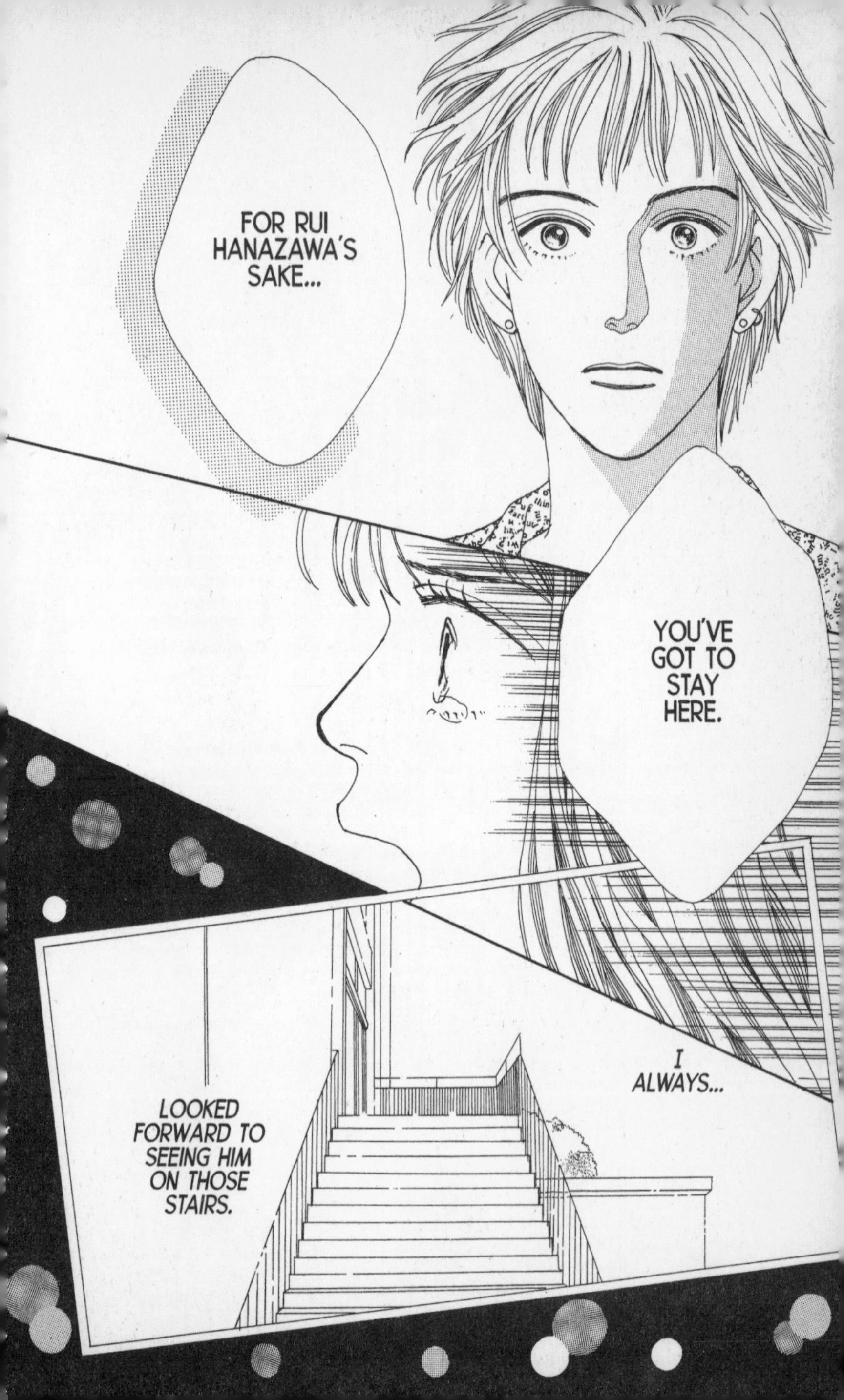
FOR RUI HANAZAWA'S SAKE...
YOU'VE GOT TO STAY HERE.
I ALWAYS...
LOOKED FORWARD TO SEEING HIM ON THOSE STAIRS.

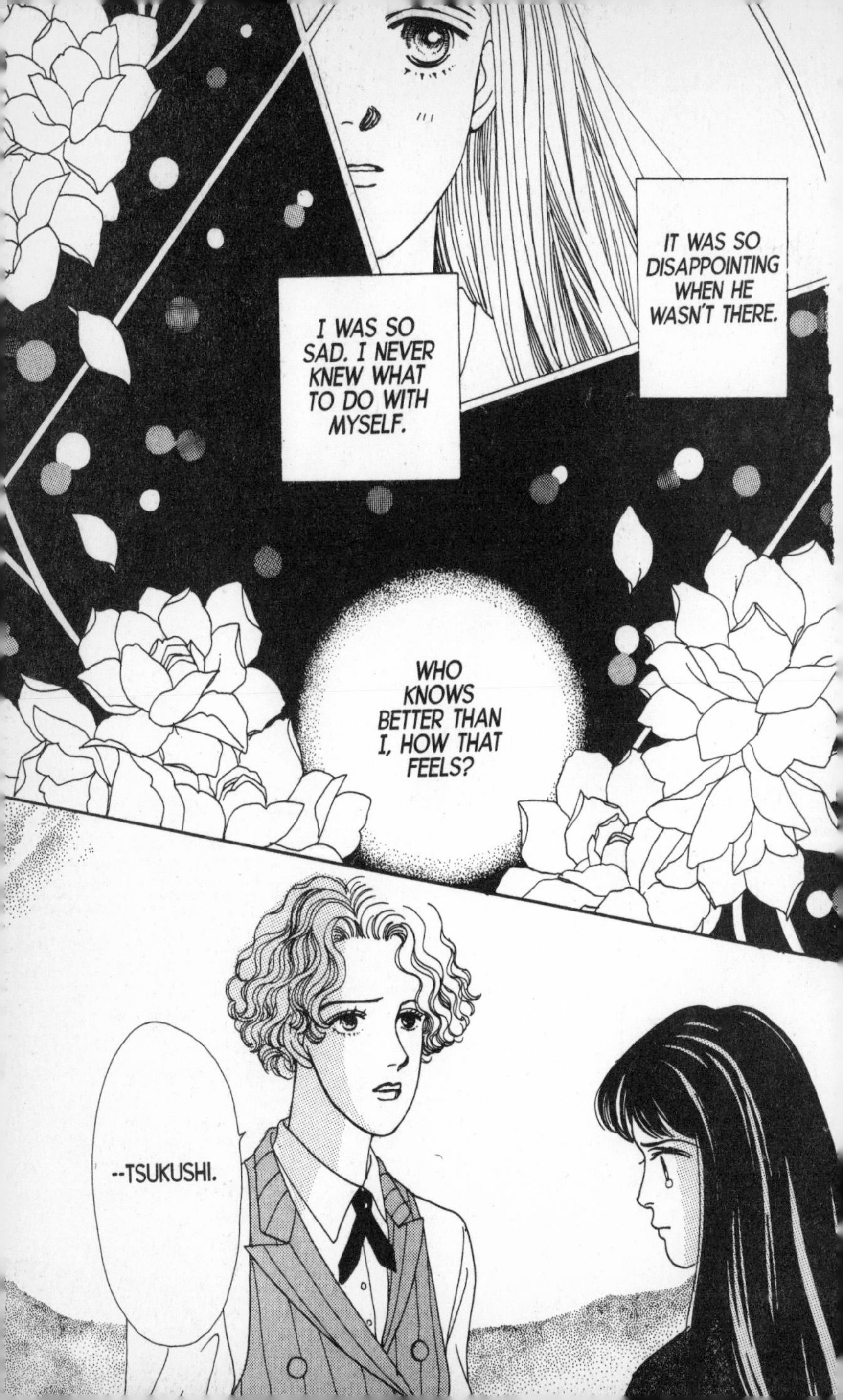
IT WAS SO DISAPPOINTING WHEN HE WASN'T THERE.
I WAS SO SAD. I NEVER KNEW WHAT TO DO WITH MYSELF.
WHO KNOWS BETTER THAN I, HOW THAT FEELS?
--TSUKUSHI.

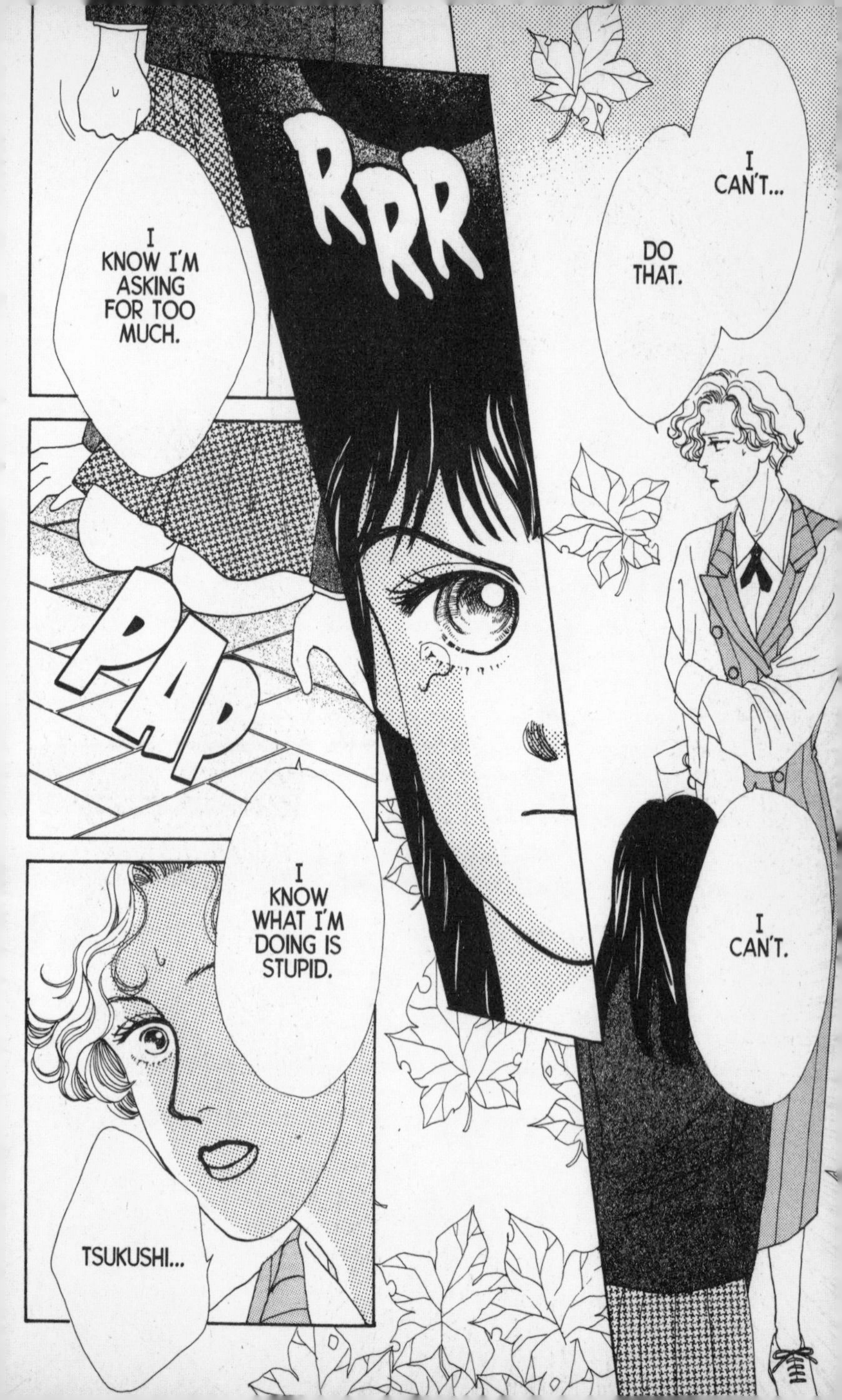
I CAN'T... DO THAT.
I CAN'T.
RRR
I KNOW I'M ASKING FOR TOO MUCH.
PAP
I KNOW WHAT I'M DOING IS STUPID.
TSUKUSHI...

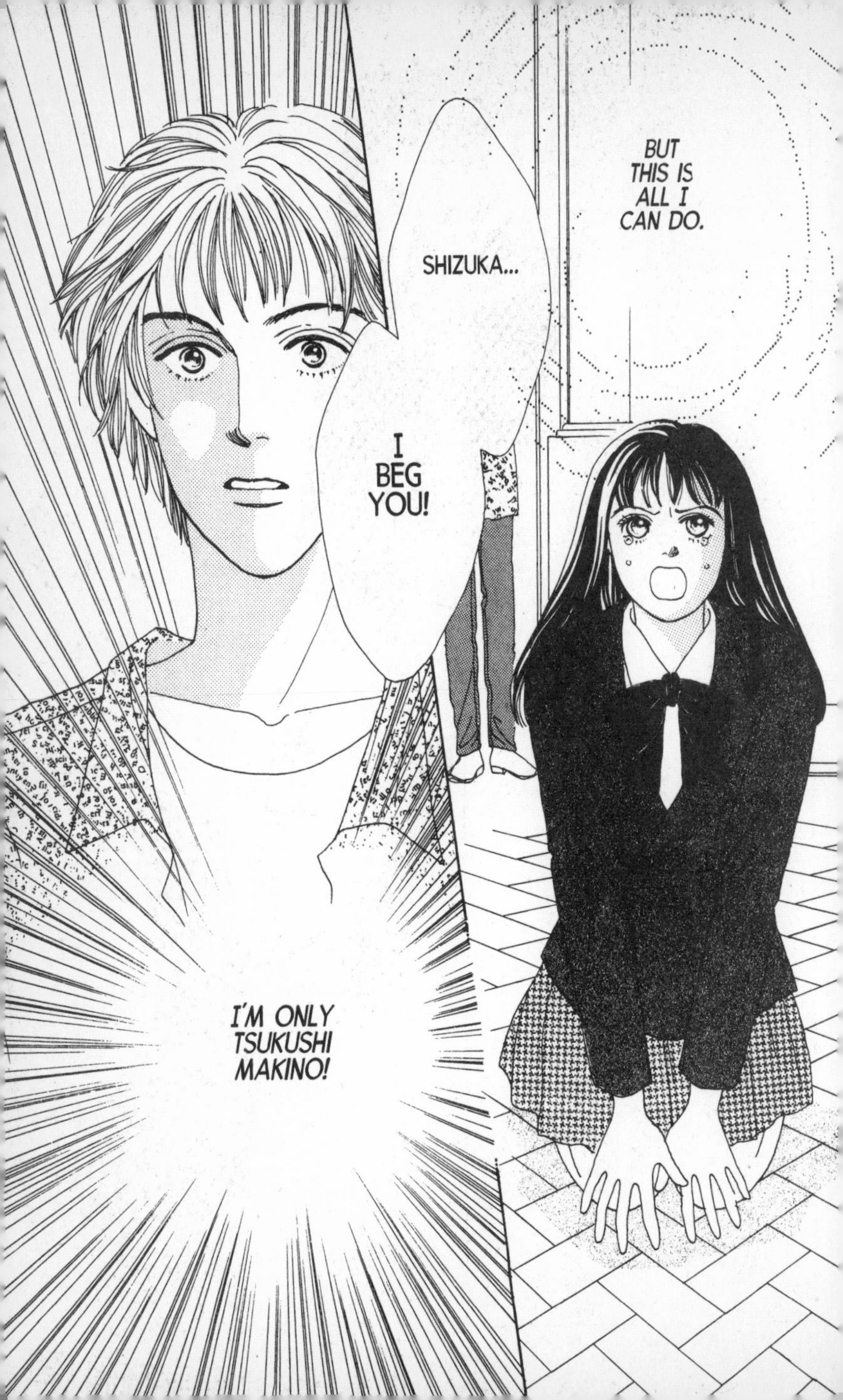
BUT THIS IS ALL I CAN DO.
SHIZUKA...
I BEG YOU!
I'M ONLY TSUKUSHI MAKINO!

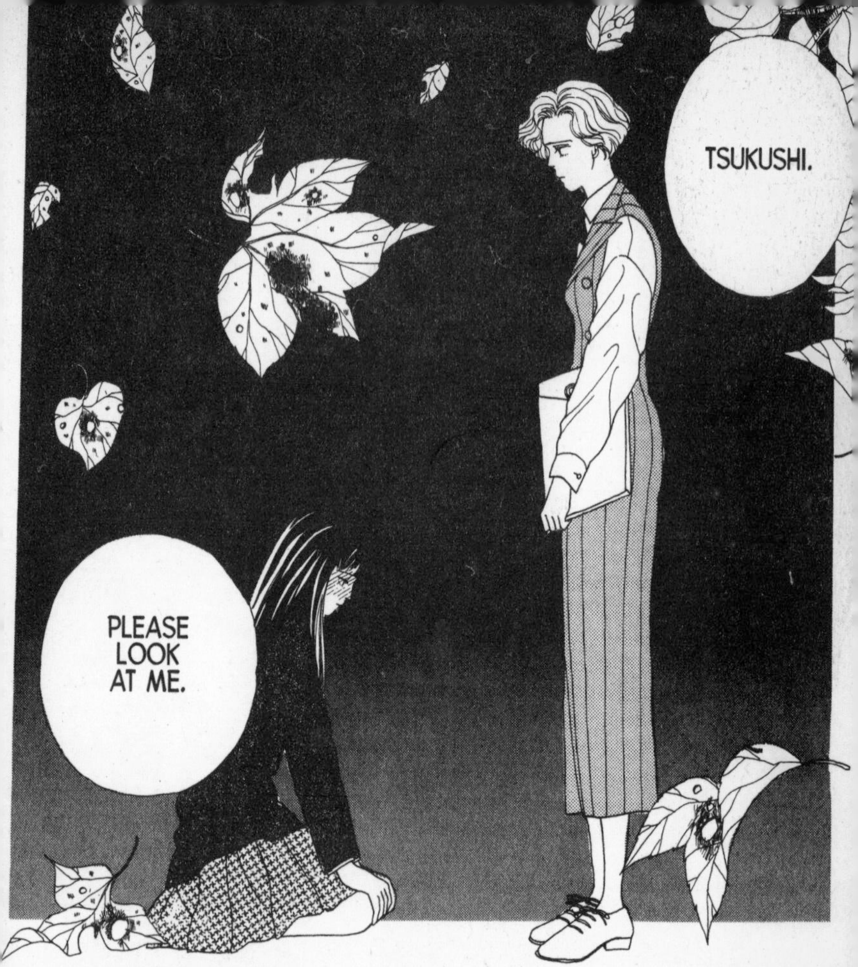
TSUKUSHI.
PLEASE LOOK AT ME.

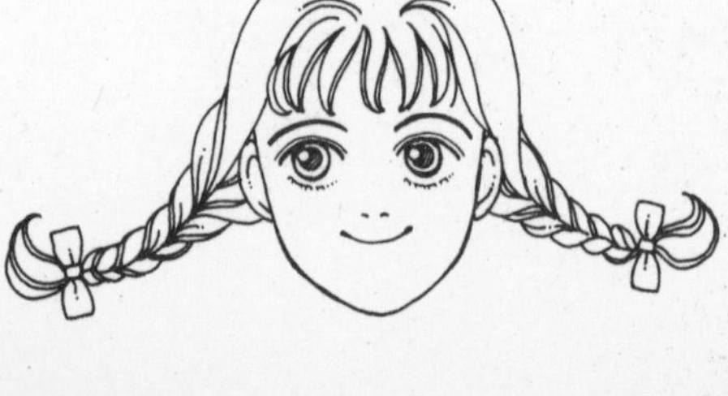

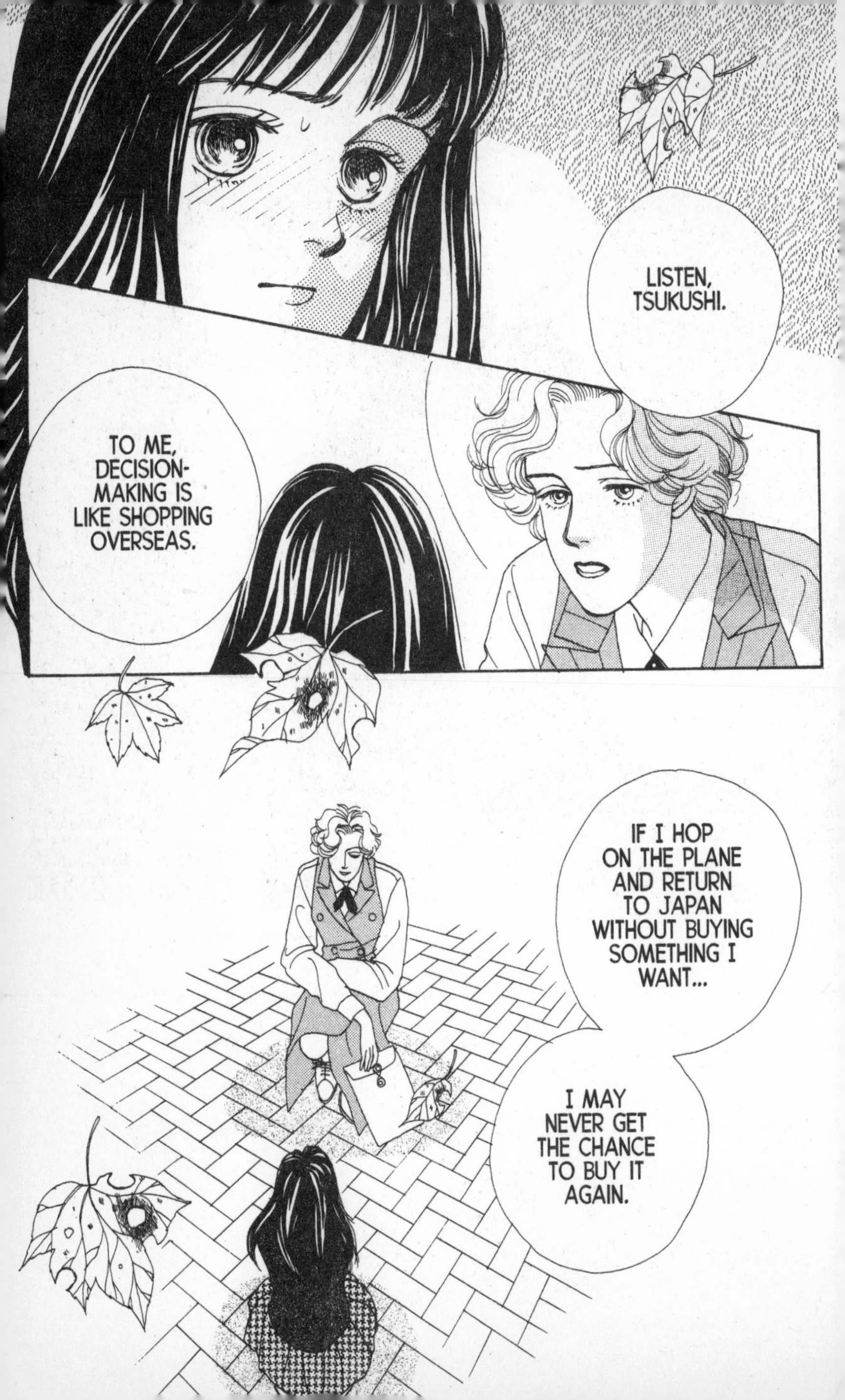
LISTEN, TSUKUSHI.
TO ME, DECISION-MAKING IS LIKE SHOPPING OVERSEAS.
IF I HOP ON THE PLANE AND RETURN TO JAPAN WITHOUT BUYING SOMETHING I WANT...
I MAY NEVER GET THE CHANCE TO BUY IT AGAIN.

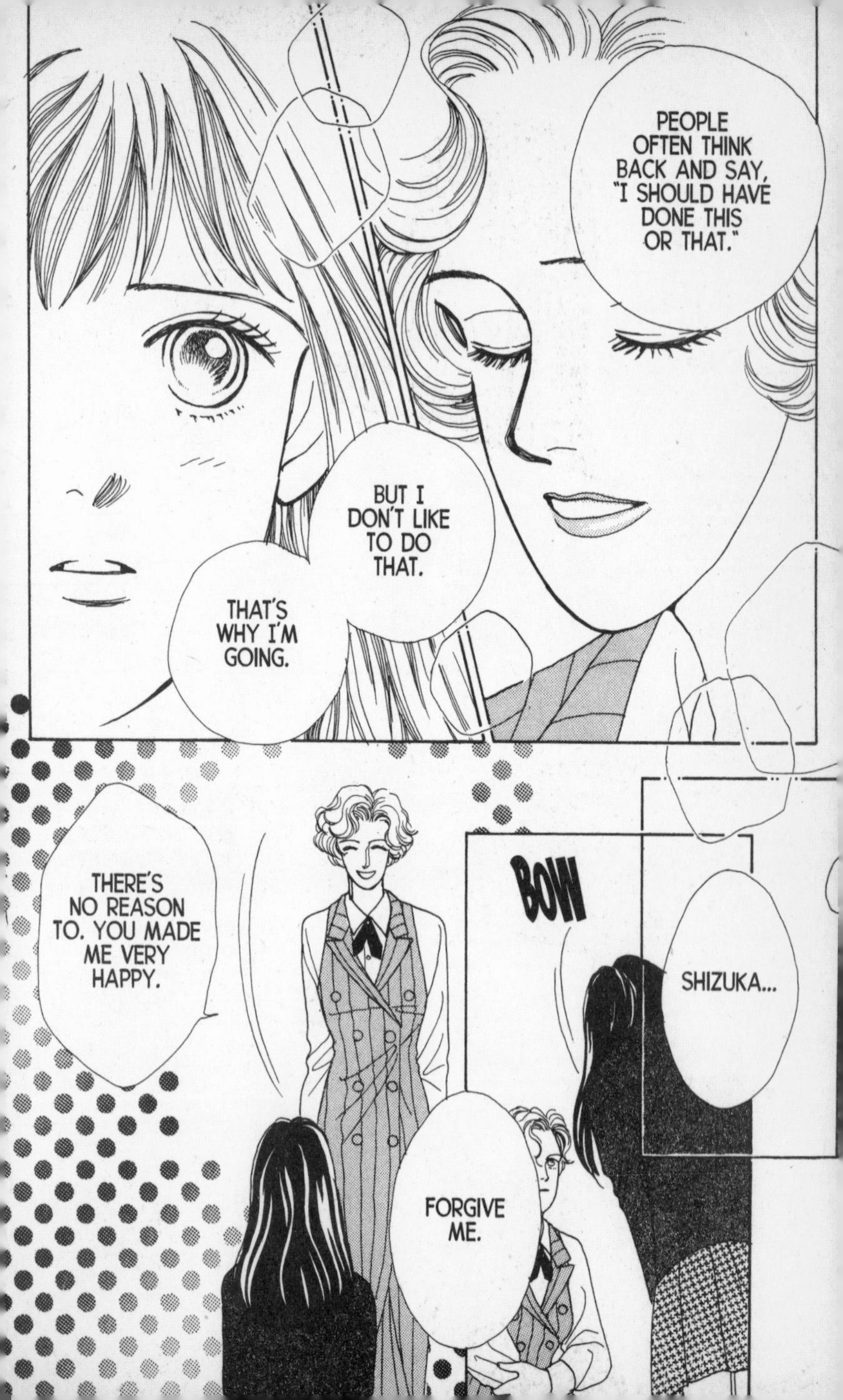
PEOPLE OFTEN THINK BACK AND SAY, "I SHOULD HAVE DONE THIS OR THAT."
BUT I DON'T LIKE TO DO THAT.
THAT'S WHY I'M GOING.
SHIZUKA...
BOW
FORGIVE ME.
THERE'S NO REASON TO. YOU MADE ME VERY HAPPY.

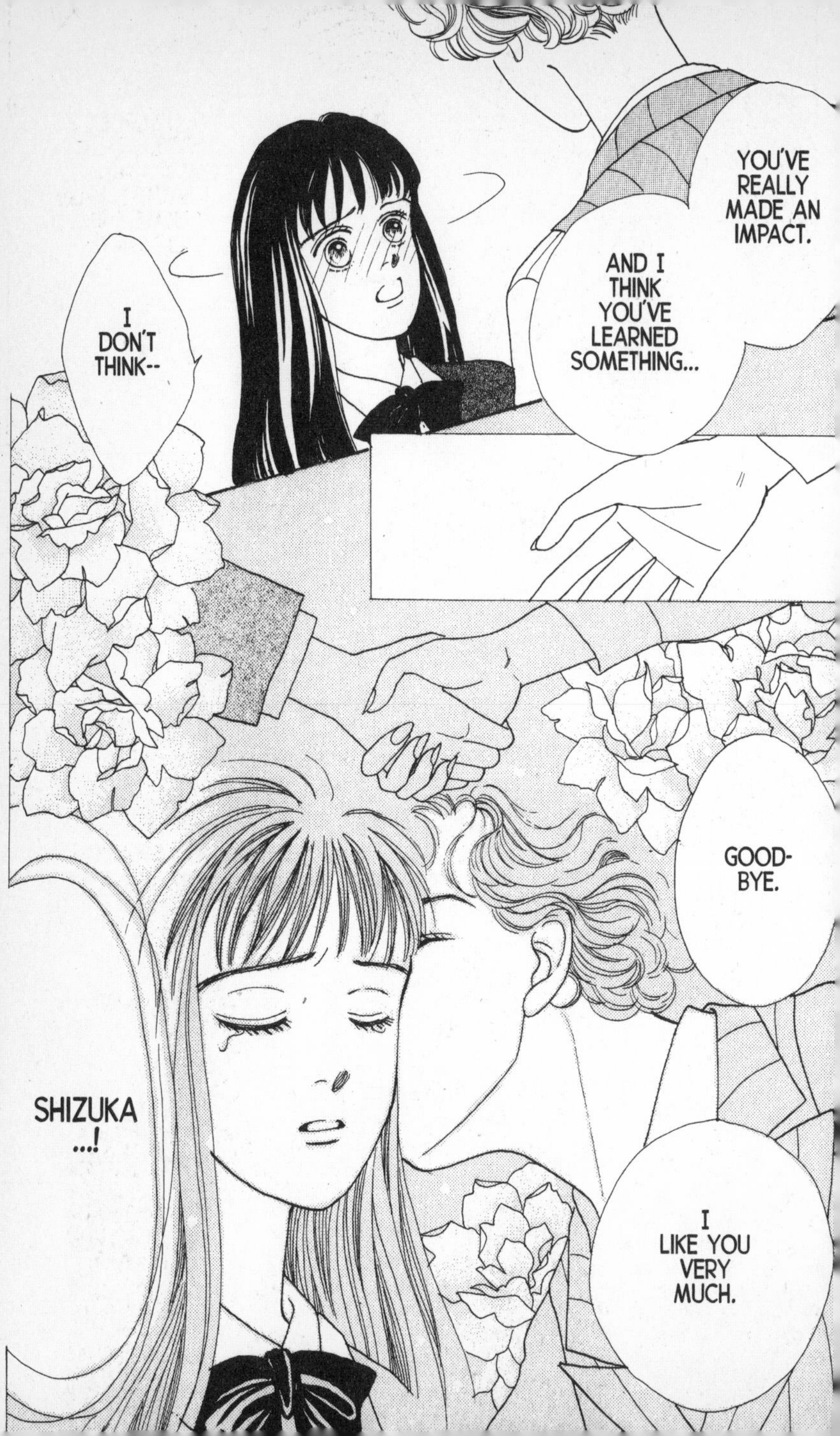
YOU'VE REALLY MADE AN IMPACT.
AND I THINK YOU'VE LEARNED SOMETHING...
I DON'T THINK--
GOOD-BYE.
I LIKE YOU VERY MUCH.
SHIZUKA ...!

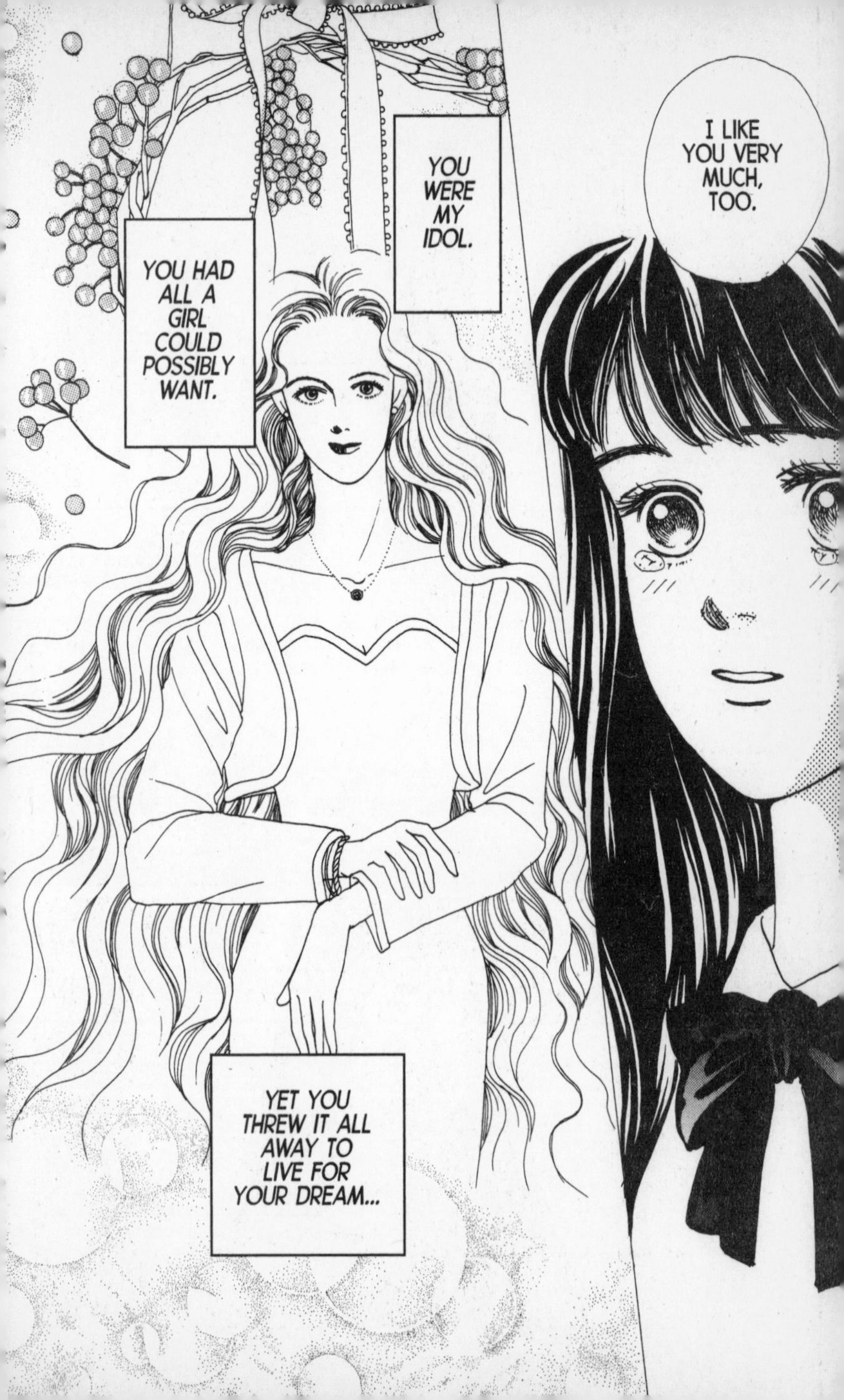
I LIKE YOU VERY MUCH, TOO.
YOU WERE MY IDOL.
YOU HAD ALL A GIRL COULD POSSIBLY WANT.
YET YOU THREW IT ALL AWAY TO LIVE FOR YOUR DREAM...

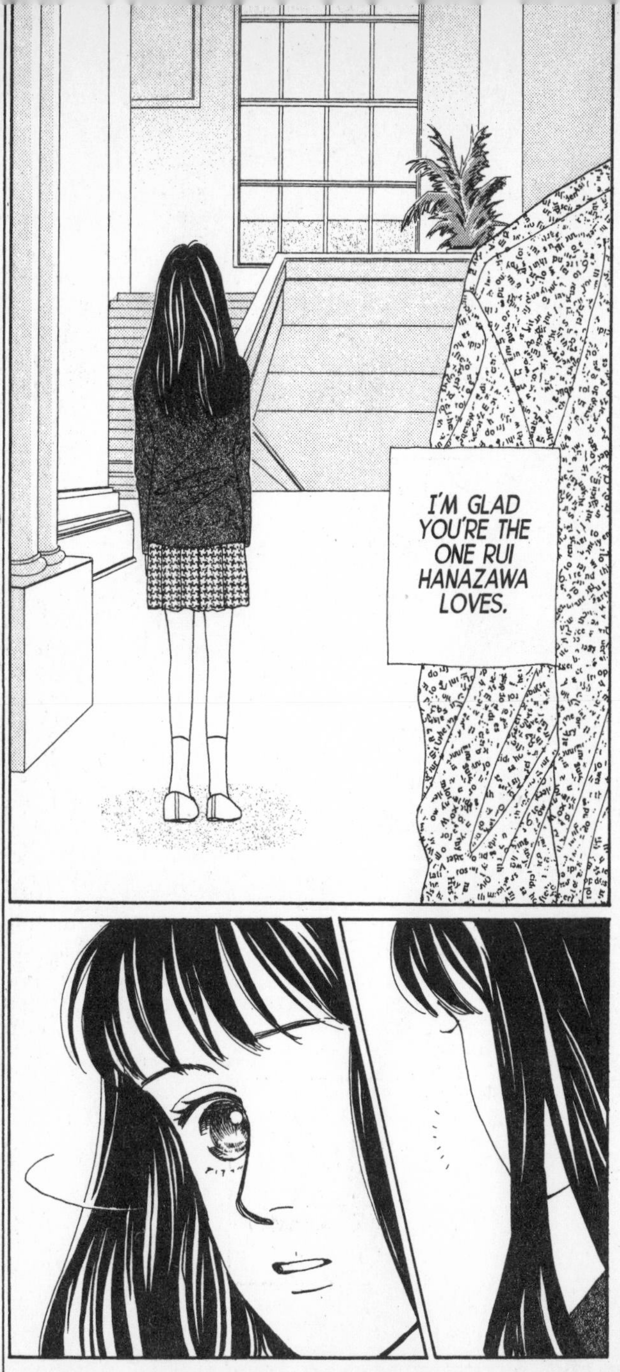
I'M GLAD YOU'RE THE ONE RUI HANAZAWA LOVES.

4

Let me say a few more words about the voice actors.

The actor who had the part of Kazuya was really into his role.

He even looked like my image of Kazuya.

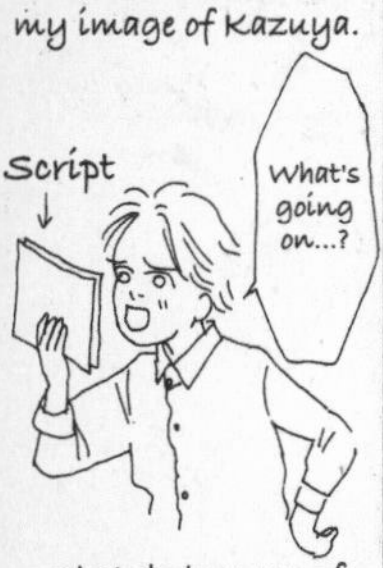
Script
What's going on...?

That dorky way of speaking...he really sounded like Kazuya.

His dialogue with Tsukasa was so funny...It made us all laugh.

That reminds me... That Kazuya character is one of my favorites, but I get some fan letters saying he's "creepy." I wonder why...

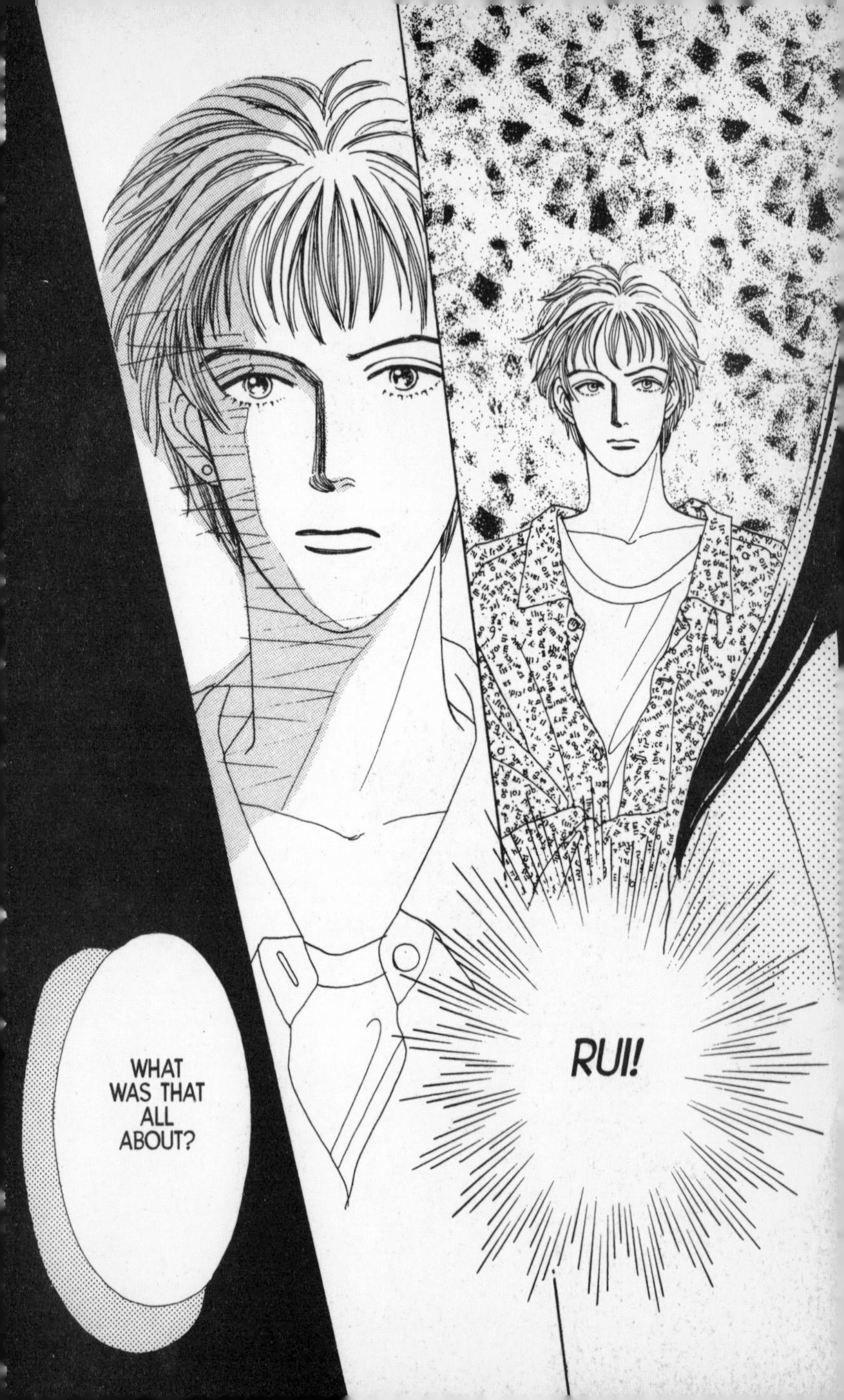
RUI!
WHAT WAS THAT ALL ABOUT?

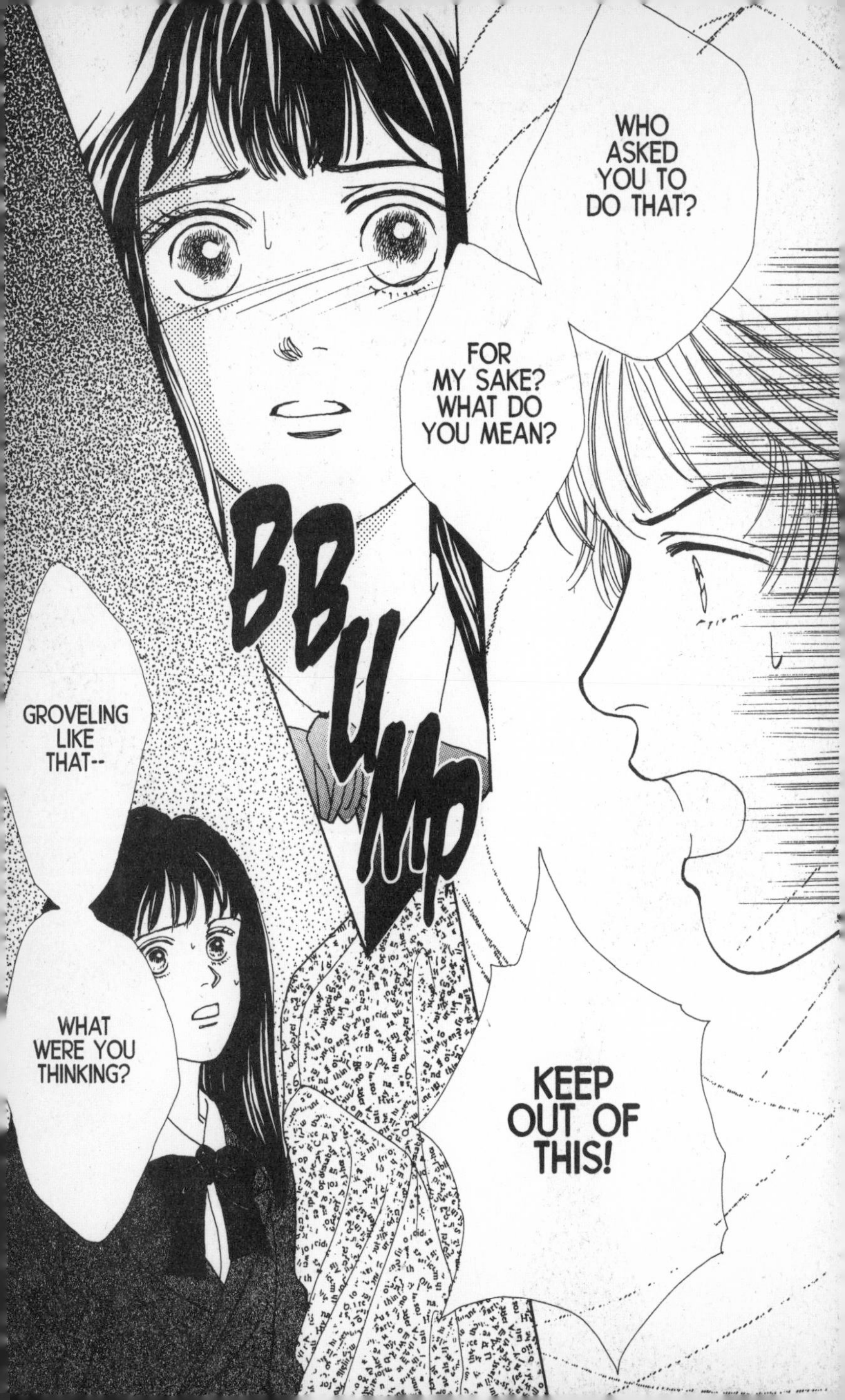
WHO ASKED YOU TO DO THAT?
FOR MY SAKE? WHAT DO YOU MEAN?
BBUMP
GROVELING LIKE THAT--
WHAT WERE YOU THINKING?
KEEP OUT OF THIS!

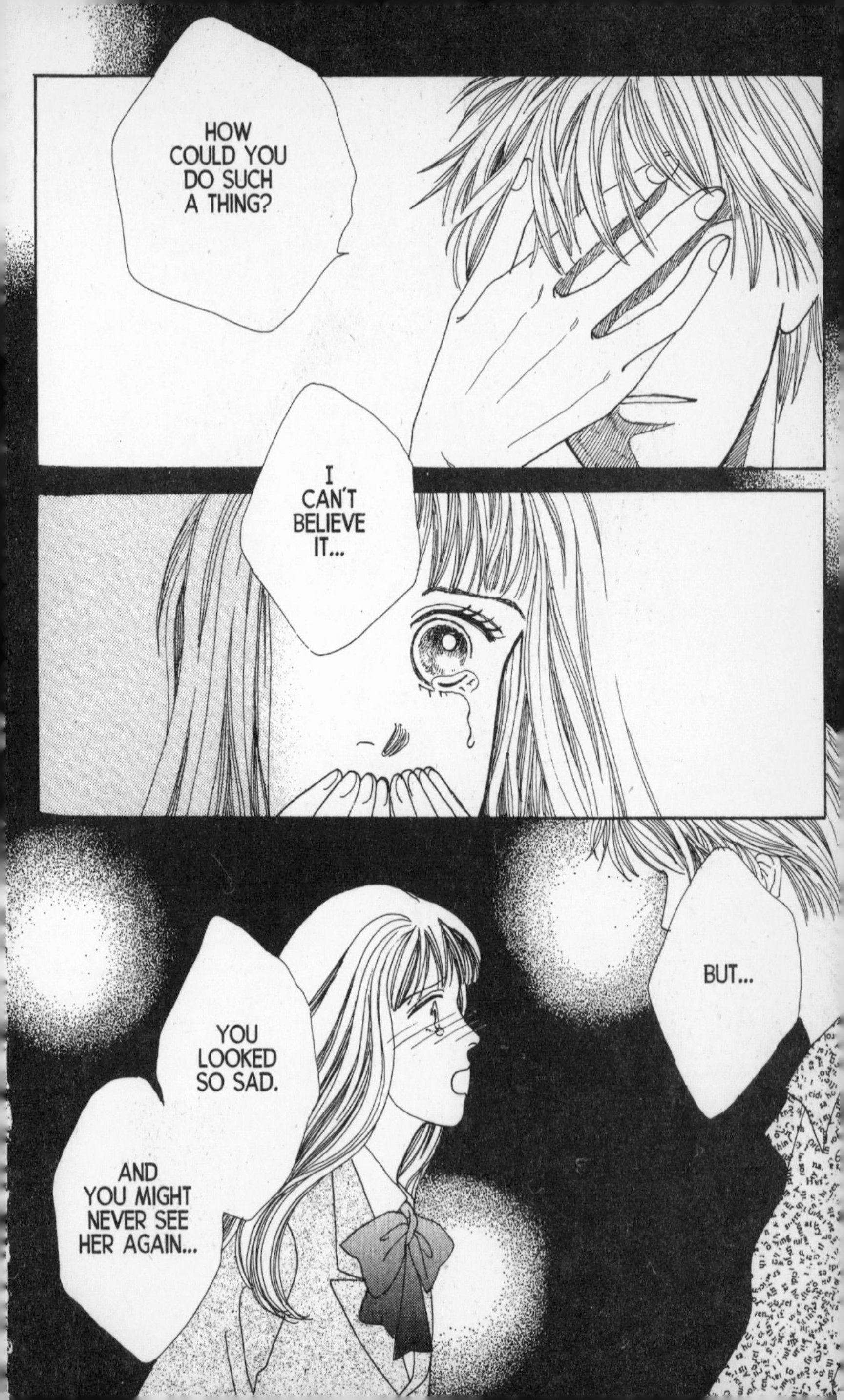
HOW COULD YOU DO SUCH A THING?
I CAN'T BELIEVE IT...
BUT...
YOU LOOKED SO SAD.
AND YOU MIGHT NEVER SEE HER AGAIN...

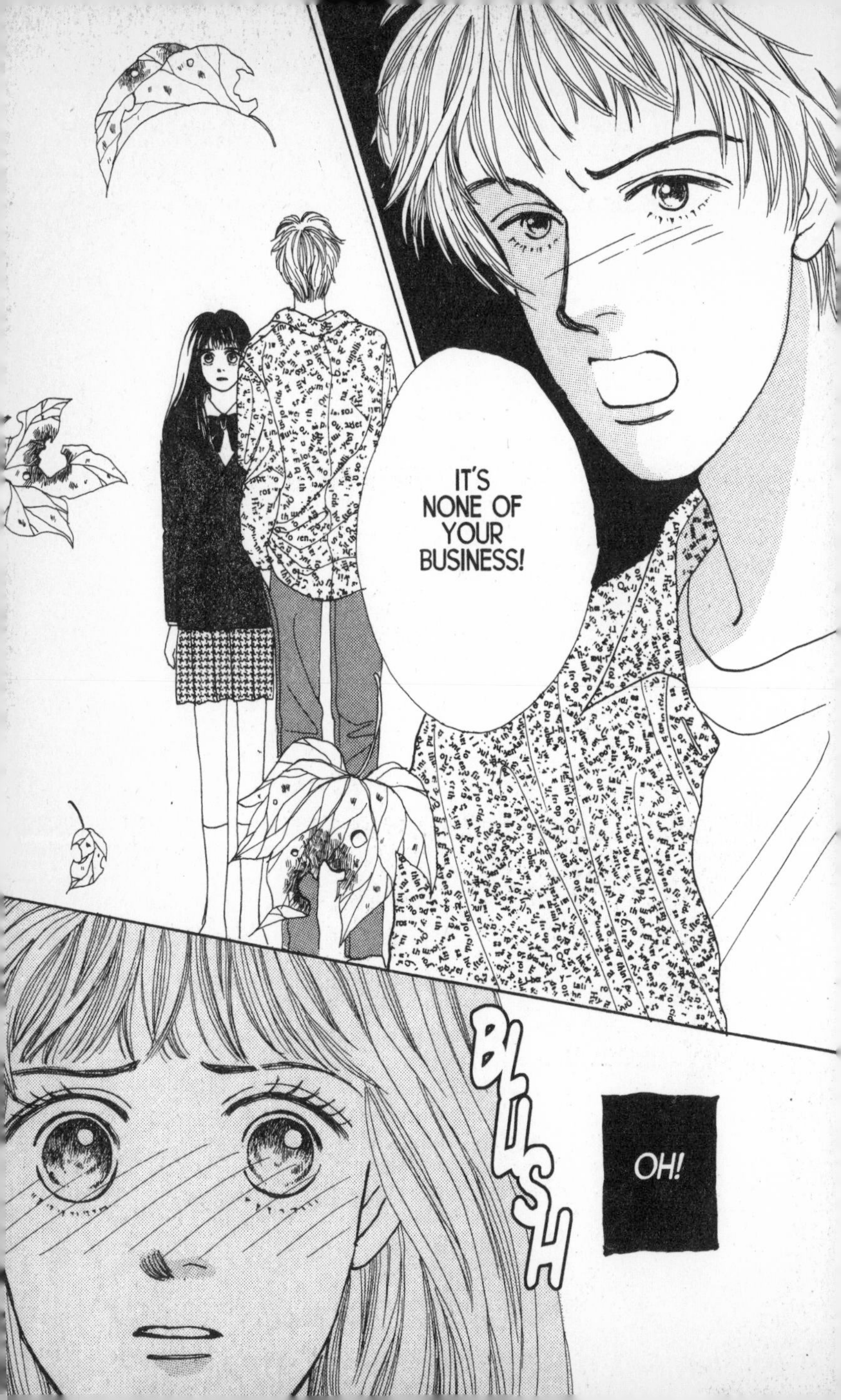
IT'S NONE OF YOUR BUSINESS!
BLUSH
OH!

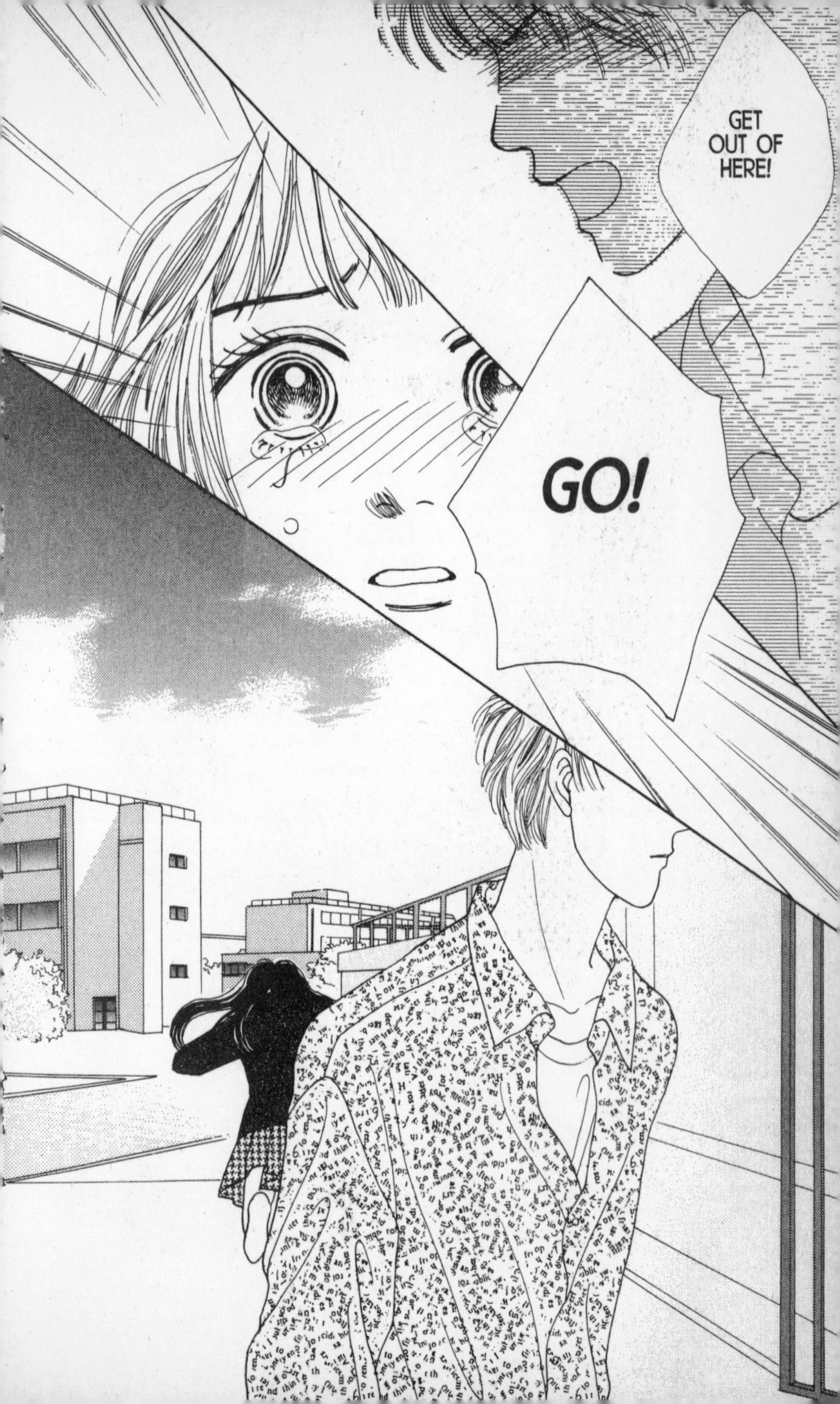
GET OUT OF HERE!
GO!

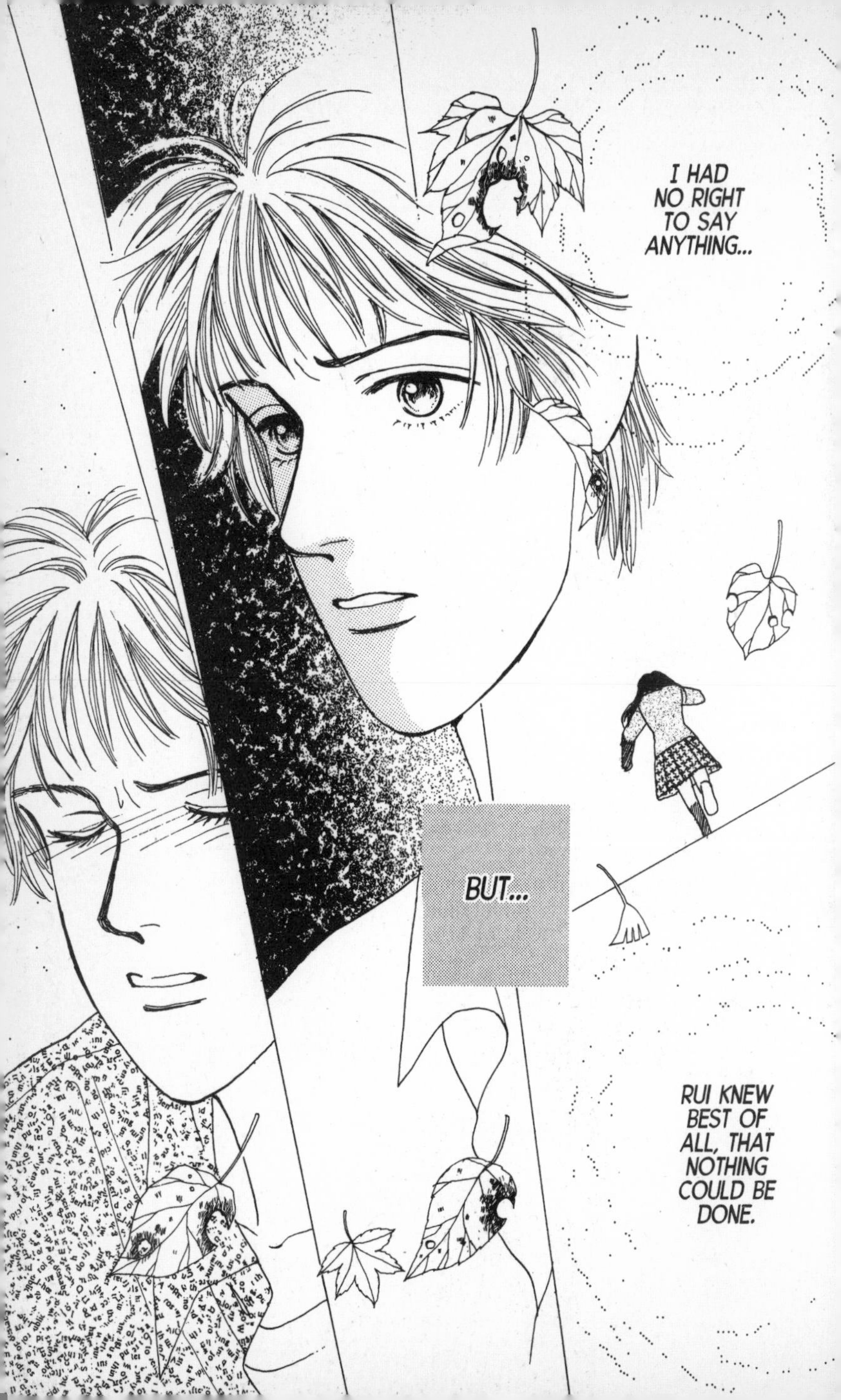
I HAD NO RIGHT TO SAY ANYTHING...
BUT...
RUI KNEW BEST OF ALL, THAT NOTHING COULD BE DONE.

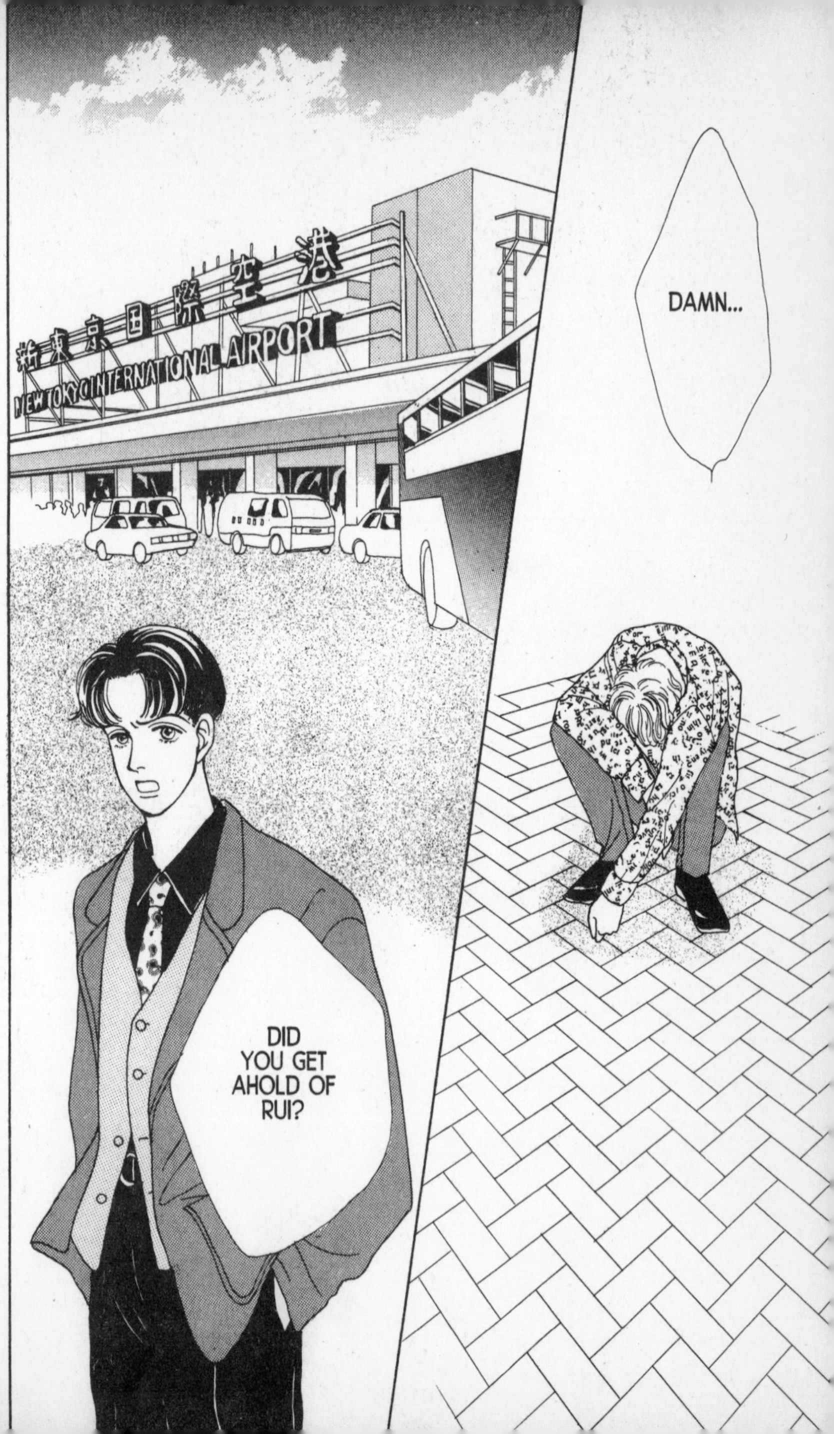
DAMN...
新東京国際空港
NEW TOKYO INTERNATIONAL AIRPORT
DID YOU GET AHOLD OF RUI?

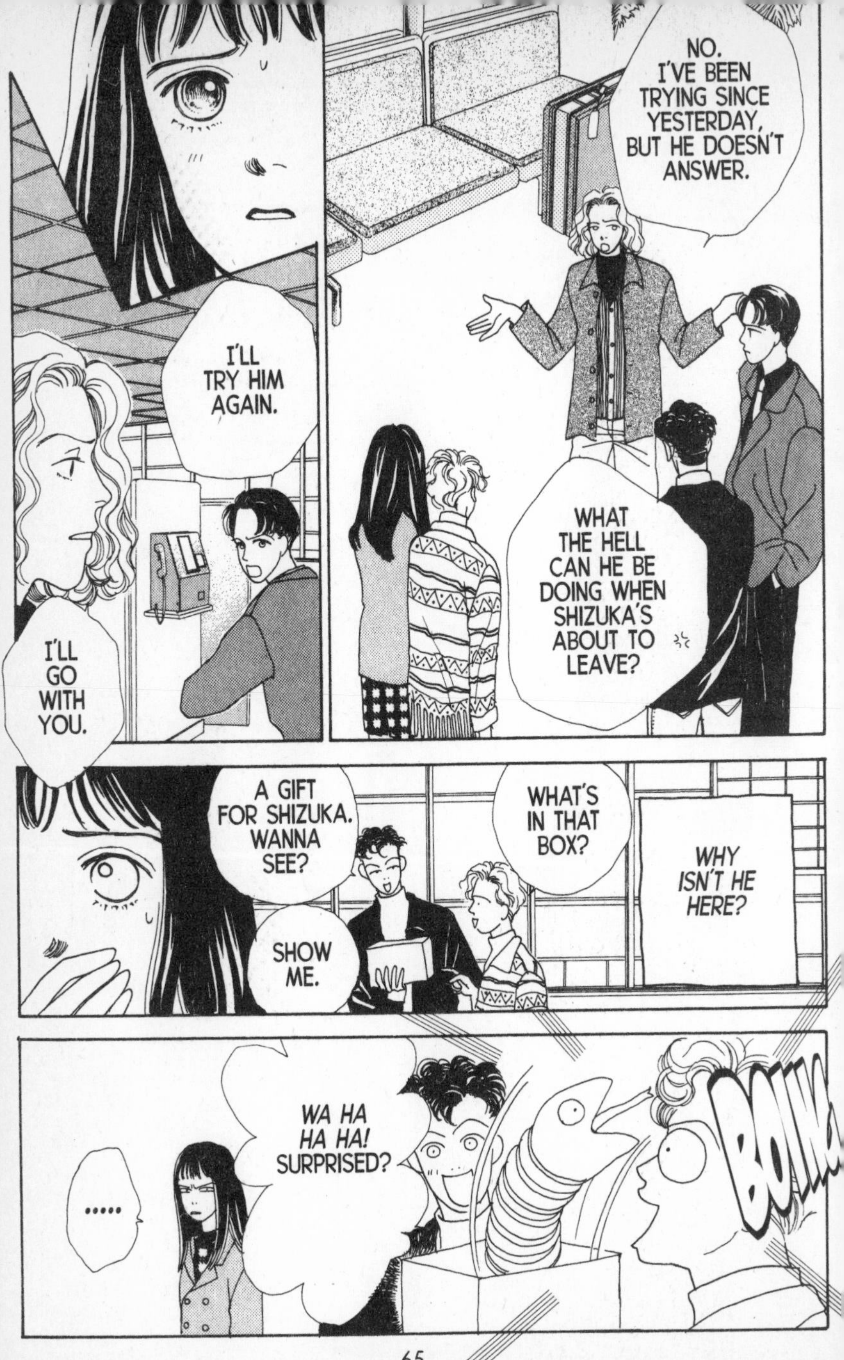
NO. I'VE BEEN TRYING SINCE YESTERDAY, BUT HE DOESN'T ANSWER.
WHAT THE HELL CAN HE BE DOING WHEN SHIZUKA'S ABOUT TO LEAVE?
I'LL TRY HIM AGAIN.
I'LL GO WITH YOU.
WHY ISN'T HE HERE?
WHAT'S IN THAT BOX?
A GIFT FOR SHIZUKA. WANNA SEE?
SHOW ME.
BOIN
WA HA HA HA! SURPRISED?
......

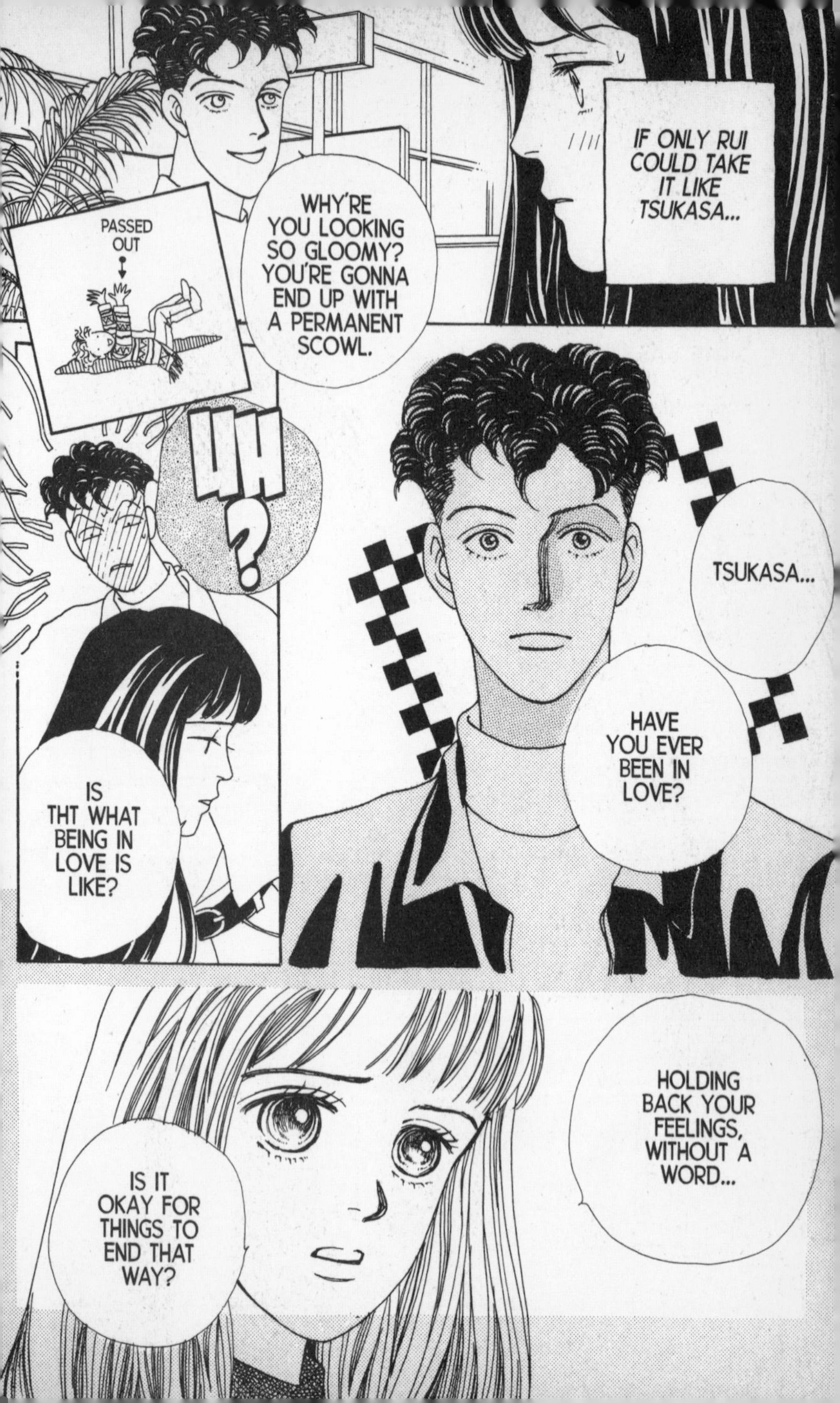
IF ONLY RUI COULD TAKE IT LIKE TSUKASA...
WHY'RE YOU LOOKING SO GLOOMY? YOU'RE GONNA END UP WITH A PERMANENT SCOWL.
PASSED OUT
TSUKASA...
HAVE YOU EVER BEEN IN LOVE?
UH?
IS THT WHAT BEING IN LOVE IS LIKE?
HOLDING BACK YOUR FEELINGS, WITHOUT A WORD...
IS IT OKAY FOR THINGS TO END THAT WAY?

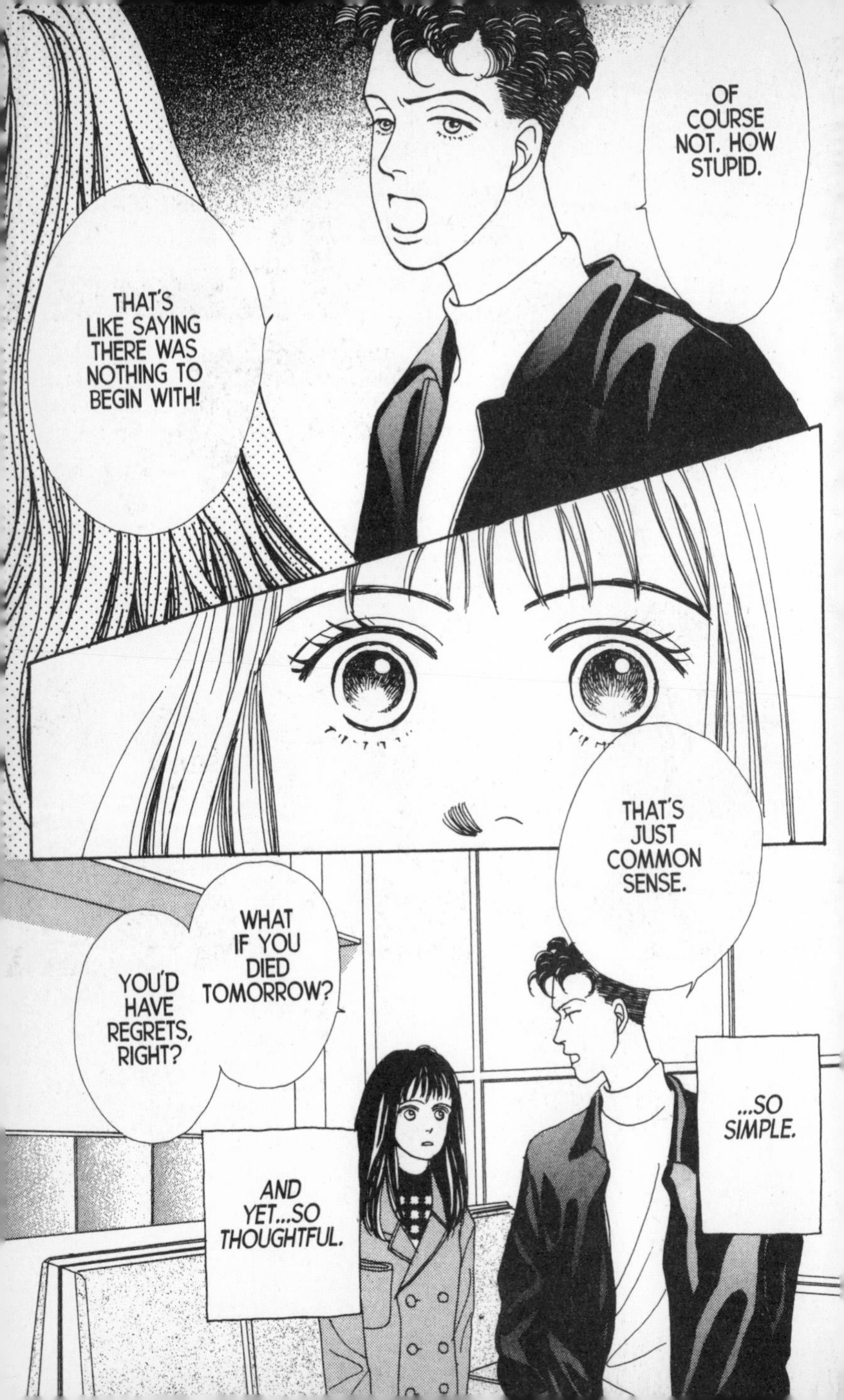
OF COURSE NOT. HOW STUPID.
THAT'S LIKE SAYING THERE WAS NOTHING TO BEGIN WITH!
THAT'S JUST COMMON SENSE.
WHAT IF YOU DIED TOMORROW?
YOU'D HAVE REGRETS, RIGHT?
...SO SIMPLE.
AND YET...SO THOUGHTFUL.

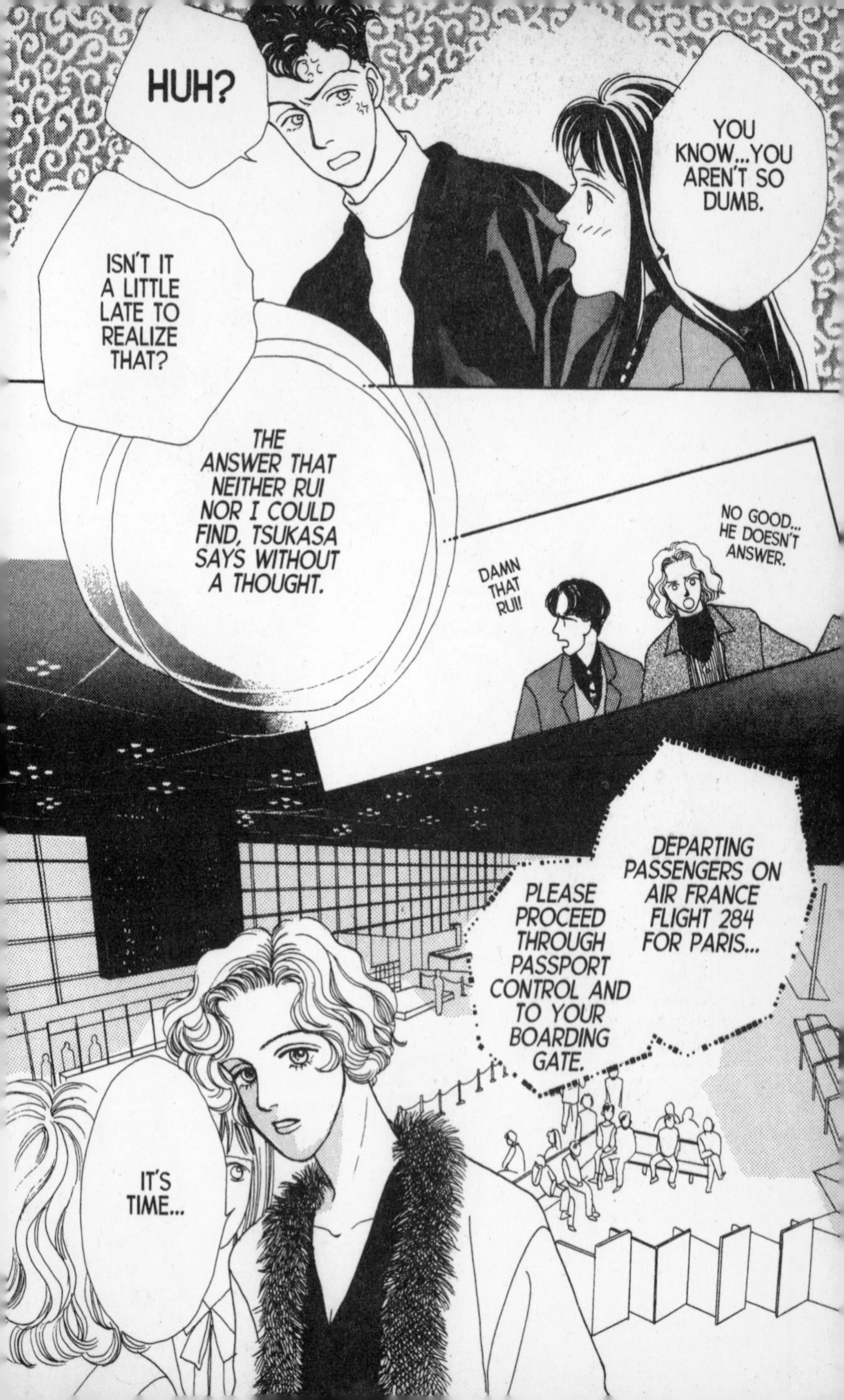

YOU KNOW...YOU AREN'T SO DUMB.
HUH?
ISN'T IT A LITTLE LATE TO REALIZE THAT?
THE ANSWER THAT NEITHER RUI NOR I COULD FIND, TSUKASA SAYS WITHOUT A THOUGHT.
NO GOOD... HE DOESN'T ANSWER.
DAMN THAT RUI!
DEPARTING PASSENGERS ON AIR FRANCE FLIGHT 284 FOR PARIS...
PLEASE PROCEED THROUGH PASSPORT CONTROL AND TO YOUR BOARDING GATE.
IT'S TIME...

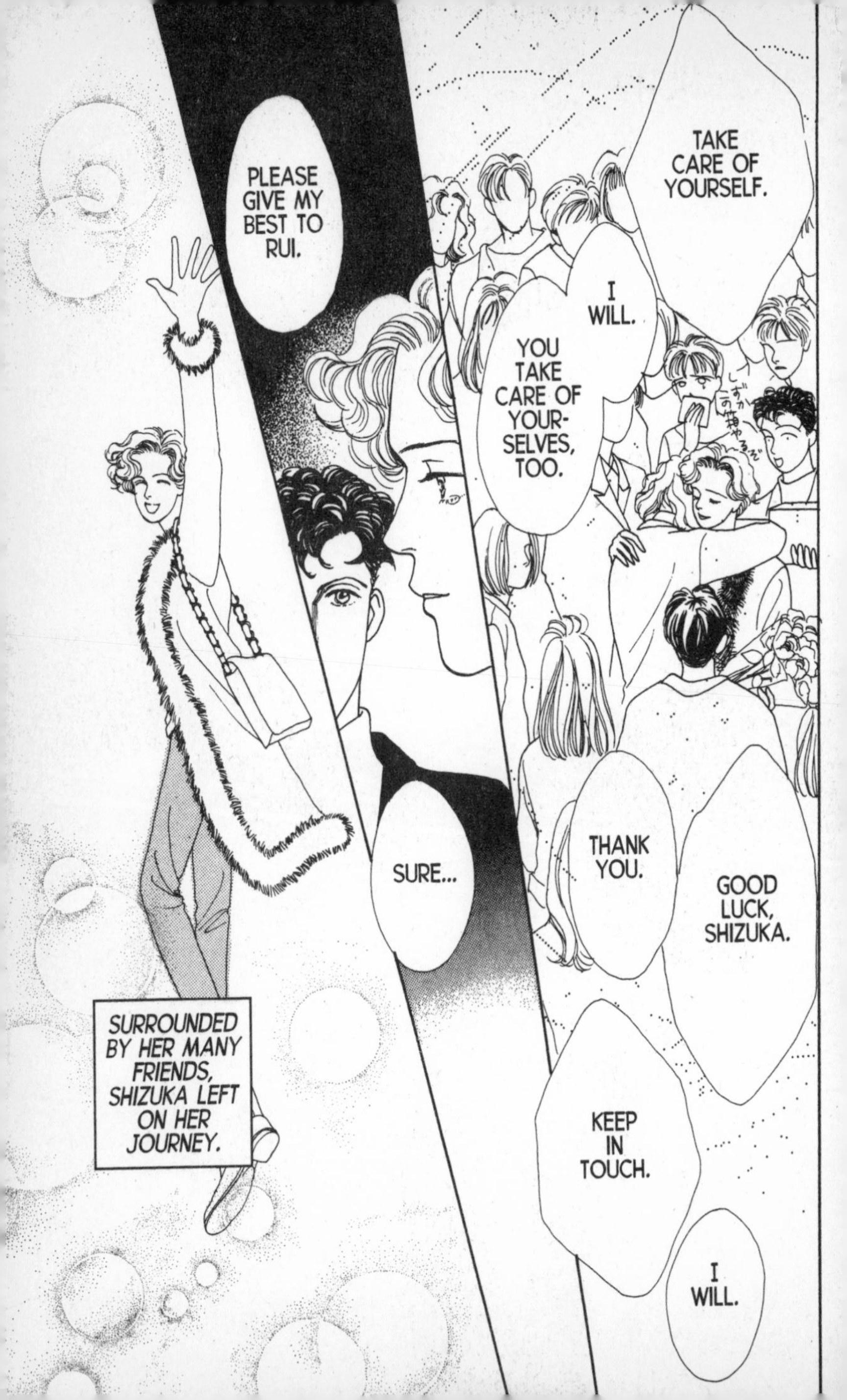
TAKE CARE OF YOURSELF.
I WILL.
YOU TAKE CARE OF YOUR-SELVES, TOO.
THANK YOU.
GOOD LUCK, SHIZUKA.
KEEP IN TOUCH.
I WILL.
PLEASE GIVE MY BEST TO RUI.
SURE...
SURROUNDED BY HER MANY FRIENDS, SHIZUKA LEFT ON HER JOURNEY.

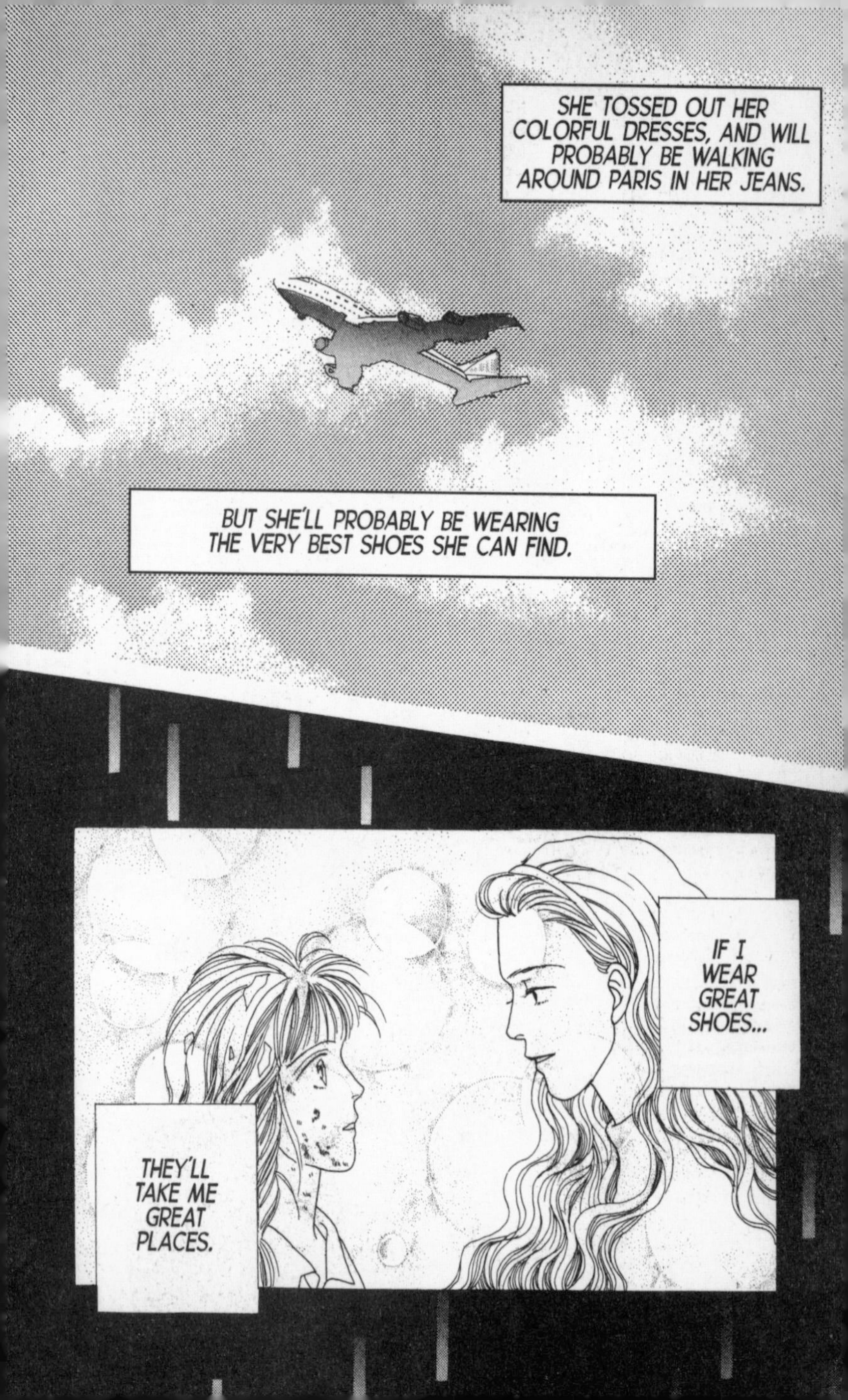
SHE TOSSED OUT HER COLORFUL DRESSES, AND WILL PROBABLY BE WALKING AROUND PARIS IN HER JEANS.
BUT SHE'LL PROBABLY BE WEARING THE VERY BEST SHOES SHE CAN FIND.
IF I WEAR GREAT SHOES...
THEY'LL TAKE ME GREAT PLACES.

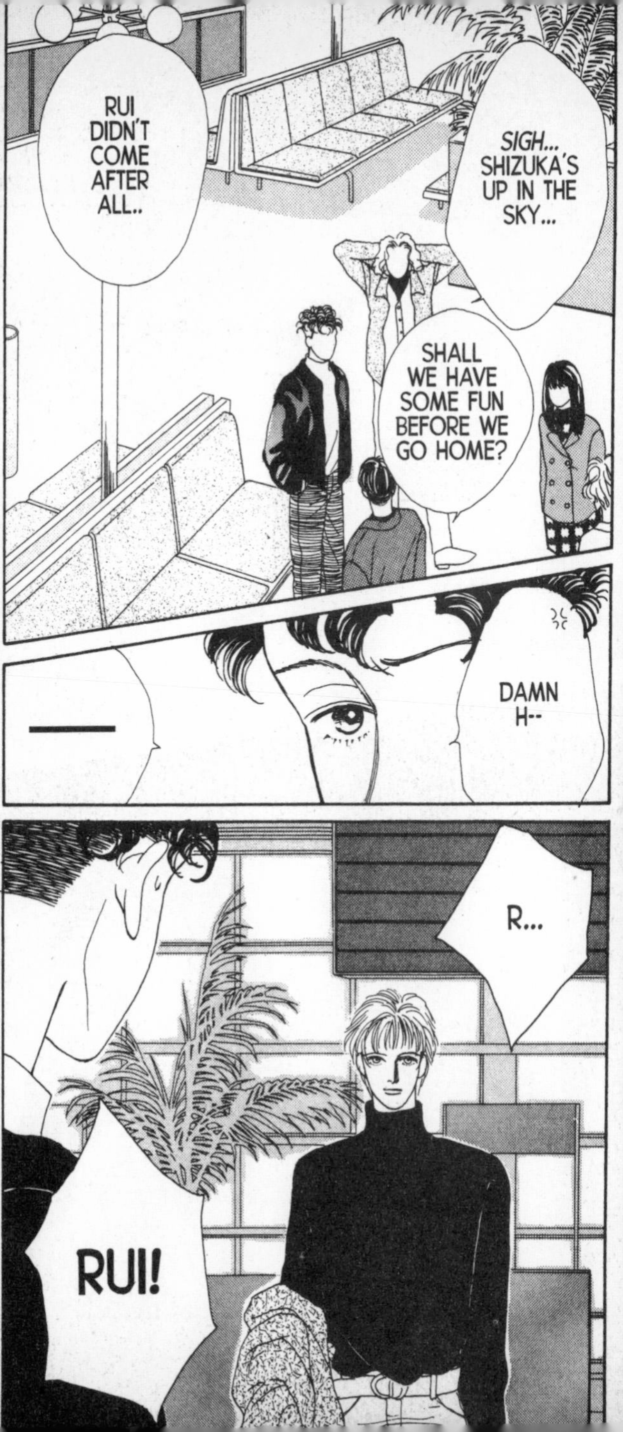
SIGH... SHIZUKA'S UP IN THE SKY...
RUI DIDN'T COME AFTER ALL..
SHALL WE HAVE SOME FUN BEFORE WE GO HOME?
DAMN H--
—
R...
RUI!

5

About the "Boys over Flowers" CD...

The story turned out a little differently from the original, but I'm satisfied with the results.

Of course, it's the first time my work has had a voice over. It's been a very interesting experience.

I'm very grateful to the writer, Watanabe, who created a script out of this somewhat incoherent work.

But, more than anything, I think I owe much to my very supportive readers.

Really, truly...

This job made me glad to be a cartoonist.

Next, I'll report on my interview with Takuya Kimura.

I mentioned my interview in Volume 3, and the response was stunning. Readers asked, "Please tell us more." And, "I envy you! Please tell us everything!" Takuya is certainly very popular!

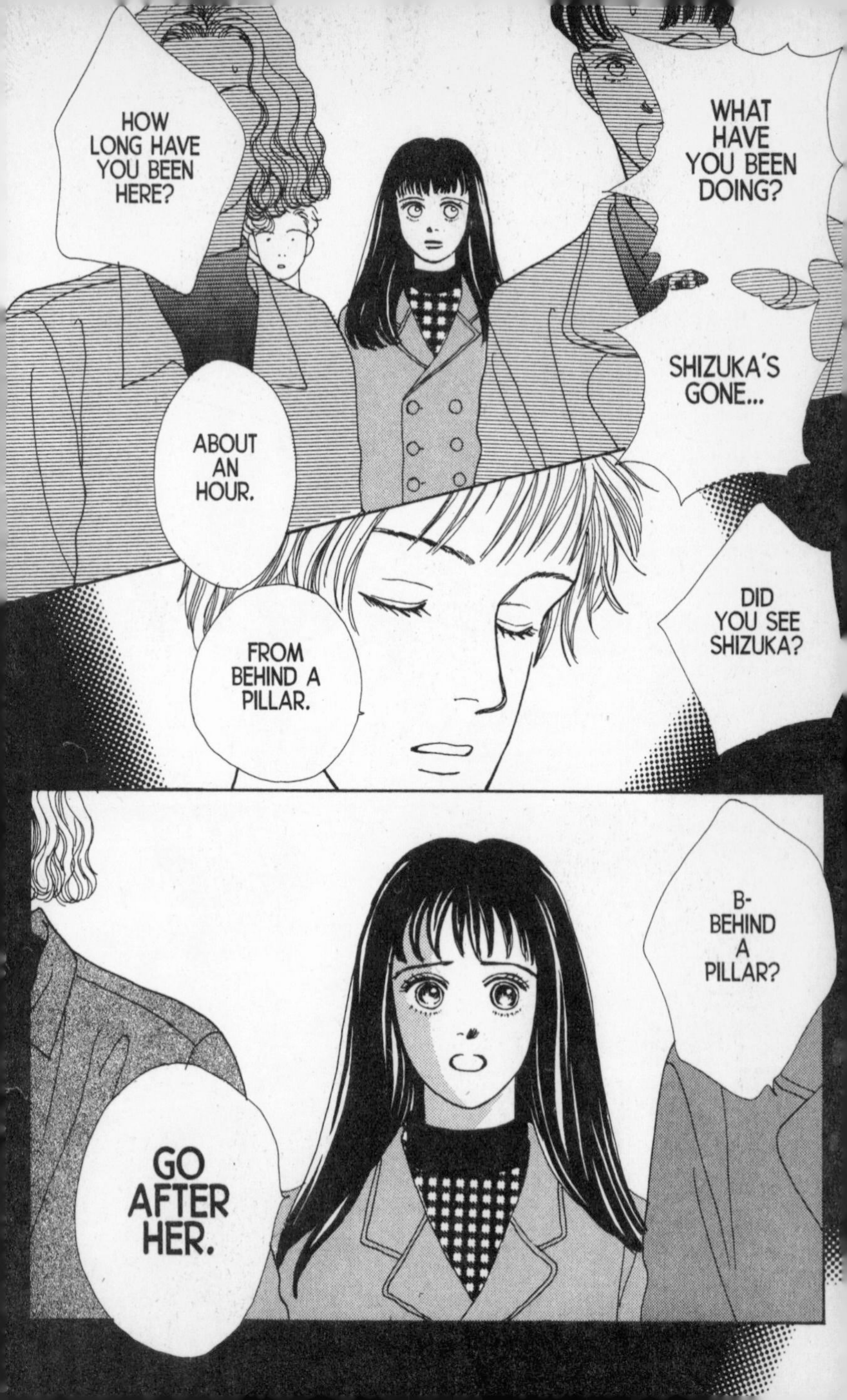
WHAT HAVE YOU BEEN DOING?
HOW LONG HAVE YOU BEEN HERE?
SHIZUKA'S GONE...
ABOUT AN HOUR.
DID YOU SEE SHIZUKA?
FROM BEHIND A PILLAR.
B- BEHIND A PILLAR?
GO AFTER HER.

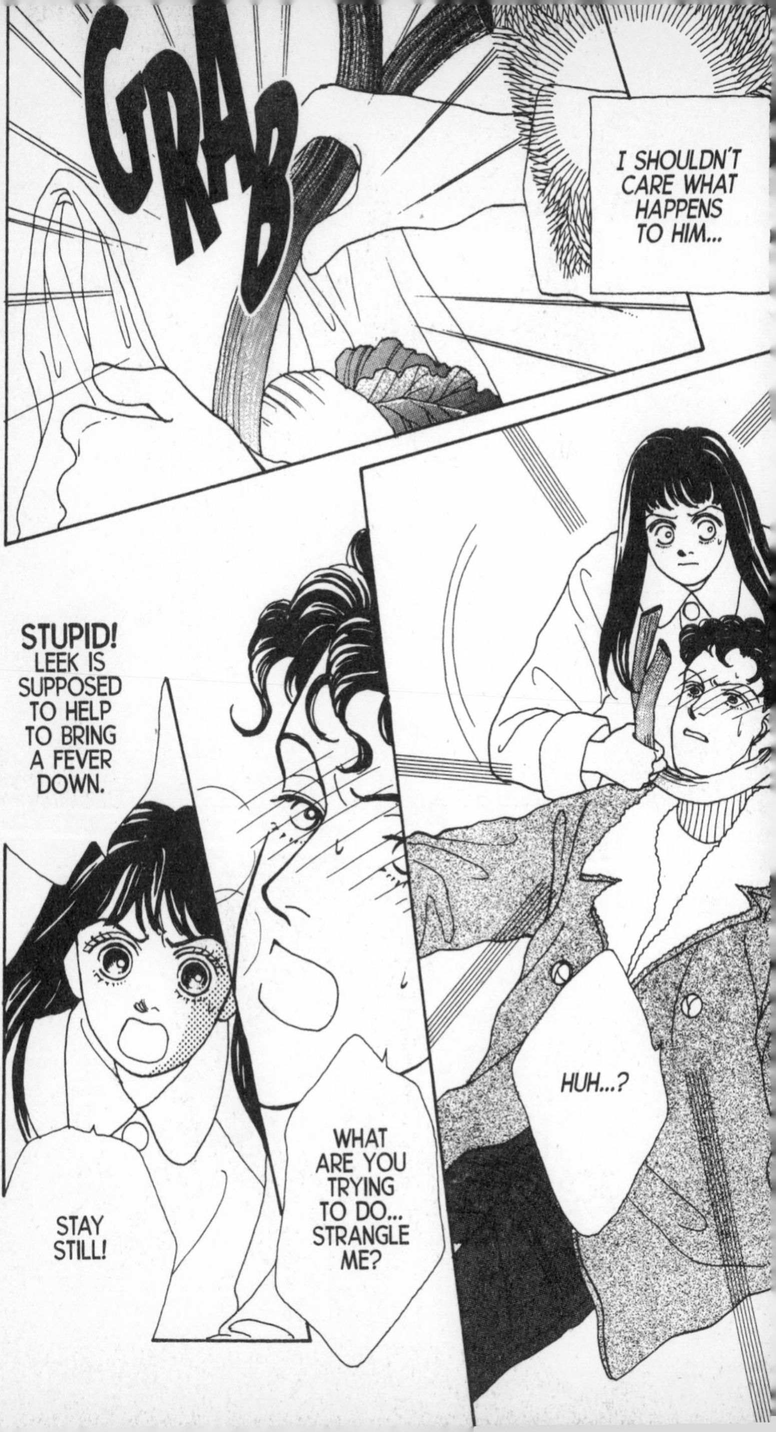
I SHOULDN'T CARE WHAT HAPPENS TO HIM...
GRAB
HUH...?
WHAT ARE YOU TRYING TO DO... STRANGLE ME?
STUPID! LEEK IS SUPPOSED TO HELP TO BRING A FEVER DOWN.
STAY STILL!

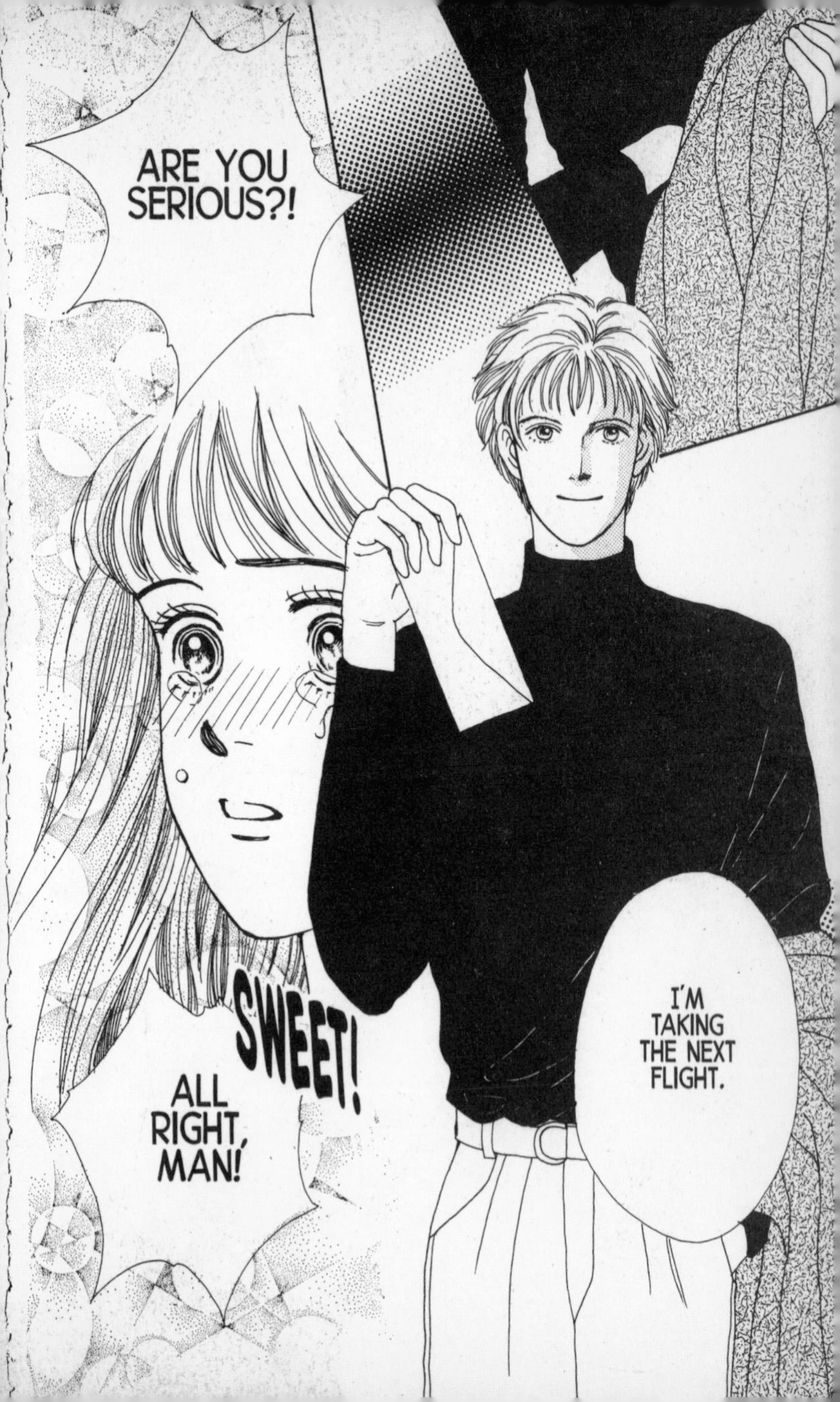
I'M TAKING THE NEXT FLIGHT.
ARE YOU SERIOUS?!
SWEET!
ALL RIGHT, MAN!

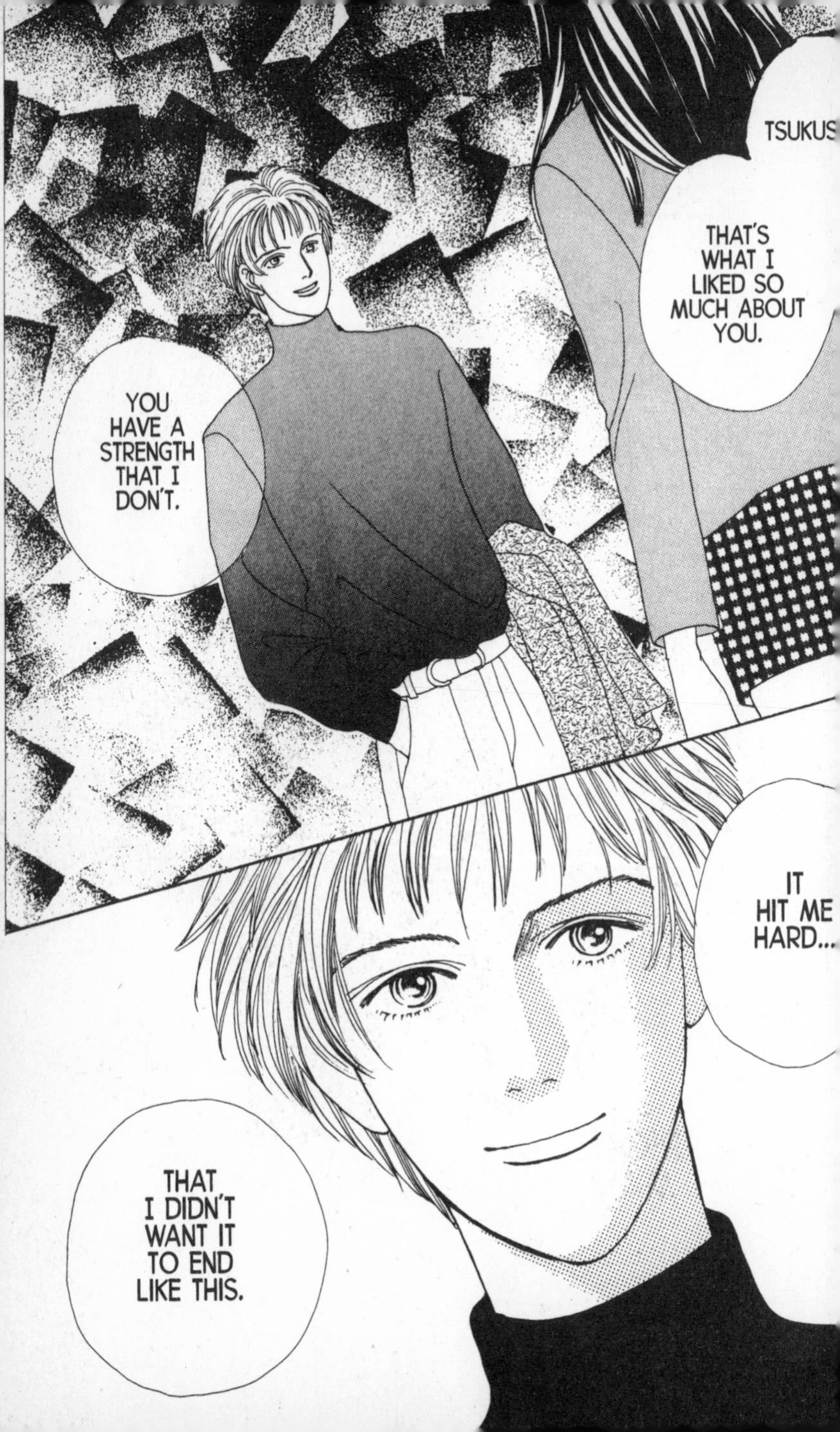
TSUKUS
THAT'S WHAT I LIKED SO MUCH ABOUT YOU.
YOU HAVE A STRENGTH THAT I DON'T.
IT HIT ME HARD...
THAT I DIDN'T WANT IT TO END LIKE THIS.

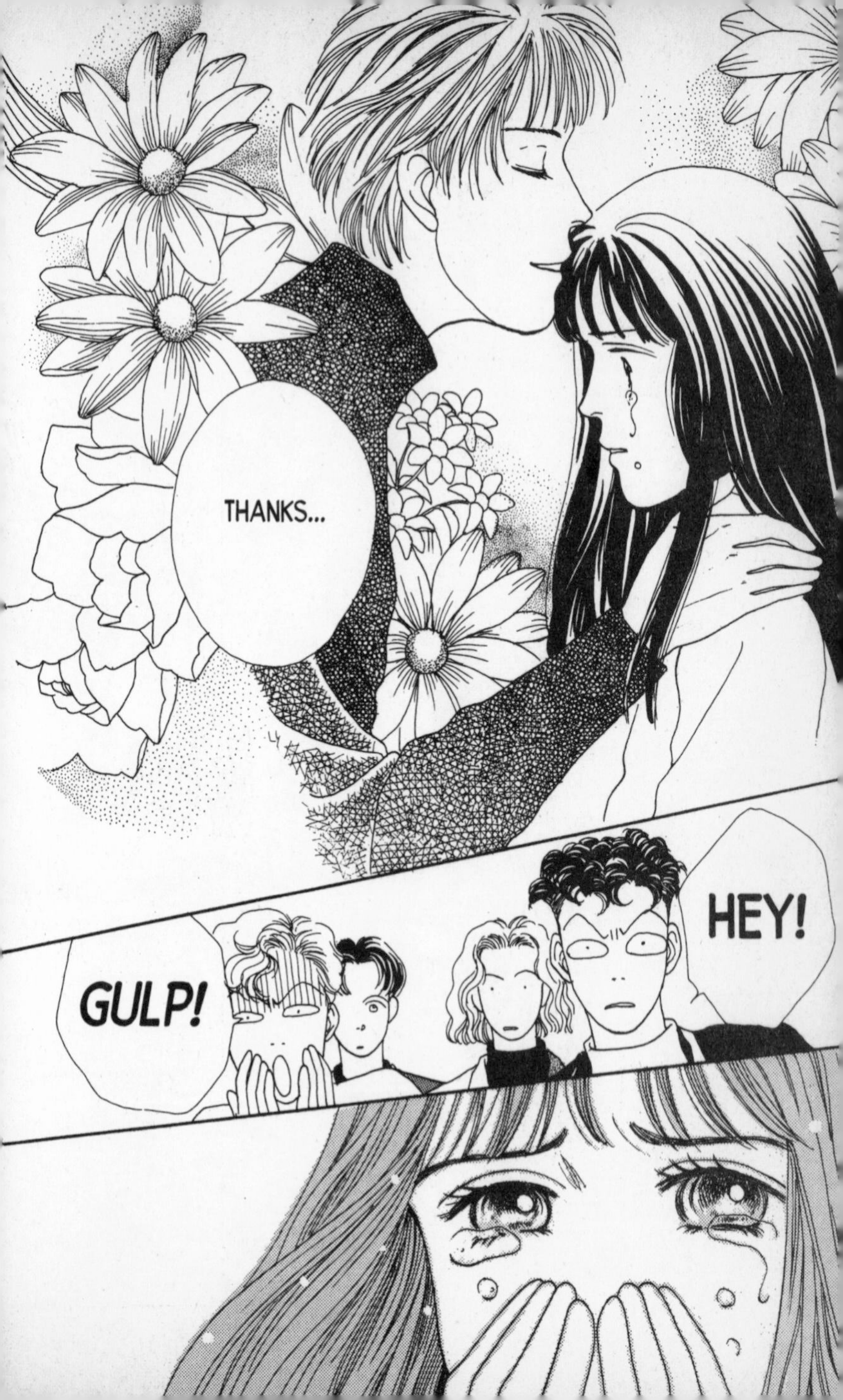
THANKS...
HEY!
GULP!

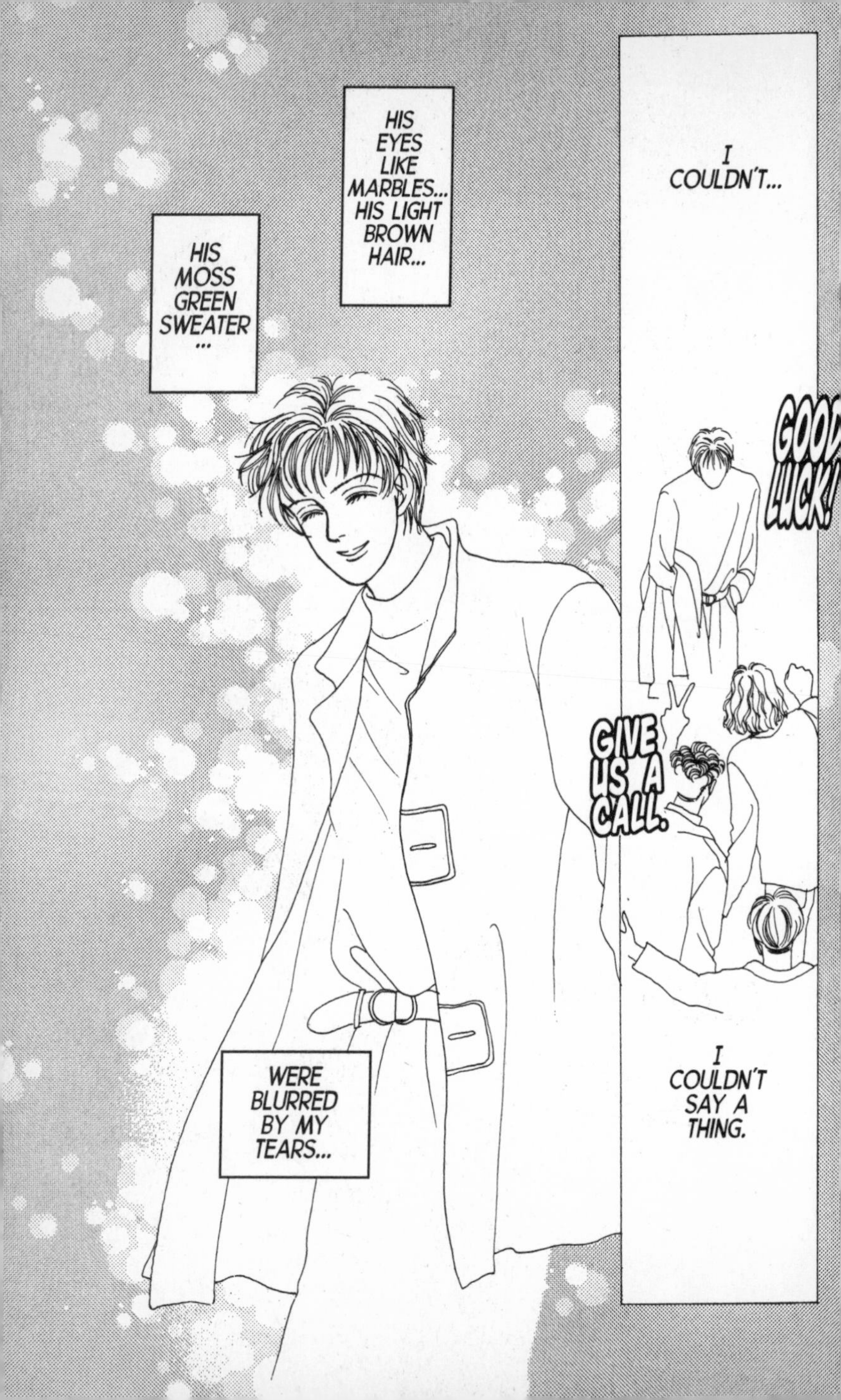
I COULDN'T...
GOOD LUCK!
GIVE US A CALL.
I COULDN'T SAY A THING.
HIS EYES LIKE MARBLES... HIS LIGHT BROWN HAIR...
HIS MOSS GREEN SWEATER ...
WERE BLURRED BY MY TEARS...

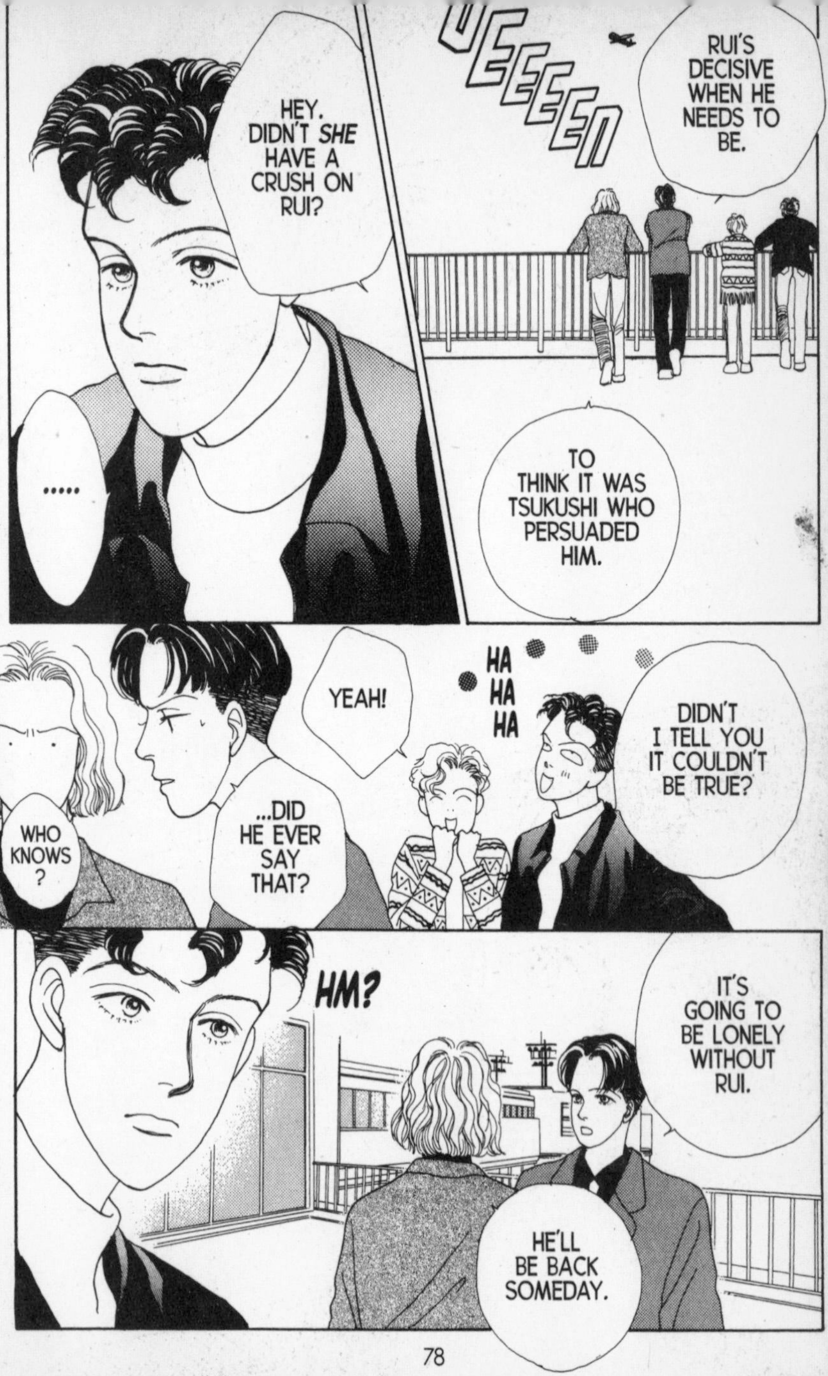
RUI'S DECISIVE WHEN HE NEEDS TO BE.
TO THINK IT WAS TSUKUSHI WHO PERSUADED HIM.
HEY. DIDN'T *SHE* HAVE A CRUSH ON RUI?
......
DIDN'T I TELL YOU IT COULDN'T BE TRUE?
HA HA HA
YEAH!
...DID HE EVER SAY THAT?
WHO KNOWS?
IT'S GOING TO BE LONELY WITHOUT RUI.
HE'LL BE BACK SOMEDAY.
HM?

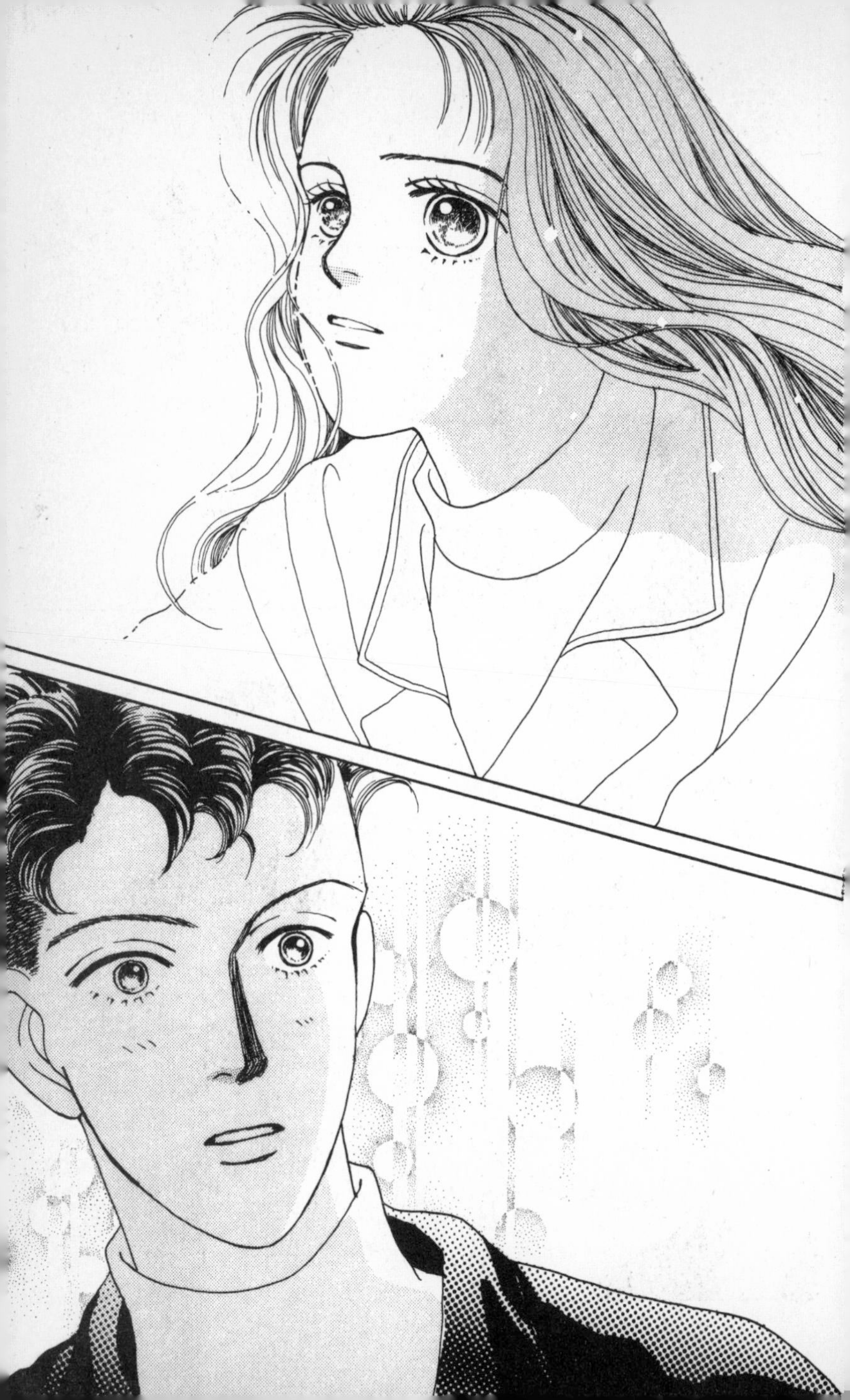

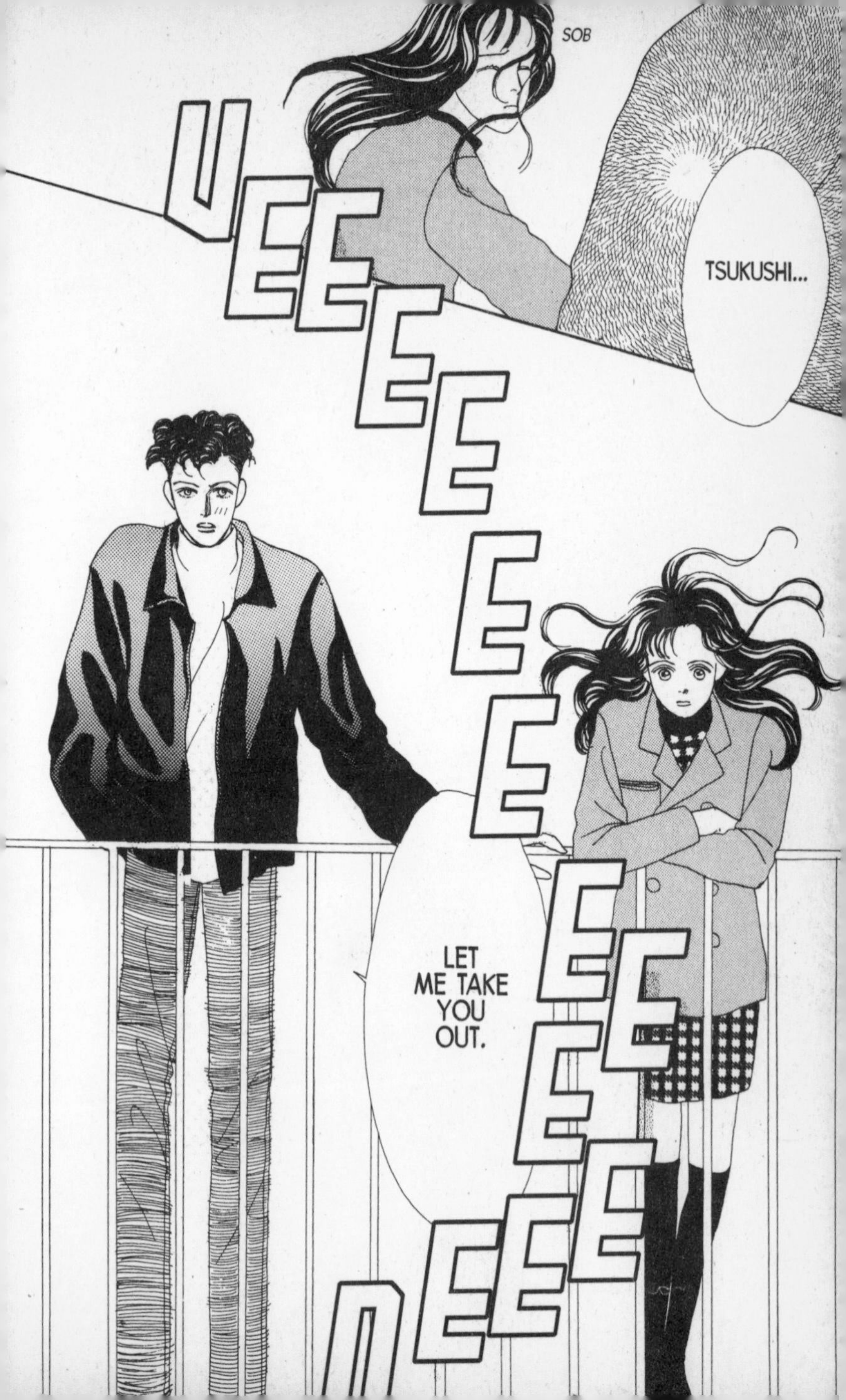
SOB
TSUKUSHI...
UEEEEEEEEEEEEN
LET ME TAKE YOU OUT.

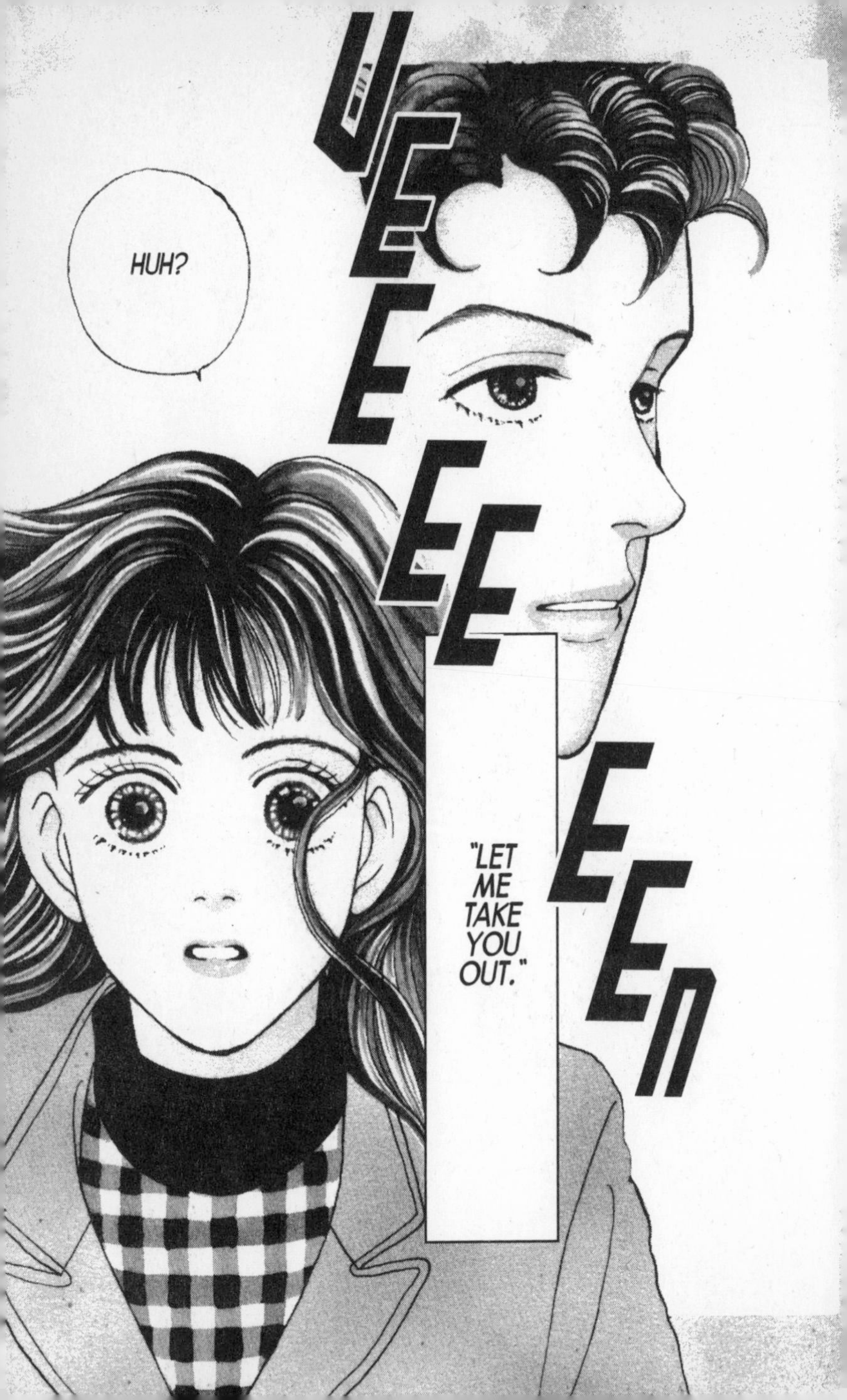

UEEEEEEEEN
"LET ME TAKE YOU OUT."
HUH?

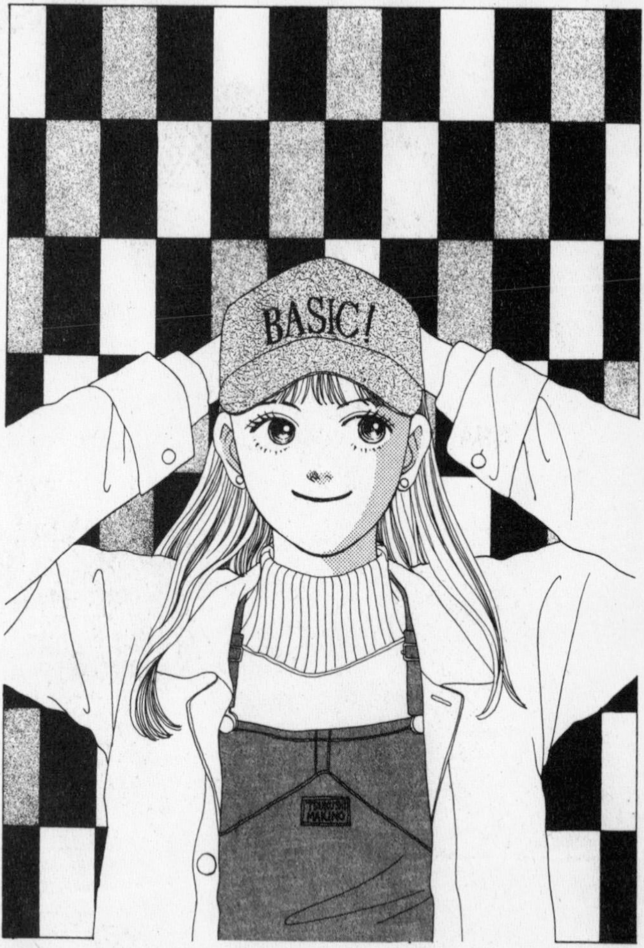
BASIC!

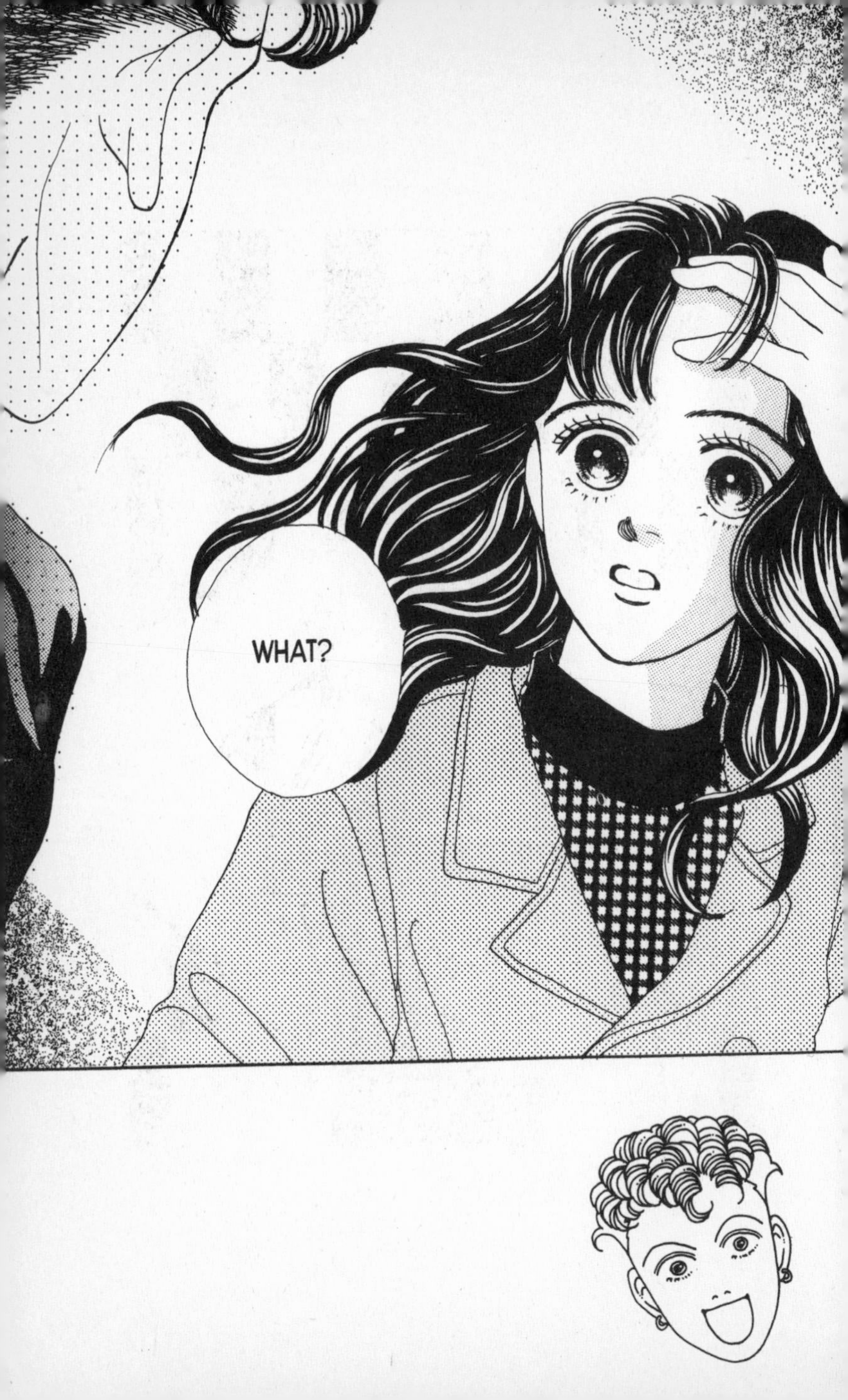
WHAT?

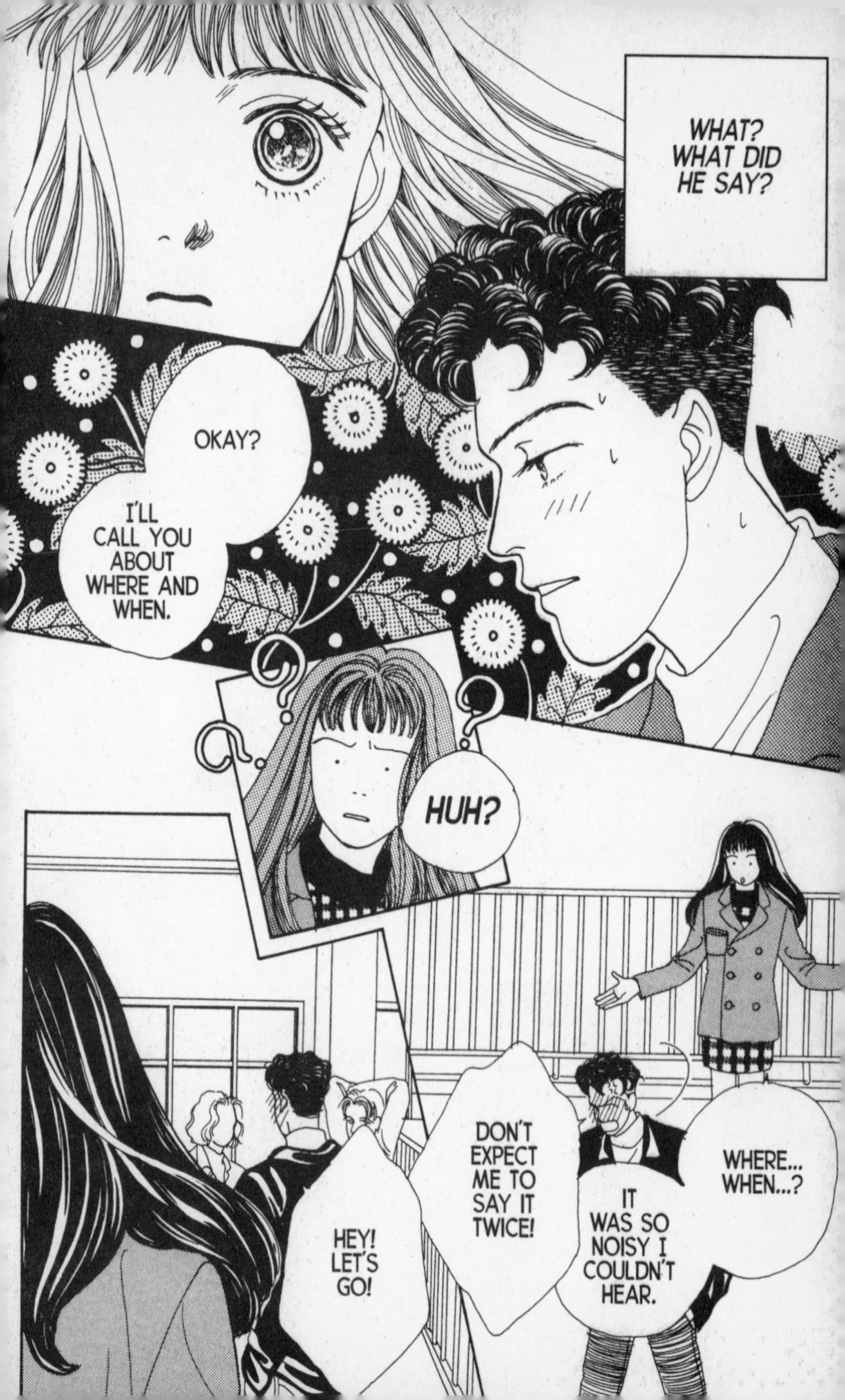
WHAT? WHAT DID HE SAY?
OKAY?
I'LL CALL YOU ABOUT WHERE AND WHEN.
HUH?
WHERE... WHEN...?
IT WAS SO NOISY I COULDN'T HEAR.
DON'T EXPECT ME TO SAY IT TWICE!
HEY! LET'S GO!

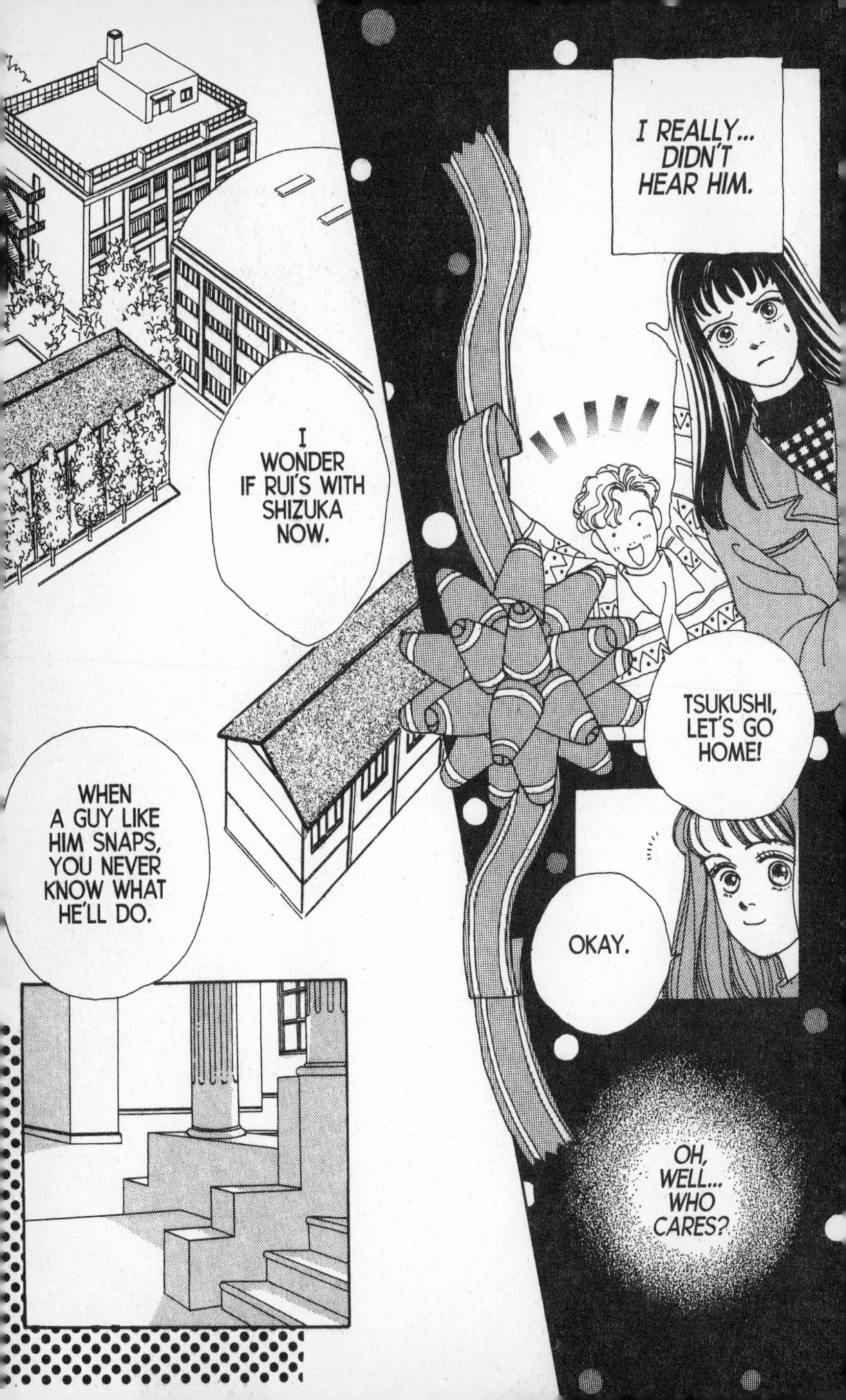
I REALLY... DIDN'T HEAR HIM.
TSUKUSHI, LET'S GO HOME!
OKAY.
OH, WELL... WHO CARES?
I WONDER IF RUI'S WITH SHIZUKA NOW.
WHEN A GUY LIKE HIM SNAPS, YOU NEVER KNOW WHAT HE'LL DO.

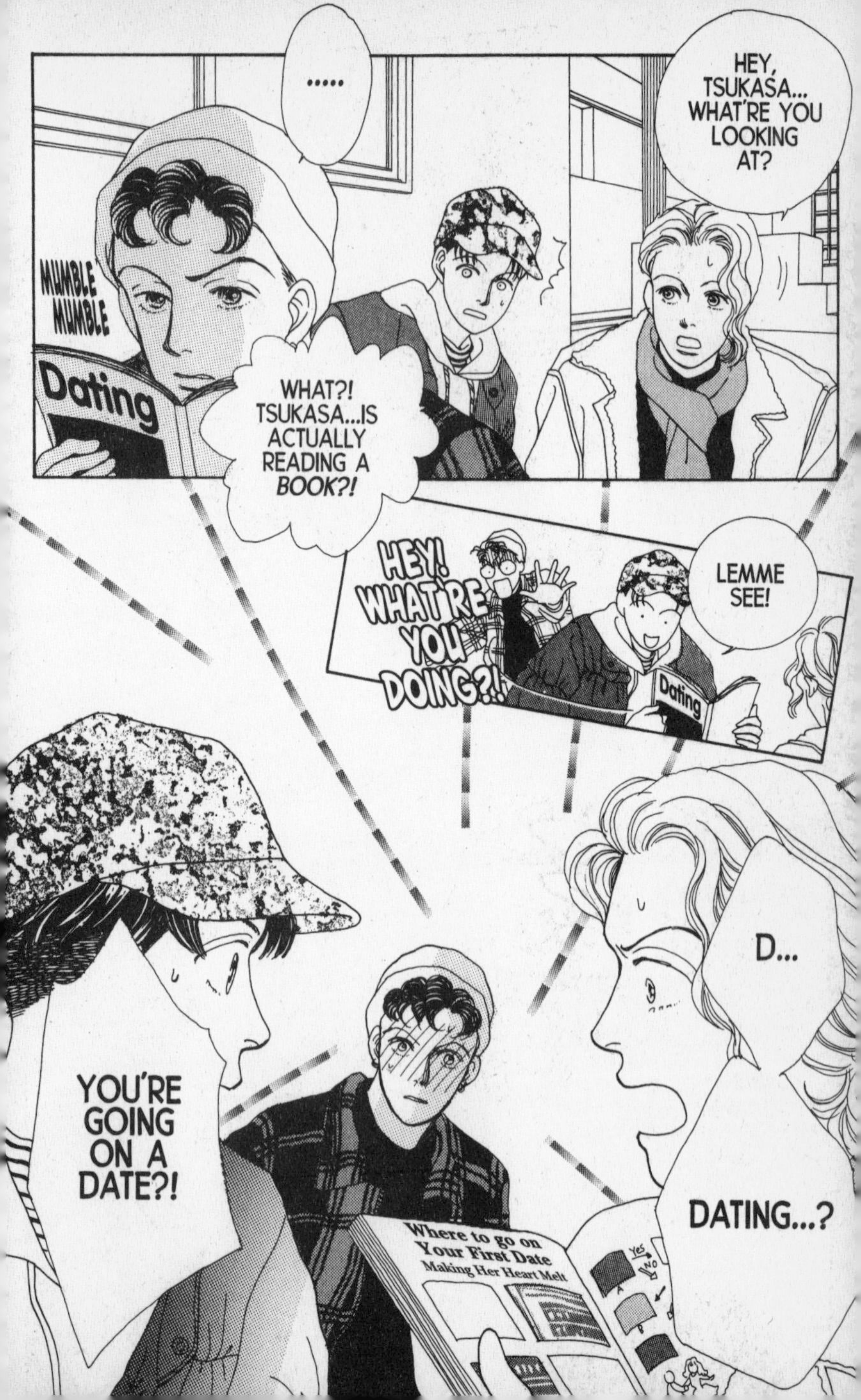
HEY, TSUKASA... WHAT'RE YOU LOOKING AT?
.....
MUMBLE MUMBLE
Dating
WHAT?! TSUKASA...IS ACTUALLY READING A *BOOK*?!
LEMME SEE!
HEY! WHAT'RE YOU DOING?!
Dating
D...
DATING...?
YOU'RE GOING ON A DATE?!
Where to go on Your First Date
Making Her Heart Melt

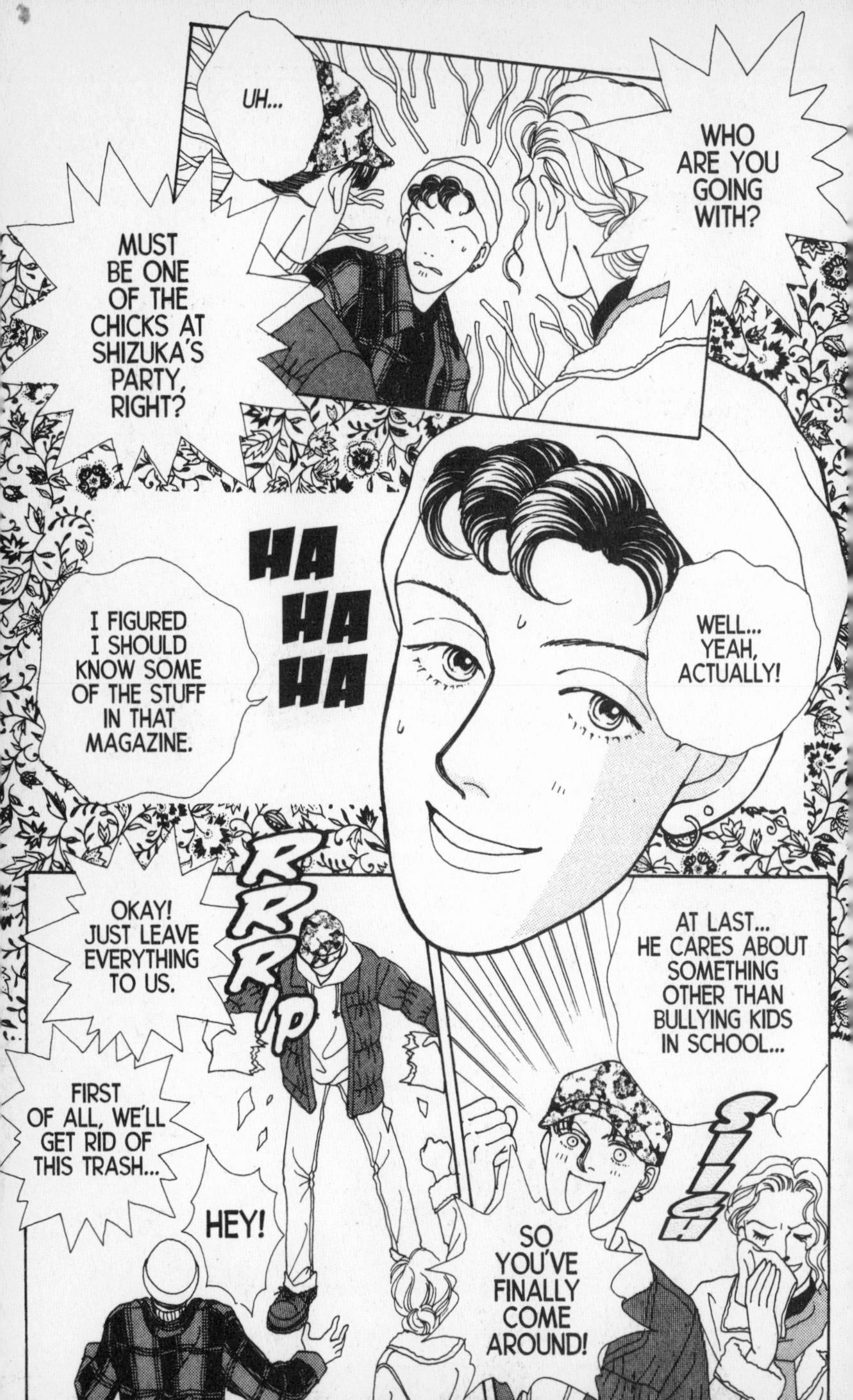
WHO ARE YOU GOING WITH?
UH...
MUST BE ONE OF THE CHICKS AT SHIZUKA'S PARTY, RIGHT?
WELL... YEAH, ACTUALLY!
HA HA HA
I FIGURED I SHOULD KNOW SOME OF THE STUFF IN THAT MAGAZINE.
AT LAST... HE CARES ABOUT SOMETHING OTHER THAN BULLYING KIDS IN SCHOOL...
SIGH
SO YOU'VE FINALLY COME AROUND!
OKAY! JUST LEAVE EVERYTHING TO US.
RRRIP
FIRST OF ALL, WE'LL GET RID OF THIS TRASH...
HEY!

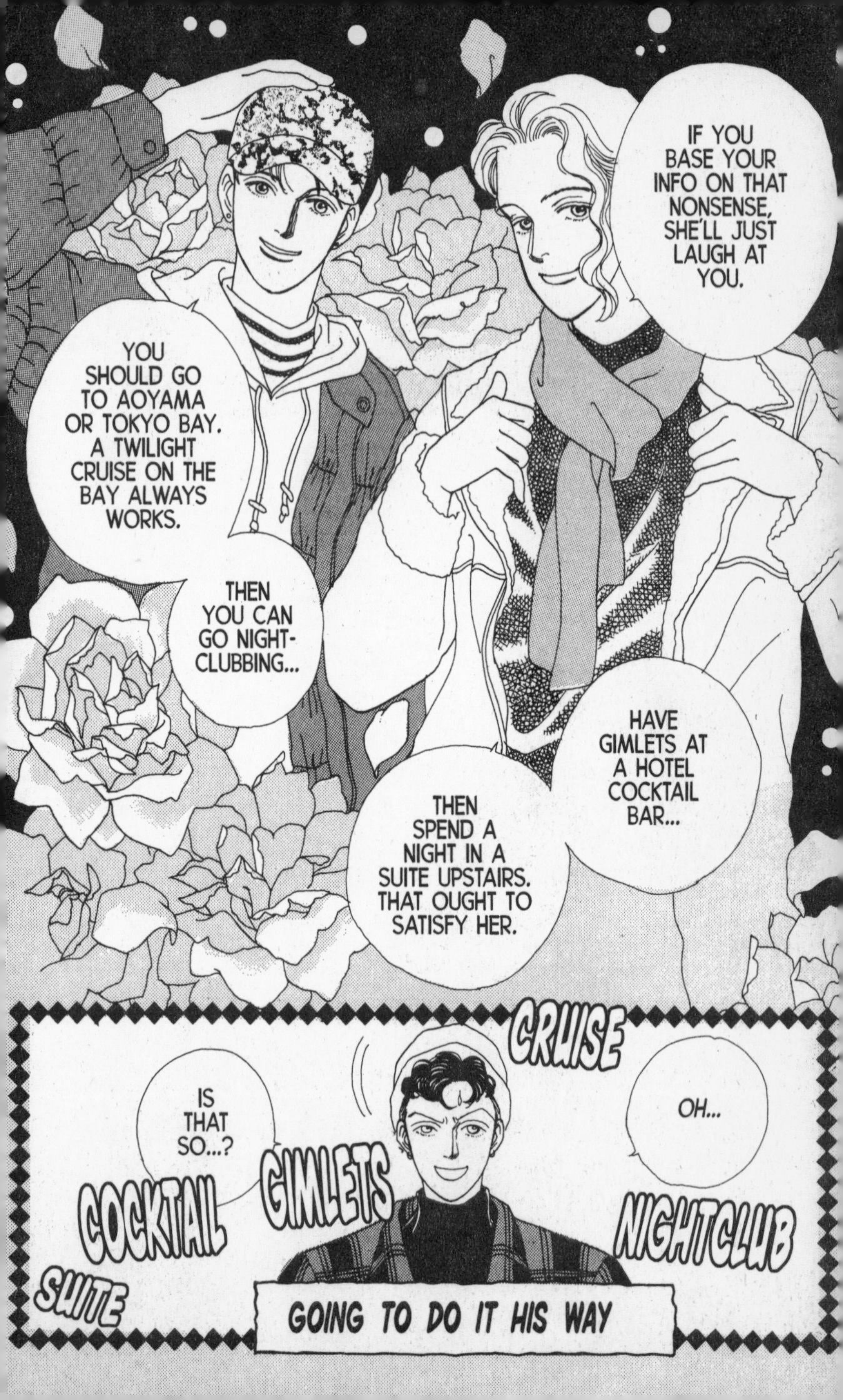
IF YOU BASE YOUR INFO ON THAT NONSENSE, SHE'LL JUST LAUGH AT YOU.
YOU SHOULD GO TO AOYAMA OR TOKYO BAY. A TWILIGHT CRUISE ON THE BAY ALWAYS WORKS.
THEN YOU CAN GO NIGHT-CLUBBING...
HAVE GIMLETS AT A HOTEL COCKTAIL BAR...
THEN SPEND A NIGHT IN A SUITE UPSTAIRS. THAT OUGHT TO SATISFY HER.
CRUISE
OH...
IS THAT SO...?
GIMLETS
NIGHTCLUB
COCKTAIL
SUITE
GOING TO DO IT HIS WAY

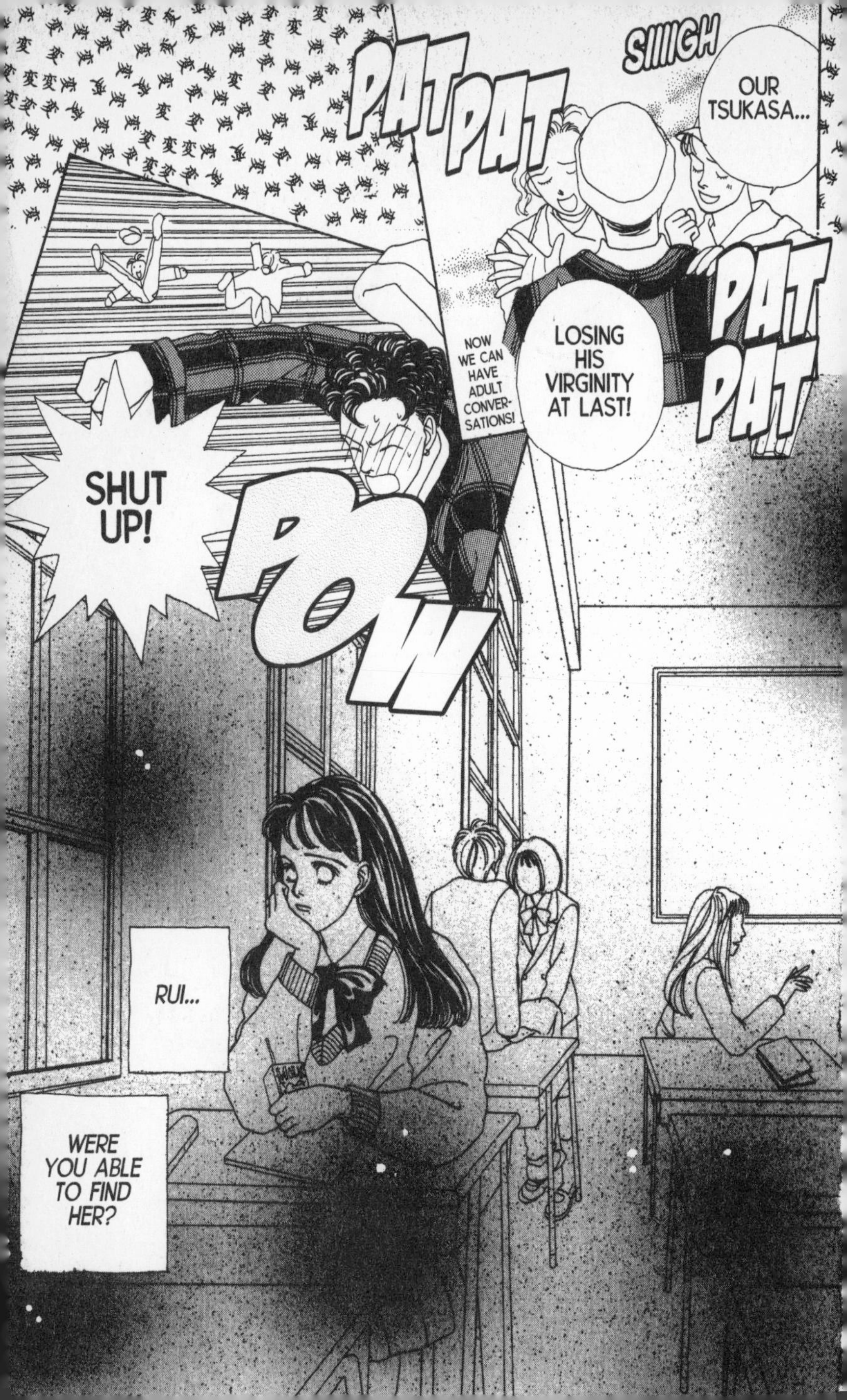
OUR TSUKASA...
SIIIIGH
PAT PAT
PAT PAT
LOSING HIS VIRGINITY AT LAST!
NOW WE CAN HAVE ADULT CONVER-SATIONS!
SHUT UP!
POW
RUI...
WERE YOU ABLE TO FIND HER?

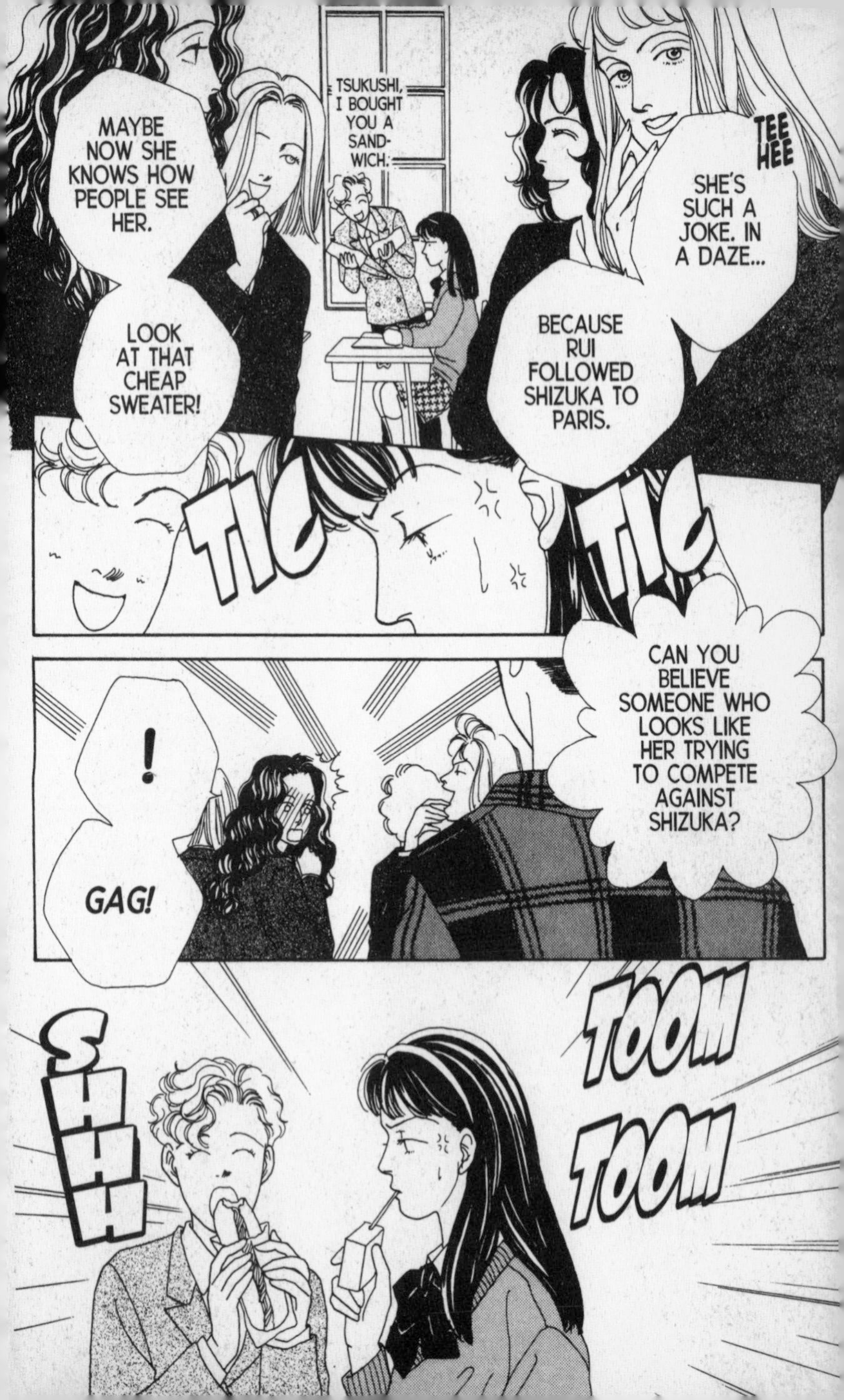
TEE HEE
SHE'S SUCH A JOKE. IN A DAZE...
BECAUSE RUI FOLLOWED SHIZUKA TO PARIS.
TSUKUSHI, I BOUGHT YOU A SAND-WICH.
MAYBE NOW SHE KNOWS HOW PEOPLE SEE HER.
LOOK AT THAT CHEAP SWEATER!
TIC
TIC
CAN YOU BELIEVE SOMEONE WHO LOOKS LIKE HER TRYING TO COMPETE AGAINST SHIZUKA?
!
GAG!
TOOM TOOM
SHHHH

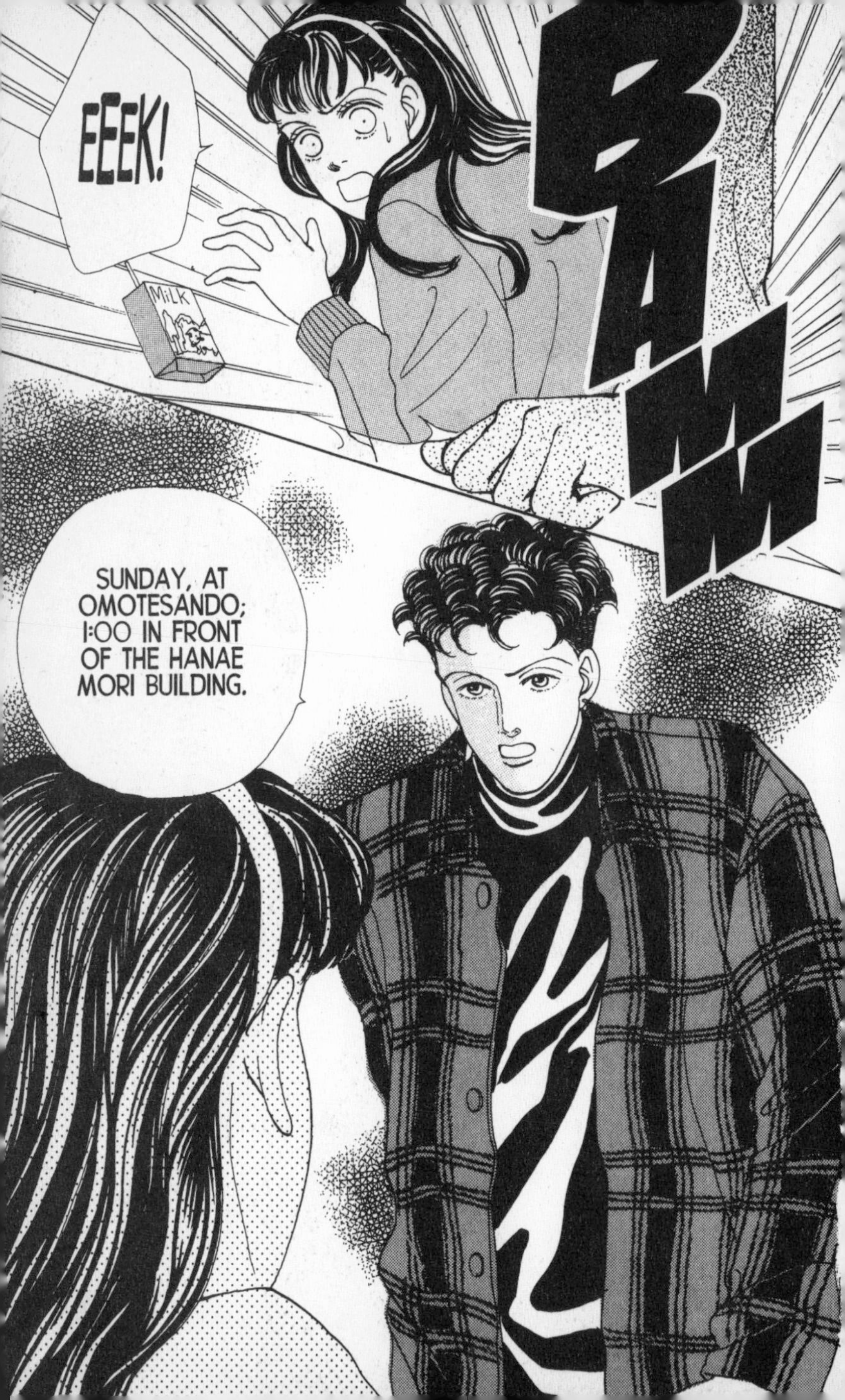
BAMMM
EEEK!
MiLK
SUNDAY, AT OMOTESANDO; 1:00 IN FRONT OF THE HANAE MORI BUILDING.

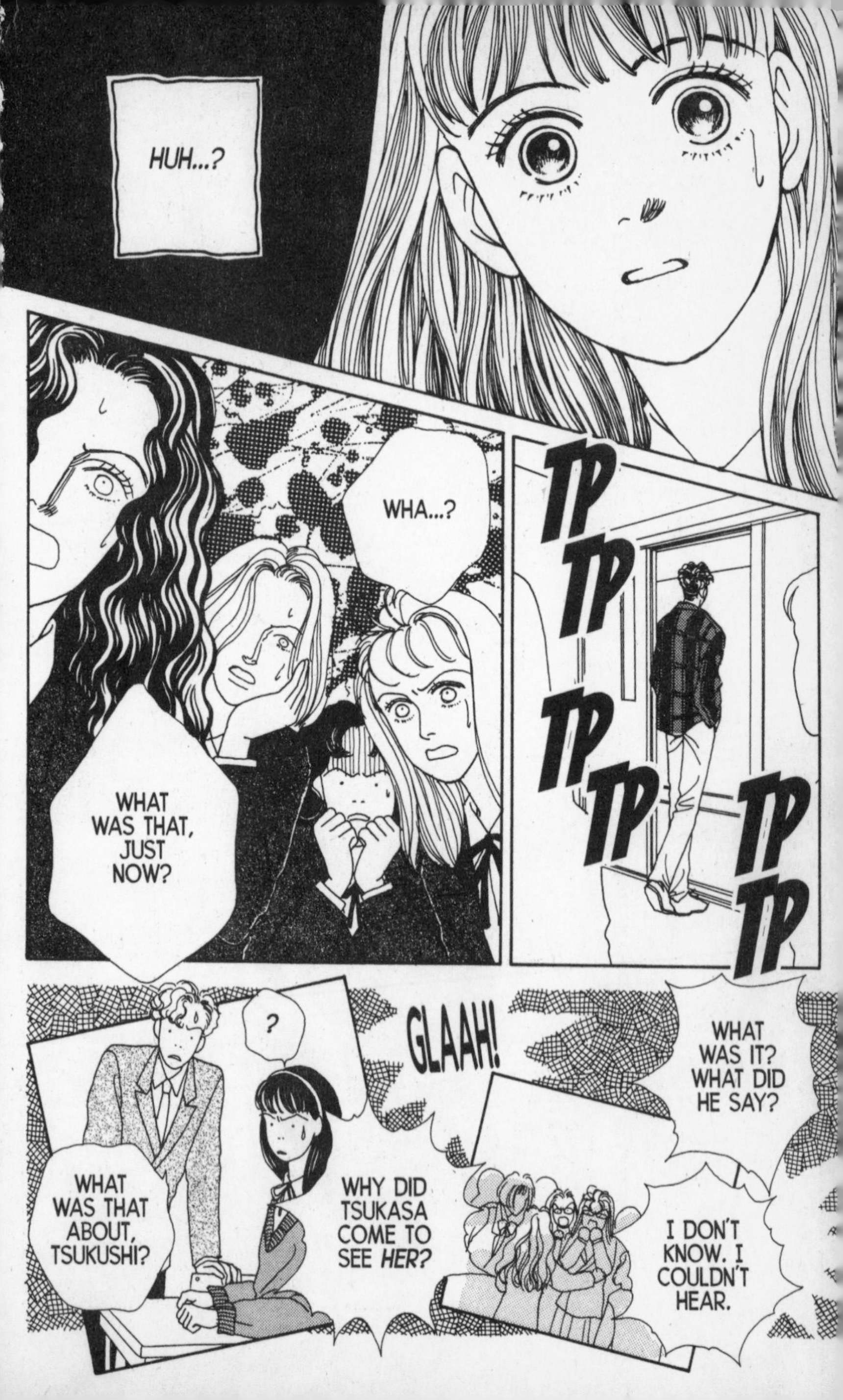
HUH...?
TP TP TP TP TP TP
WHA...?
WHAT WAS THAT, JUST NOW?
WHAT WAS IT? WHAT DID HE SAY?
I DON'T KNOW. I COULDN'T HEAR.
GLAAH!
?
WHY DID TSUKASA COME TO SEE *HER*?
WHAT WAS THAT ABOUT, TSUKUSHI?

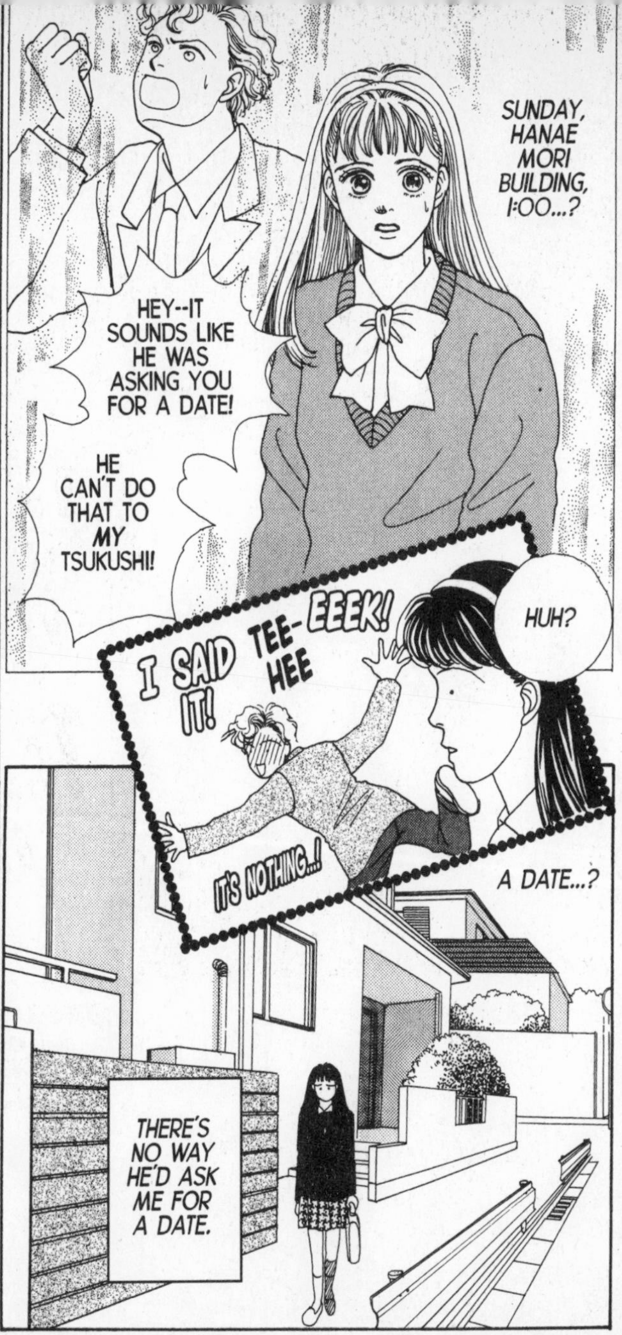
SUNDAY, HANAE MORI BUILDING, 1:00...?
HEY--IT SOUNDS LIKE HE WAS ASKING YOU FOR A DATE!
HE CAN'T DO THAT TO MY TSUKUSHI!
HUH?
I SAID IT! TEE-HEE
EEEK!
IT'S NOTHING..!
A DATE...?
THERE'S NO WAY HE'D ASK ME FOR A DATE.

6

Our interview wasn't anything formal. It was more like a chat.

It was like I was asking Takuya questions as a representative of his fans.

We didn't have much time, so I asked him several questions in the car on our way to the studio.

I asked him what the name of his dog was, and what kinds of girls he liked.

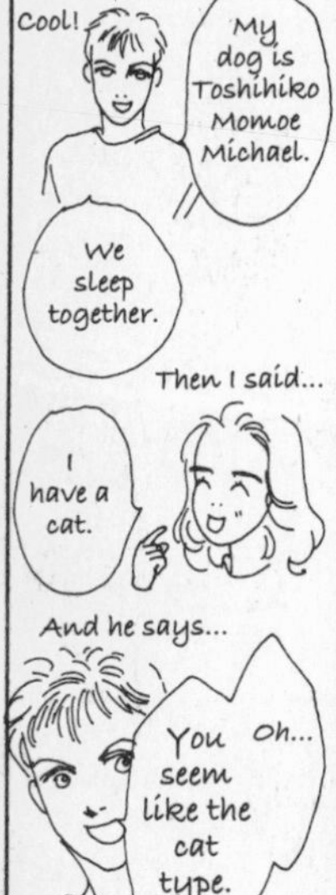
Cool!
My dog is Toshihiko Momoe Michael.
We sleep together.
Then I said...
I have a cat.
And he says...
Oh...
You seem like the cat type.

I wonder what he meant by that.

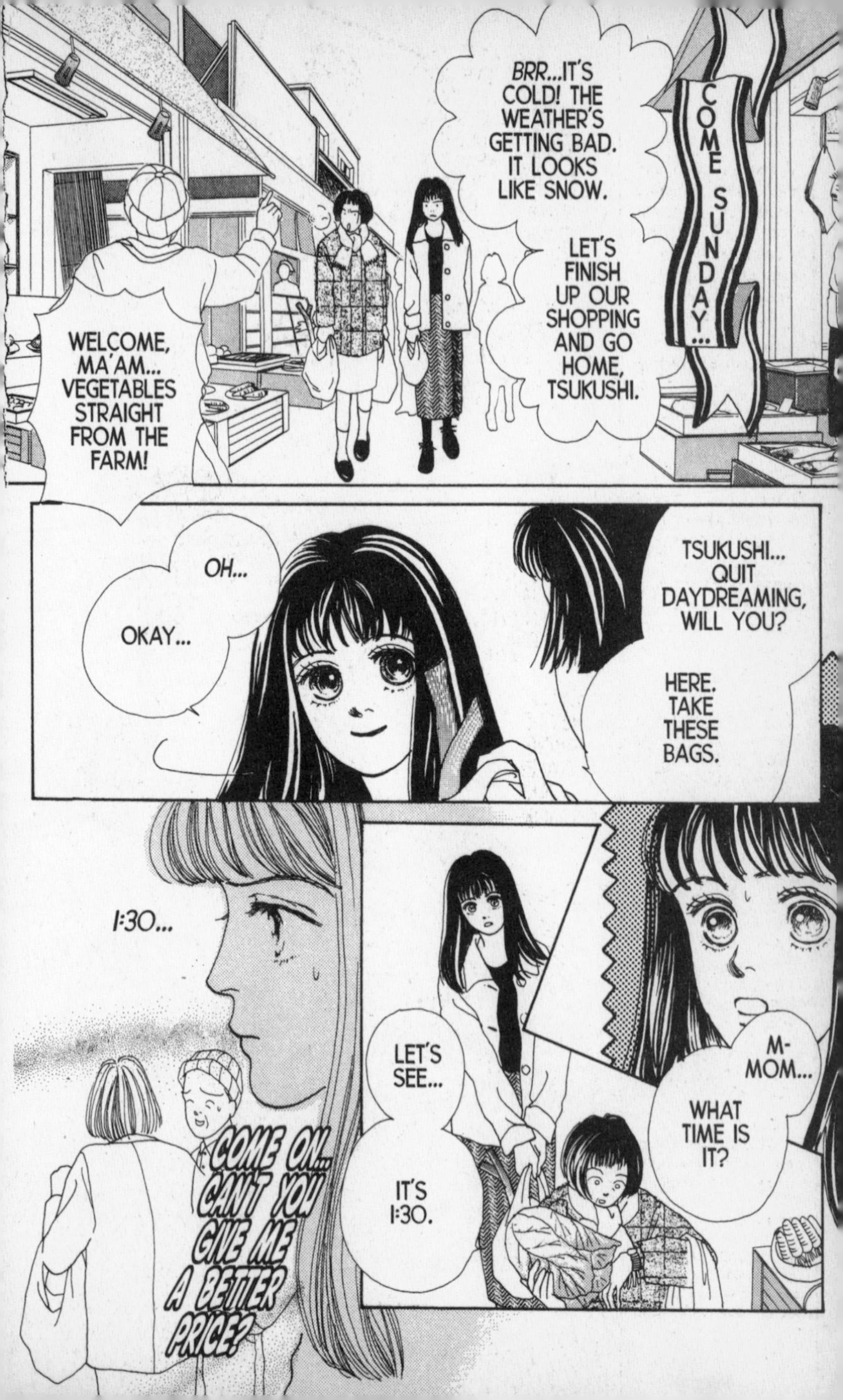
COME SUNDAY...
BRR...IT'S COLD! THE WEATHER'S GETTING BAD. IT LOOKS LIKE SNOW.
LET'S FINISH UP OUR SHOPPING AND GO HOME, TSUKUSHI.
WELCOME, MA'AM... VEGETABLES STRAIGHT FROM THE FARM!
TSUKUSHI... QUIT DAYDREAMING, WILL YOU?
HERE. TAKE THESE BAGS.
OH...
OKAY...
M-MOM...
WHAT TIME IS IT?
LET'S SEE...
IT'S 1:30.
1:30...
COME ON... CAN'T YOU GIVE ME A BETTER PRICE?

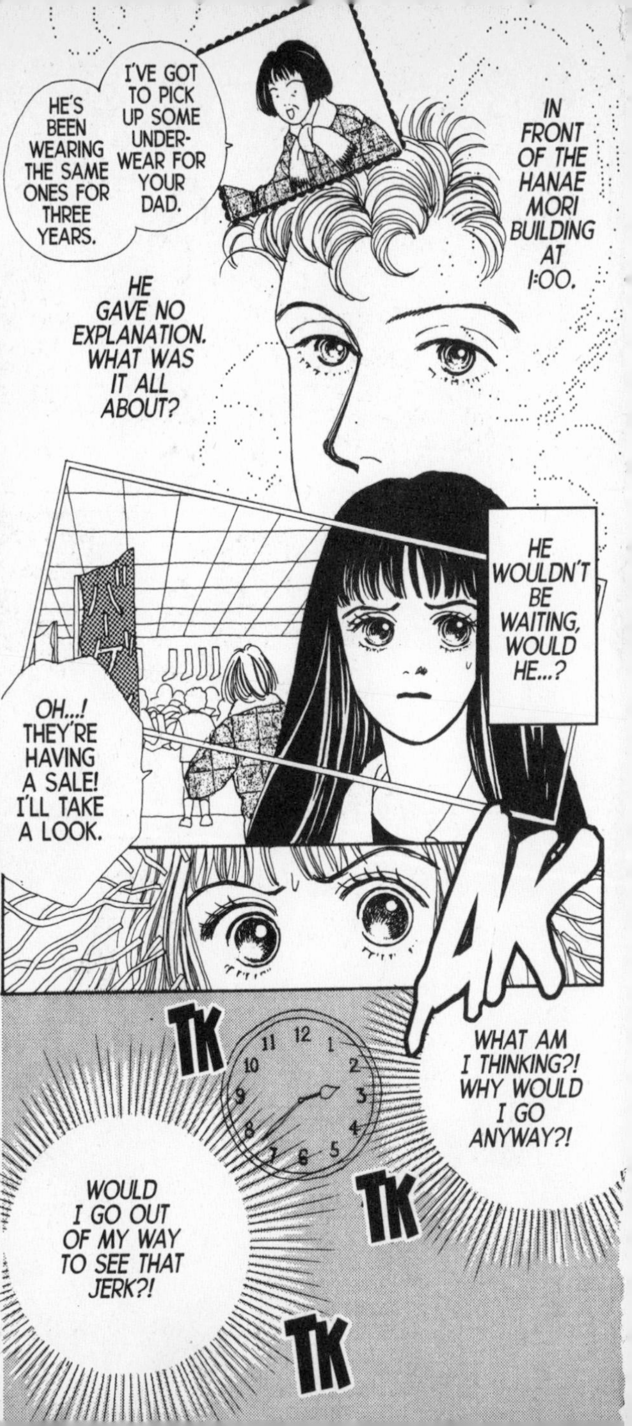
IN FRONT OF THE HANAE MORI BUILDING AT 1:00.
I'VE GOT TO PICK UP SOME UNDER-WEAR FOR YOUR DAD.
HE'S BEEN WEARING THE SAME ONES FOR THREE YEARS.
HE GAVE NO EXPLANATION. WHAT WAS IT ALL ABOUT?
HE WOULDN'T BE WAITING, WOULD HE...?
OH...! THEY'RE HAVING A SALE! I'LL TAKE A LOOK.
AK
WHAT AM I THINKING?! WHY WOULD I GO ANYWAY?!
TK
TK
WOULD I GO OUT OF MY WAY TO SEE THAT JERK?!
TK

7

When we got to the studio, we took some photos for the cover of Margaret. Takuya is quite the pro. Whatever the pose, or the expression, he looked great.

And he doesn't blink much. he kept his eye on the camera at all times.

Then I had some pictures taken of the two of us. I was so tense...having my picture taken with such a hot guy. Anybody would be nervous. Heck, he's prettier than most of the girls on the street.

But...

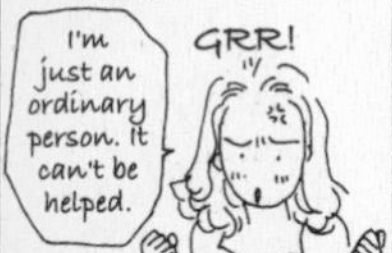
I'm just an ordinary person. It can't be helped.
GRR!

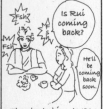

I swallowed my pride and had the photos taken. It was embarrassing.

Takuya talked to me about this and that, trying to get me to relax. He was so thoughtful.

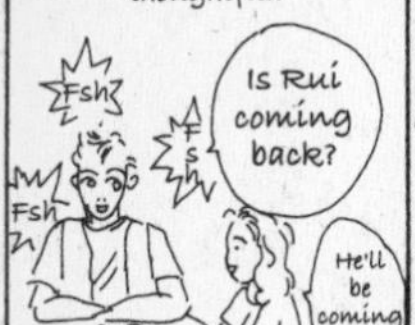
Fsh
Fsh
Fsh
Is Rui coming back?
He'll be coming back soon.

Thanks to him, I was able to relax, and have the pictures taken.

Except they turned out awful. Even my friends said, "Those pictures are pretty bad." Which, considering what I look like, couldn't be helped...

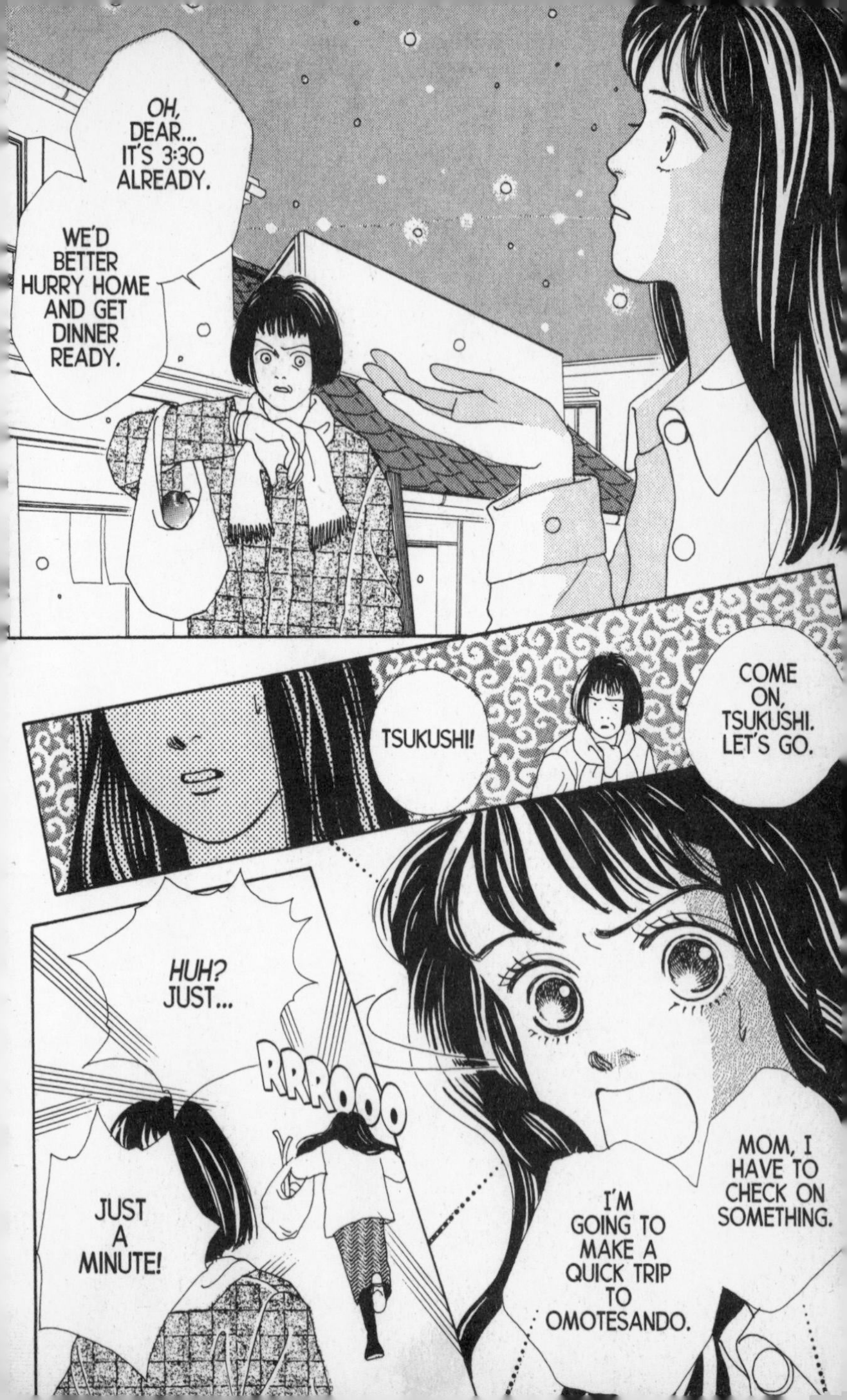

OH, DEAR... IT'S 3:30 ALREADY.
WE'D BETTER HURRY HOME AND GET DINNER READY.
COME ON, TSUKUSHI. LET'S GO.
TSUKUSHI!
MOM, I HAVE TO CHECK ON SOMETHING.
I'M GOING TO MAKE A QUICK TRIP TO OMOTESANDO.
HUH? JUST...
RRROOO
JUST A MINUTE!

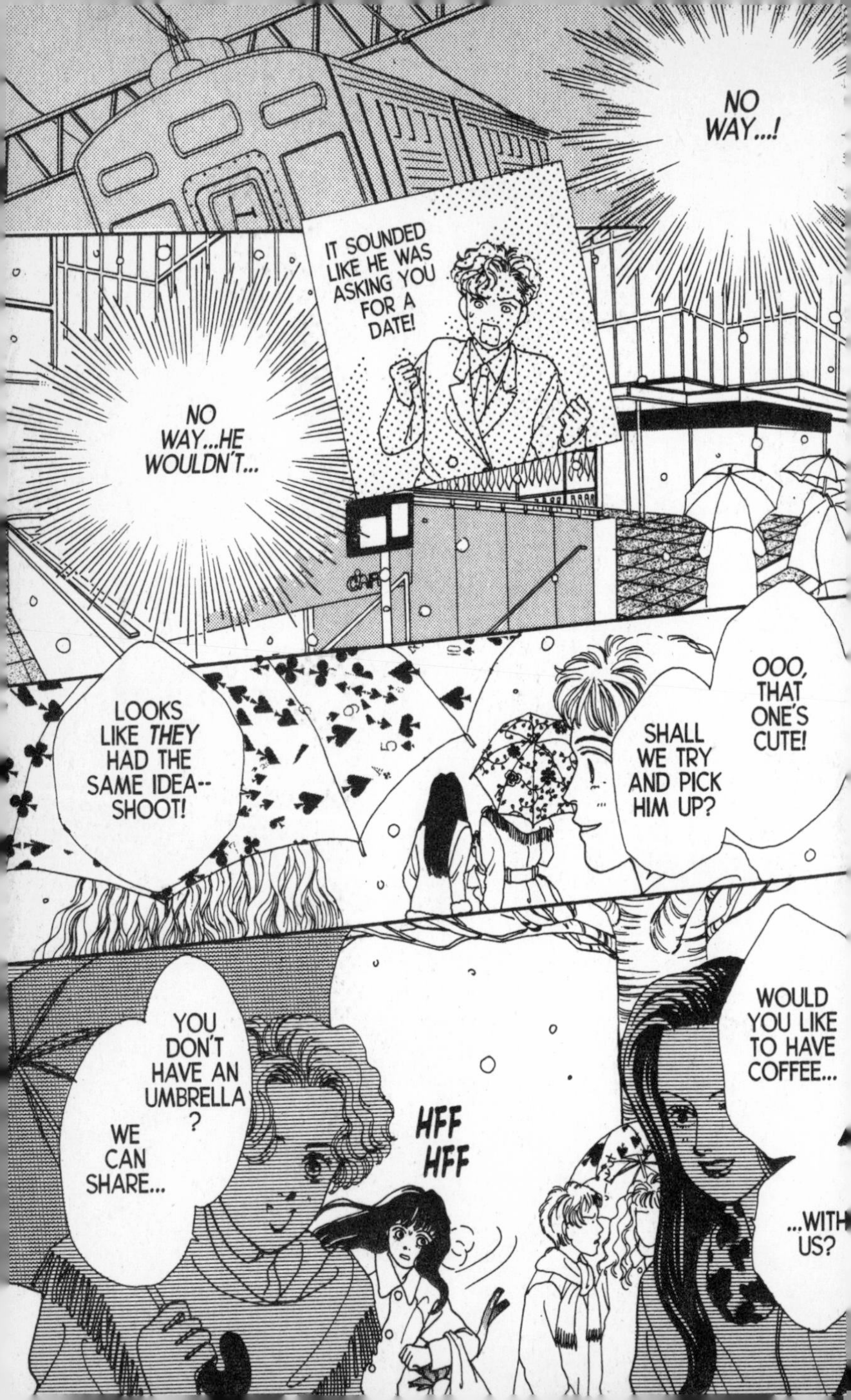
NO WAY...!
IT SOUNDED LIKE HE WAS ASKING YOU FOR A DATE!
NO WAY...HE WOULDN'T...
OOO, THAT ONE'S CUTE!
SHALL WE TRY AND PICK HIM UP?
LOOKS LIKE *THEY* HAD THE SAME IDEA-- SHOOT!
WOULD YOU LIKE TO HAVE COFFEE...
...WITH US?
HFF HFF
YOU DON'T HAVE AN UMBRELLA?
WE CAN SHARE...

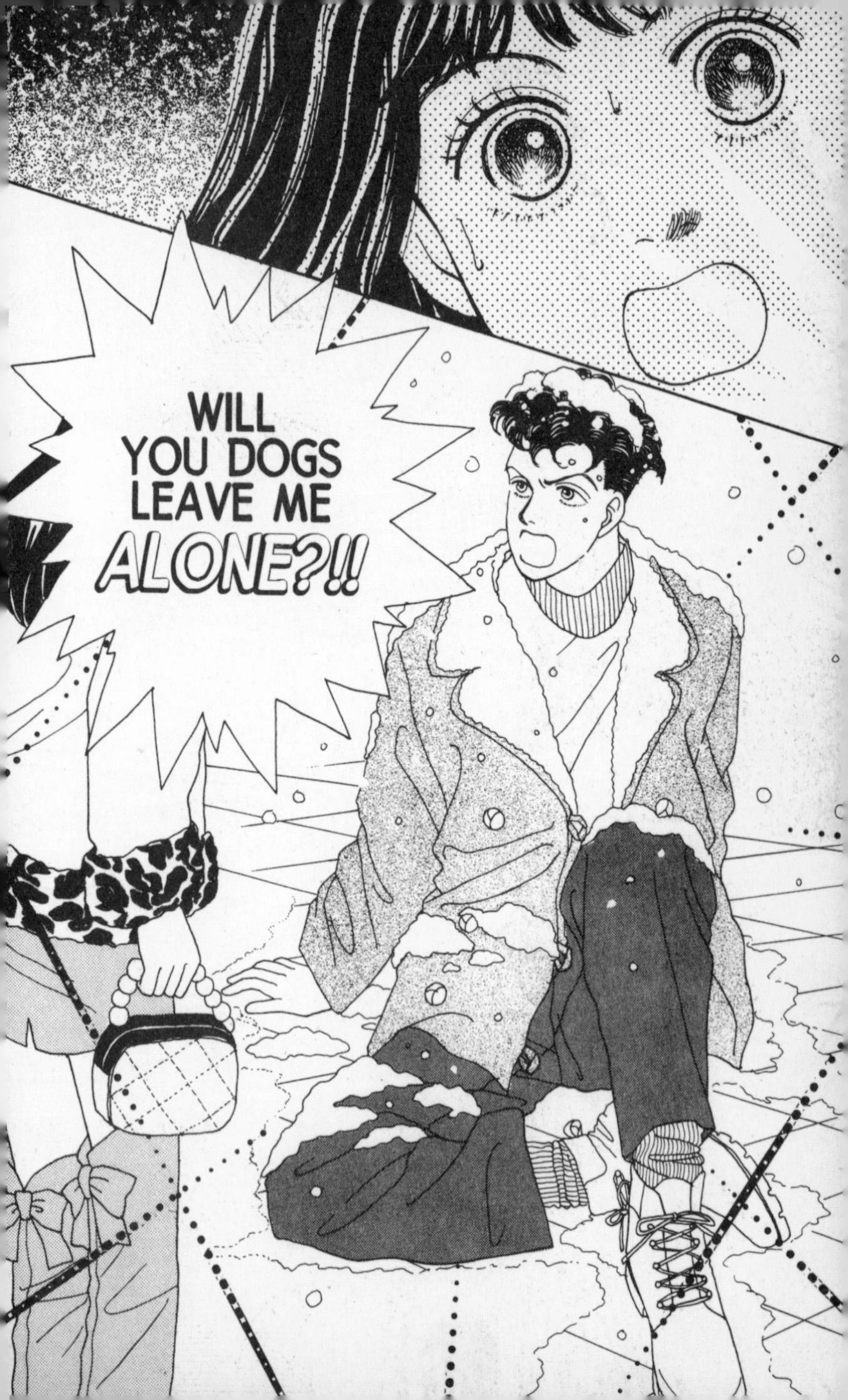
WILL YOU DOGS LEAVE ME ALONE?!!

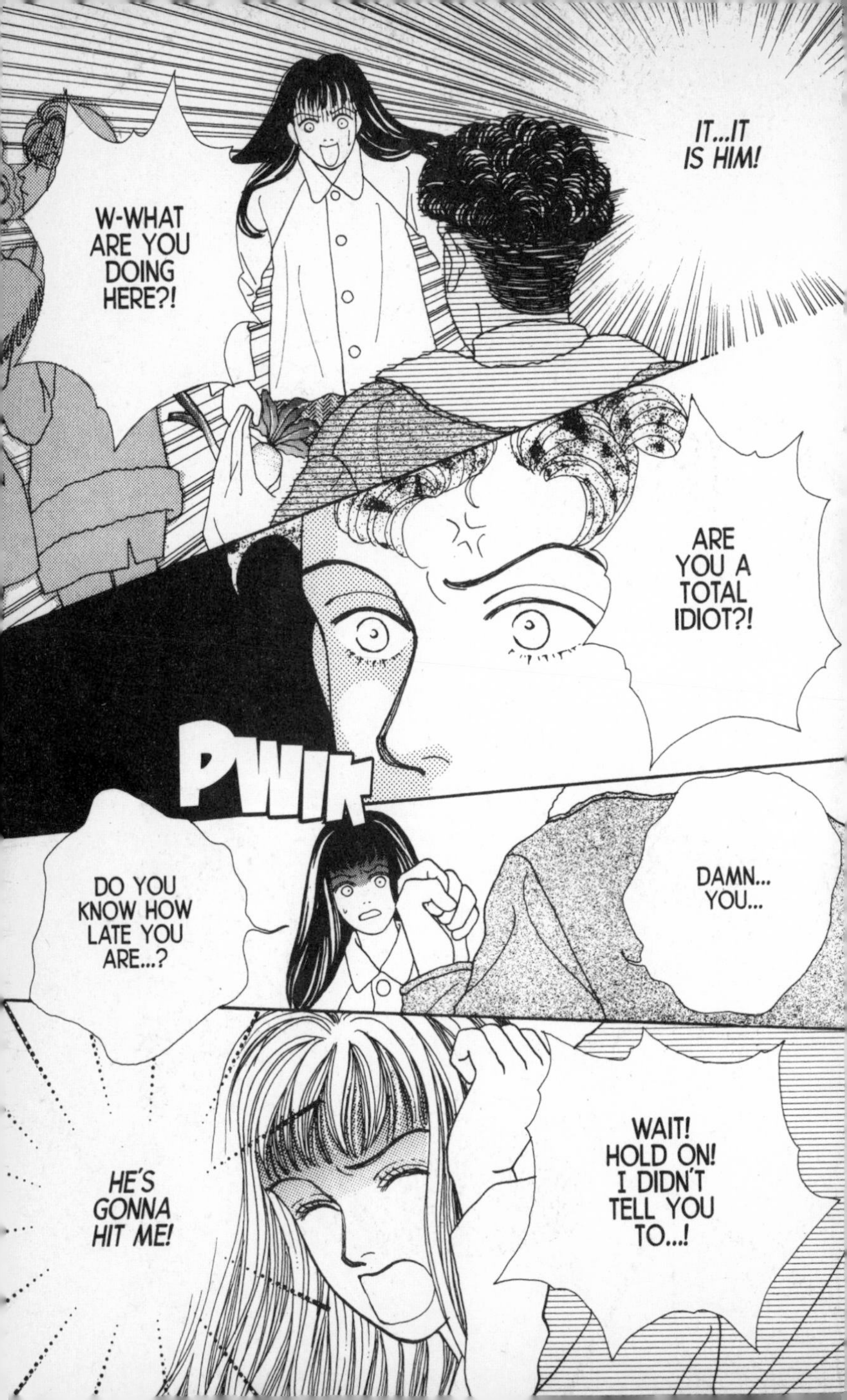
IT...IT IS HIM!
W-WHAT ARE YOU DOING HERE?!
ARE YOU A TOTAL IDIOT?!
PWIK
DAMN... YOU...
DO YOU KNOW HOW LATE YOU ARE...?
WAIT! HOLD ON! I DIDN'T TELL YOU TO...!
HE'S GONNA HIT ME!

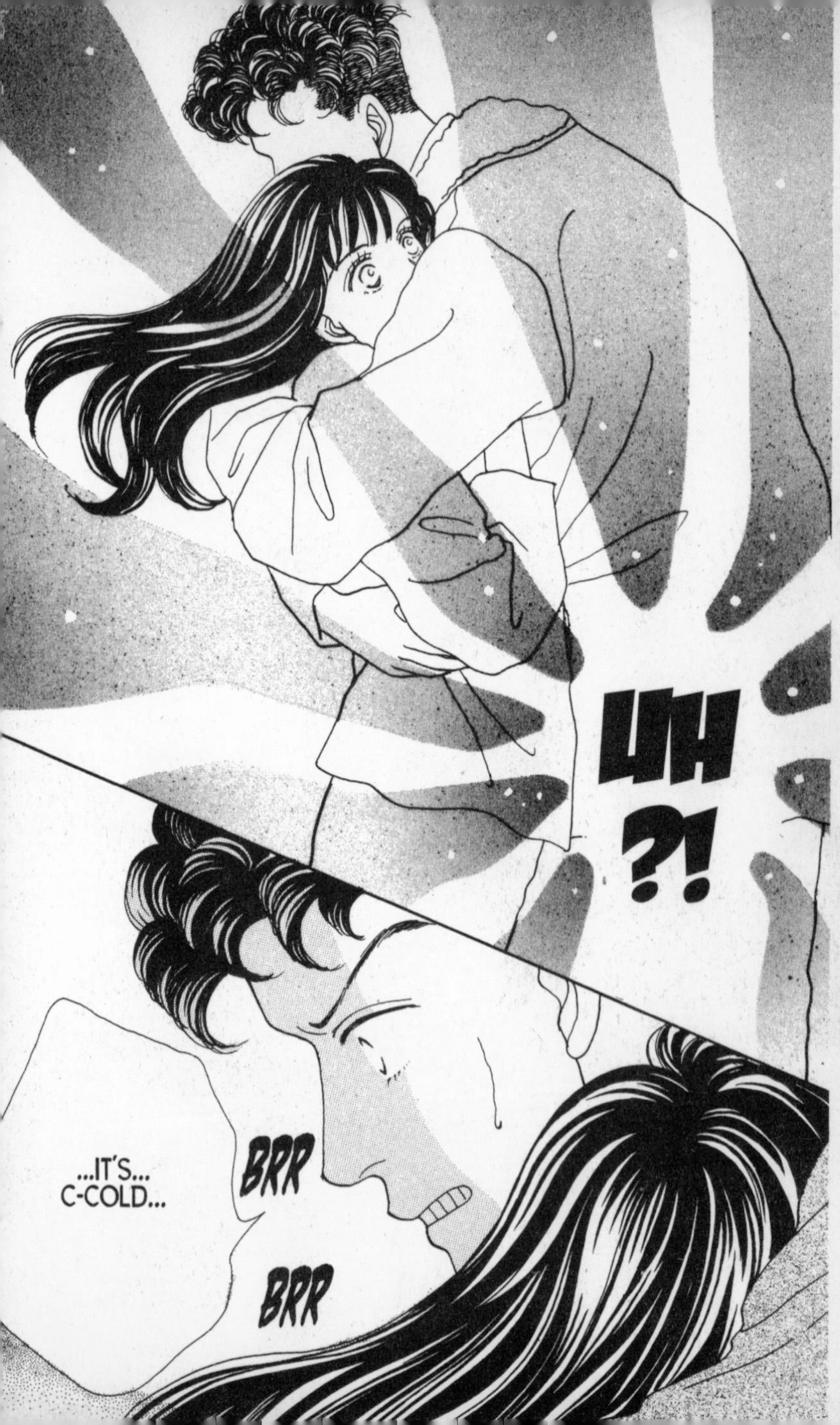
UH ?!
BRR
...IT'S... C-COLD...
BRR

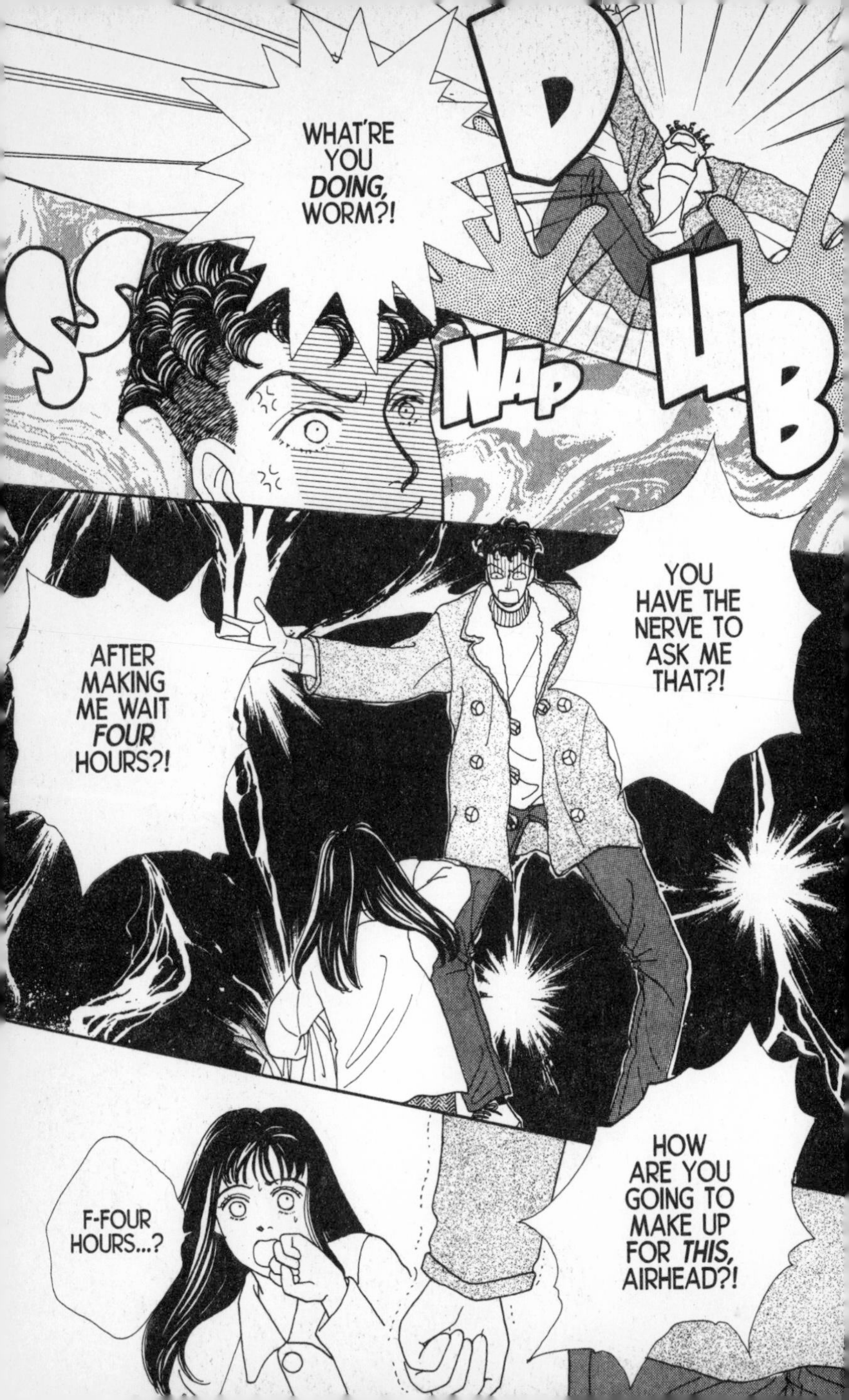
WHAT'RE YOU *DOING,* WORM?!
YOU HAVE THE NERVE TO ASK ME THAT?!
AFTER MAKING ME WAIT *FOUR* HOURS?!
HOW ARE YOU GOING TO MAKE UP FOR *THIS,* AIRHEAD?!
F-FOUR HOURS...?

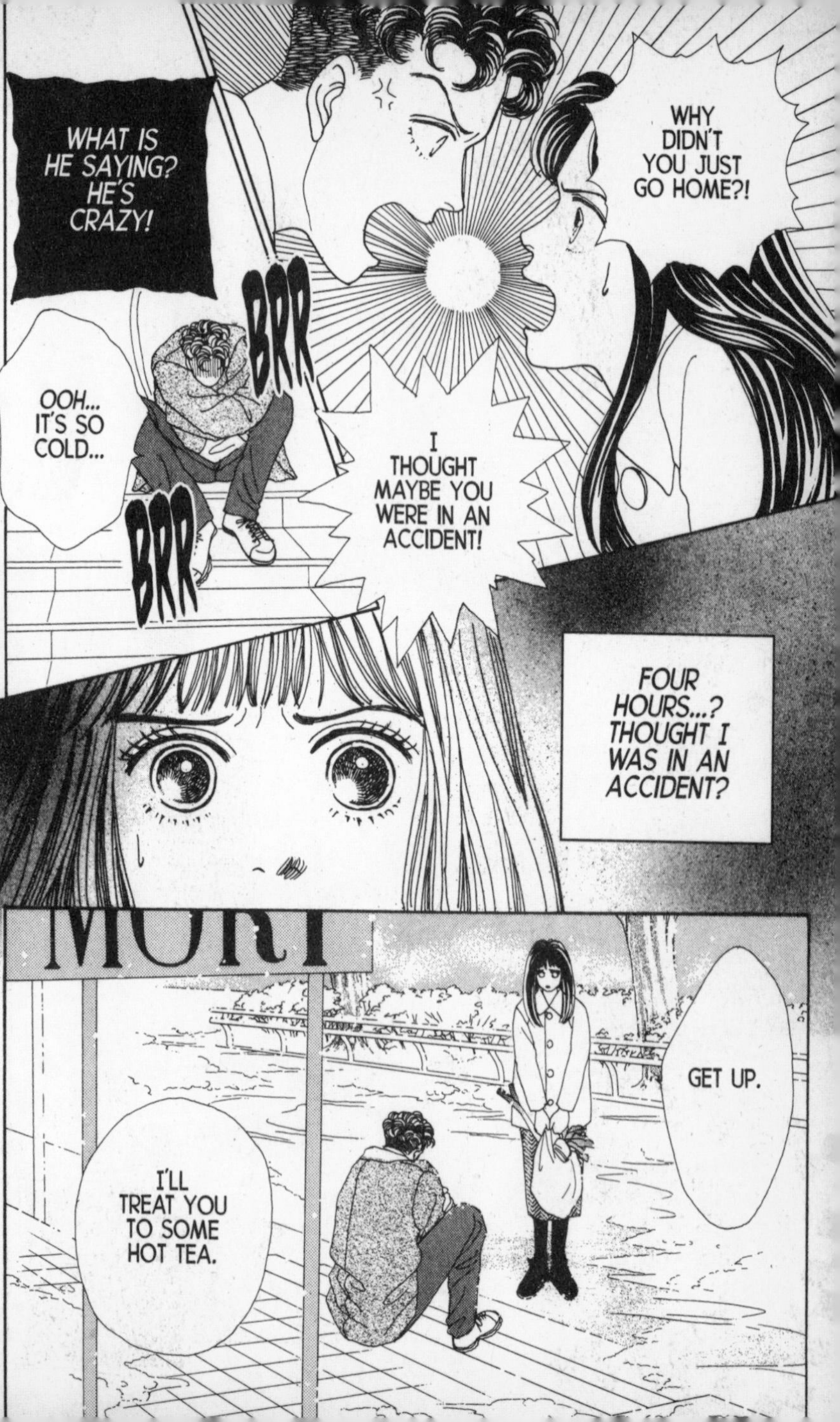
WHY DIDN'T YOU JUST GO HOME?!
I THOUGHT MAYBE YOU WERE IN AN ACCIDENT!
WHAT IS HE SAYING? HE'S CRAZY!
OOH... IT'S SO COLD...
BRR
BRR
FOUR HOURS...? THOUGHT I WAS IN AN ACCIDENT?
MORI
GET UP.
I'LL TREAT YOU TO SOME HOT TEA.

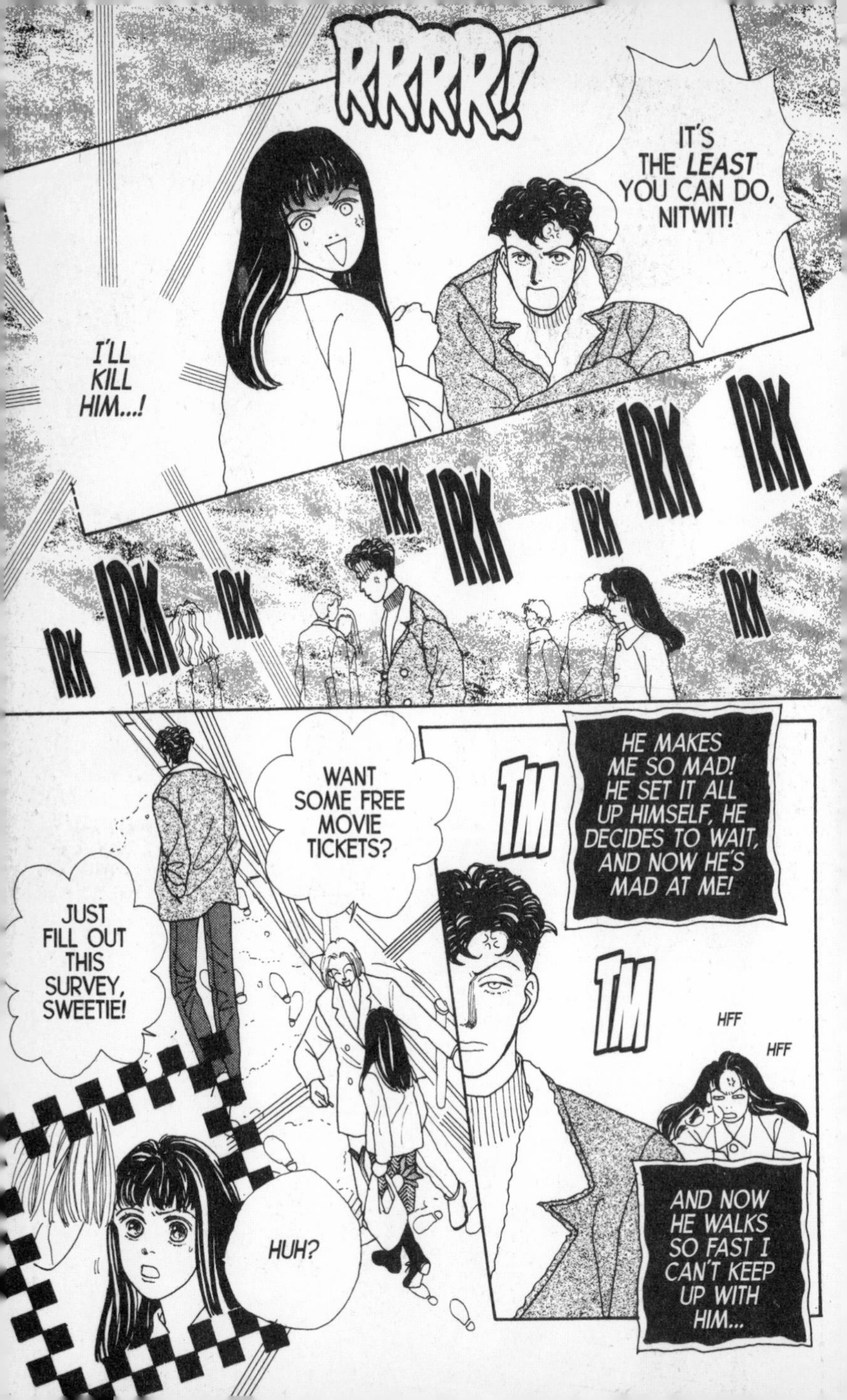
RRRR!
IT'S THE *LEAST* YOU CAN DO, NITWIT!
I'LL KILL HIM...!
IRK
IRK
IRK
IRK
IRK
IRK
IRK
IRK
IRK
TM
HE MAKES ME SO MAD! HE SET IT ALL UP HIMSELF, HE DECIDES TO WAIT, AND NOW HE'S MAD AT ME!
TM
HFF
HFF
AND NOW HE WALKS SO FAST I CAN'T KEEP UP WITH HIM...
WANT SOME FREE MOVIE TICKETS?
JUST FILL OUT THIS SURVEY, SWEETIE!
HUH?

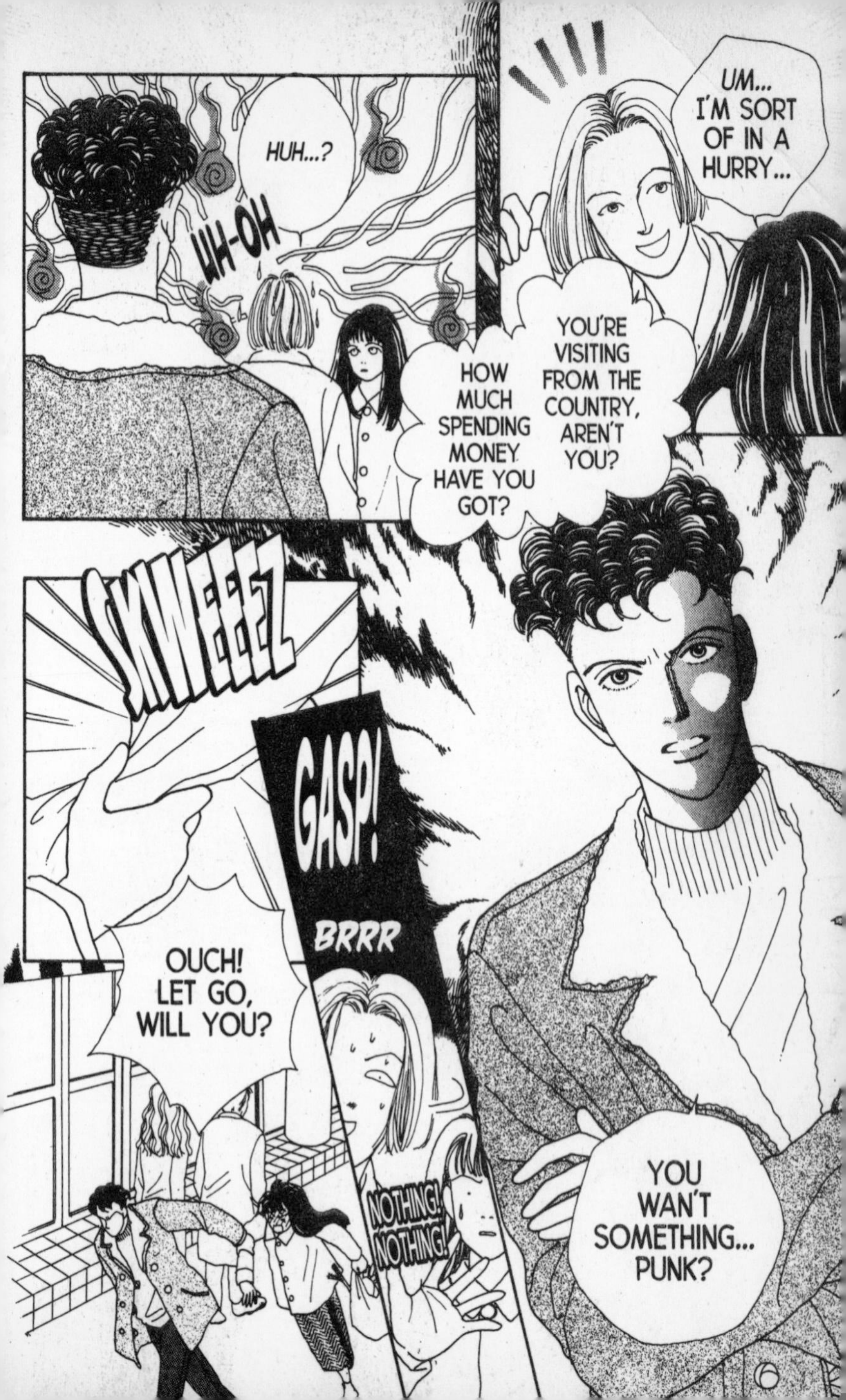
UM... I'M SORT OF IN A HURRY...
YOU'RE VISITING FROM THE COUNTRY, AREN'T YOU?
HOW MUCH SPENDING MONEY HAVE YOU GOT?
HUH...?
UH-OH
YOU WAN'T SOMETHING... PUNK?
SKWEEEZ
OUCH! LET GO, WILL YOU?
GASP!
BRRR
NOTHING! NOTHING!

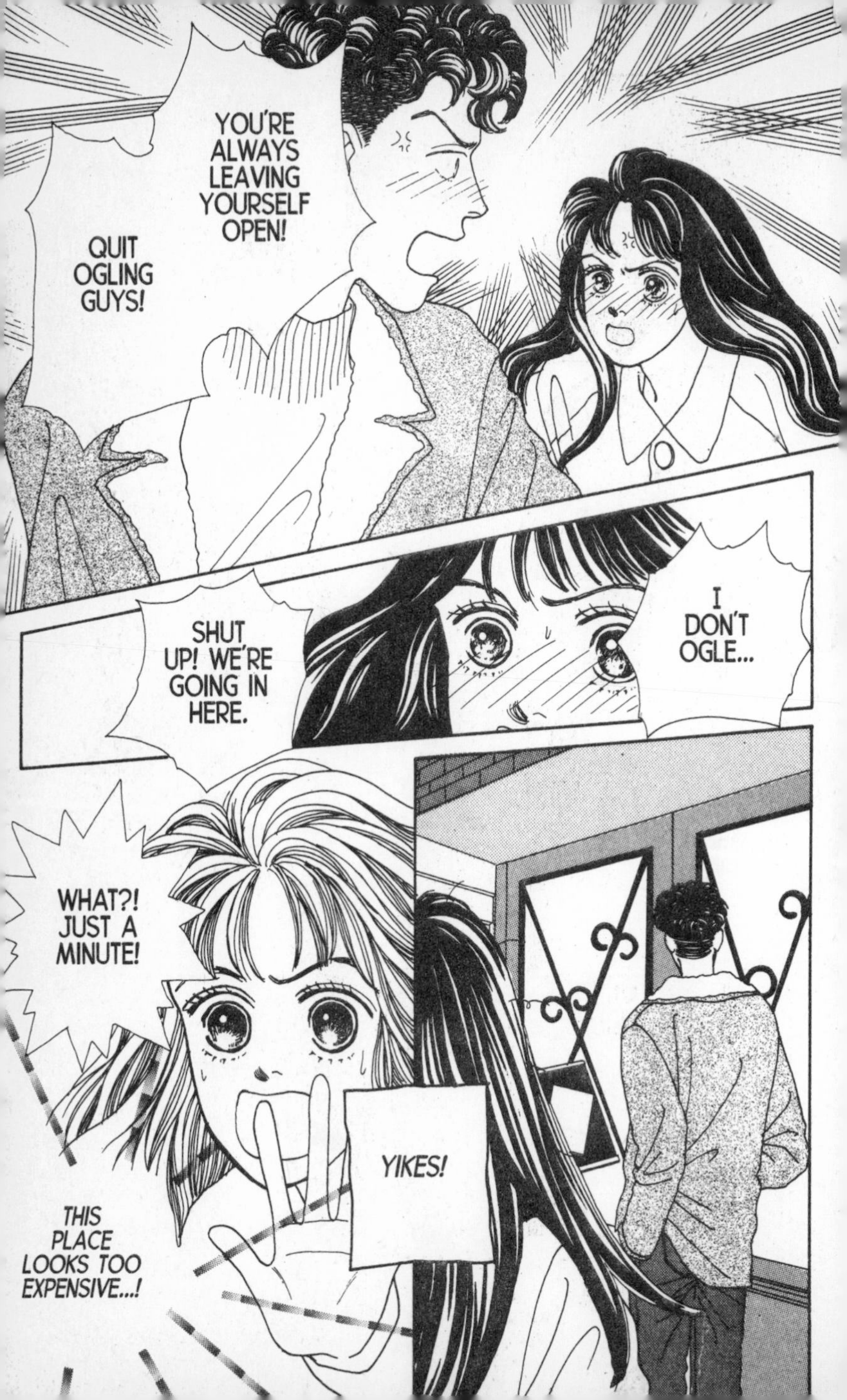
YOU'RE ALWAYS LEAVING YOURSELF OPEN!
QUIT OGLING GUYS!
I DON'T OGLE...
SHUT UP! WE'RE GOING IN HERE.
WHAT?! JUST A MINUTE!
YIKES!
THIS PLACE LOOKS TOO EXPENSIVE...!

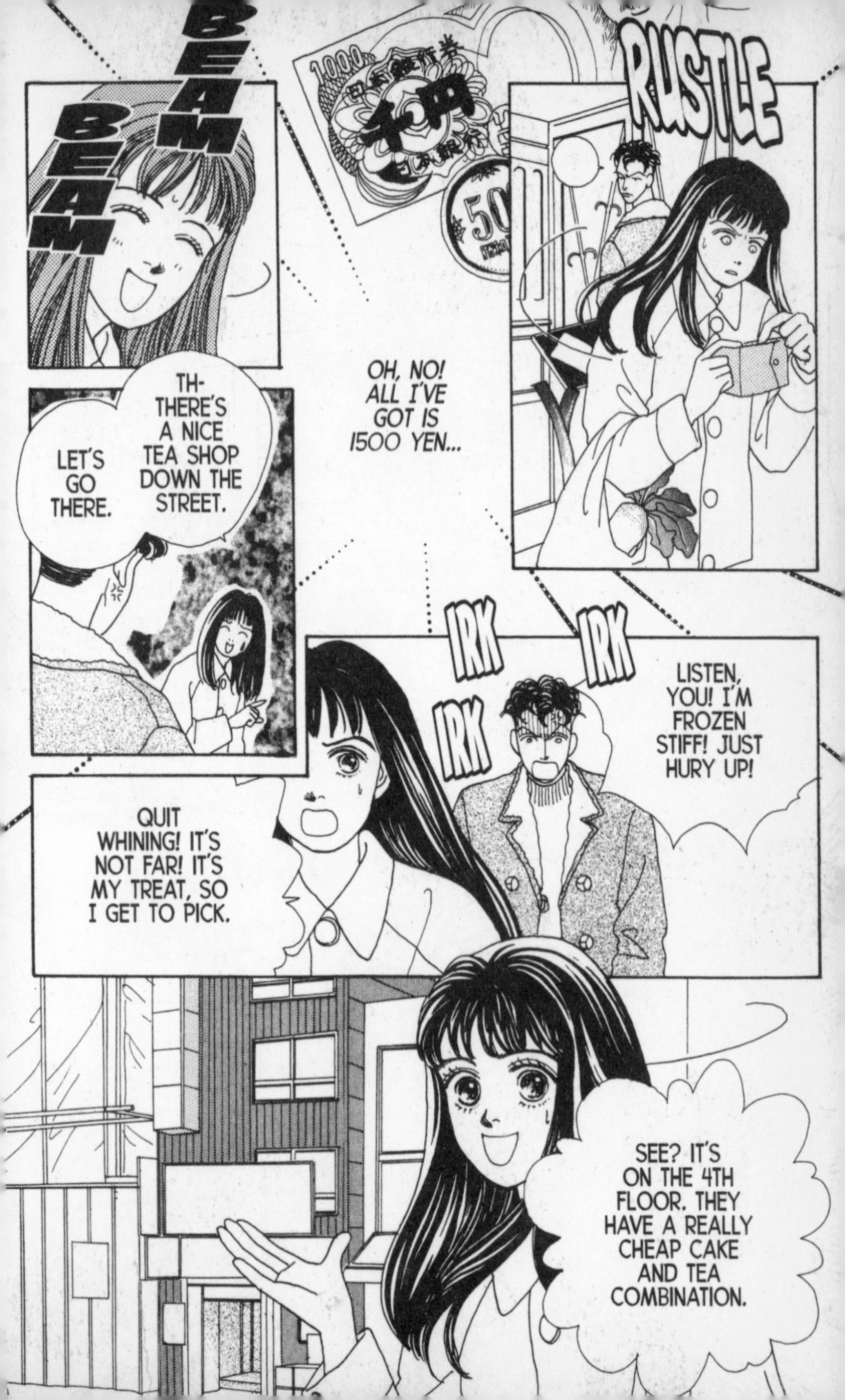
RUSTLE
OH, NO! ALL I'VE GOT IS 1500 YEN...
BEAM
BEAM
TH-THERE'S A NICE TEA SHOP DOWN THE STREET.
LET'S GO THERE.
IRK
IRK
IRK
LISTEN, YOU! I'M FROZEN STIFF! JUST HURY UP!
QUIT WHINING! IT'S NOT FAR! IT'S MY TREAT, SO I GET TO PICK.
SEE? IT'S ON THE 4TH FLOOR. THEY HAVE A REALLY CHEAP CAKE AND TEA COMBINATION.

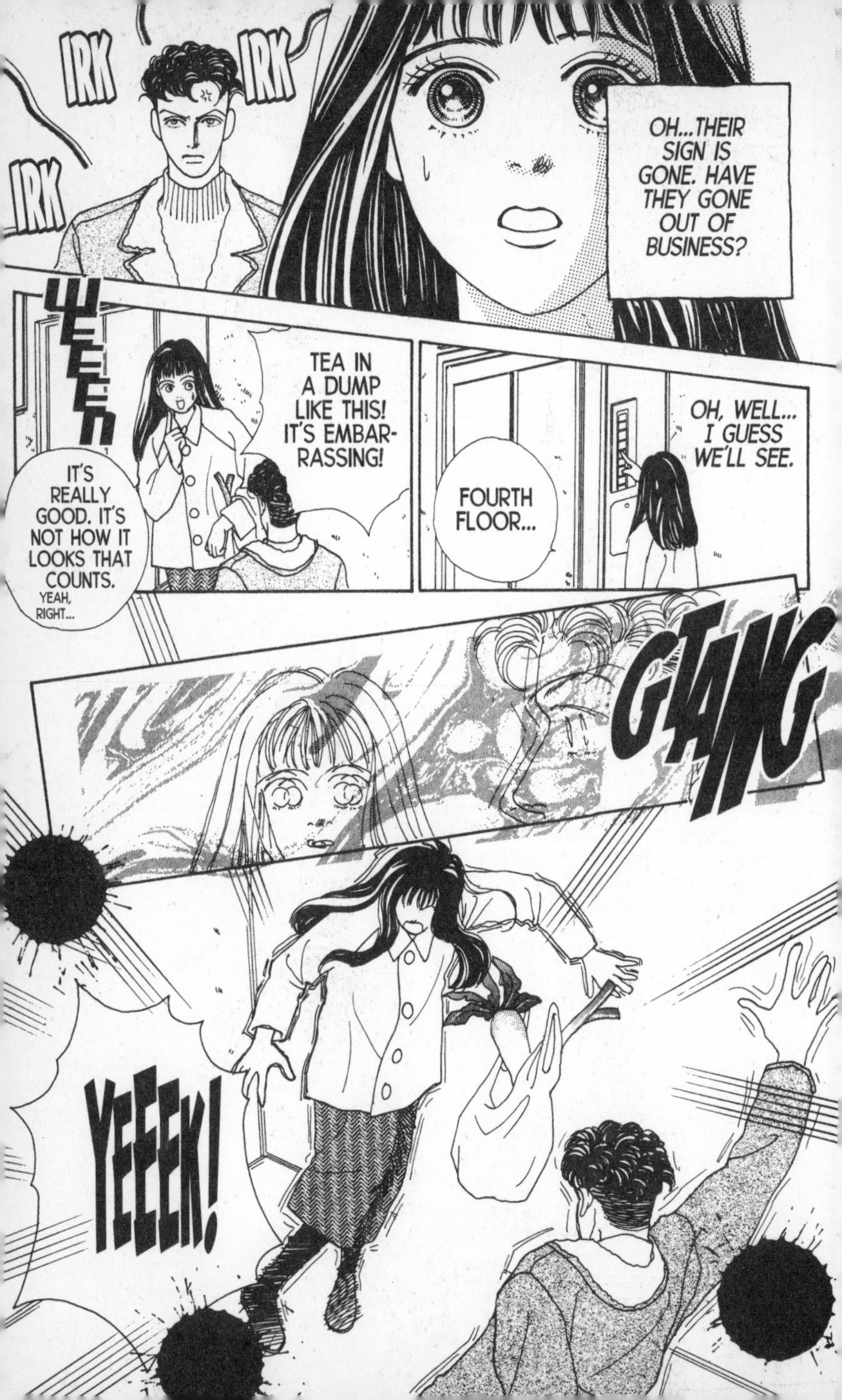
OH...THEIR SIGN IS GONE. HAVE THEY GONE OUT OF BUSINESS?
IRK
IRK
IRK
OH, WELL... I GUESS WE'LL SEE.
FOURTH FLOOR...
TEA IN A DUMP LIKE THIS! IT'S EMBARRASSING!
WEEEN
IT'S REALLY GOOD. IT'S NOT HOW IT LOOKS THAT COUNTS.
YEAH, RIGHT...
GTANG
YEEEK!

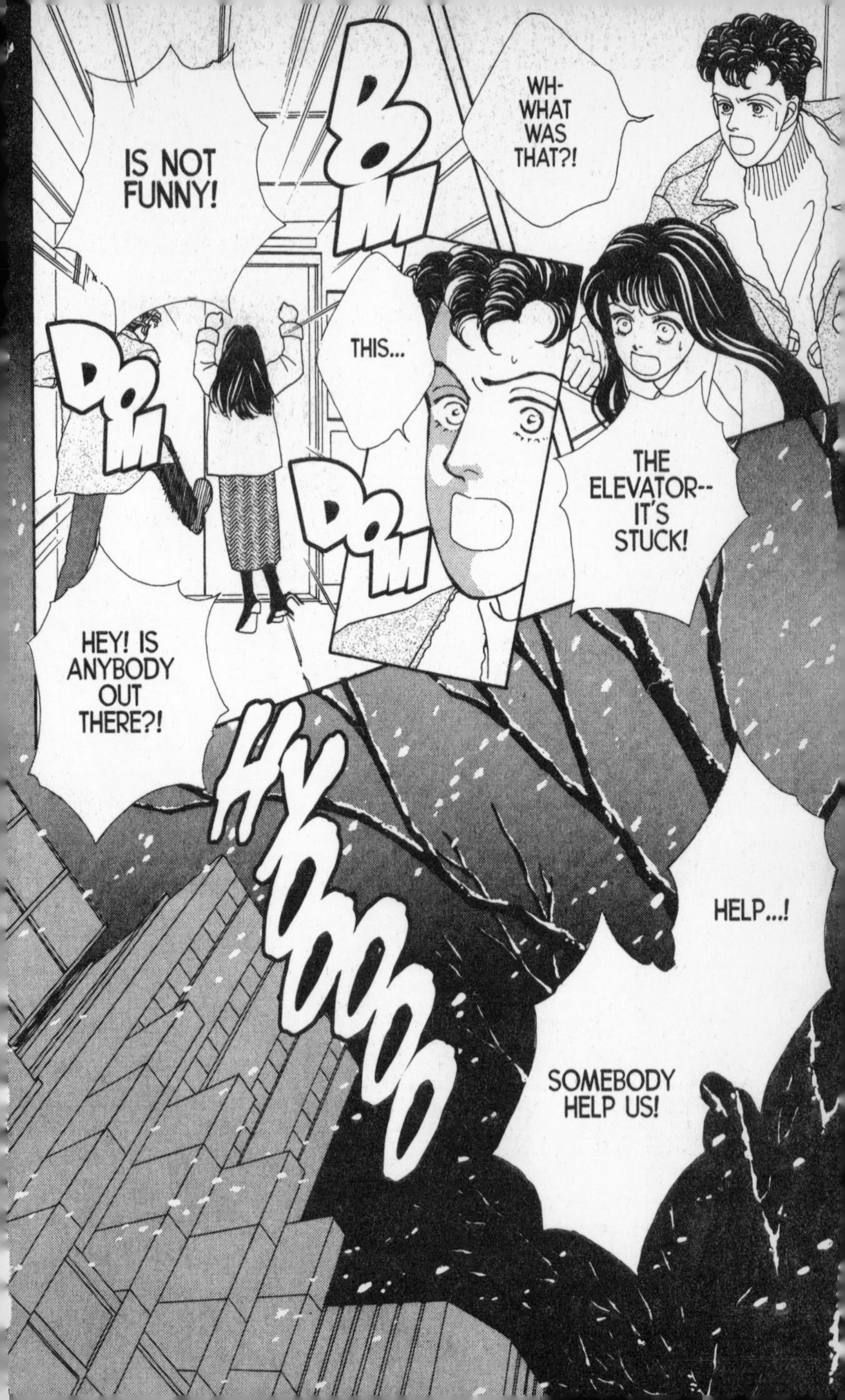
WH- WHAT WAS THAT?!
BOM
THE ELEVATOR-- IT'S STUCK!
THIS...
IS NOT FUNNY!
DOM
DOM
HEY! IS ANYBODY OUT THERE?!
HYOOOOOO
HELP...!
SOMEBODY HELP US!

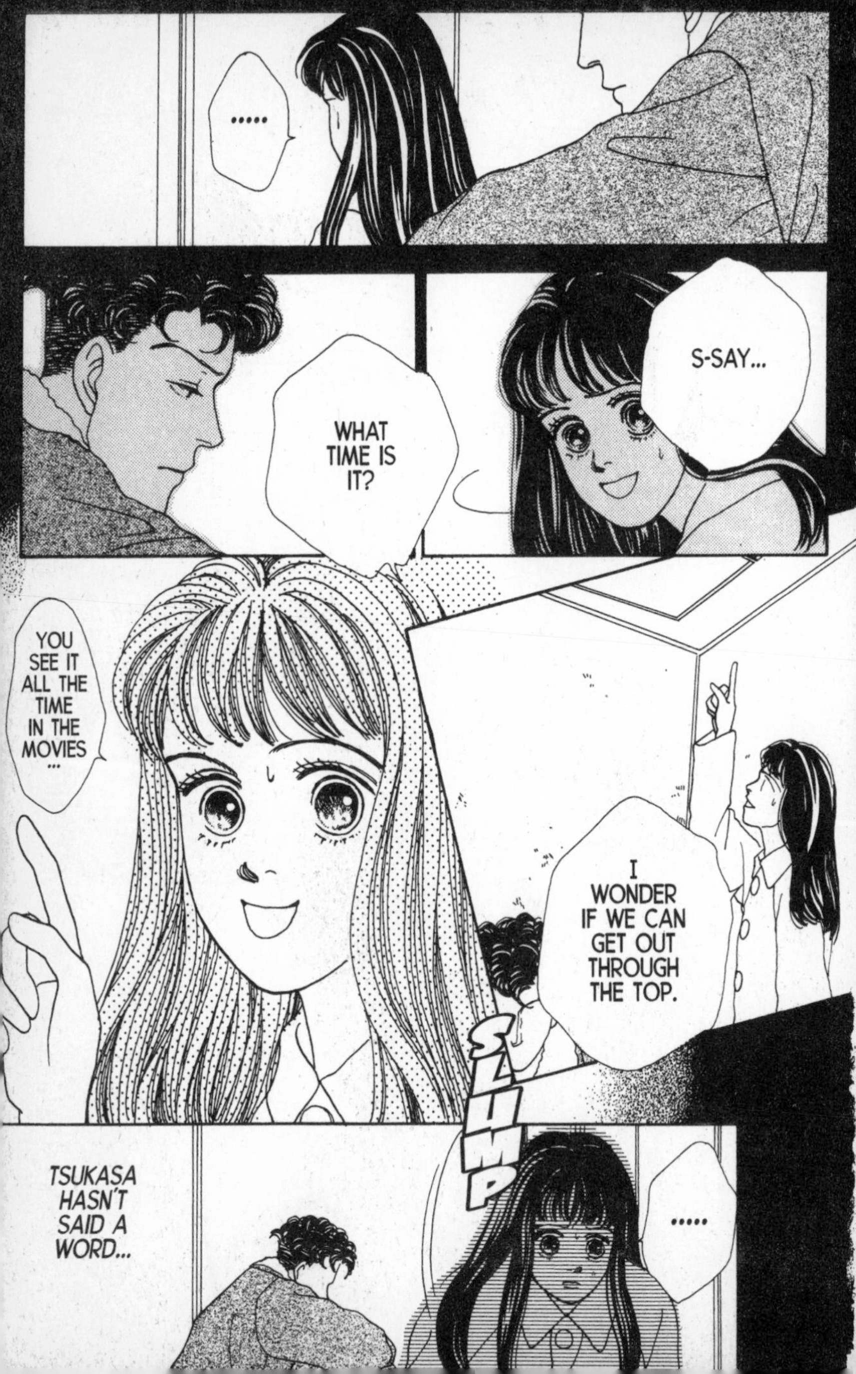
.....
S-SAY...
WHAT TIME IS IT?
I WONDER IF WE CAN GET OUT THROUGH THE TOP.
YOU SEE IT ALL THE TIME IN THE MOVIES ...
SLUMP
.....
TSUKASA HASN'T SAID A WORD...

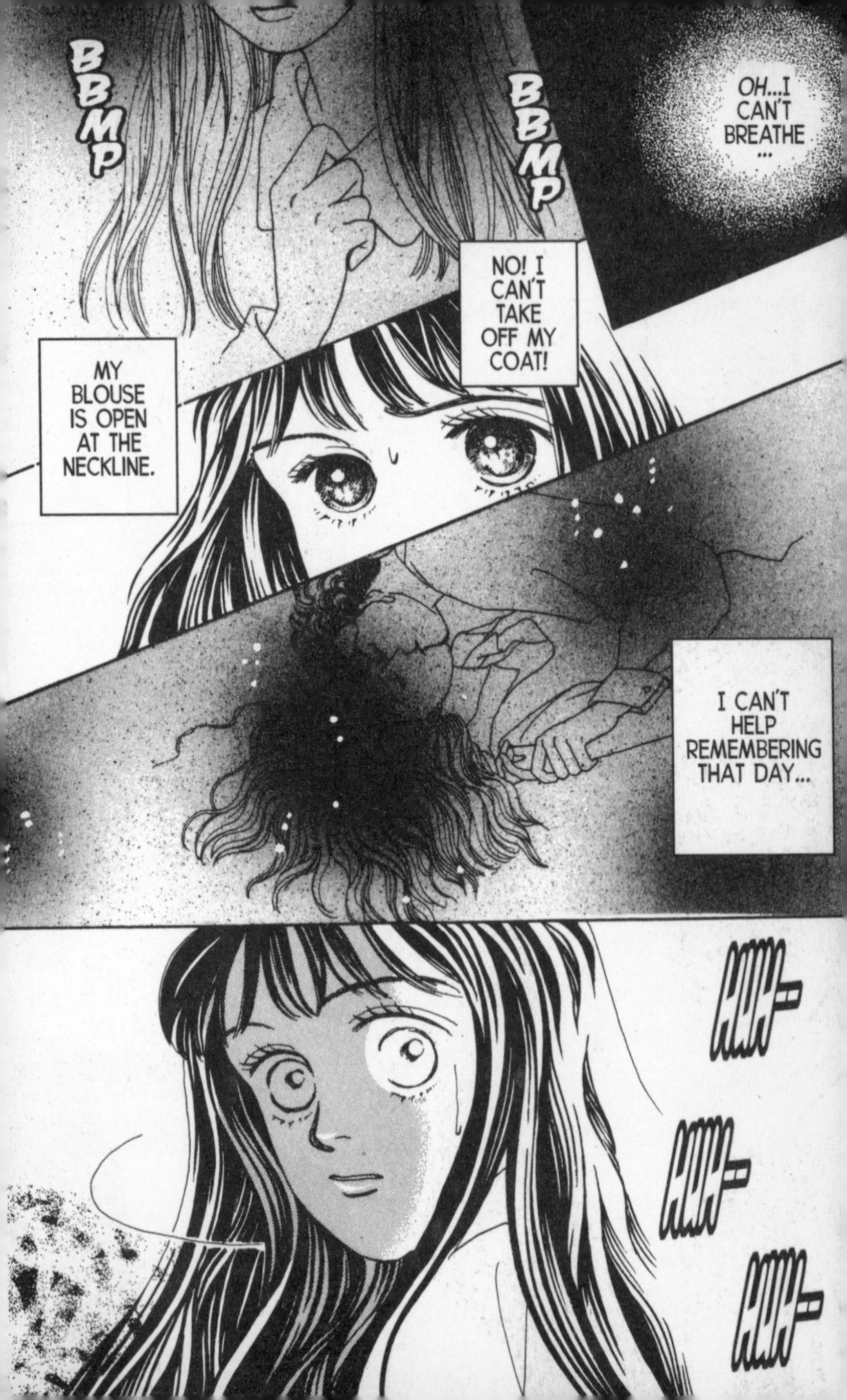
OH...I CAN'T BREATHE...
BBMP
BBMP
NO! I CAN'T TAKE OFF MY COAT!
MY BLOUSE IS OPEN AT THE NECKLINE.
I CAN'T HELP REMEMBERING THAT DAY...

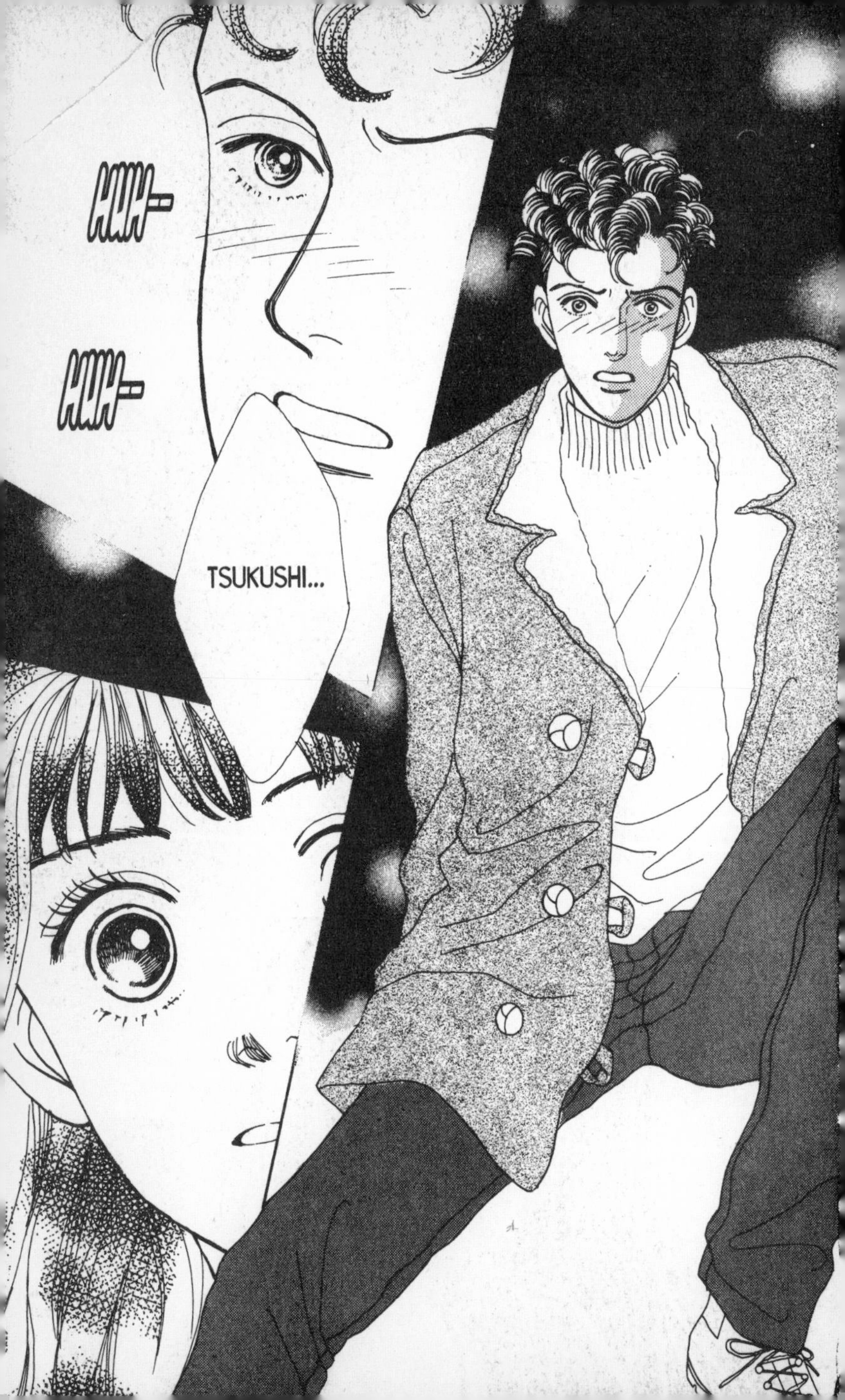
HUH—
HUH—
TSUKUSHI...

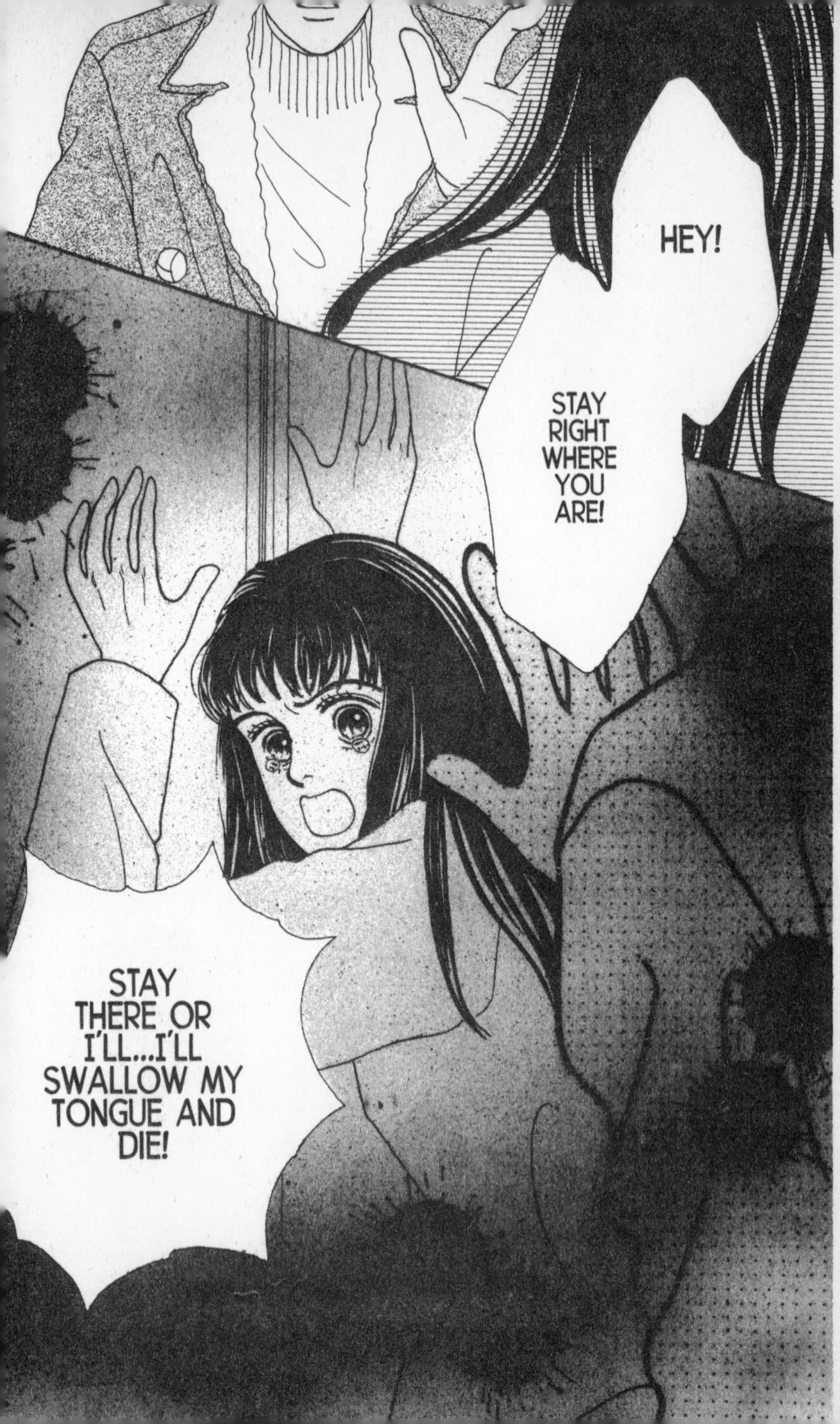
HEY!
STAY RIGHT WHERE YOU ARE!
STAY THERE OR I'LL...I'LL SWALLOW MY TONGUE AND DIE!

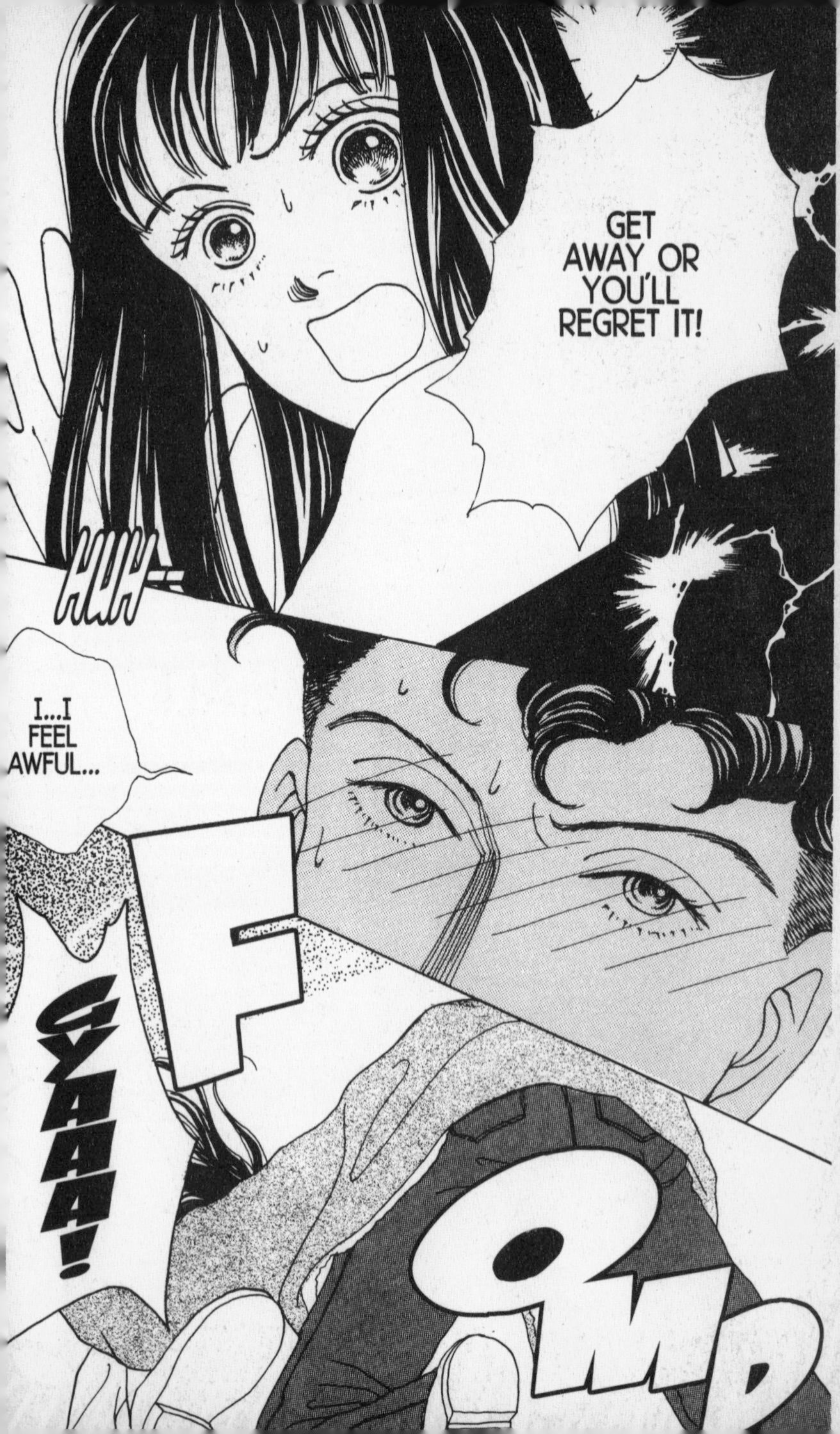
GET AWAY OR YOU'LL REGRET IT!
HUH--
I...I FEEL AWFUL...
F
GYAAAA!

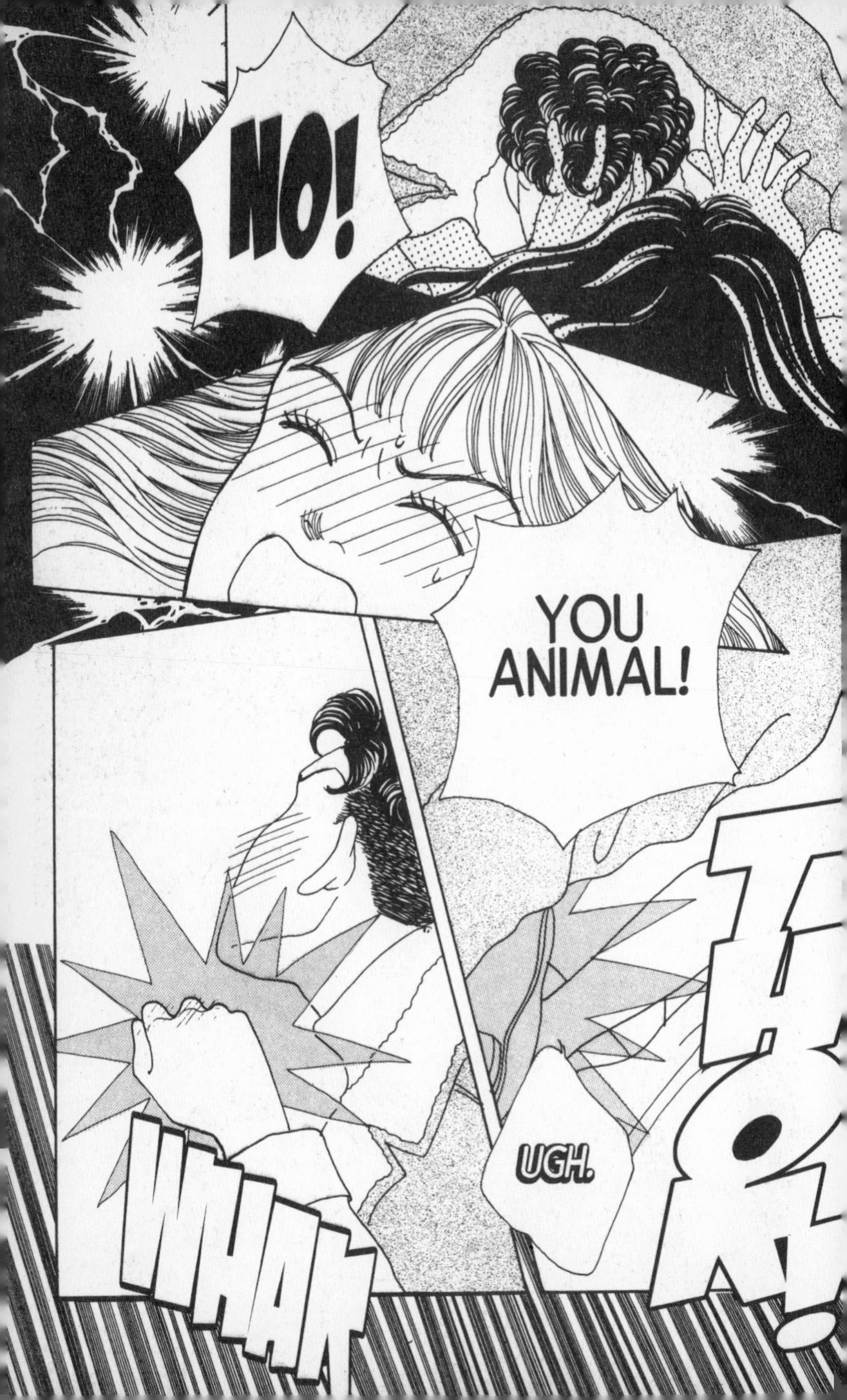
NO!
YOU ANIMAL!
UGH.

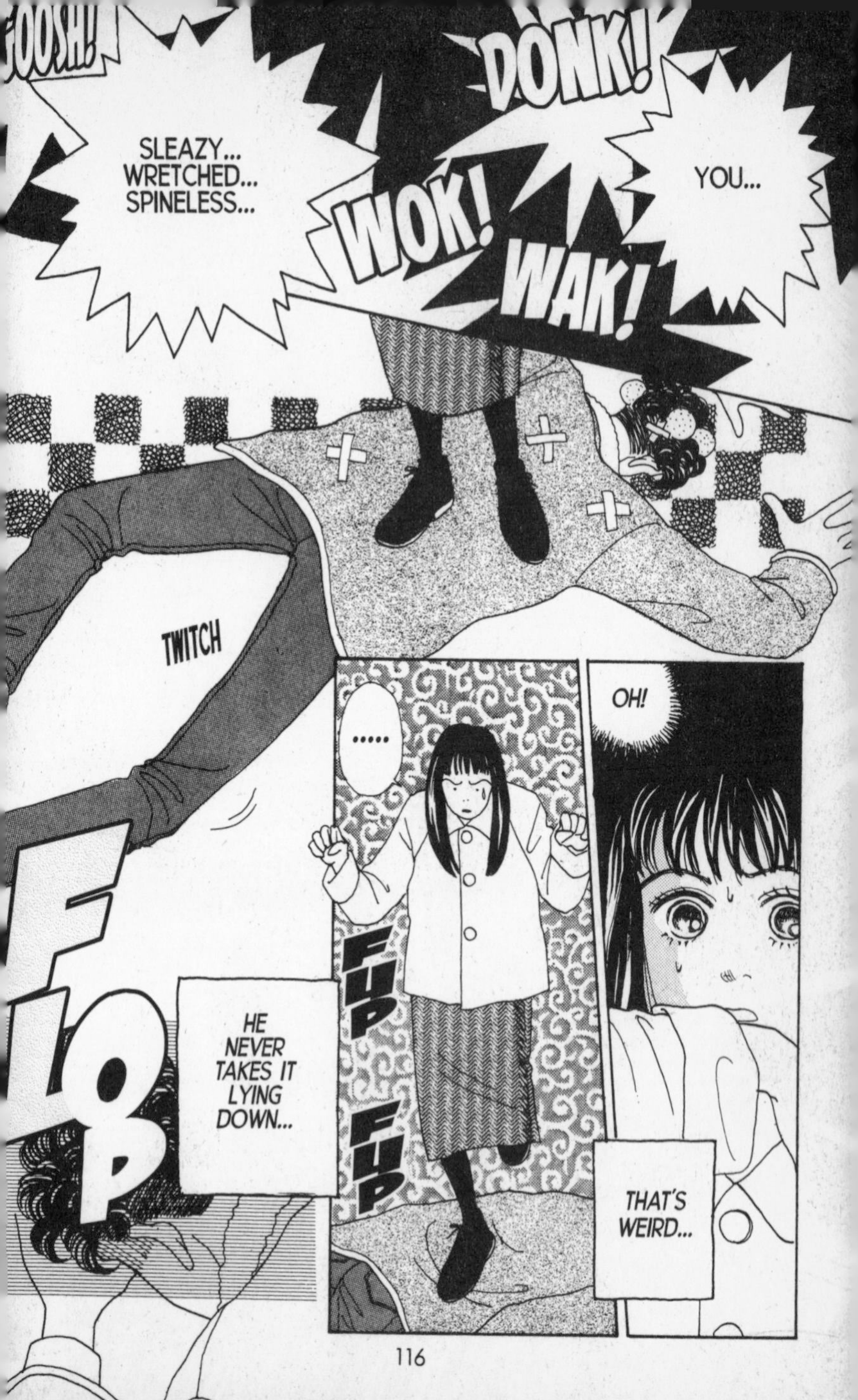
DONK!
YOU...
WAK!
WOK!
SLEAZY... WRETCHED... SPINELESS...
OOSH!
OH!
THAT'S WEIRD...
.....
FLIP
FLIP
TWITCH
FLOP
HE NEVER TAKES IT LYING DOWN...

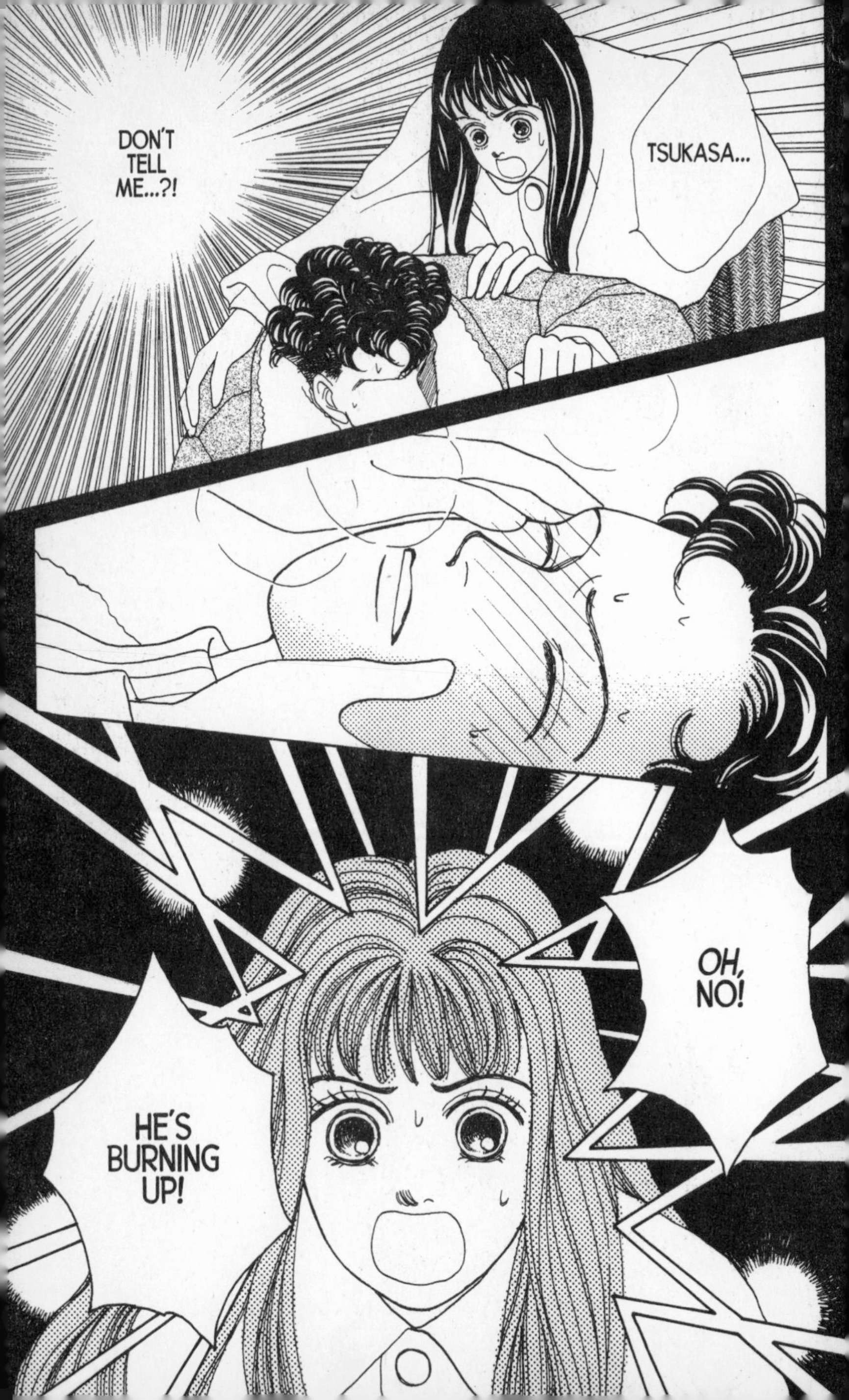
TSUKASA...
DON'T TELL ME...?!
OH, NO!
HE'S BURNING UP!

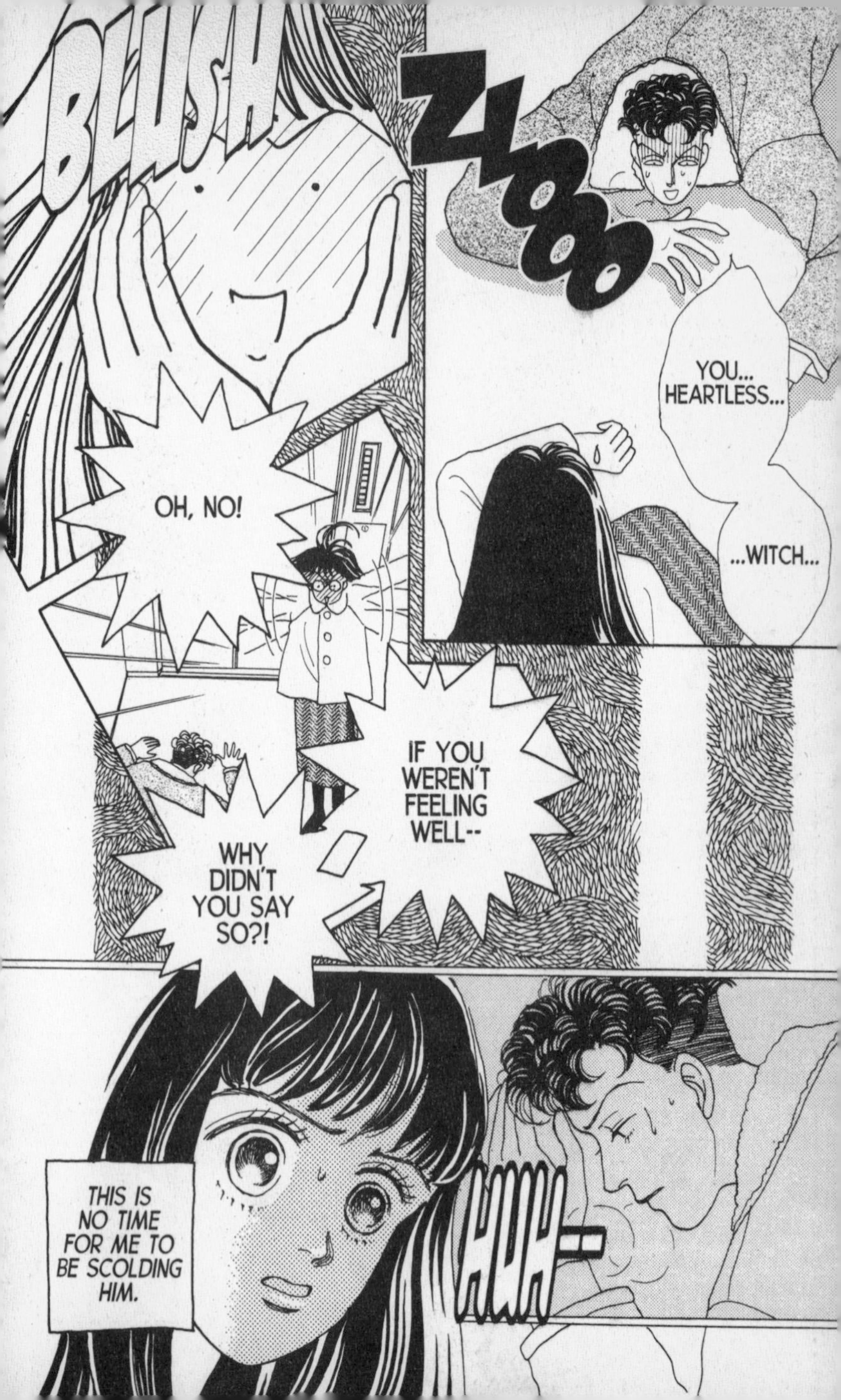
YOU... HEARTLESS...
...WITCH...
BLUSH
OH, NO!
IF YOU WEREN'T FEELING WELL--
WHY DIDN'T YOU SAY SO?!
THIS IS NO TIME FOR ME TO BE SCOLDING HIM.

8

Everything was over by 9:00pm. We were all starving so about 10 of us went to a Chinese restaurant to eat.

Why, thank you.

Here you go, Ms. Kamio.

Please, that's enough.

I was very lucky to have Mr. Kimura pouring me drinks. I must apologize to all his fans. It makes me nervous to think someone might send me a razor blade in the mail.

Glint

Everyone was in a good mood—talking about working on a second volume—when we ended for the night.

I'm sure there are a lot more things for me to write about, but this is as far as I'll go right now.

If you're interested, please listen to our CD. And with that, I end my report on the Hana yori Dango CD.

THE ELEVATOR'S OUT OF ORDER AND NO ONE'S COMING TO HELP US.

AND TSUKASA HAS A FEVER...

IT'S COLD...

BUT IT'S HIS FAULT FOR WAITING IN THE SNOW.

WHY SHOULD I CARE ...?

HE DID WORSE THINGS TO ME.

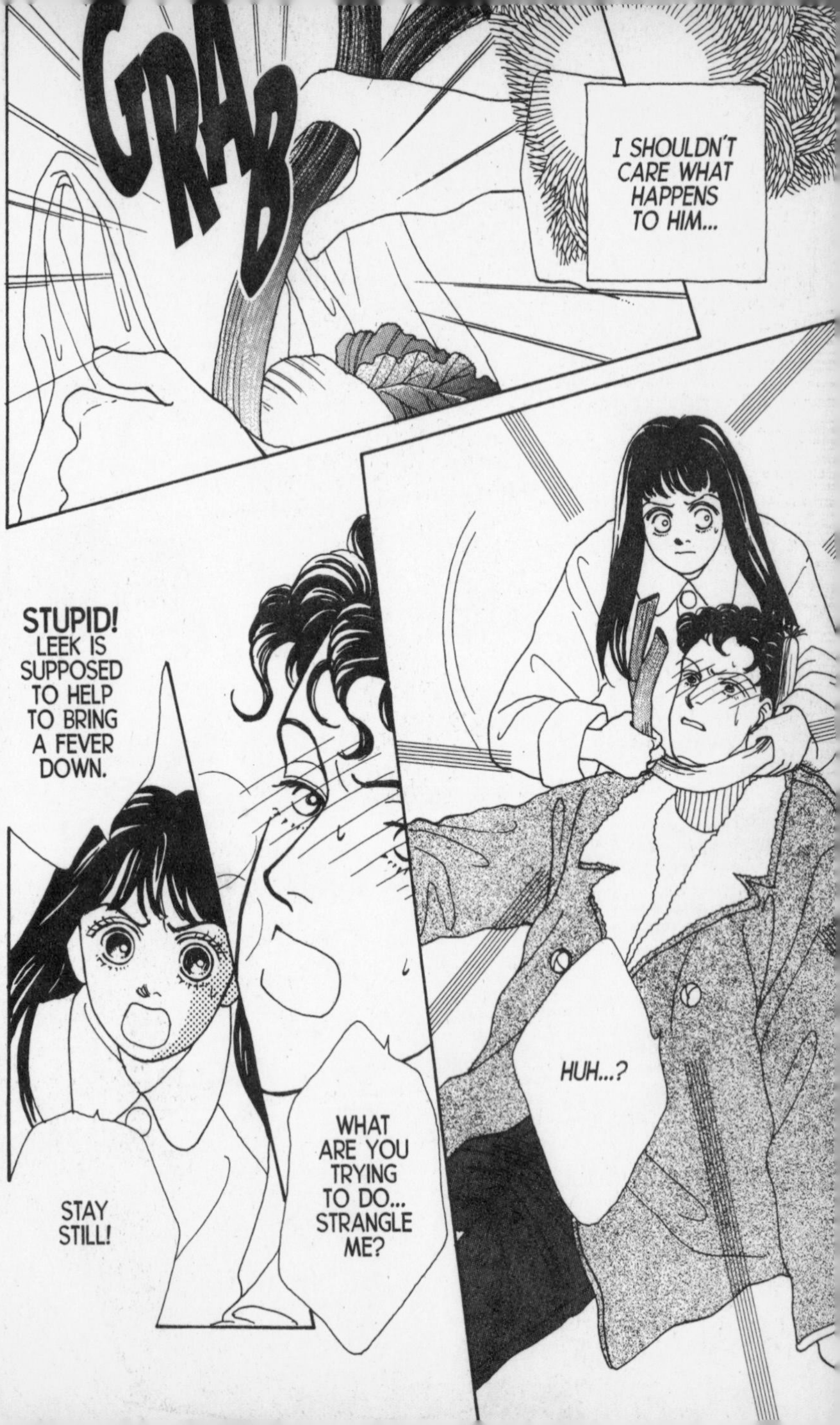
I SHOULDN'T CARE WHAT HAPPENS TO HIM...
GRAB
HUH...?
WHAT ARE YOU TRYING TO DO... STRANGLE ME?
STUPID! LEEK IS SUPPOSED TO HELP TO BRING A FEVER DOWN.
STAY STILL!

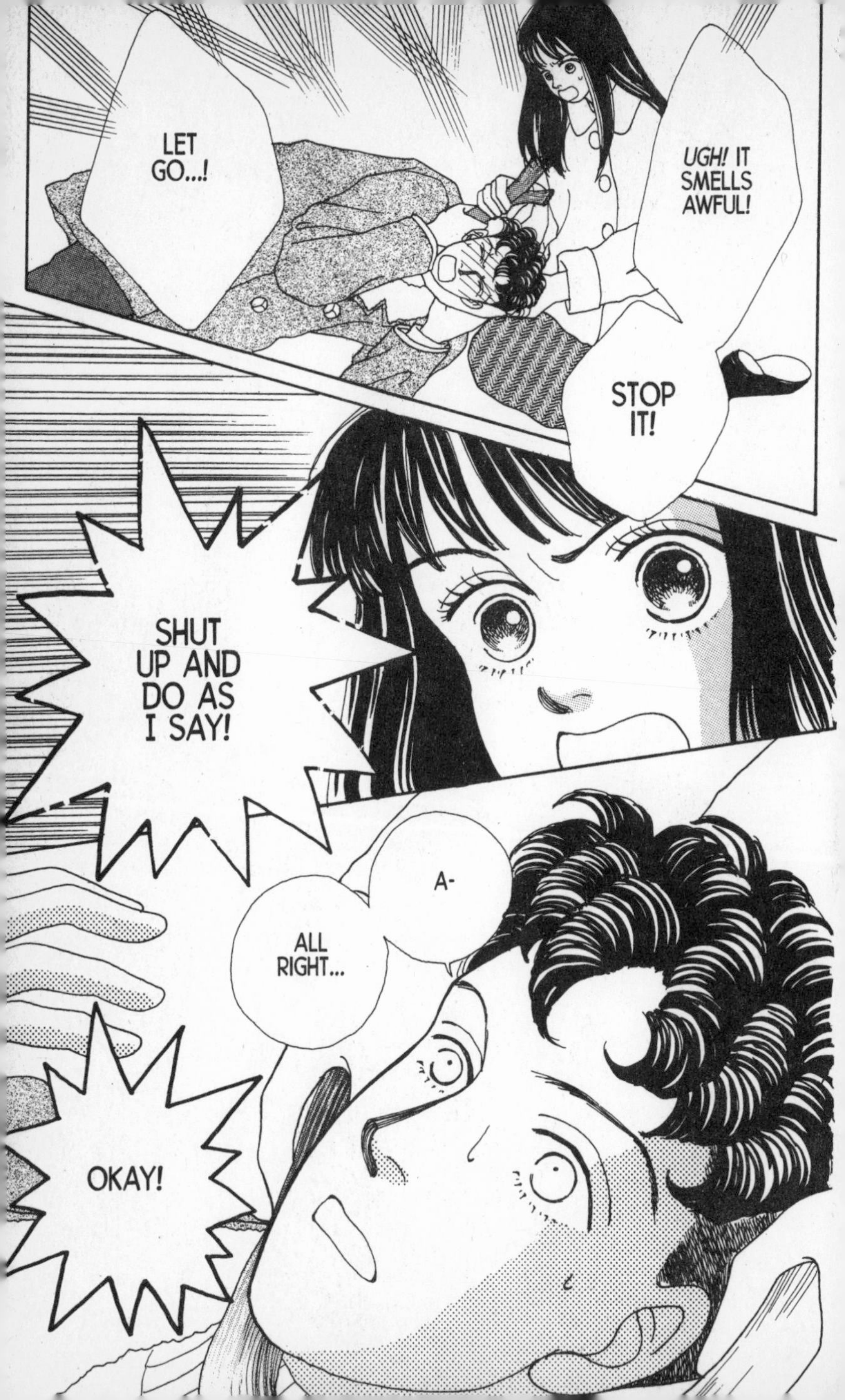
UGH! IT SMELLS AWFUL!
LET GO...!
STOP IT!
SHUT UP AND DO AS I SAY!
A-
ALL RIGHT...
OKAY!

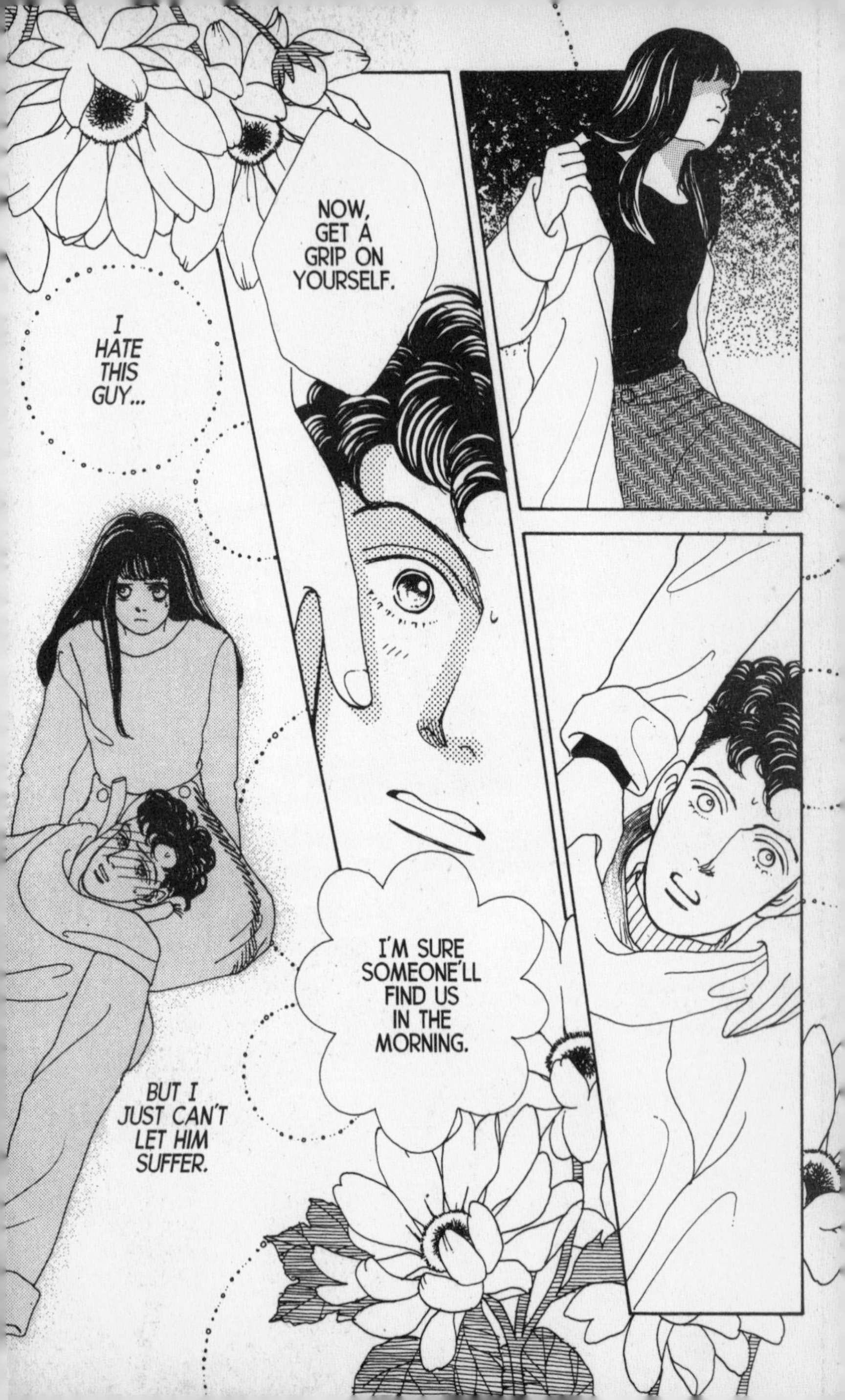
NOW, GET A GRIP ON YOURSELF.
I'M SURE SOMEONE'LL FIND US IN THE MORNING.
I HATE THIS GUY...
BUT I JUST CAN'T LET HIM SUFFER.

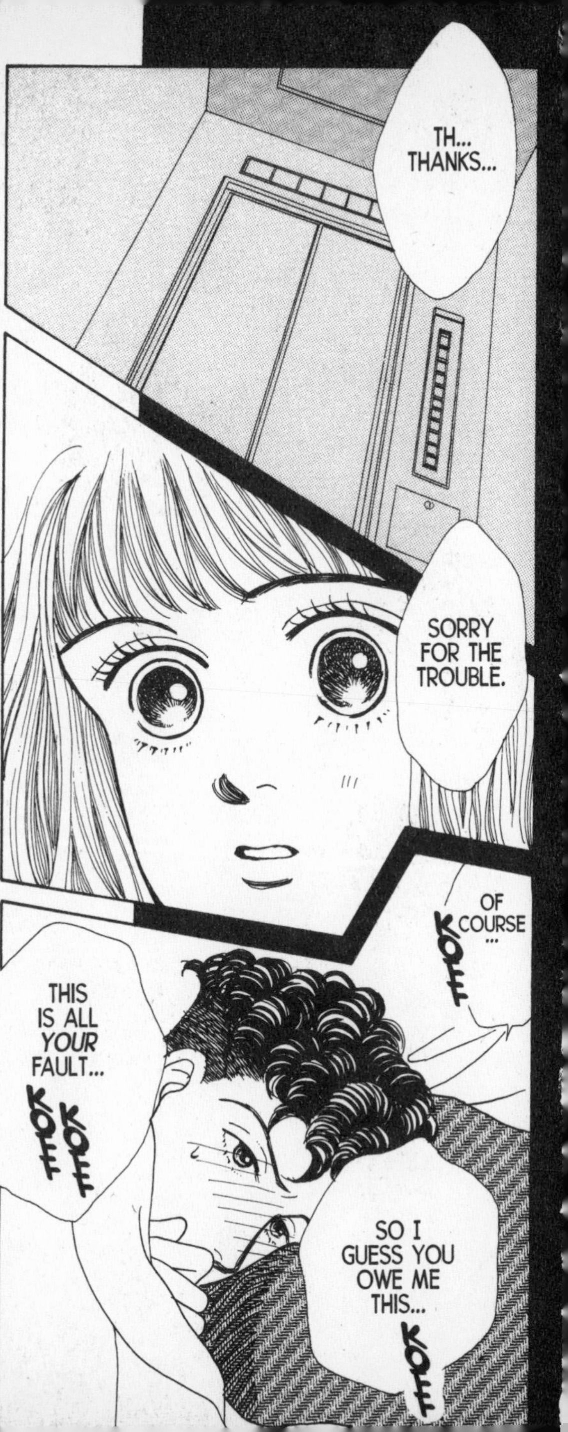
TH... THANKS...
SORRY FOR THE TROUBLE.
OF COURSE...
KOFF
THIS IS ALL *YOUR* FAULT...
KOFF KOFF
SO I GUESS YOU OWE ME THIS...
KOFF

9

June 29th was my birthday but, of course, I worked that day. It was the same last year, and the year before. (Sob) I was grateful to be busy, but it was still a little sad.

However, my assistants brought a fireworks set and we set them off to celebrate. I was so happy.

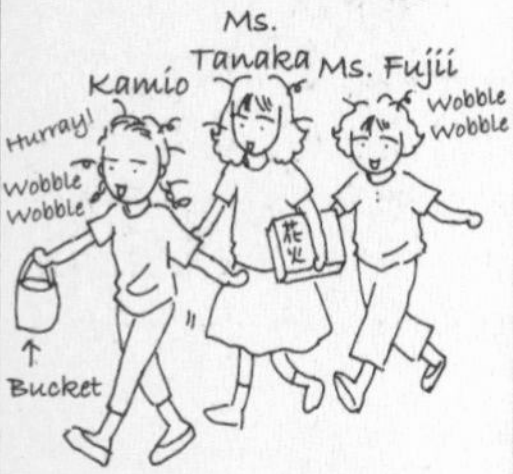
Ms. Tanaka
Ms. Fujii
Kamio
Hurray!
Wobble Wobble
Wobble Wobble
Bucket

Three haggard women bringing fireworks and a bucket to the playground.

Anyone who saw us probably thought we were weird.

We hadn't done fireworks in a long time, so it was a lot of fun.

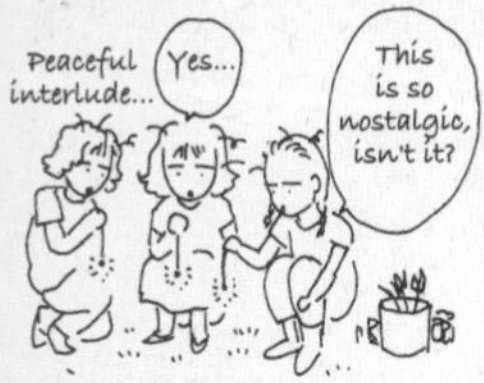
Peaceful interlude...
Yes...
This is so nostalgic, isn't it?

We saved the sparklers for last. I hope this is a good year for me.

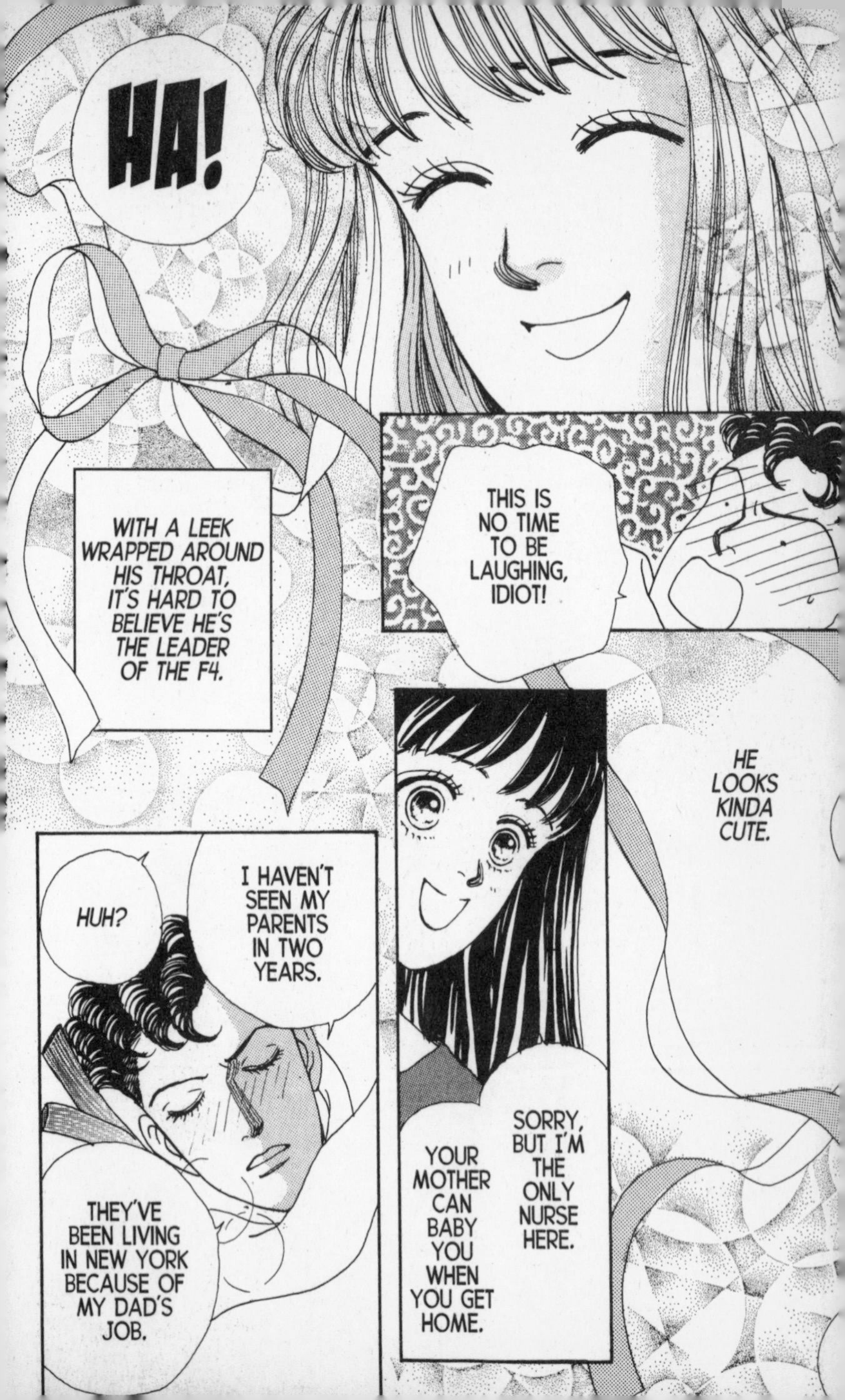
HA!
THIS IS NO TIME TO BE LAUGHING, IDIOT!
WITH A LEEK WRAPPED AROUND HIS THROAT, IT'S HARD TO BELIEVE HE'S THE LEADER OF THE F4.
HE LOOKS KINDA CUTE.
SORRY, BUT I'M THE ONLY NURSE HERE.
YOUR MOTHER CAN BABY YOU WHEN YOU GET HOME.
HUH?
I HAVEN'T SEEN MY PARENTS IN TWO YEARS.
THEY'VE BEEN LIVING IN NEW YORK BECAUSE OF MY DAD'S JOB.

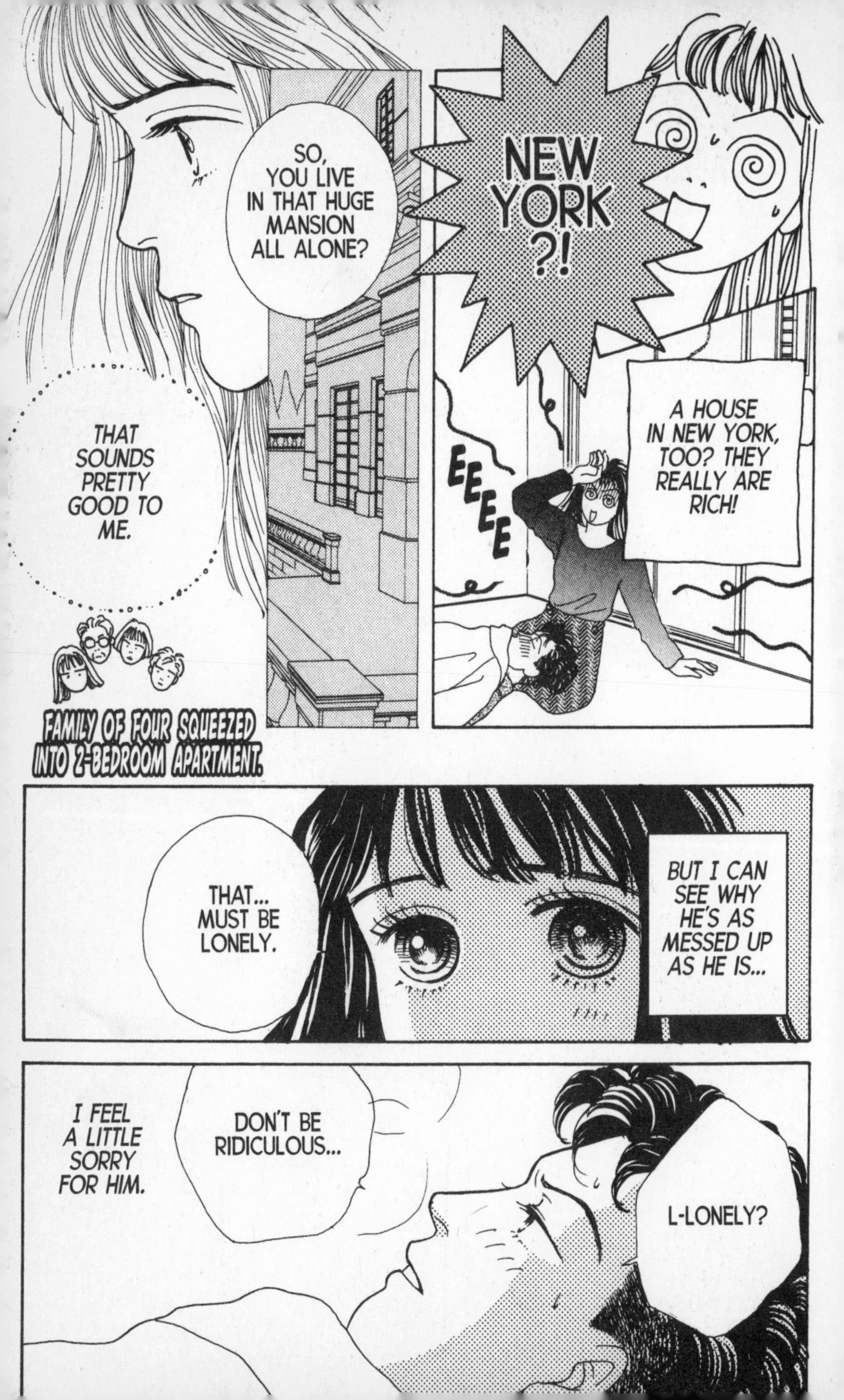
NEW YORK?!
A HOUSE IN NEW YORK, TOO? THEY REALLY ARE RICH!
EEEE
SO, YOU LIVE IN THAT HUGE MANSION ALL ALONE?
THAT SOUNDS PRETTY GOOD TO ME.
FAMILY OF FOUR SQUEEZED INTO 2-BEDROOM APARTMENT.
BUT I CAN SEE WHY HE'S AS MESSED UP AS HE IS...
THAT... MUST BE LONELY.
L-LONELY?
DON'T BE RIDICULOUS...
I FEEL A LITTLE SORRY FOR HIM.

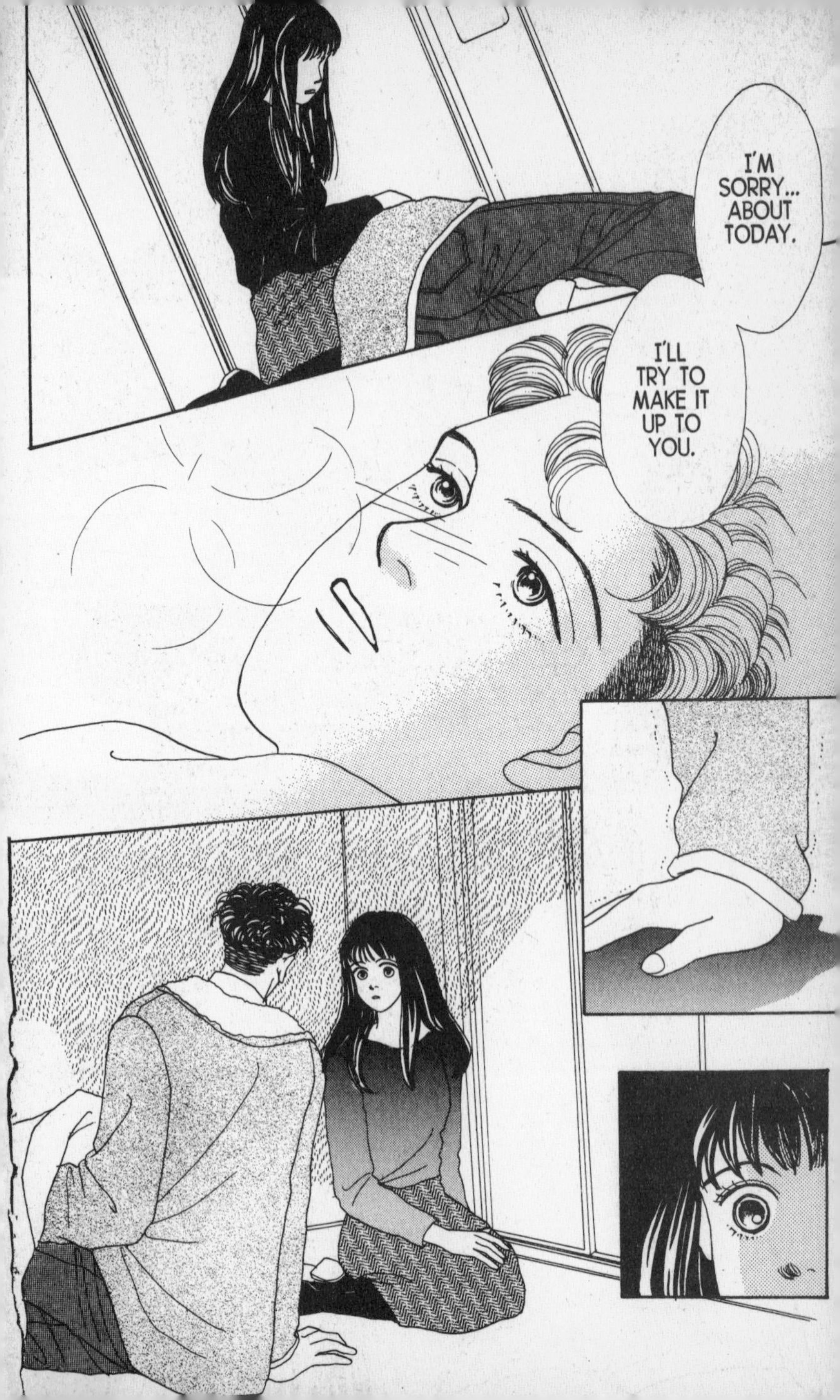
I'M SORRY... ABOUT TODAY.
I'LL TRY TO MAKE IT UP TO YOU.

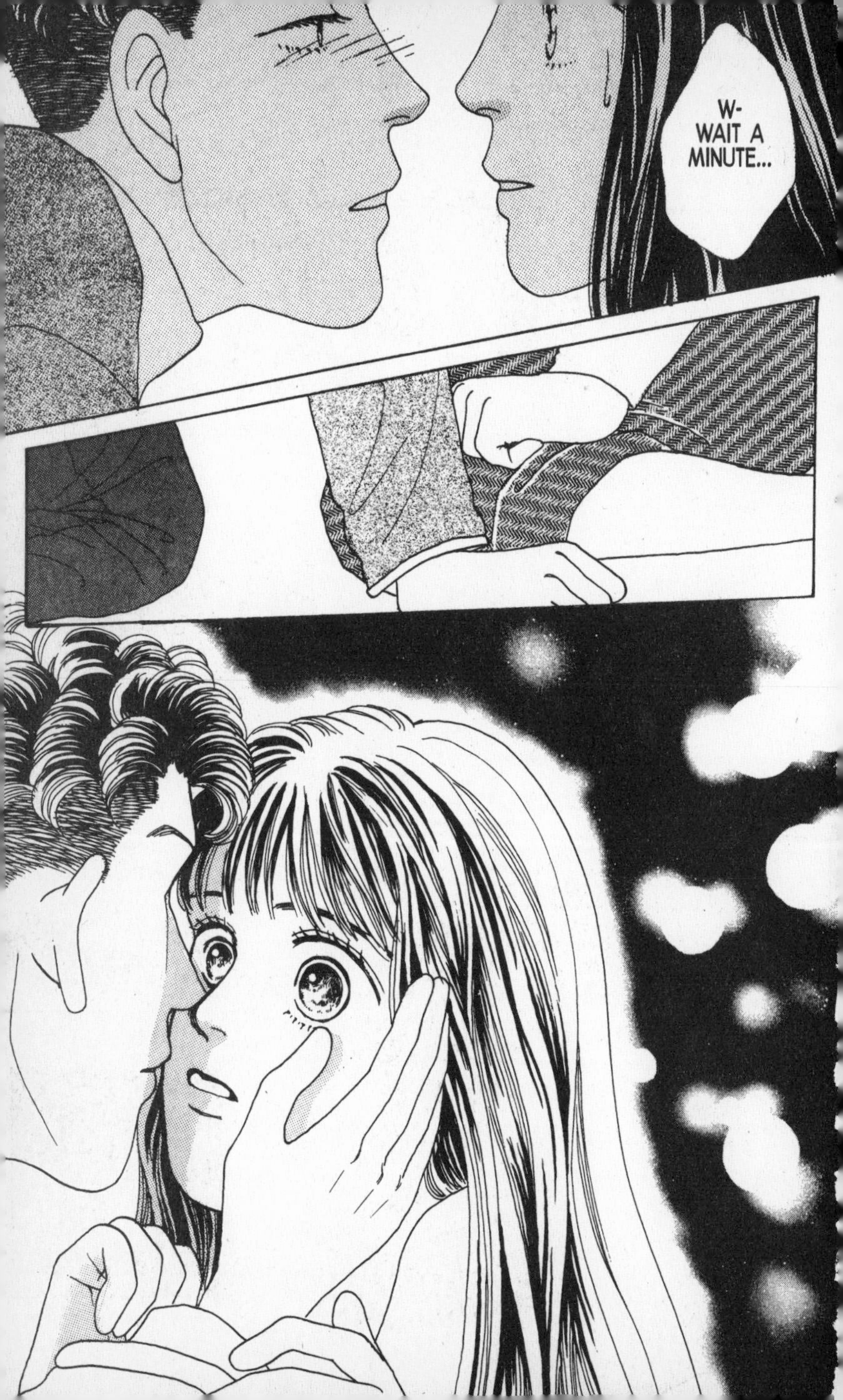
W- WAIT A MINUTE...

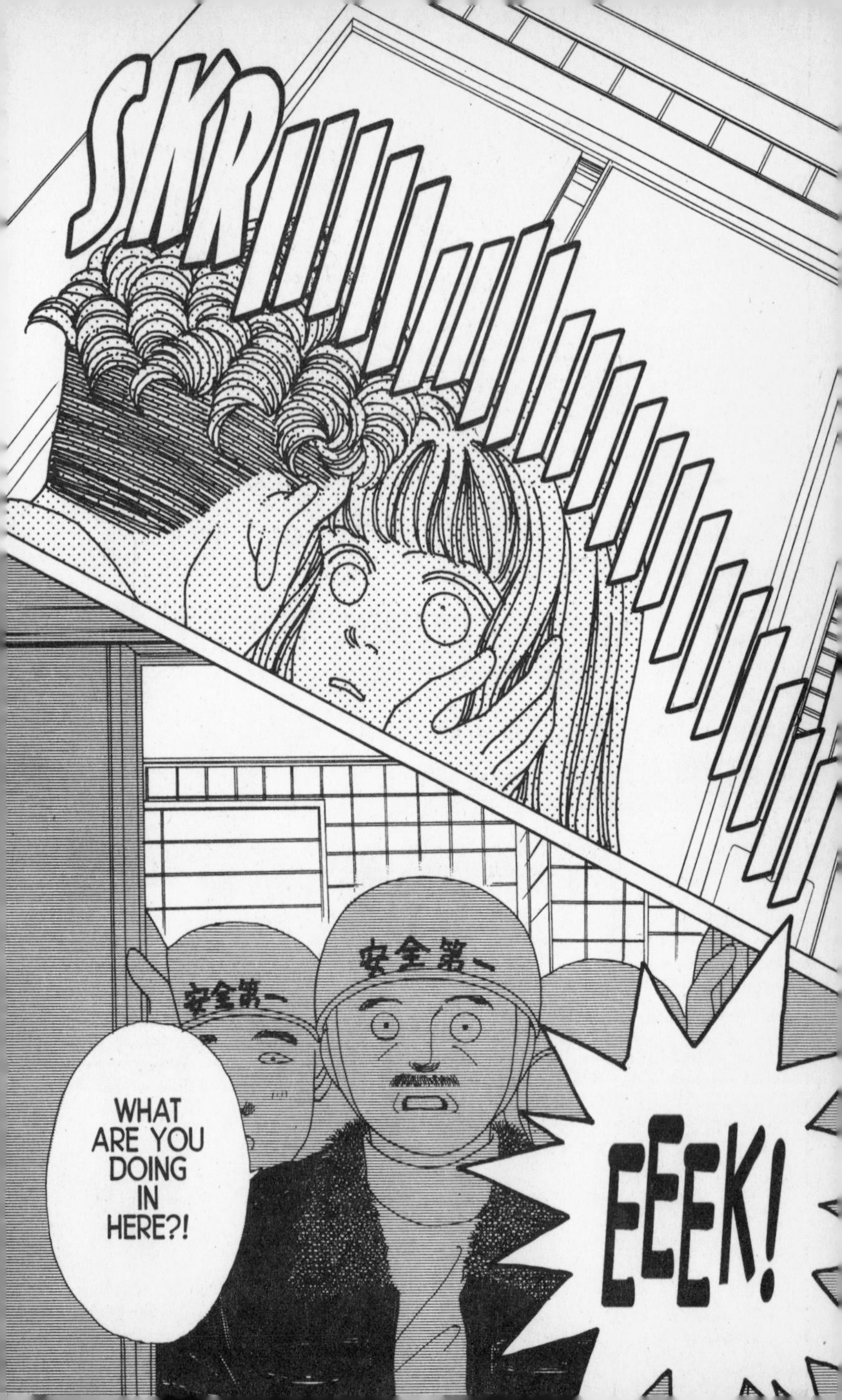
SKRIIIIIIIIIIIIIIIIIIII
EEEK!
安全第一
安全第一
WHAT ARE YOU DOING IN HERE?!

10

I didn't feel very well, not long ago, so I decided to get a complete physical. It took half a day. I drank barium for the first time. I hear it's much easier to drink now that they've given it a fruit flavor. A little bit might taste fine, but to swallow 400ml at once...It was thick like a milk shake. I thought I was going to puke it all up.

The doctor wasn't very sympathetic:

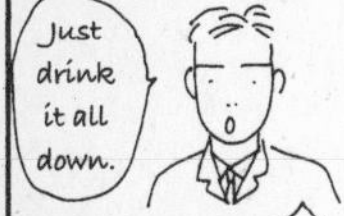
Just drink it all down.

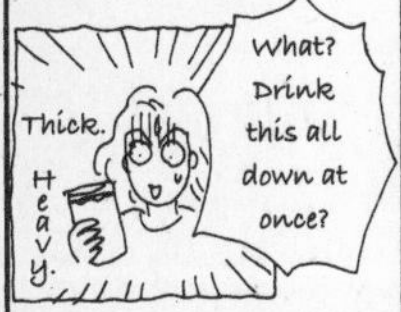
What? Drink this all down at once?
Thick.
Heavy.

I drank it. They said I'd have to drink another one if I stopped halfway.

After the test, I was told I had a slight problem with my liver. Oh, dear...! I like to drink, but I really don't drink a lot. I wonder if I've been working too hard.

I guess it's true--you need your health. I hope you'll all take good care of yourselves!

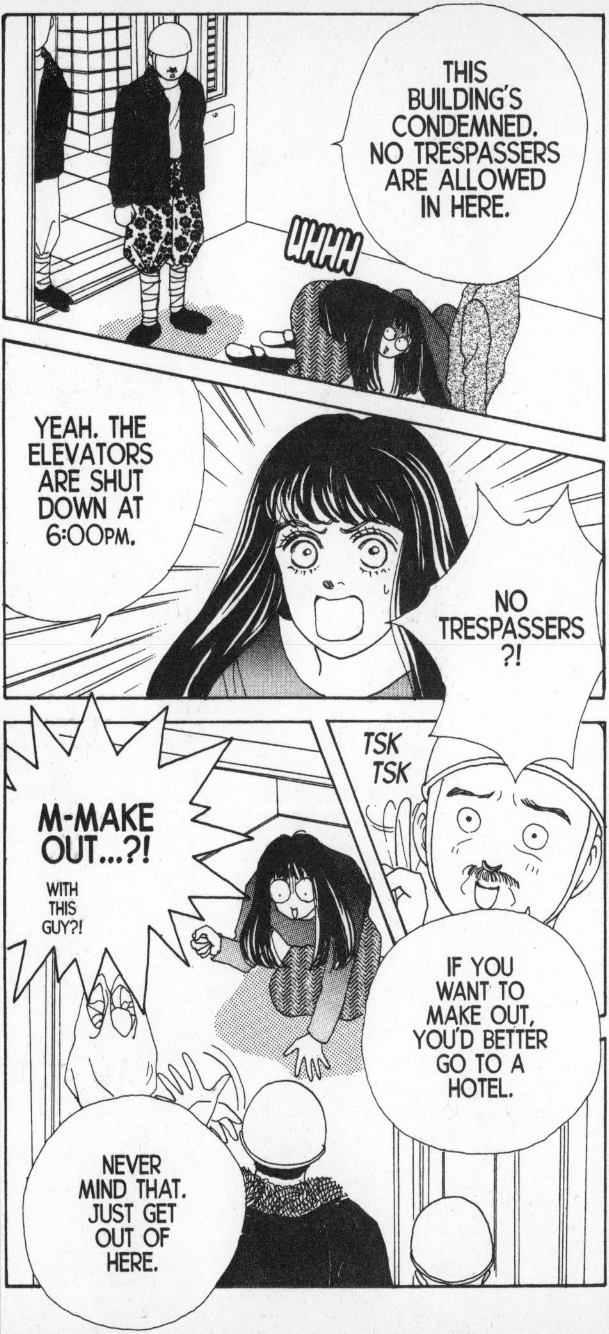
THIS BUILDING'S CONDEMNED. NO TRESPASSERS ARE ALLOWED IN HERE.
UHHH
NO TRESPASSERS ?!
YEAH. THE ELEVATORS ARE SHUT DOWN AT 6:00PM.
TSK TSK
IF YOU WANT TO MAKE OUT, YOU'D BETTER GO TO A HOTEL.
M-MAKE OUT...?!
WITH THIS GUY?!
NEVER MIND THAT. JUST GET OUT OF HERE.

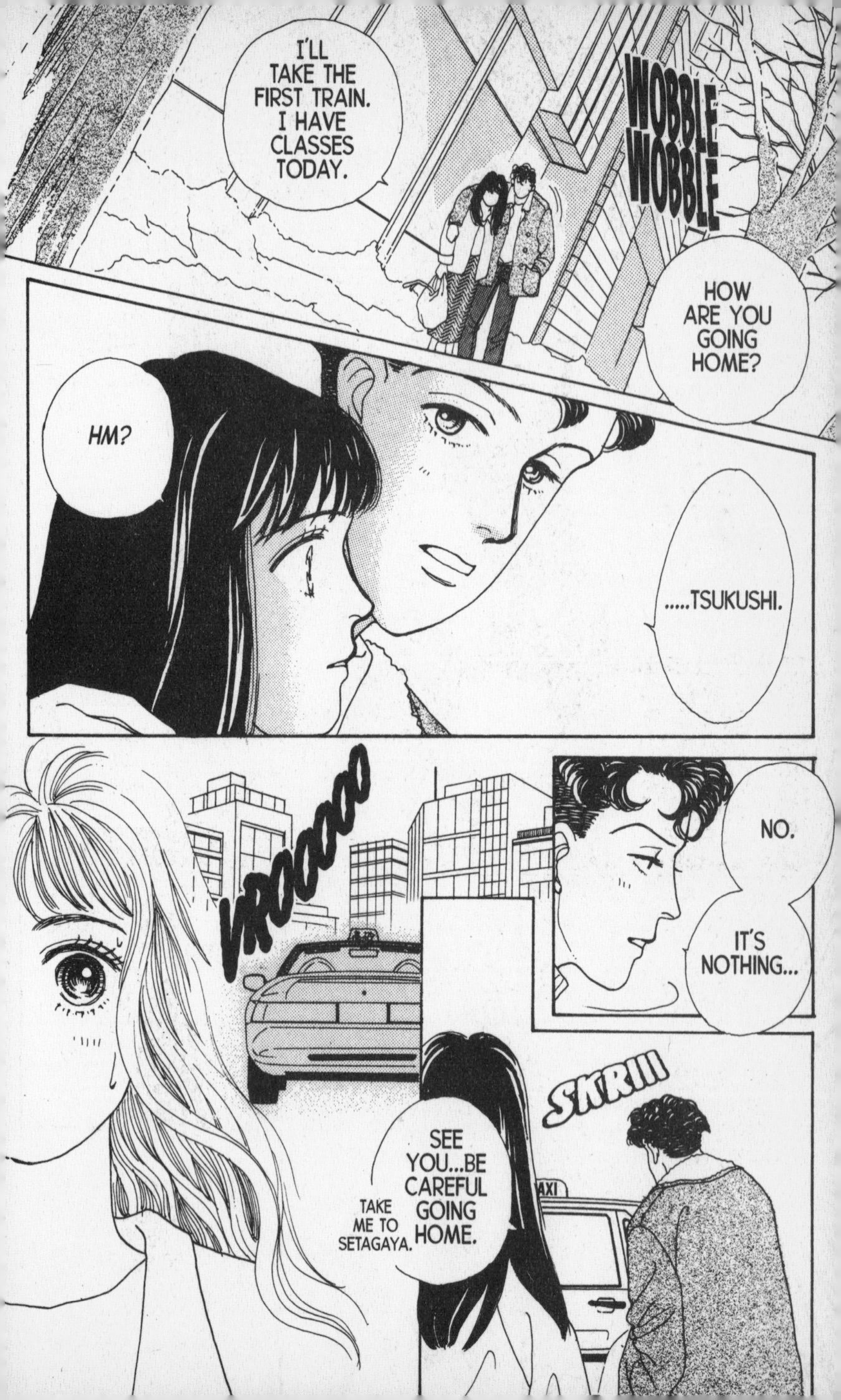
WOBBLE WOBBLE
I'LL TAKE THE FIRST TRAIN. I HAVE CLASSES TODAY.
HOW ARE YOU GOING HOME?
.....TSUKUSHI.
HM?
NO.
IT'S NOTHING...
VROOOOO
SKRIII
SEE YOU...BE CAREFUL GOING HOME.
TAKE ME TO SETAGAYA.

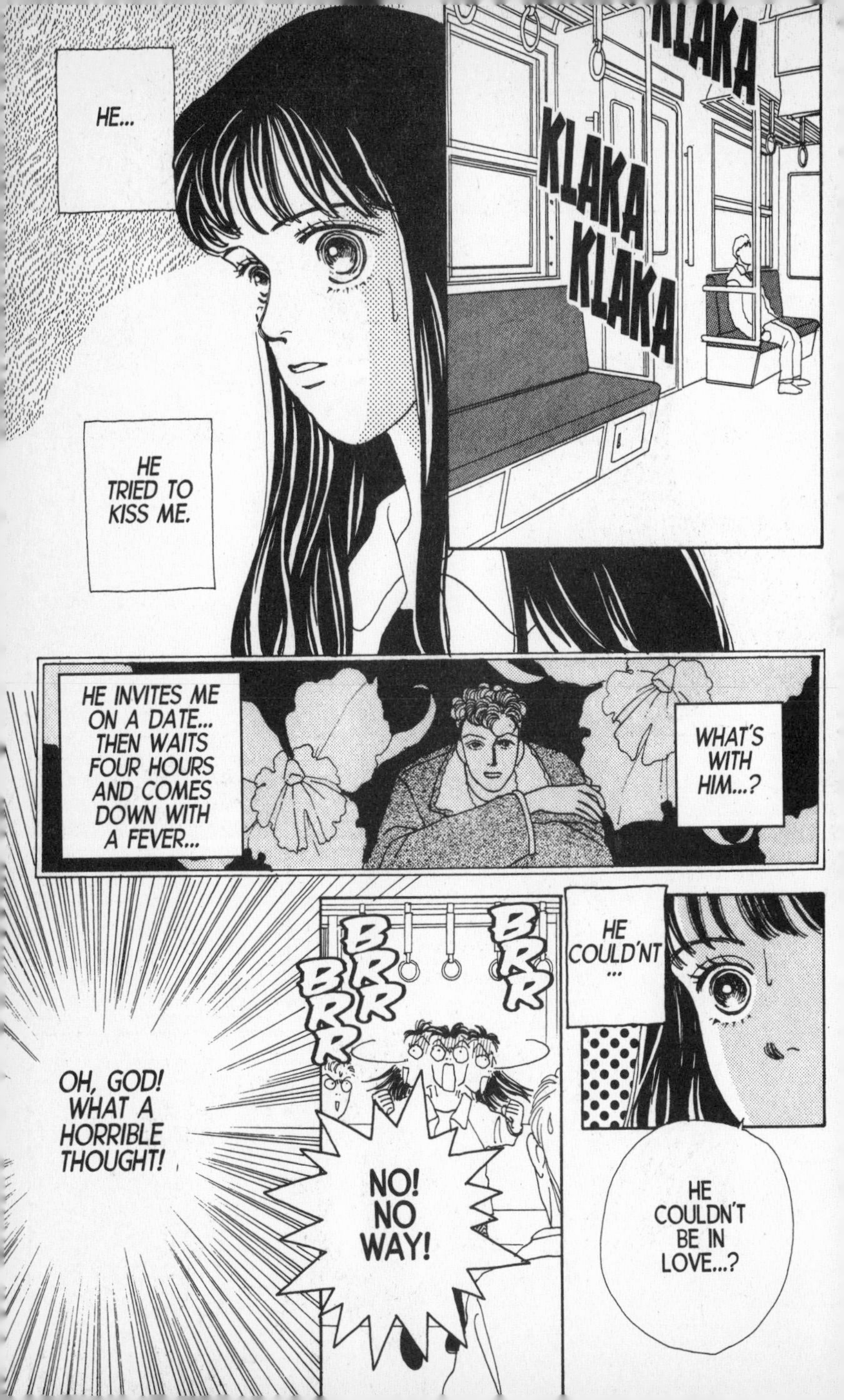

KLAKA
KLAKA
KLAKA
KLAKA
HE...
HE TRIED TO KISS ME.
WHAT'S WITH HIM...?
HE INVITES ME ON A DATE... THEN WAITS FOUR HOURS AND COMES DOWN WITH A FEVER...
HE COULD'NT ...
HE COULDN'T BE IN LOVE...?
BRRR
BRRR
BRRR
NO! NO WAY!
OH, GOD! WHAT A HORRIBLE THOUGHT!

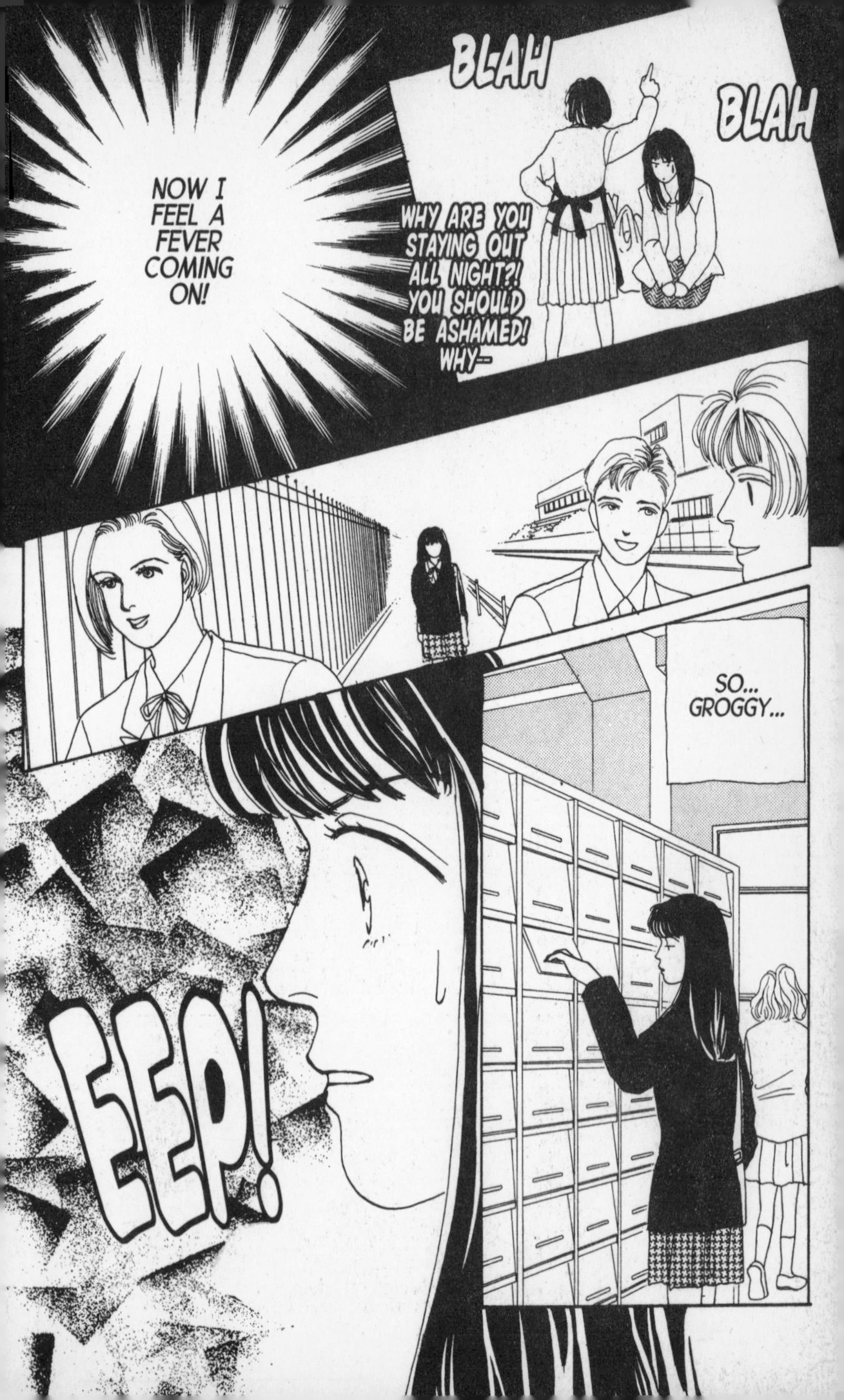
BLAH
BLAH
WHY ARE YOU STAYING OUT ALL NIGHT?! YOU SHOULD BE ASHAMED! WHY--
NOW I FEEL A FEVER COMING ON!
SO... GROGGY...
EEP!

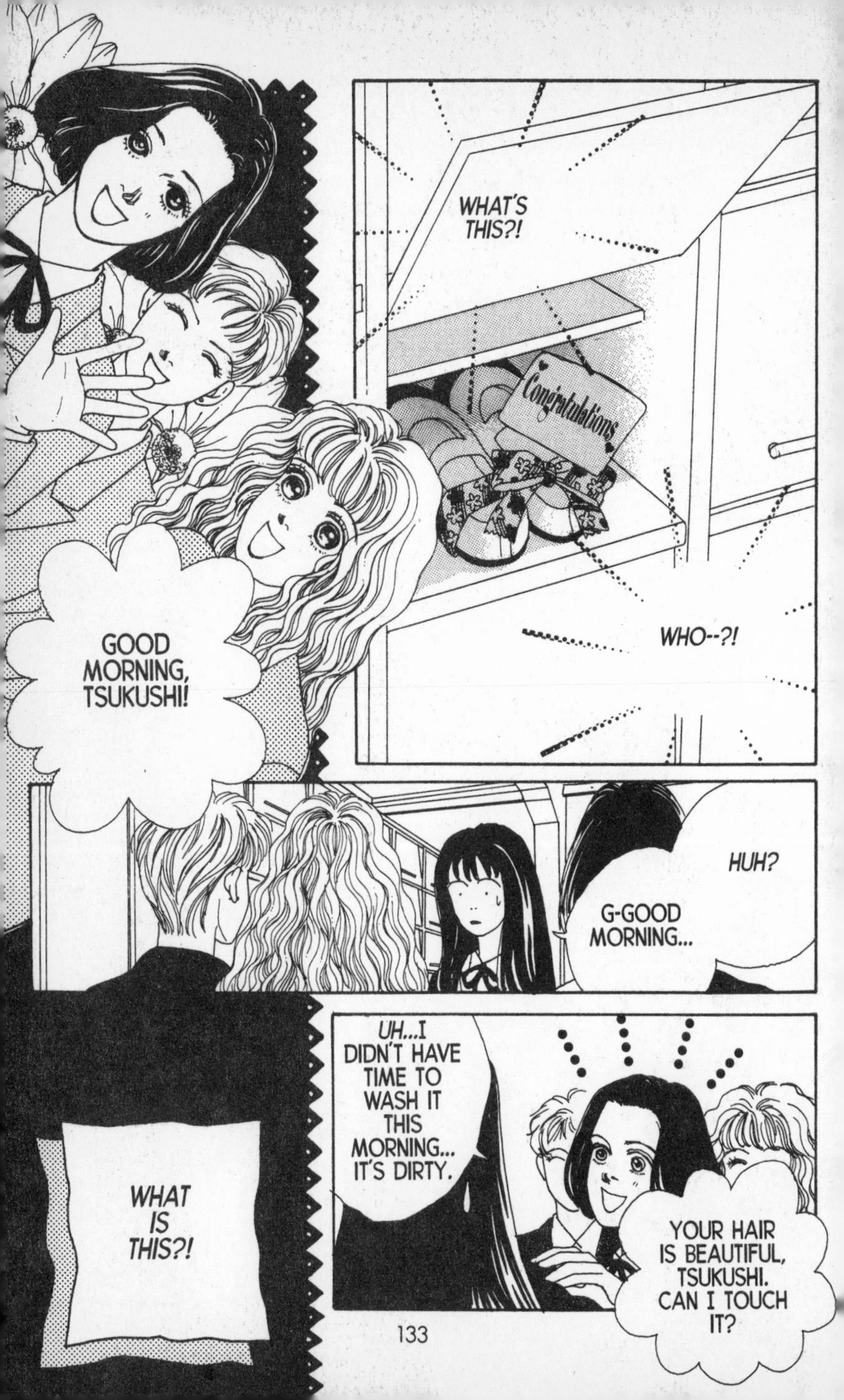
Congratulations
WHAT'S THIS?!
WHO--?!
GOOD MORNING, TSUKUSHI!
HUH?
G-GOOD MORNING...
YOUR HAIR IS BEAUTIFUL, TSUKUSHI. CAN I TOUCH IT?
UH...I DIDN'T HAVE TIME TO WASH IT THIS MORNING... IT'S DIRTY.
WHAT IS THIS?!

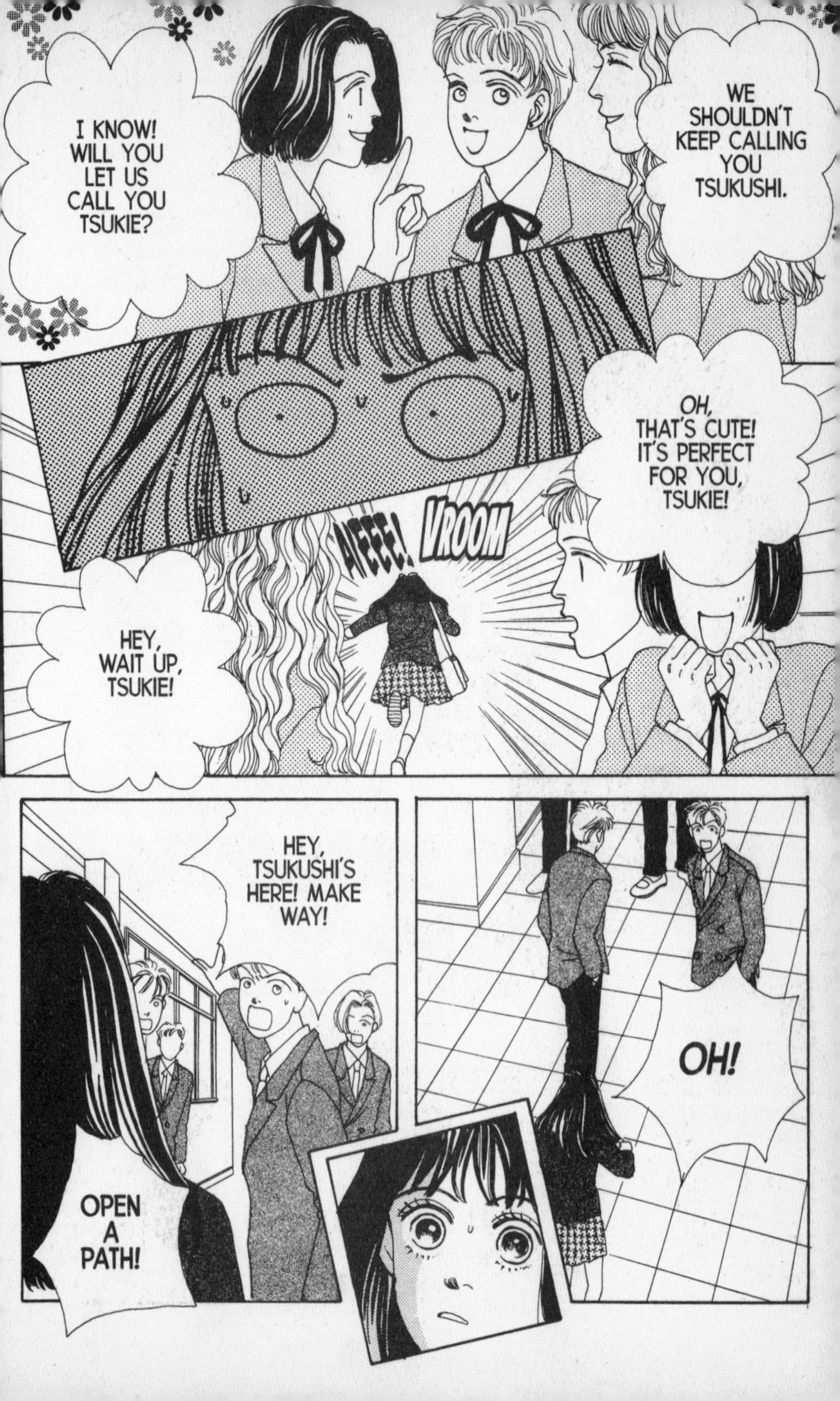
WE SHOULDN'T KEEP CALLING YOU TSUKUSHI.
I KNOW! WILL YOU LET US CALL YOU TSUKIE?
OH, THAT'S CUTE! IT'S PERFECT FOR YOU, TSUKIE!
VROOM
AIEEE!
HEY, WAIT UP, TSUKIE!
OH!
HEY, TSUKUSHI'S HERE! MAKE WAY!
OPEN A PATH!

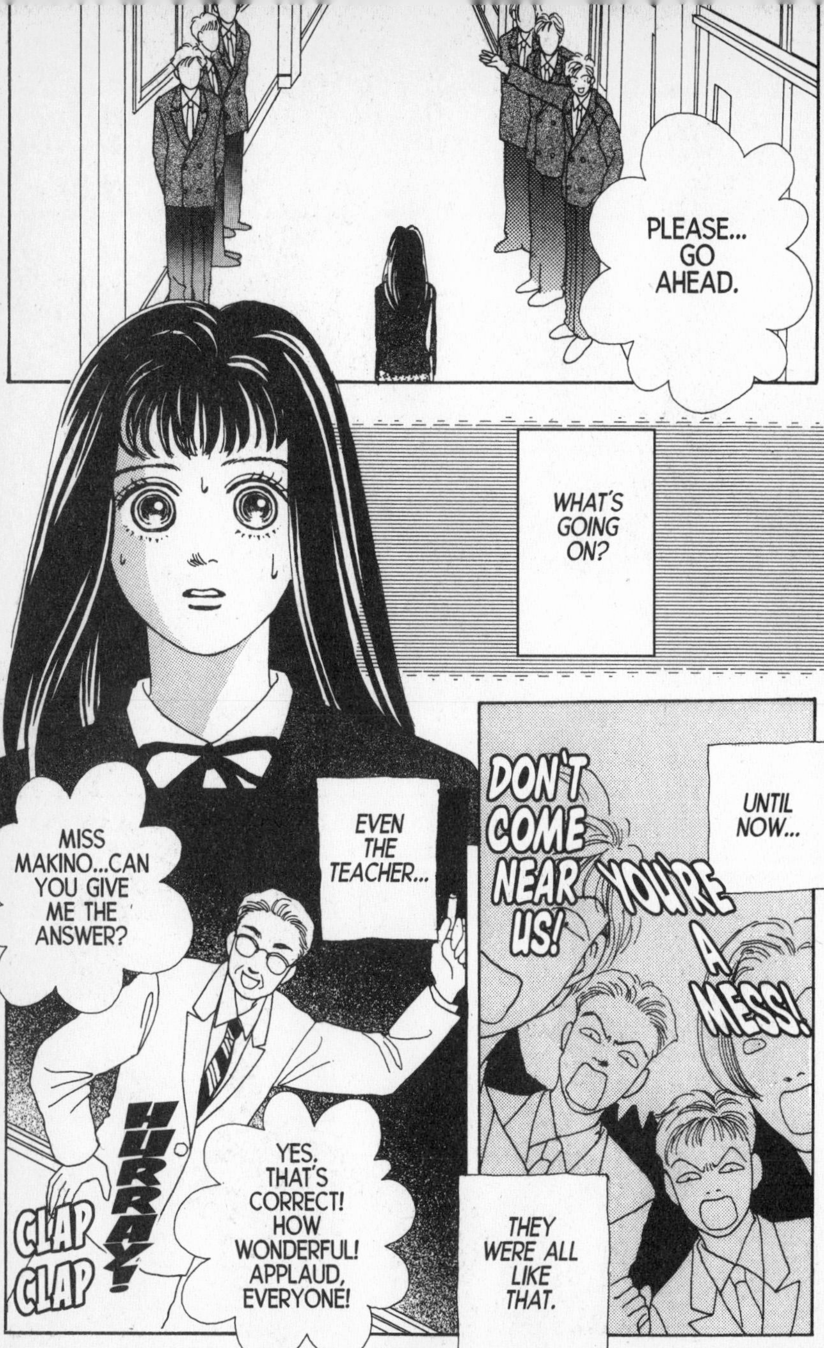
PLEASE... GO AHEAD.
WHAT'S GOING ON?
UNTIL NOW...
DON'T COME NEAR US!
YOU'RE A MESS!
THEY WERE ALL LIKE THAT.
EVEN THE TEACHER...
MISS MAKINO...CAN YOU GIVE ME THE ANSWER?
YES. THAT'S CORRECT! HOW WONDERFUL! APPLAUD, EVERYONE!
HURRAY!
CLAP CLAP

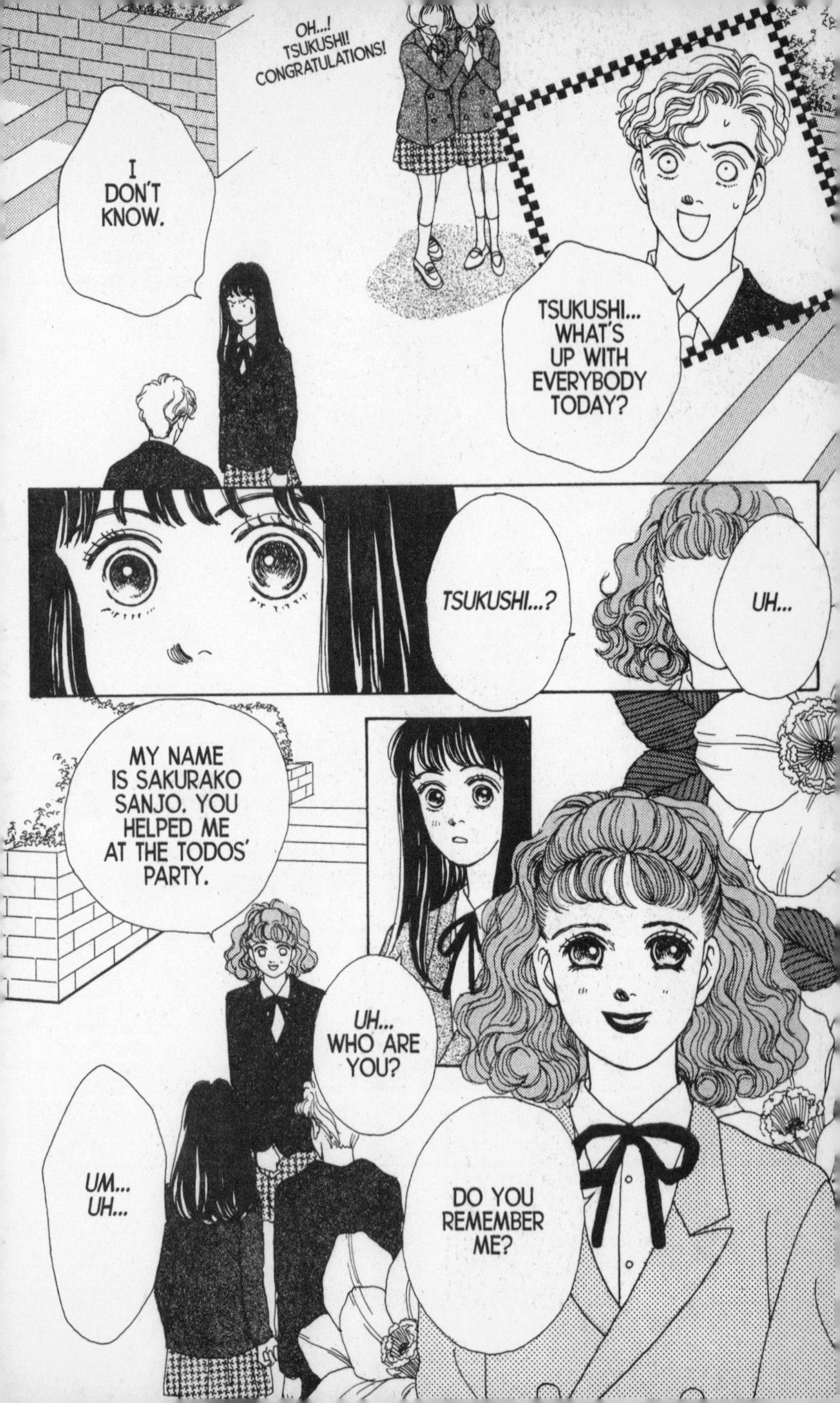

OH...! TSUKUSHI! CONGRATULATIONS!
TSUKUSHI... WHAT'S UP WITH EVERYBODY TODAY?
I DON'T KNOW.
UH...
TSUKUSHI...?
DO YOU REMEMBER ME?
UH... WHO ARE YOU?
MY NAME IS SAKURAKO SANJO. YOU HELPED ME AT THE TODOS' PARTY.
UM... UH...

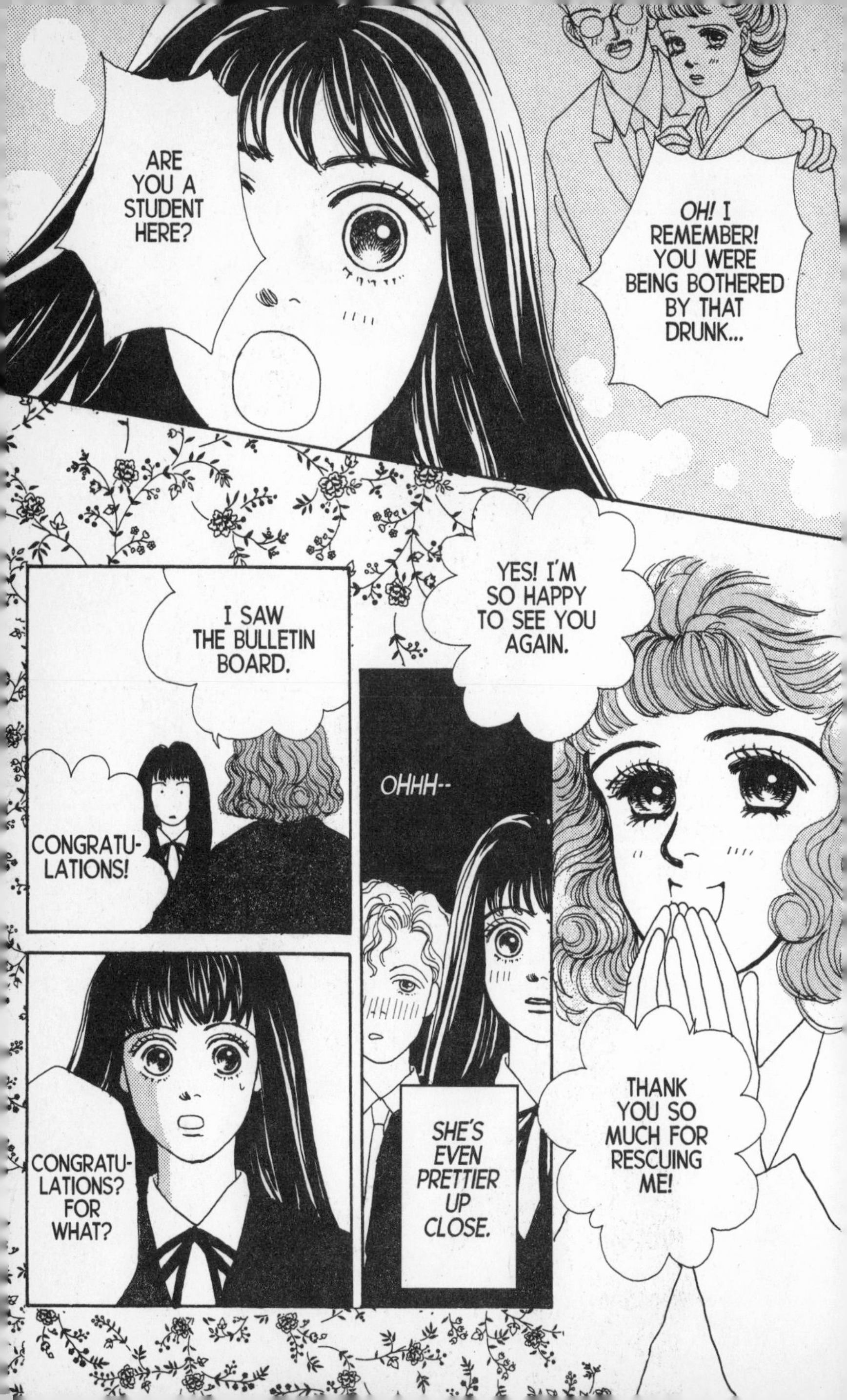
OH! I REMEMBER! YOU WERE BEING BOTHERED BY THAT DRUNK...
ARE YOU A STUDENT HERE?
YES! I'M SO HAPPY TO SEE YOU AGAIN.
THANK YOU SO MUCH FOR RESCUING ME!
OHHH--
SHE'S EVEN PRETTIER UP CLOSE.
I SAW THE BULLETIN BOARD.
CONGRATU-LATIONS!
CONGRATU-LATIONS? FOR WHAT?

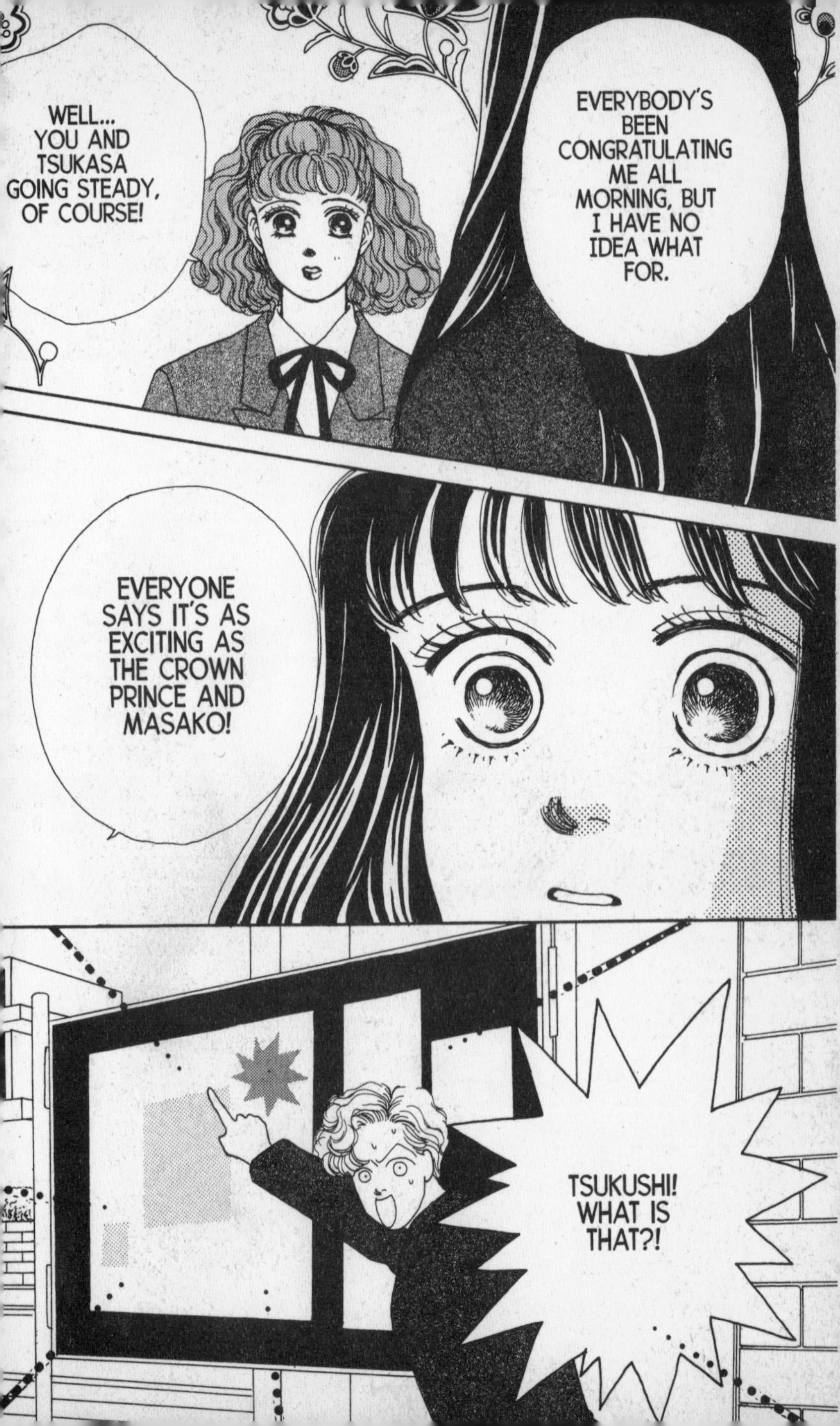
EVERYBODY'S BEEN CONGRATULATING ME ALL MORNING, BUT I HAVE NO IDEA WHAT FOR.
WELL... YOU AND TSUKASA GOING STEADY, OF COURSE!
EVERYONE SAYS IT'S AS EXCITING AS THE CROWN PRINCE AND MASAKO!
TSUKUSHI! WHAT IS THAT?!

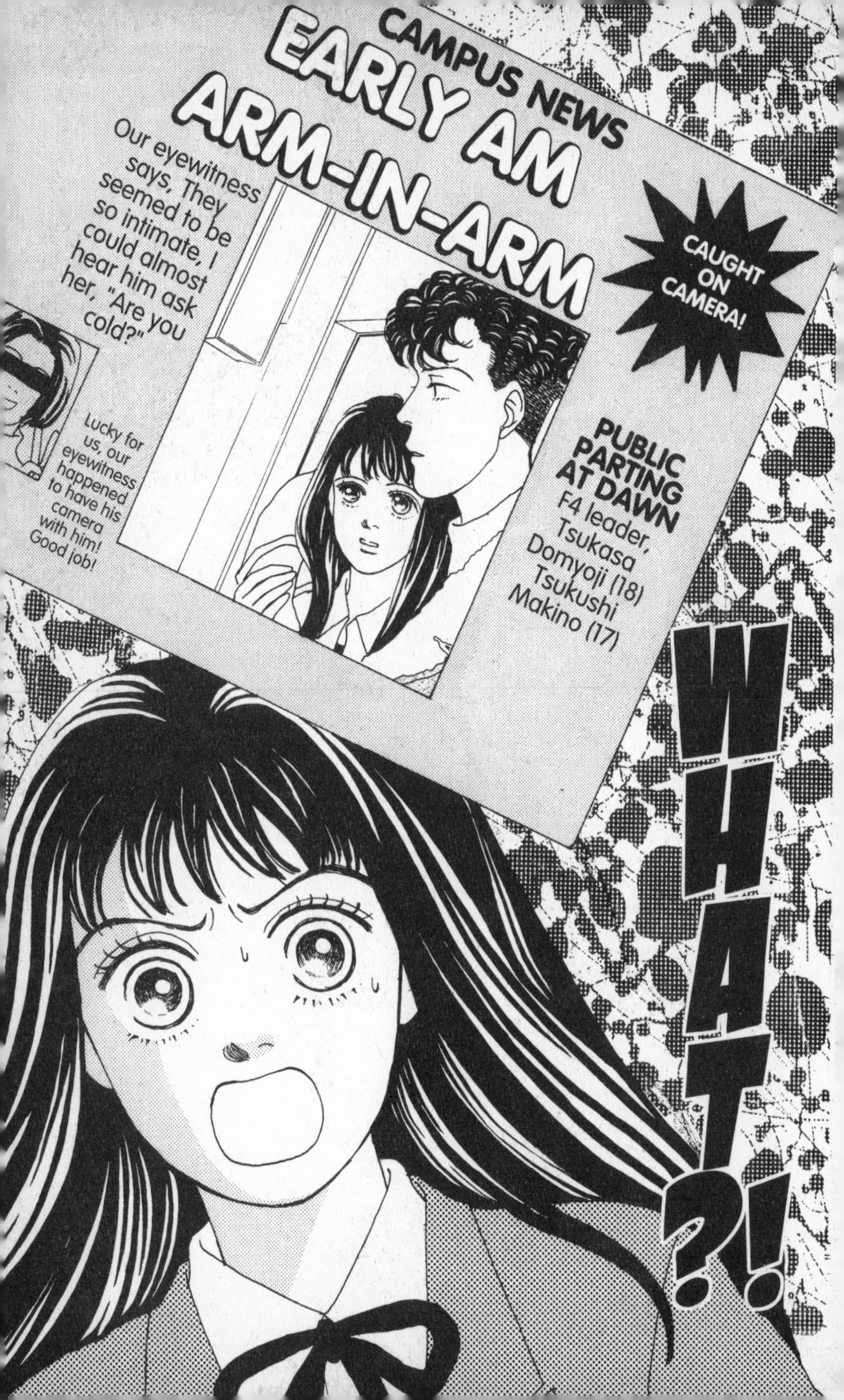
CAMPUS NEWS
EARLY AM ARM-IN-ARM
CAUGHT ON CAMERA!
Our eyewitness says, They seemed to be so intimate, I could almost hear him ask her, "Are you cold?"
PUBLIC PARTING AT DAWN
F4 leader, Tsukasa Domyoji (18) Tsukushi Makino (17)
Lucky for us, our eyewitness happened to have his camera with him! Good job!
WHAT?!

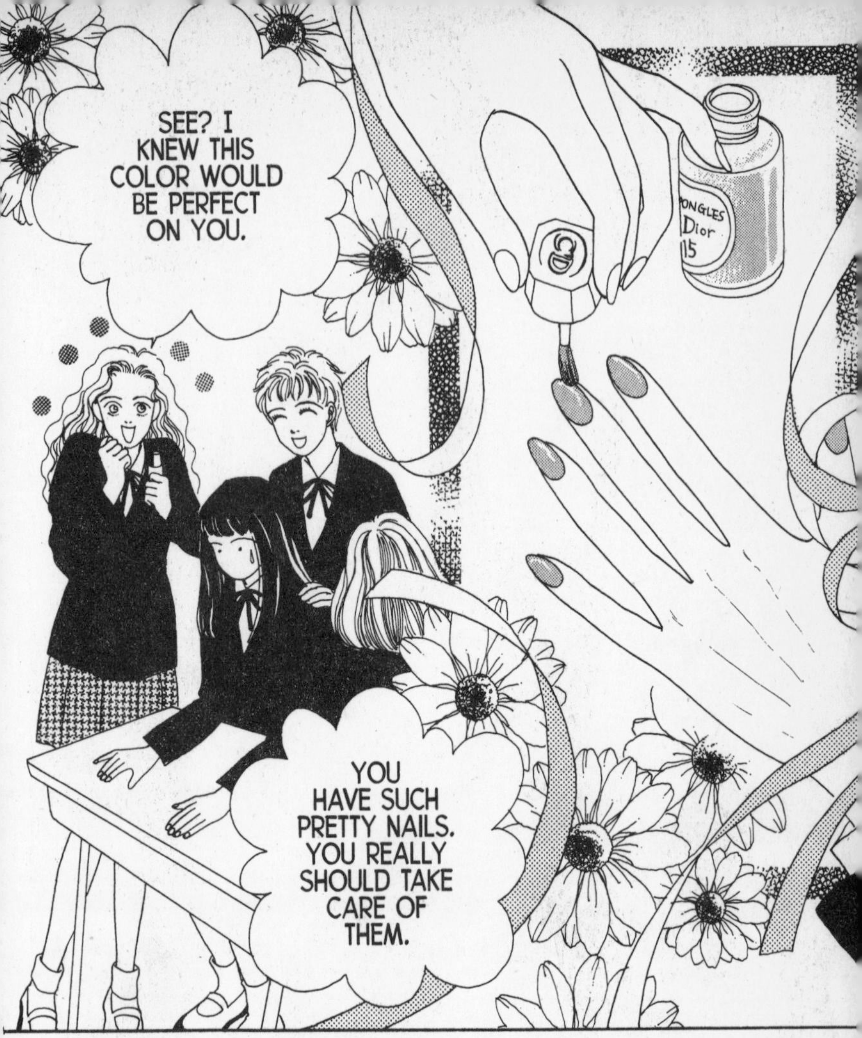
SEE? I KNEW THIS COLOR WOULD BE PERFECT ON YOU.
Dior
YOU HAVE SUCH PRETTY NAILS. YOU REALLY SHOULD TAKE CARE OF THEM.

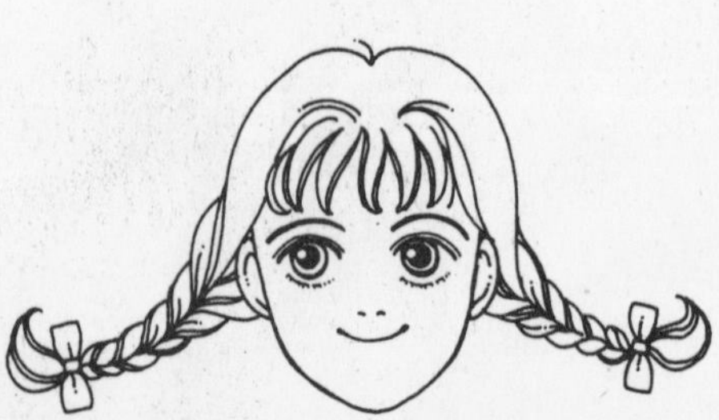

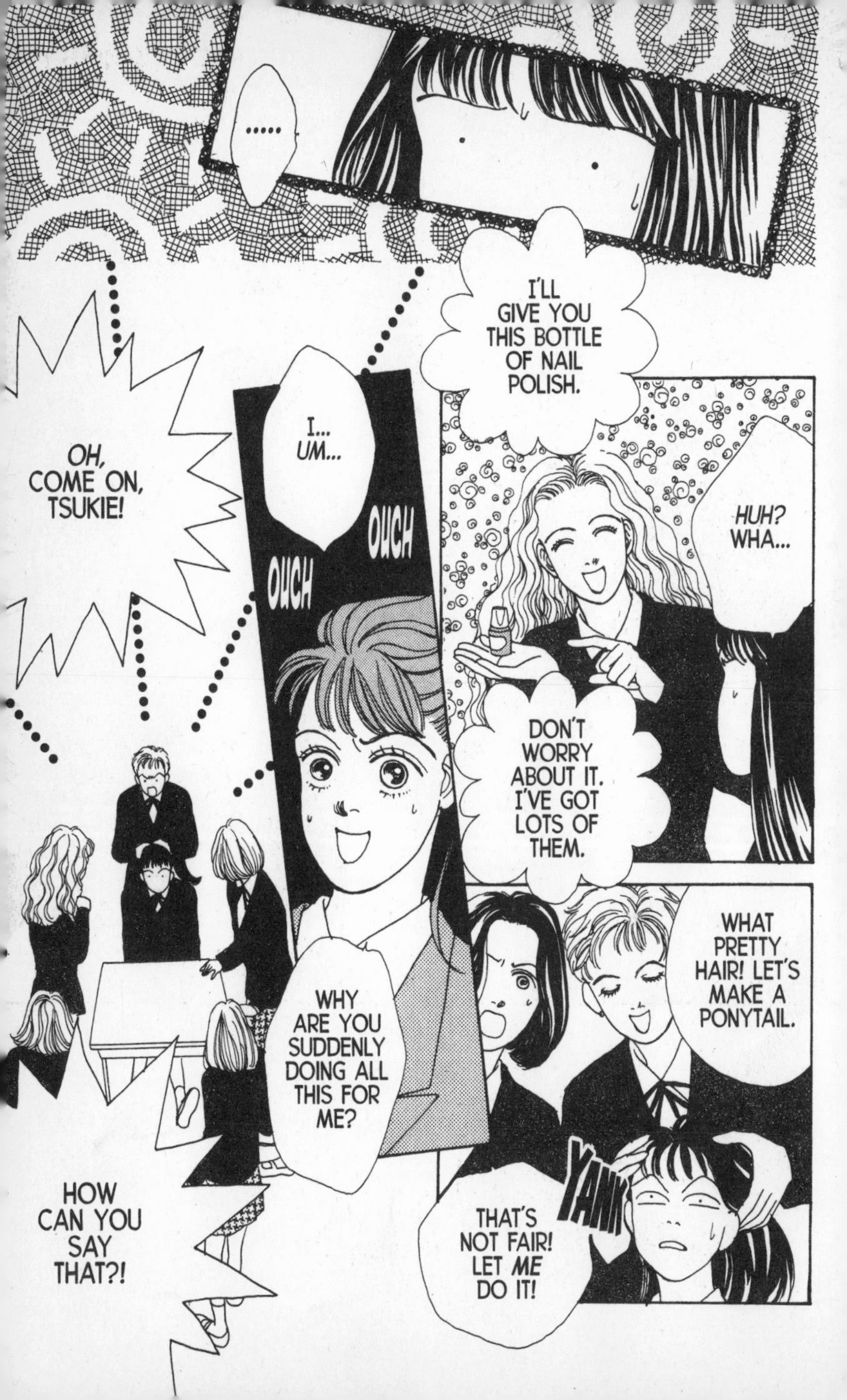
.....
I'LL GIVE YOU THIS BOTTLE OF NAIL POLISH.
HUH? WHA...
DON'T WORRY ABOUT IT. I'VE GOT LOTS OF THEM.
WHAT PRETTY HAIR! LET'S MAKE A PONYTAIL.
YANK
THAT'S NOT FAIR! LET *ME* DO IT!
I... *UM*...
OUCH
OUCH
WHY ARE YOU SUDDENLY DOING ALL THIS FOR ME?
OH, COME ON, TSUKIE!
HOW CAN YOU SAY THAT?!

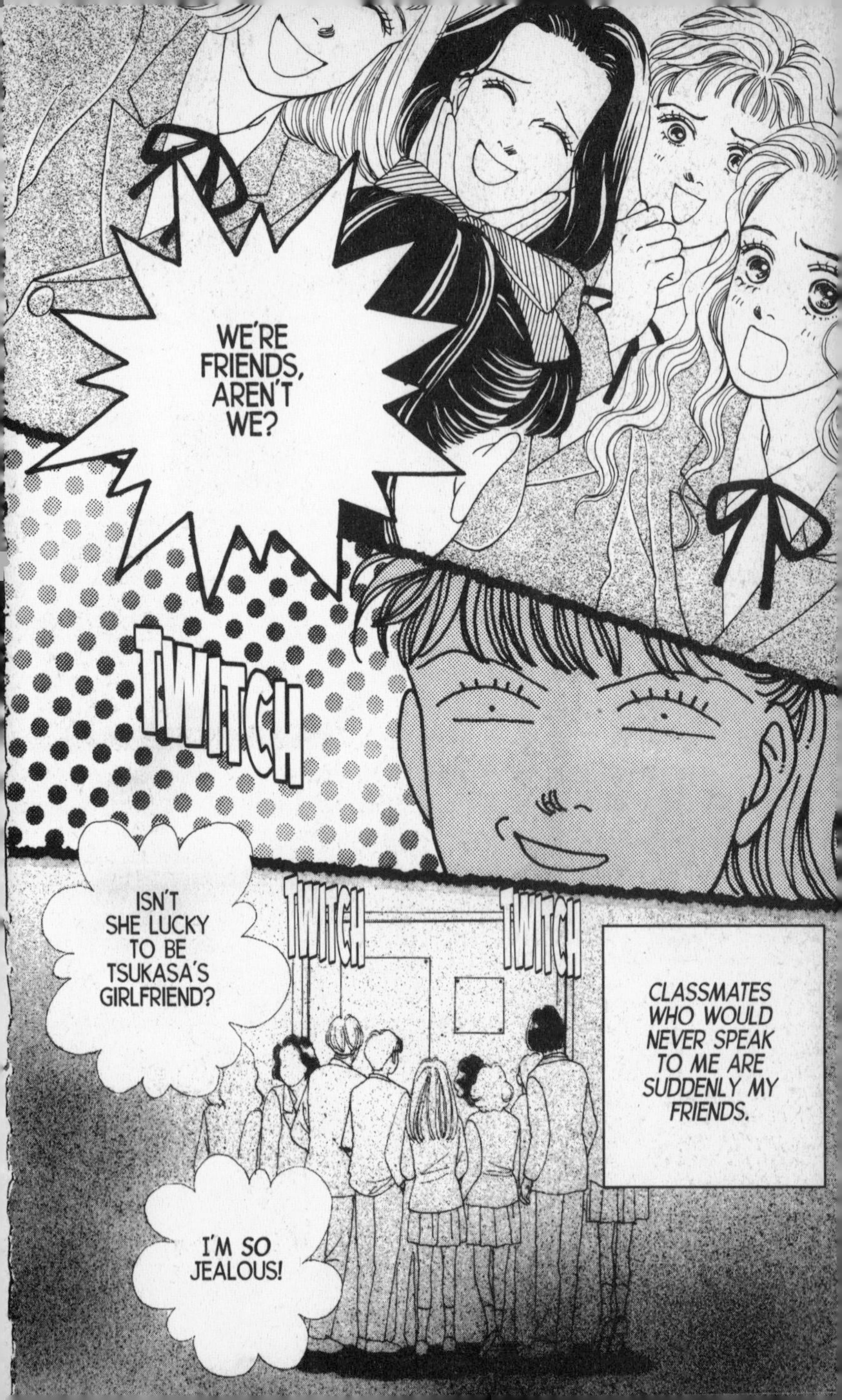
WE'RE FRIENDS, AREN'T WE?
TWITCH
CLASSMATES WHO WOULD NEVER SPEAK TO ME ARE SUDDENLY MY FRIENDS.
TWITCH
TWITCH
ISN'T SHE LUCKY TO BE TSUKASA'S GIRLFRIEND?
I'M SO JEALOUS!

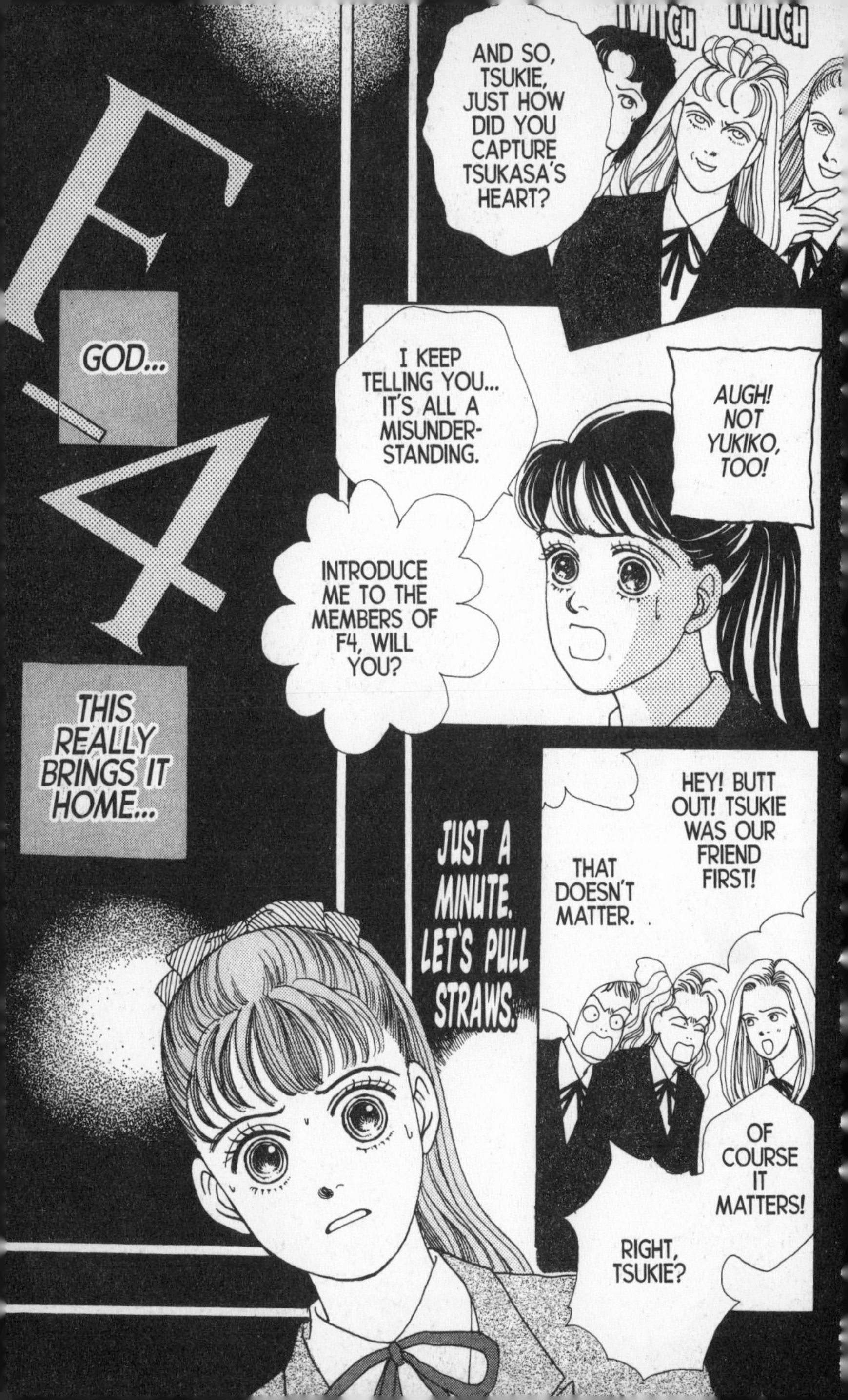
TWITCH TWITCH
AND SO, TSUKIE, JUST HOW DID YOU CAPTURE TSUKASA'S HEART?
AUGH! NOT YUKIKO, TOO!
I KEEP TELLING YOU... IT'S ALL A MISUNDER-STANDING.
INTRODUCE ME TO THE MEMBERS OF F4, WILL YOU?
HEY! BUTT OUT! TSUKIE WAS OUR FRIEND FIRST!
THAT DOESN'T MATTER.
OF COURSE IT MATTERS!
RIGHT, TSUKIE?
F4!
GOD...
THIS REALLY BRINGS IT HOME...
JUST A MINUTE. LET'S PULL STRAWS.

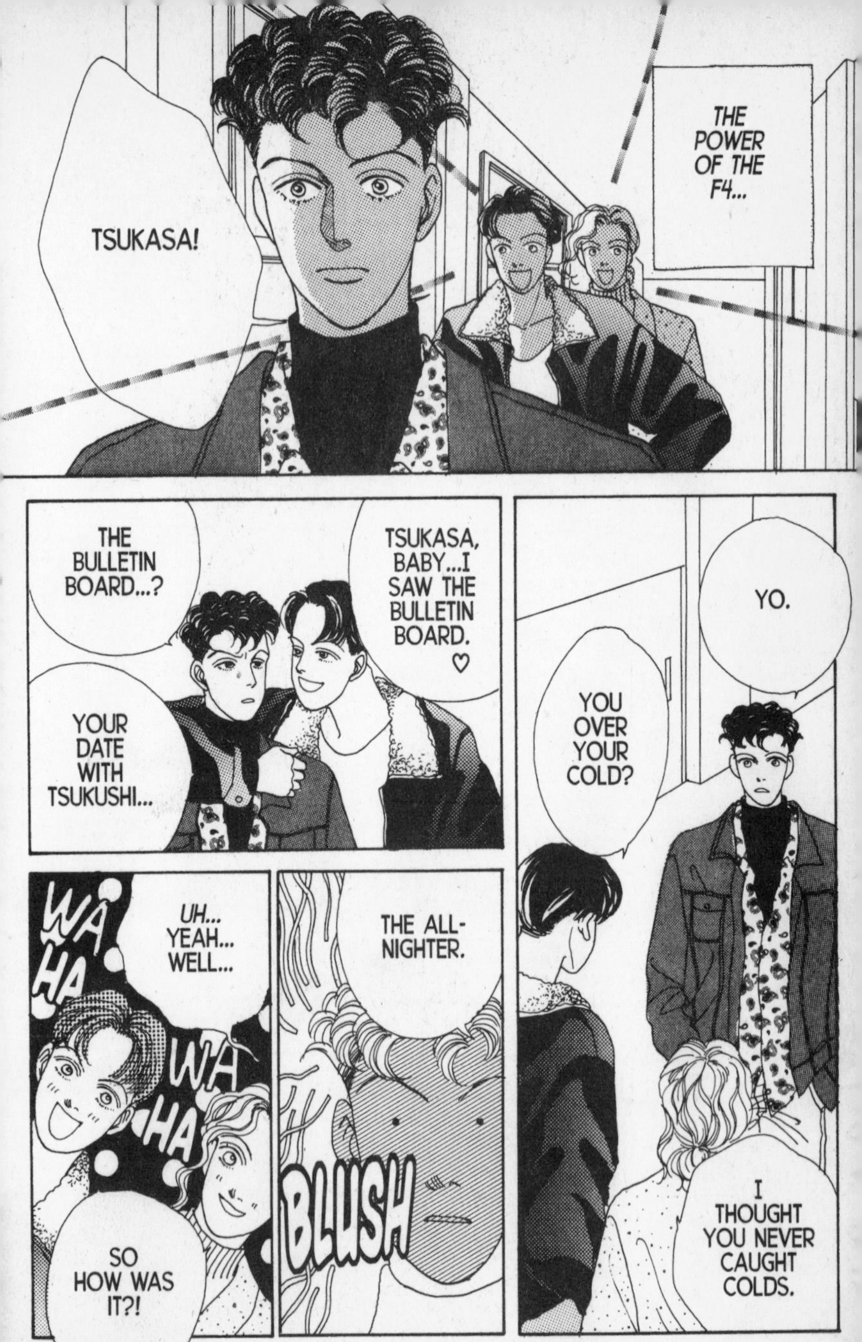
THE POWER OF THE F4...
TSUKASA!
YO.
YOU OVER YOUR COLD?
I THOUGHT YOU NEVER CAUGHT COLDS.
TSUKASA, BABY...I SAW THE BULLETIN BOARD. ♡
THE BULLETIN BOARD...?
YOUR DATE WITH TSUKUSHI...
THE ALL-NIGHTER.
BLUSH
UH... YEAH... WELL...
WA HA
WA HA
SO HOW WAS IT?!

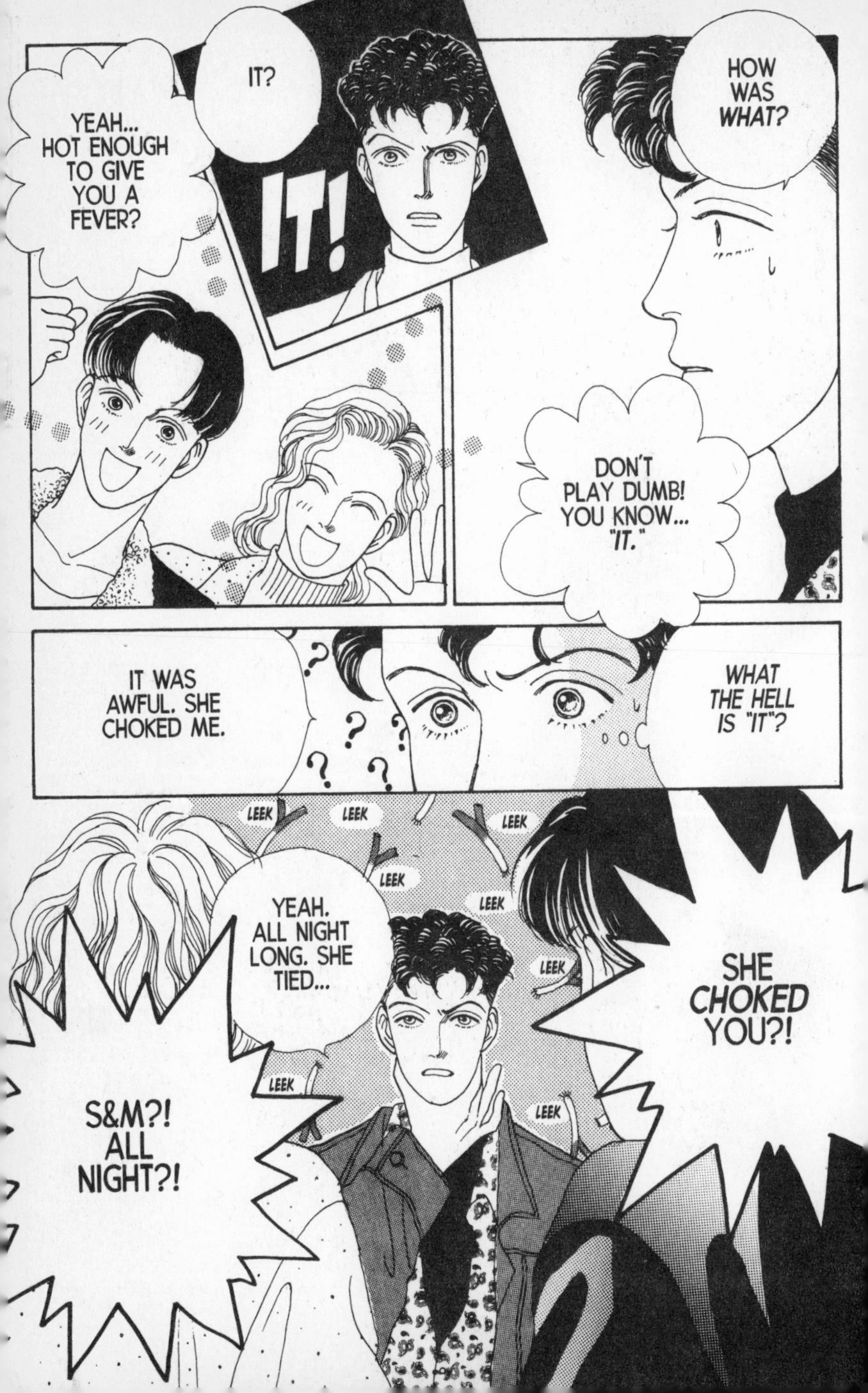
HOW WAS *WHAT?*
DON'T PLAY DUMB! YOU KNOW... *"IT."*
IT?
IT!
YEAH... HOT ENOUGH TO GIVE YOU A FEVER?
WHAT THE HELL IS "IT"?
IT WAS AWFUL. SHE CHOKED ME.
LEEK
LEEK
LEEK
LEEK
LEEK
LEEK
LEEK
LEEK
SHE *CHOKED* YOU?!
YEAH. ALL NIGHT LONG. SHE TIED...
S&M?! ALL NIGHT?!

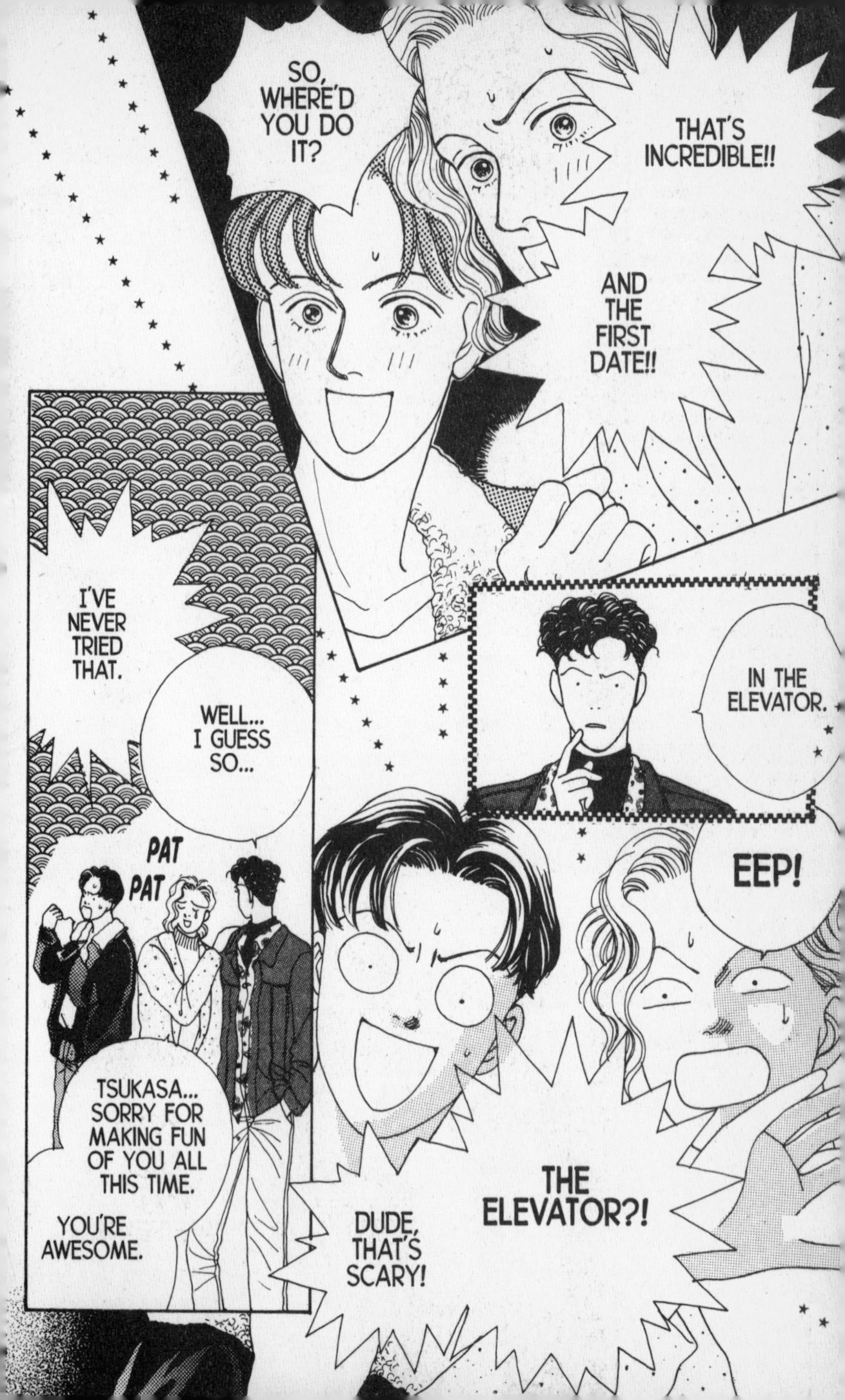
THAT'S INCREDIBLE!!
AND THE FIRST DATE!!
SO, WHERE'D YOU DO IT?
IN THE ELEVATOR.
EEP!
THE ELEVATOR?!
DUDE, THAT'S SCARY!
I'VE NEVER TRIED THAT.
WELL... I GUESS SO...
PAT PAT
TSUKASA... SORRY FOR MAKING FUN OF YOU ALL THIS TIME.
YOU'RE AWESOME.

11

Lately, I've been getting fan letters pointing out that I've been forgetting to draw in pierced earrings.

I sometimes draw in six fingers. That's embarrassing. Six fingers...SO embarrassing. (Please don't start looking for them!)

I've never been good at the details. I keep forgetting things. I'm not detail-oriented.

If only I could be more careful with the details, I think I'd be able to draw better. But, well...

A-ha a-ha

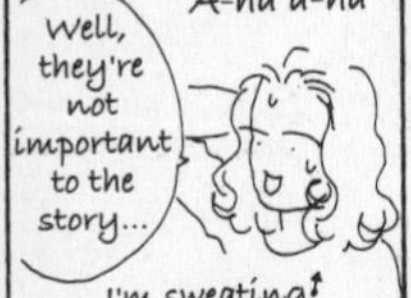
Well, they're not important to the story...

I'm sweating inside.

I shouldn't try making excuses like this.

If the missing earrings bother you, please feel free to draw them in.

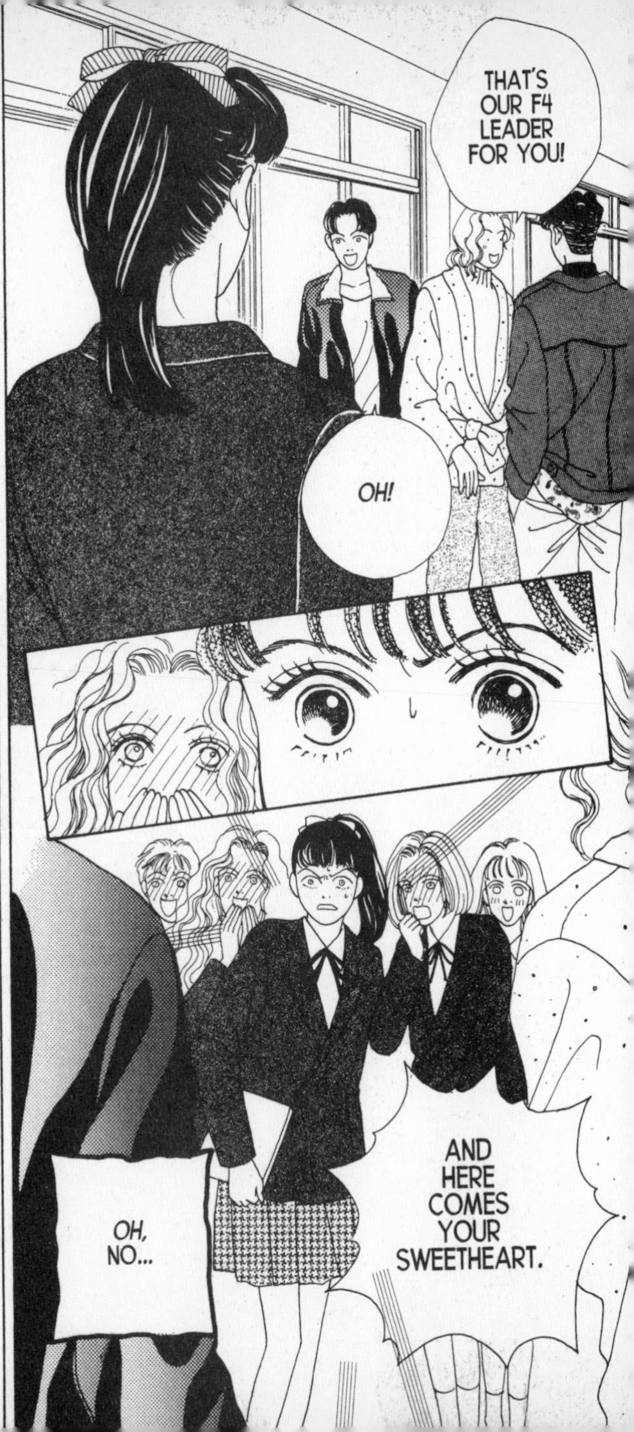
THAT'S OUR F4 LEADER FOR YOU!
OH!
AND HERE COMES YOUR SWEETHEART.
OH, NO...

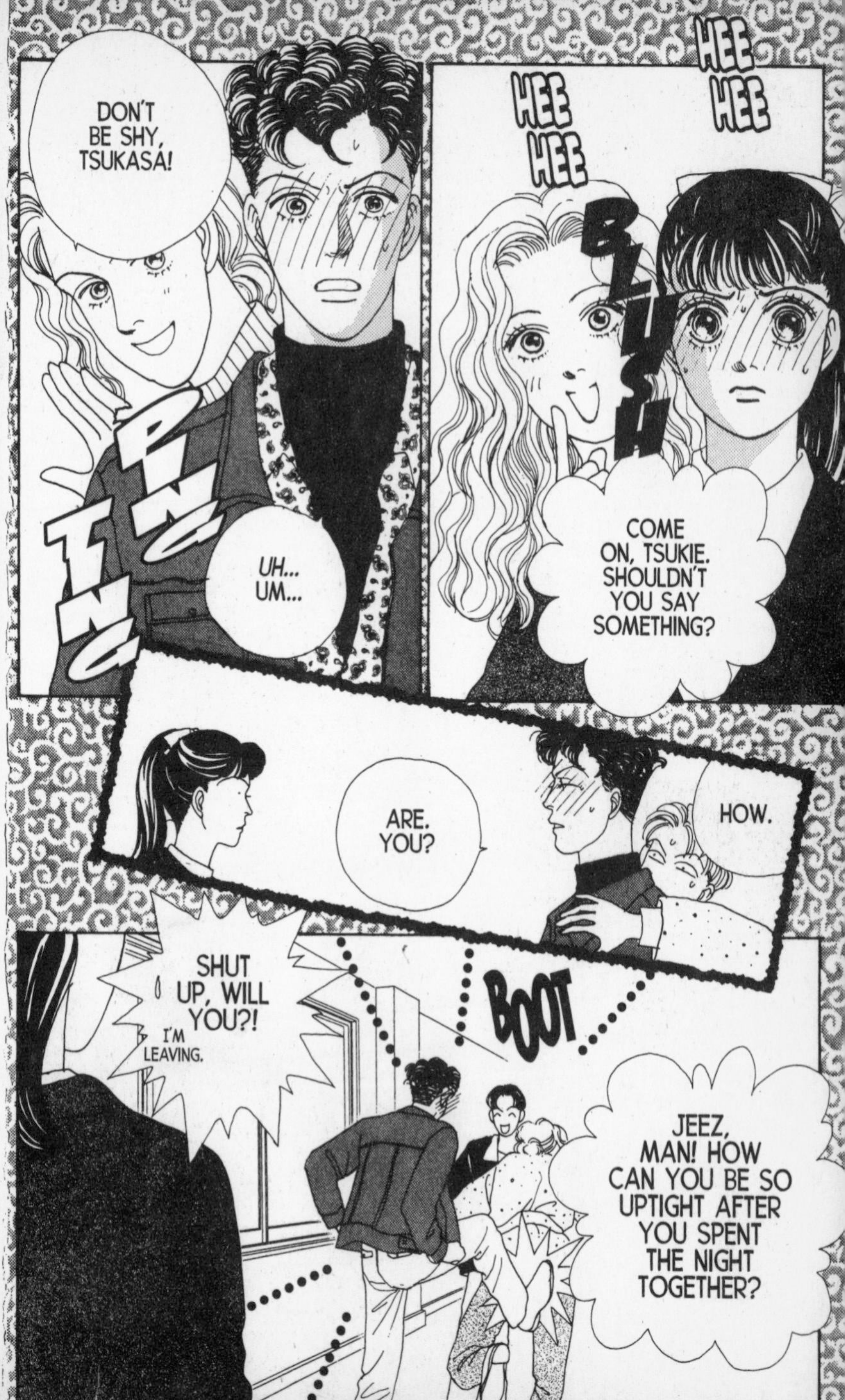
HEE HEE
HEE HEE
BLUSH
COME ON, TSUKIE. SHOULDN'T YOU SAY SOMETHING?
DON'T BE SHY, TSUKASA!
PING
TING
UH... UM...
HOW.
ARE. YOU?
JEEZ, MAN! HOW CAN YOU BE SO UPTIGHT AFTER YOU SPENT THE NIGHT TOGETHER?
BOOT
SHUT UP, WILL YOU?!
I'M LEAVING.

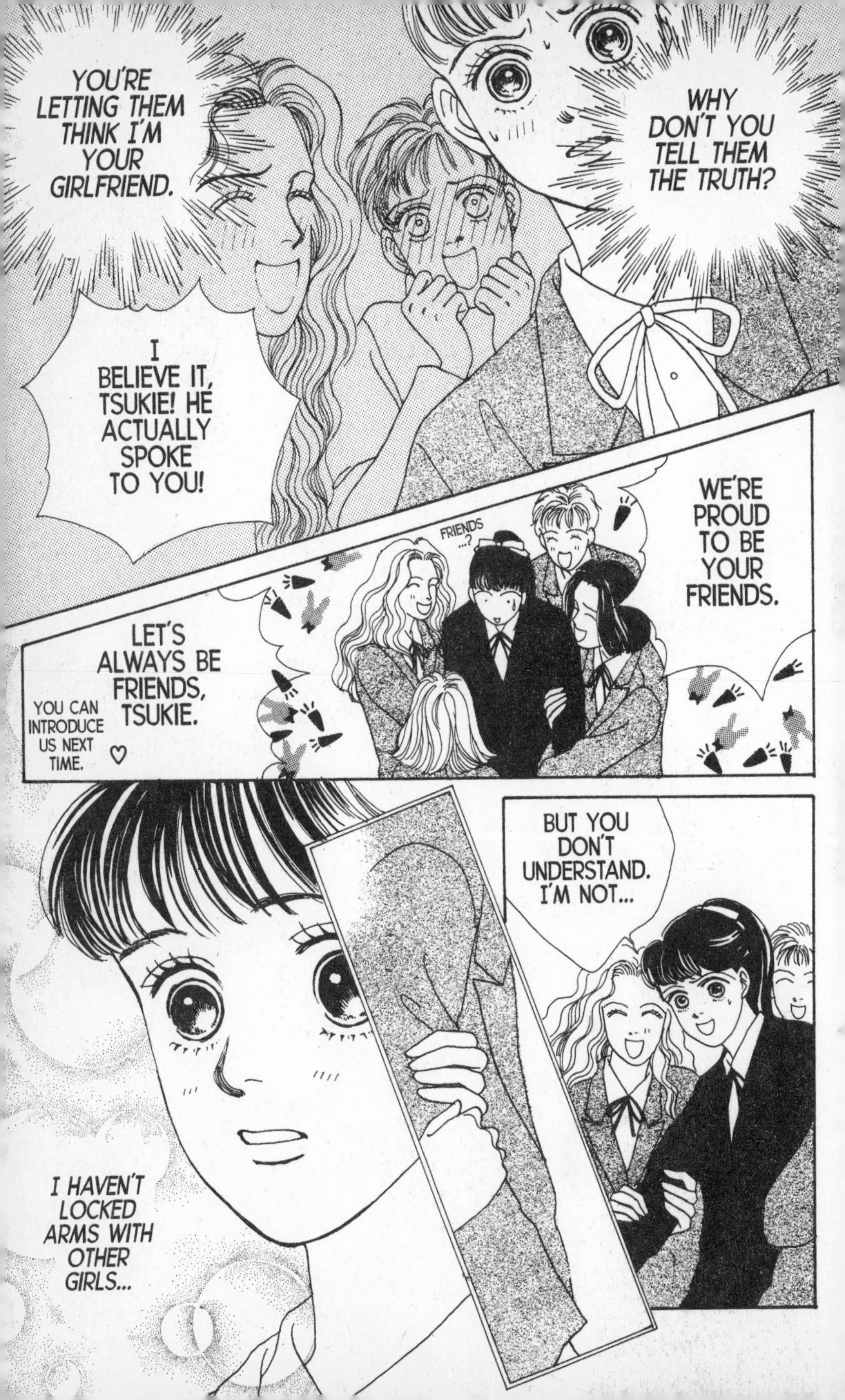

WHY DON'T YOU TELL THEM THE TRUTH?
YOU'RE LETTING THEM THINK I'M YOUR GIRLFRIEND.
I BELIEVE IT, TSUKIE! HE ACTUALLY SPOKE TO YOU!
WE'RE PROUD TO BE YOUR FRIENDS.
FRIENDS ...?
LET'S ALWAYS BE FRIENDS, TSUKIE.
YOU CAN INTRODUCE US NEXT TIME. ♡
BUT YOU DON'T UNDERSTAND. I'M NOT...
I HAVEN'T LOCKED ARMS WITH OTHER GIRLS...

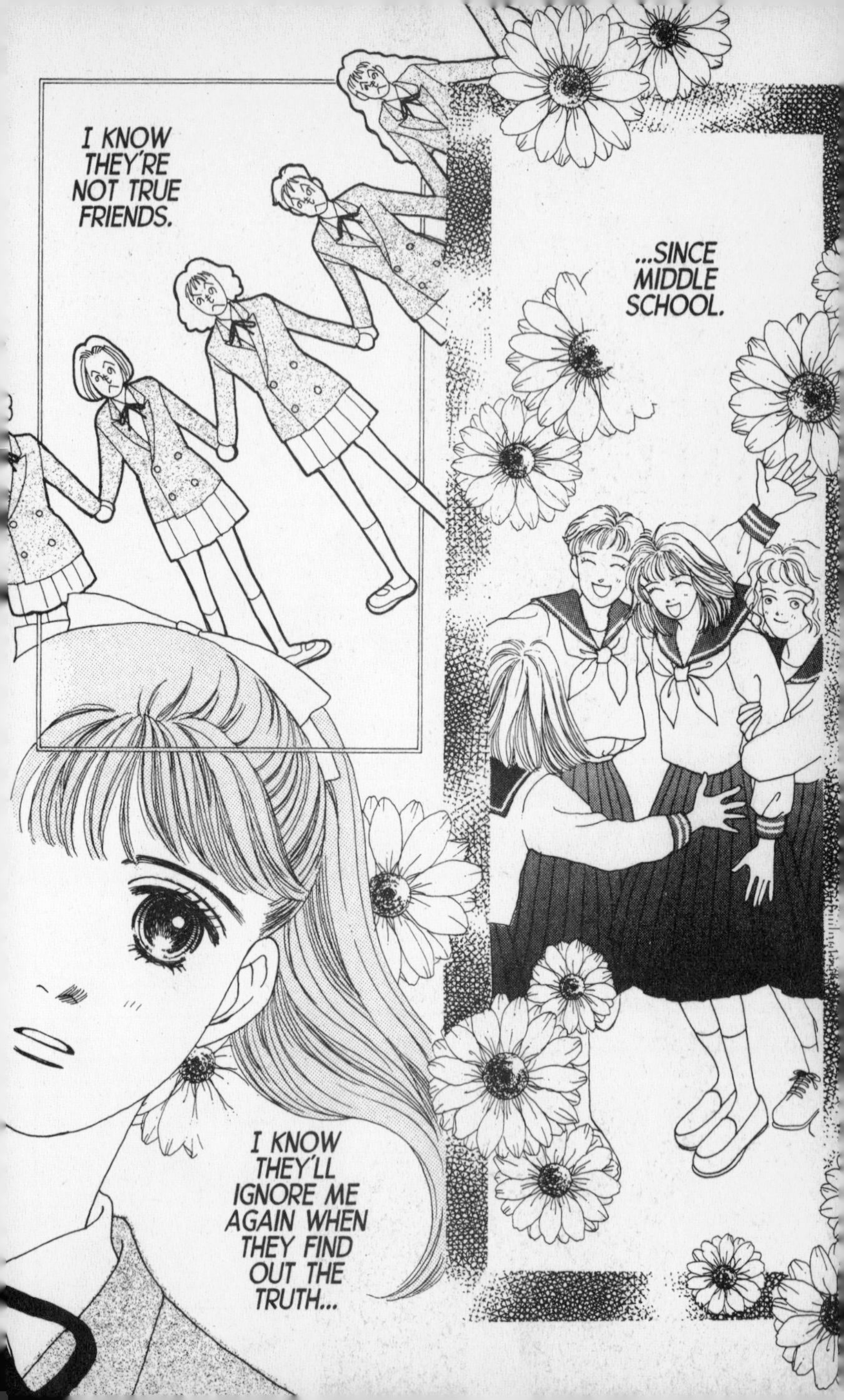
...SINCE MIDDLE SCHOOL.
I KNOW THEY'RE NOT TRUE FRIENDS.
I KNOW THEY'LL IGNORE ME AGAIN WHEN THEY FIND OUT THE TRUTH...

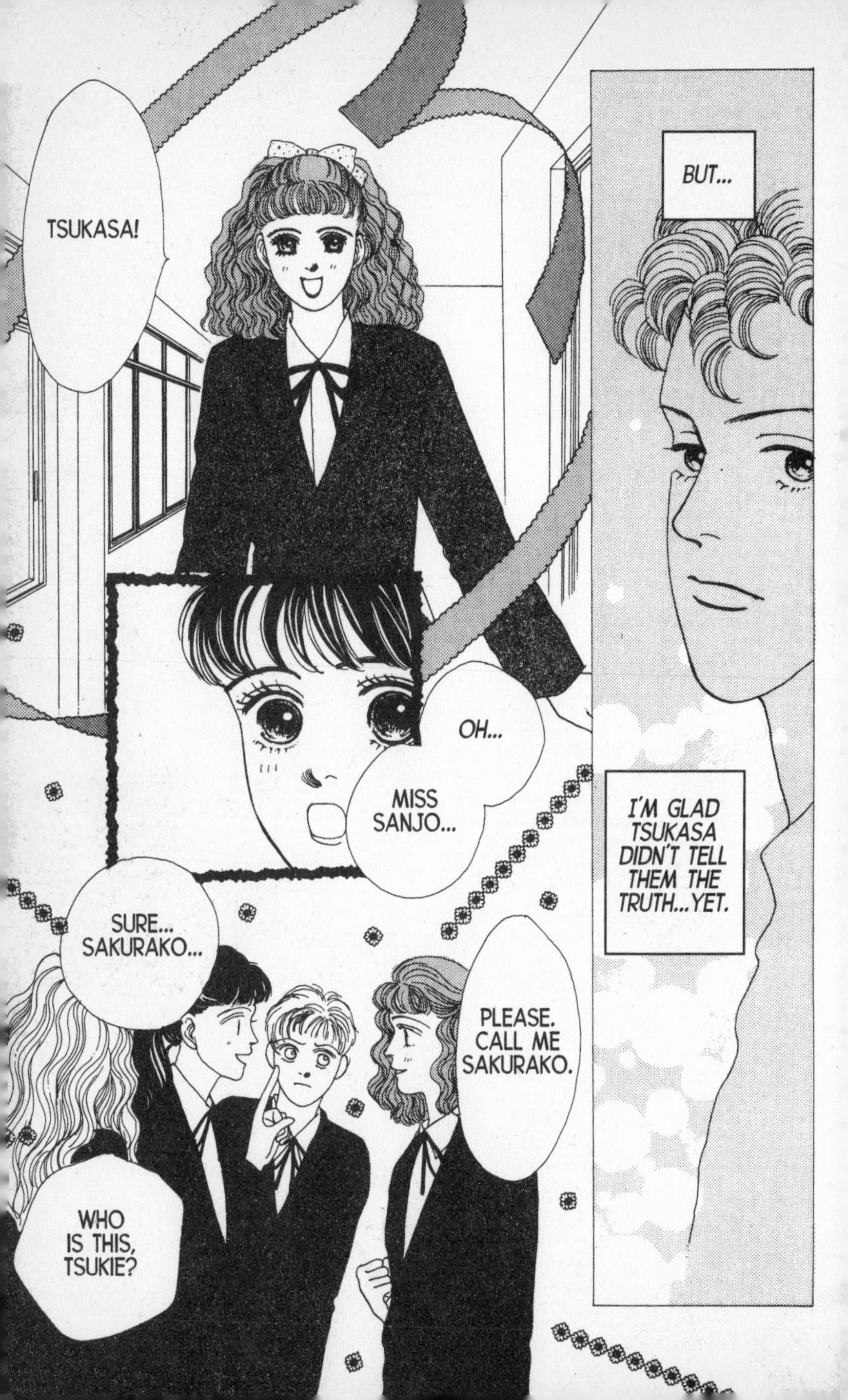
BUT...
I'M GLAD TSUKASA DIDN'T TELL THEM THE TRUTH...YET.
TSUKASA!
OH...
MISS SANJO...
PLEASE. CALL ME SAKURAKO.
SURE... SAKURAKO...
WHO IS THIS, TSUKIE?

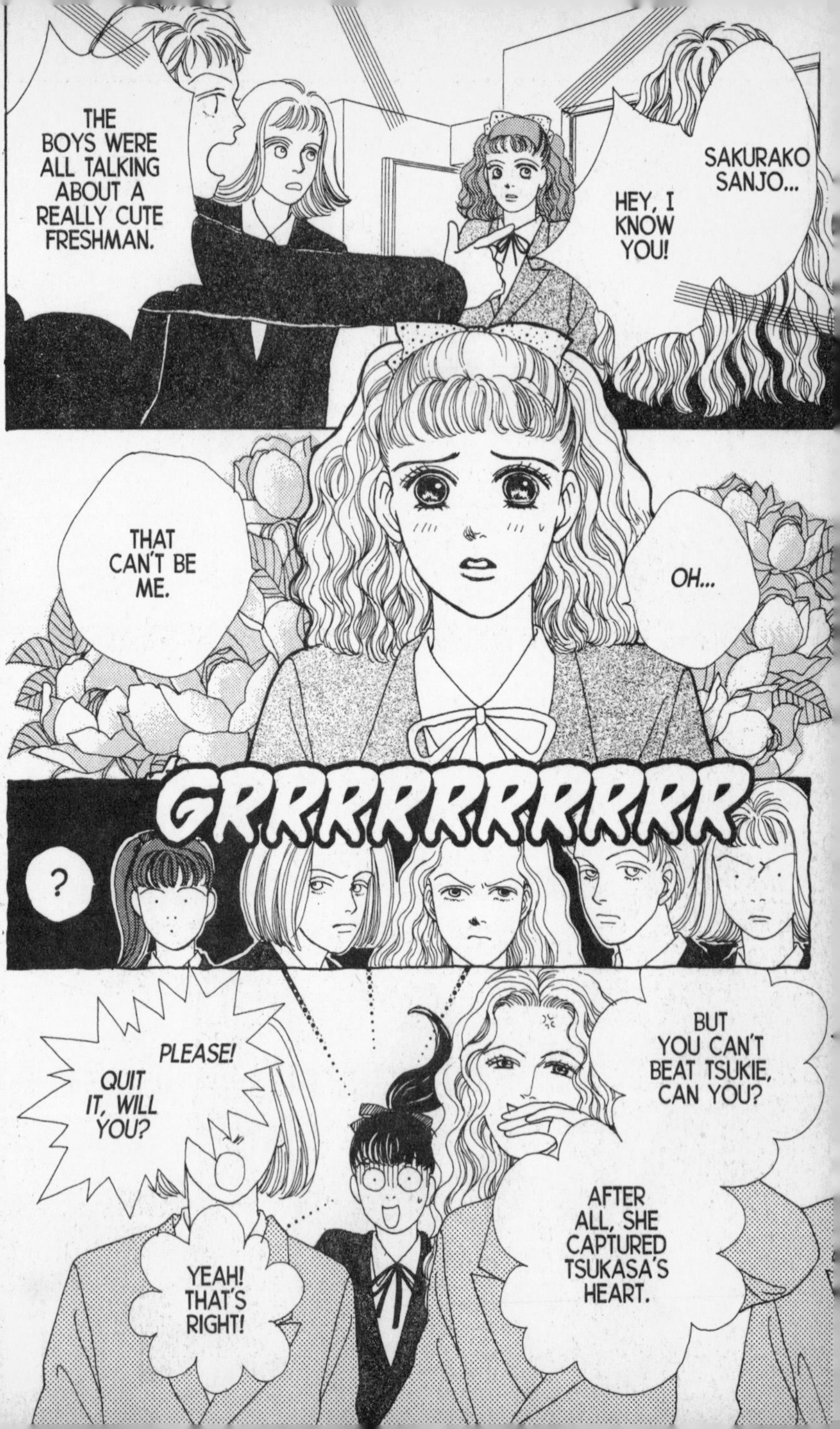
SAKURAKO SANJO...
HEY, I KNOW YOU!
THE BOYS WERE ALL TALKING ABOUT A REALLY CUTE FRESHMAN.
OH...
THAT CAN'T BE ME.
GRRRRRRRRRRR
?
BUT YOU CAN'T BEAT TSUKIE, CAN YOU?
AFTER ALL, SHE CAPTURED TSUKASA'S HEART.
YEAH! THAT'S RIGHT!
PLEASE!
QUIT IT, WILL YOU?

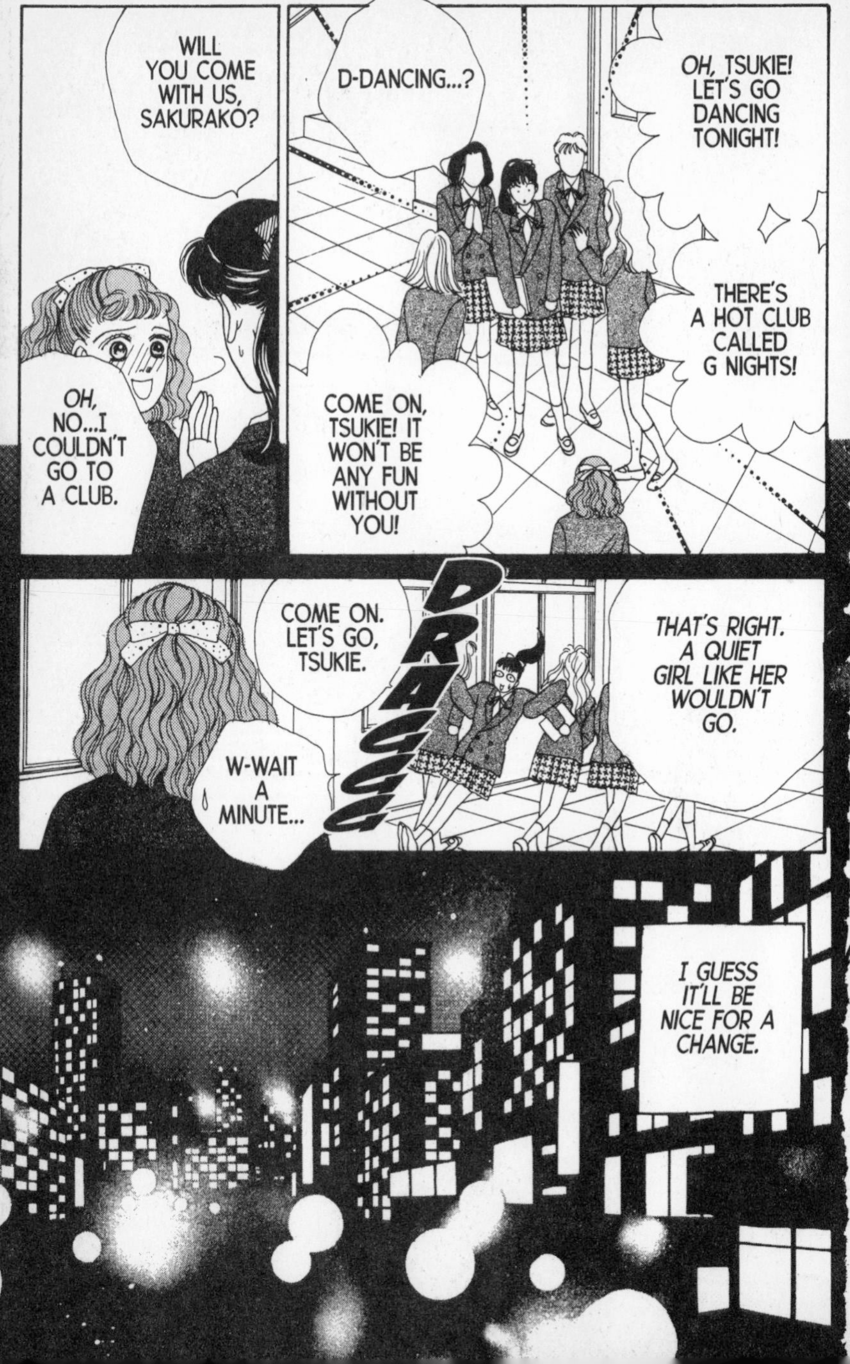

OH, TSUKIE! LET'S GO DANCING TONIGHT!
D-DANCING...?
THERE'S A HOT CLUB CALLED G NIGHTS!
COME ON, TSUKIE! IT WON'T BE ANY FUN WITHOUT YOU!
WILL YOU COME WITH US, SAKURAKO?
OH, NO...I COULDN'T GO TO A CLUB.
THAT'S RIGHT. A QUIET GIRL LIKE HER WOULDN'T GO.
COME ON. LET'S GO, TSUKIE.
DRAGGG
W-WAIT A MINUTE...
I GUESS IT'LL BE NICE FOR A CHANGE.

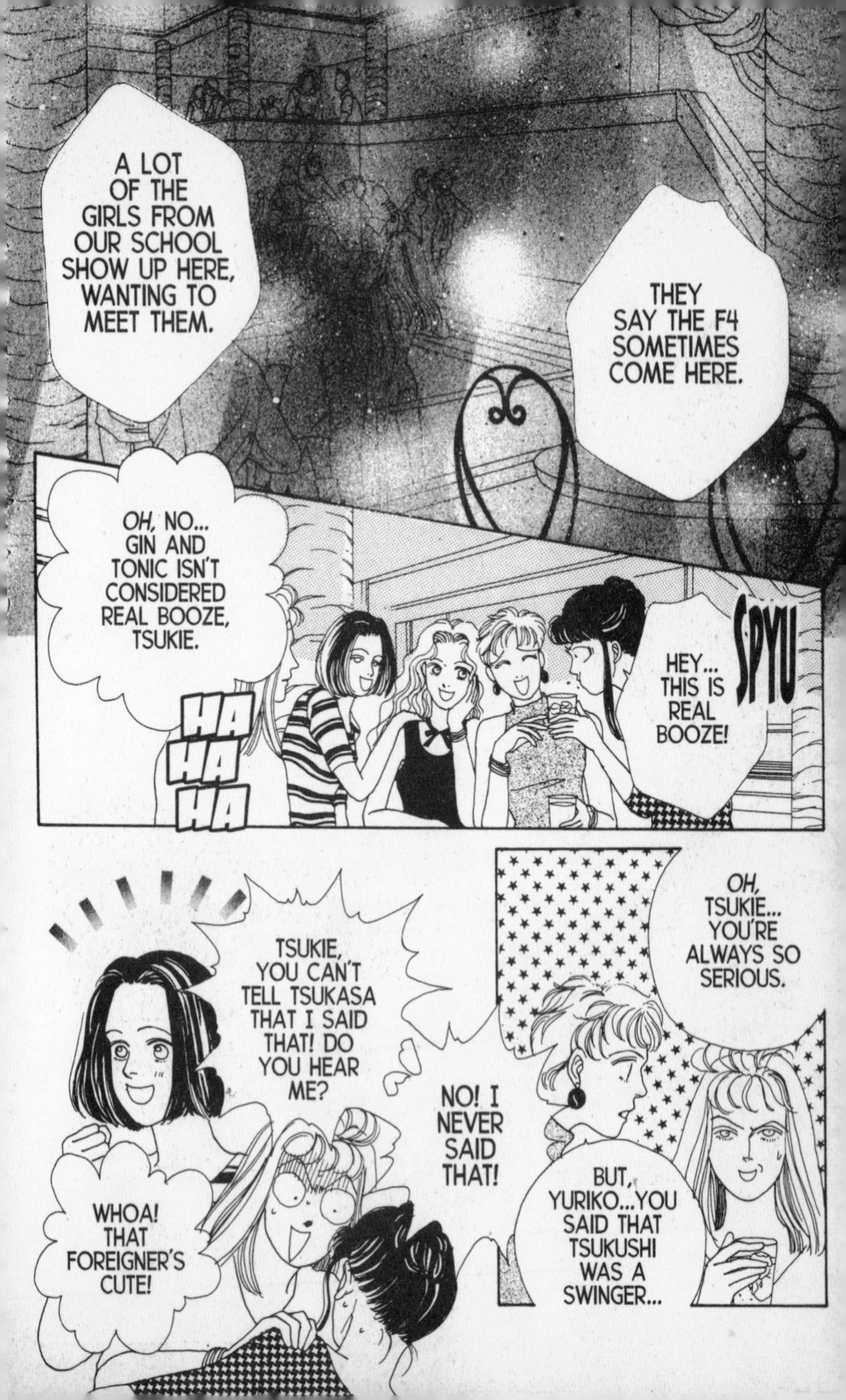
THEY SAY THE F4 SOMETIMES COME HERE.
A LOT OF THE GIRLS FROM OUR SCHOOL SHOW UP HERE, WANTING TO MEET THEM.
SPYU
HEY... THIS IS REAL BOOZE!
OH, NO... GIN AND TONIC ISN'T CONSIDERED REAL BOOZE, TSUKIE.
HA HA HA
OH, TSUKIE... YOU'RE ALWAYS SO SERIOUS.
BUT, YURIKO...YOU SAID THAT TSUKUSHI WAS A SWINGER...
NO! I NEVER SAID THAT!
TSUKIE, YOU CAN'T TELL TSUKASA THAT I SAID THAT! DO YOU HEAR ME?
WHOA! THAT FOREIGNER'S CUTE!

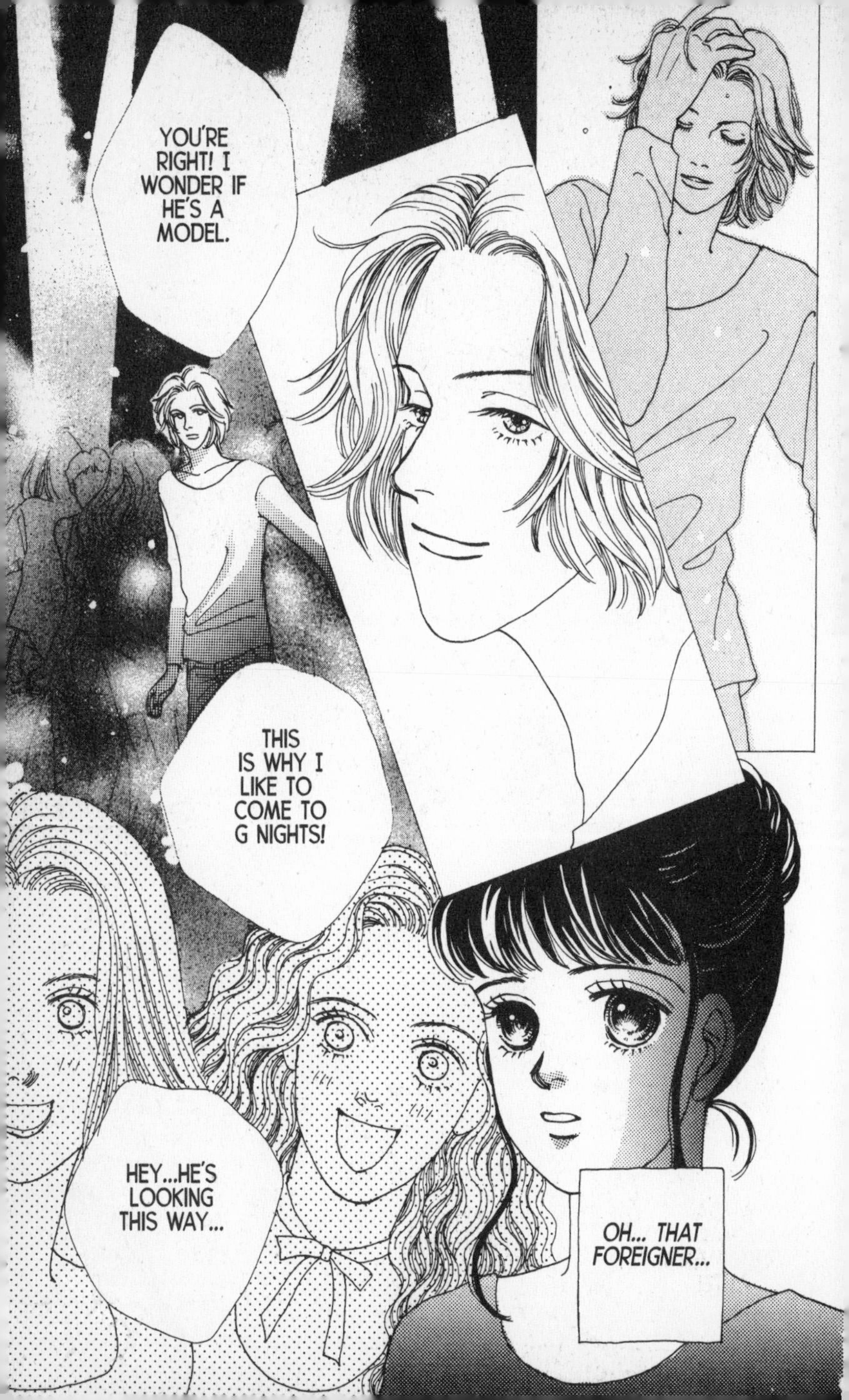
YOU'RE RIGHT! I WONDER IF HE'S A MODEL.
THIS IS WHY I LIKE TO COME TO G NIGHTS!
HEY...HE'S LOOKING THIS WAY...
OH... THAT FOREIGNER...

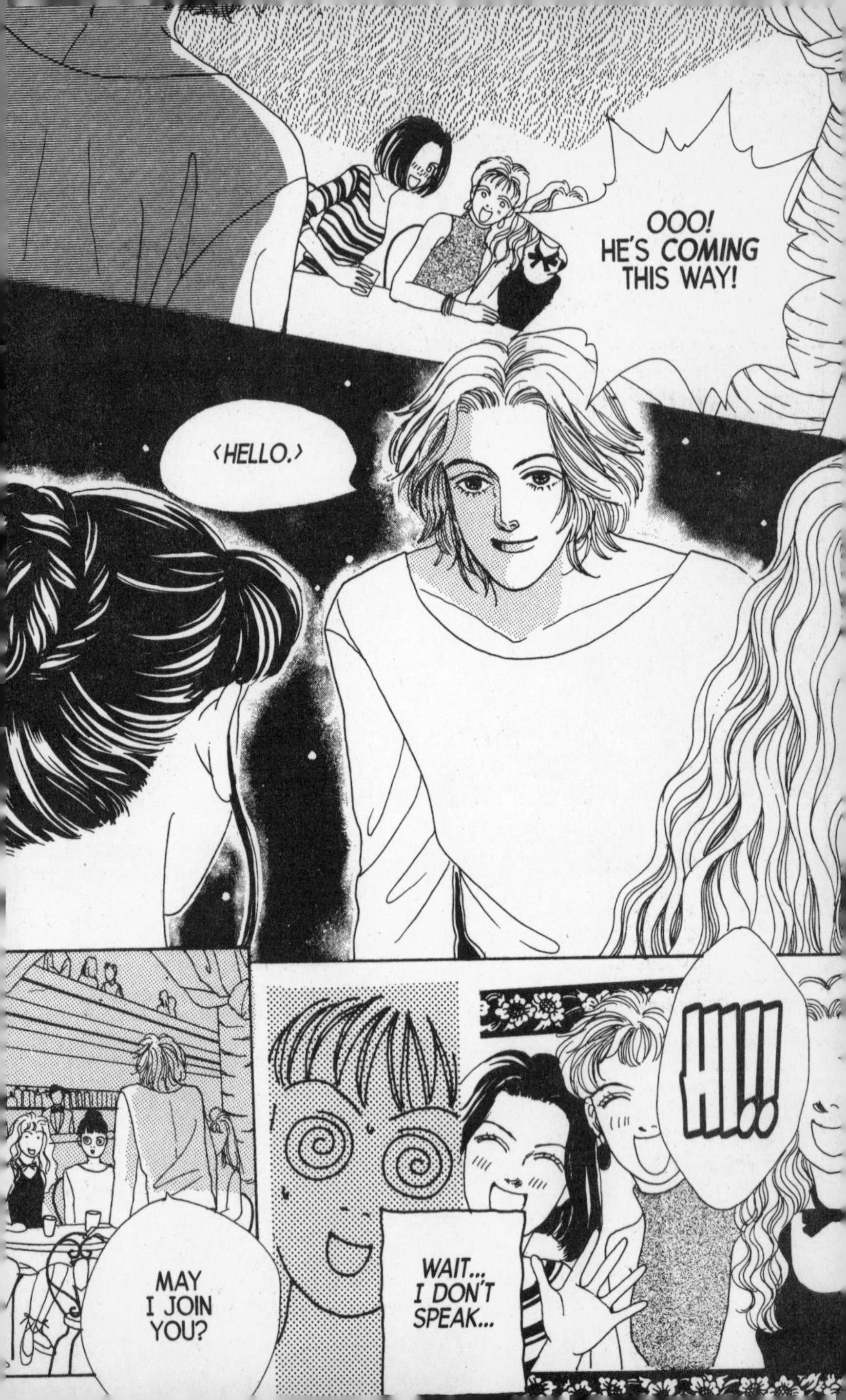
OOO! HE'S *COMING* THIS WAY!
‹HELLO.›
HI!!
WAIT... I DON'T SPEAK...
MAY I JOIN YOU?

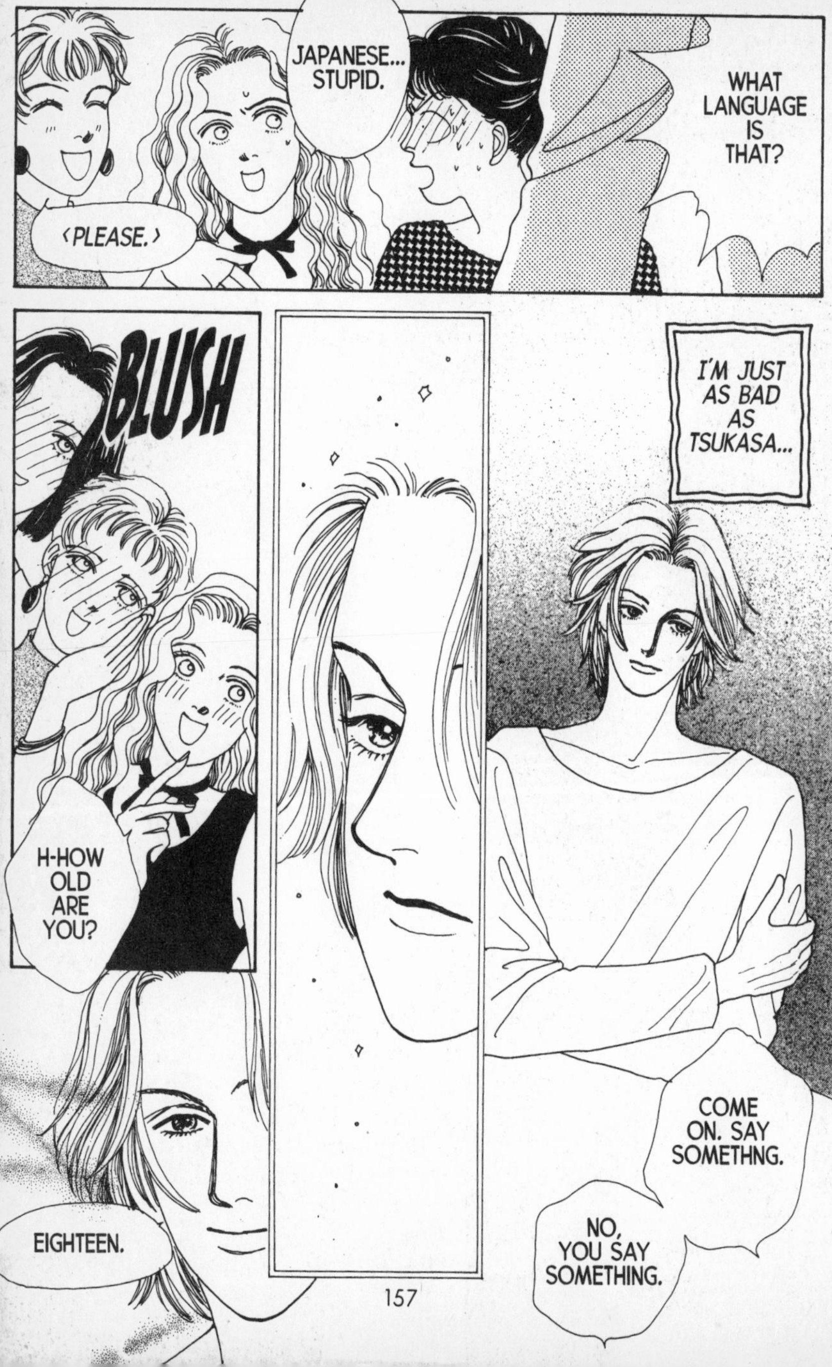
WHAT LANGUAGE IS THAT?
JAPANESE... STUPID.
‹PLEASE.›
I'M JUST AS BAD AS TSUKASA...
COME ON. SAY SOMETHNG.
NO, YOU SAY SOMETHING.
BLUSH
H-HOW OLD ARE YOU?
EIGHTEEN.

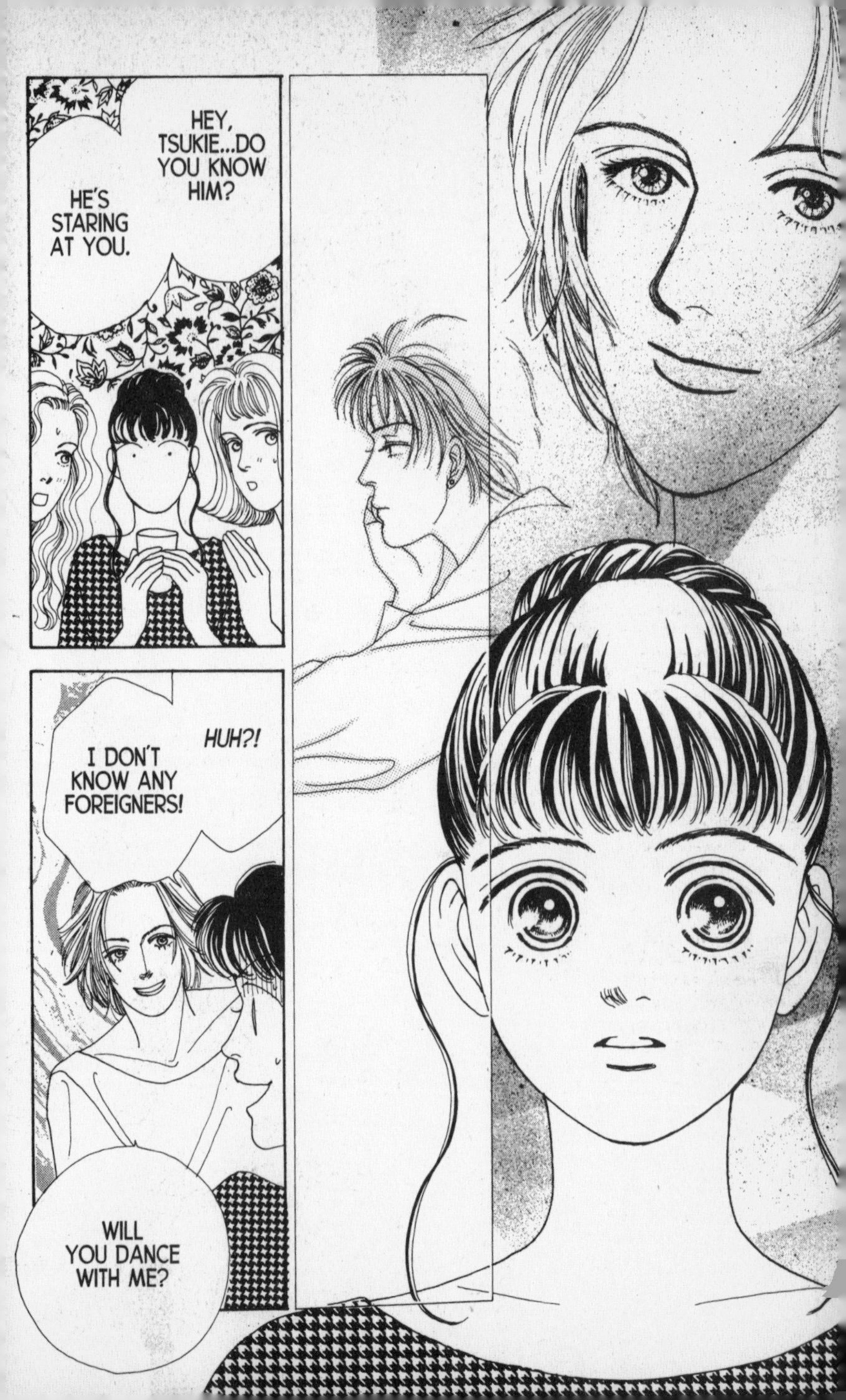
HEY, TSUKIE...DO YOU KNOW HIM?
HE'S STARING AT YOU.
HUH?!
I DON'T KNOW ANY FOREIGNERS!
WILL YOU DANCE WITH ME?

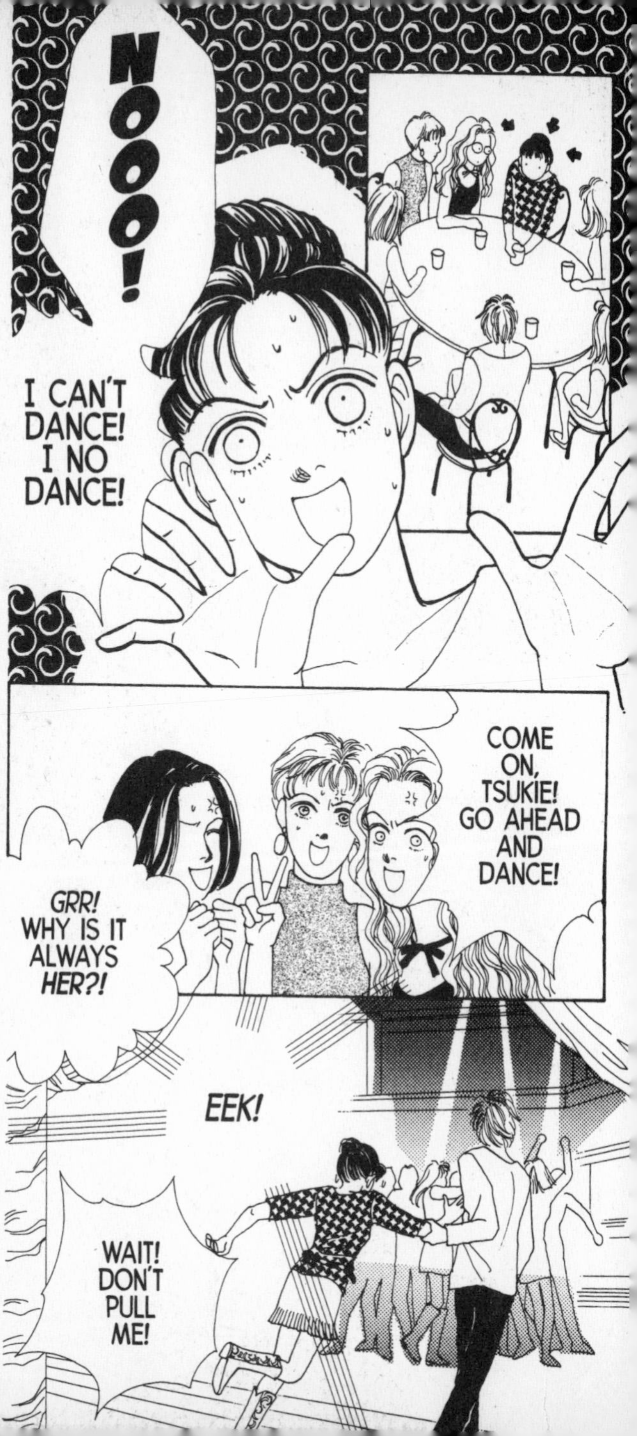
NOOOO!
I CAN'T DANCE! I NO DANCE!
COME ON, TSUKIE! GO AHEAD AND DANCE!
GRR! WHY IS IT ALWAYS HER?!
EEK!
WAIT! DON'T PULL ME!

12

What I really enjoy when I'm drawing Boys over Flowers is the fashion of the members of the F4. In fact, I dress them in my favorite styles.

Because Tsukushi comes from a poor family, I can't do much with her.

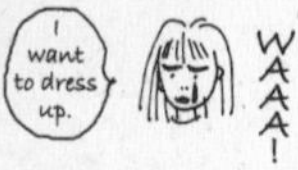
I want to dress up.
WAAAA!

Guys dress really simply nowadays--T-shirt, vest, jeans, accessories. I really like that. If a guy is really good looking, he stands out even if he isn't dressed flashily.

My absolute favorite is a guy who looks good in black. (I'm not talking about disco-style black. I hate that.)

I love the wild and sexy look. Christian Slater (Tsukasa is modeled after him) the way he looked in "Heathers" was so cool!

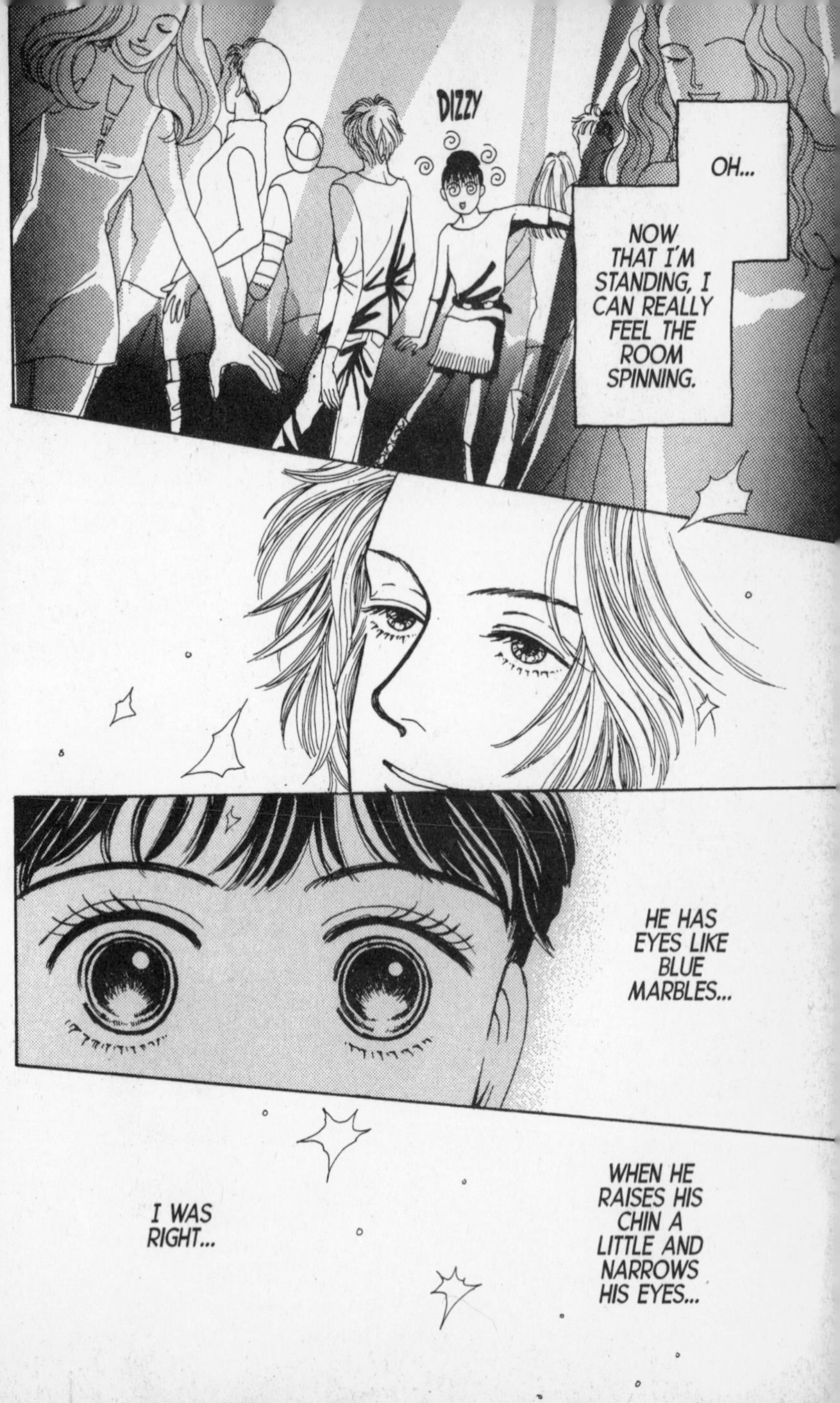
OH...
NOW THAT I'M STANDING, I CAN REALLY FEEL THE ROOM SPINNING.
DIZZY
HE HAS EYES LIKE BLUE MARBLES...
WHEN HE RAISES HIS CHIN A LITTLE AND NARROWS HIS EYES...
I WAS RIGHT...

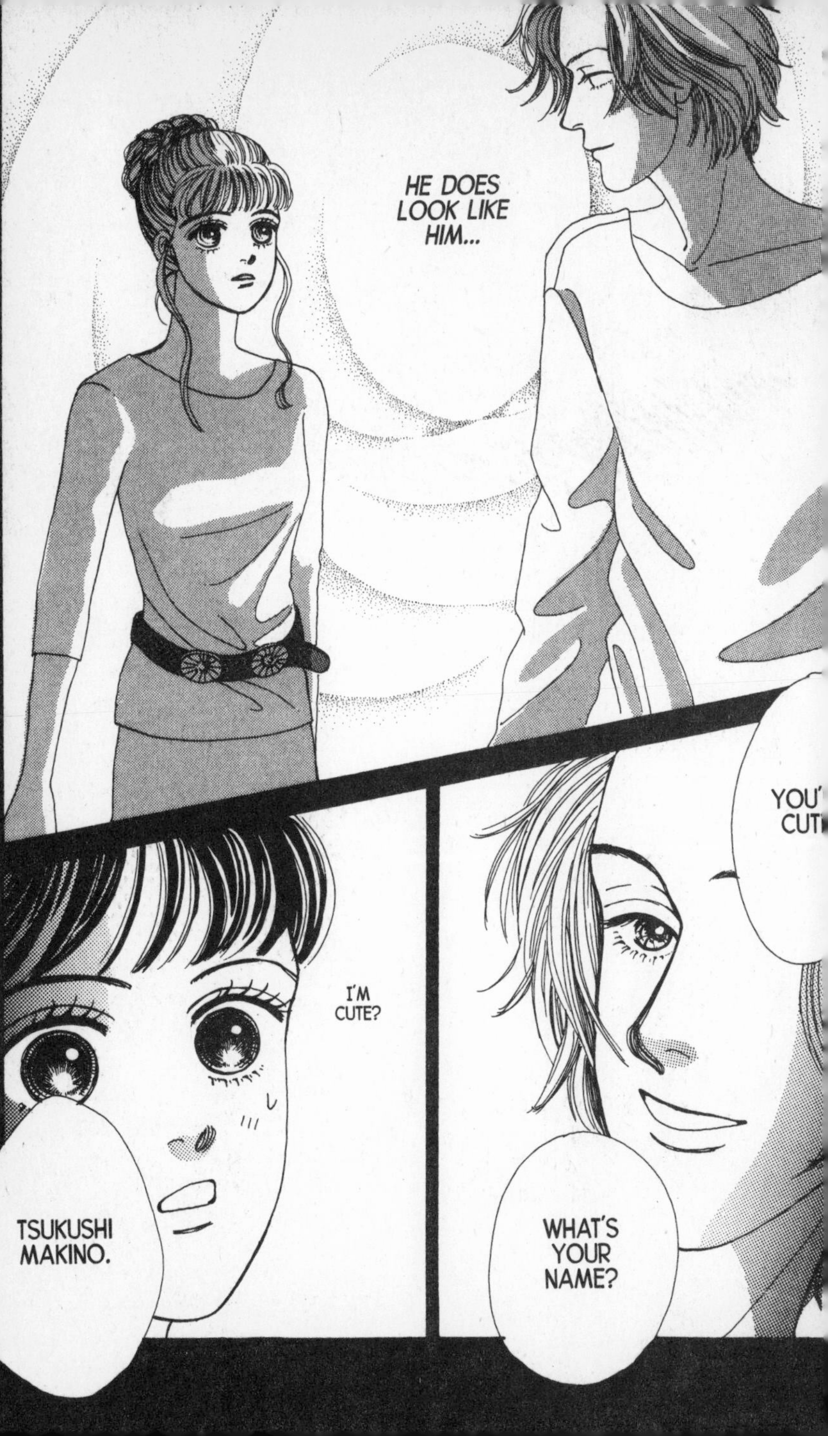
HE DOES LOOK LIKE HIM...
YOU'
CUT
WHAT'S YOUR NAME?
I'M CUTE?
TSUKUSHI MAKINO.

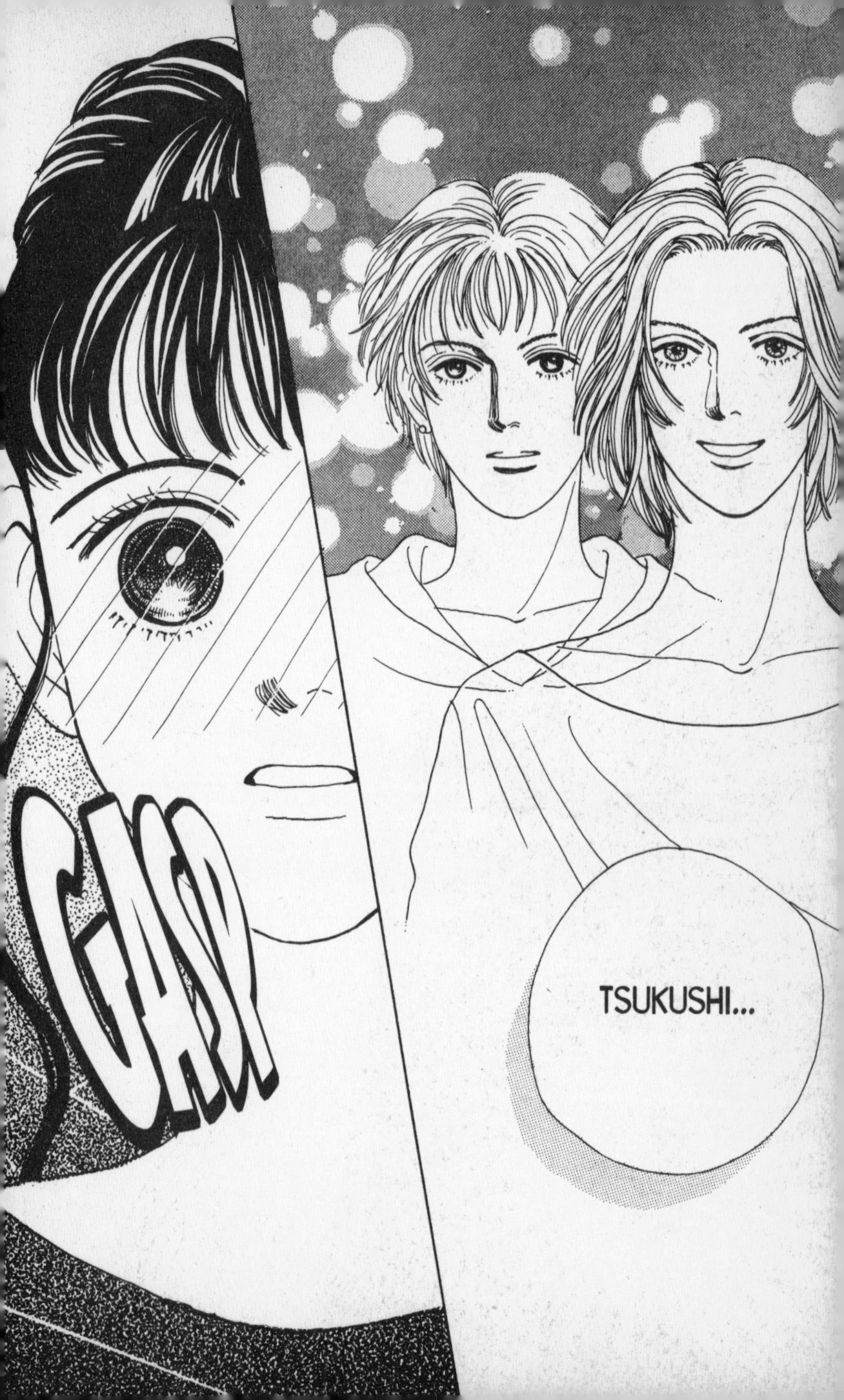
TSUKUSHI...
GASP

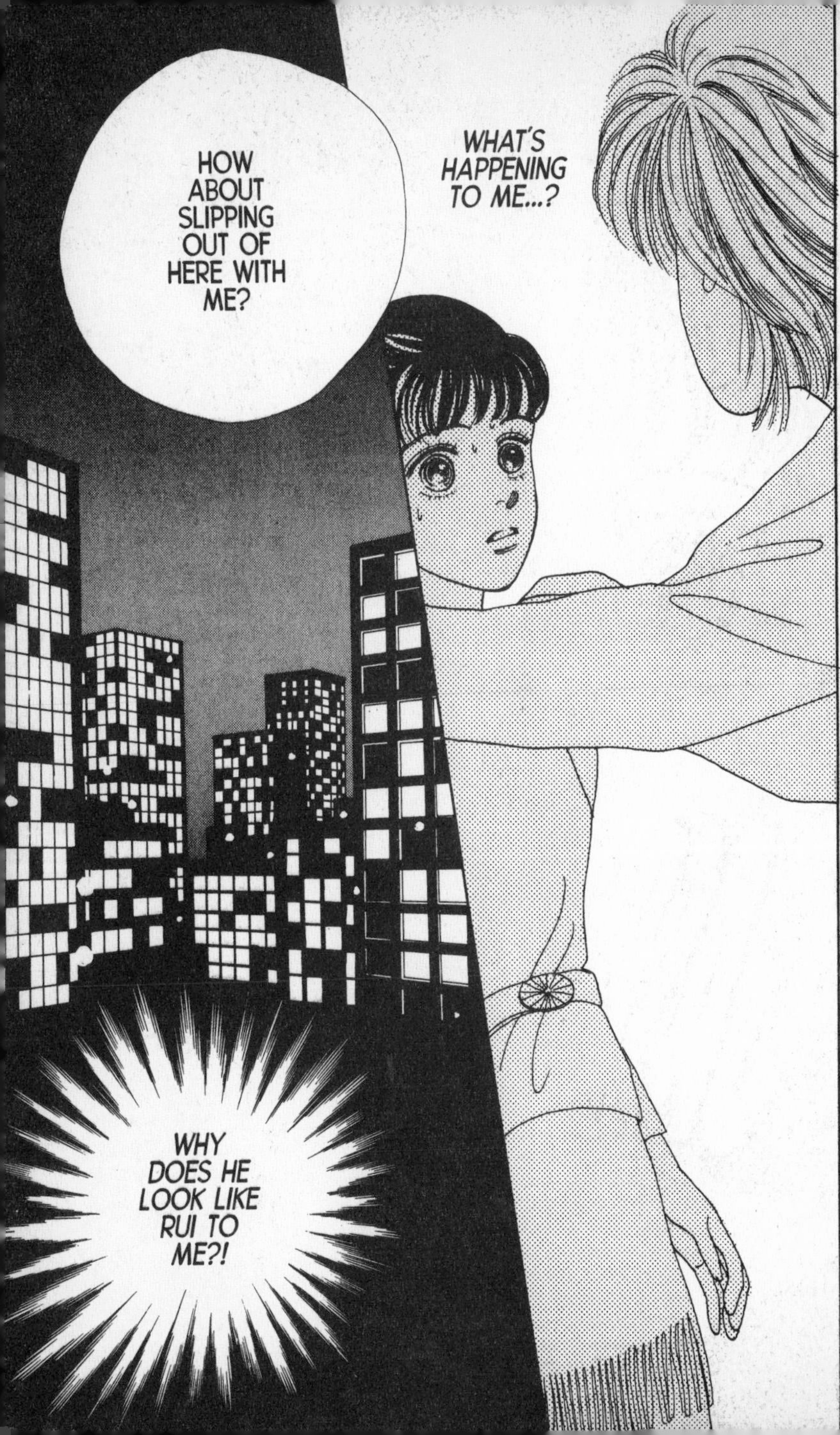
WHAT'S HAPPENING TO ME...?
HOW ABOUT SLIPPING OUT OF HERE WITH ME?
WHY DOES HE LOOK LIKE RUI TO ME?!

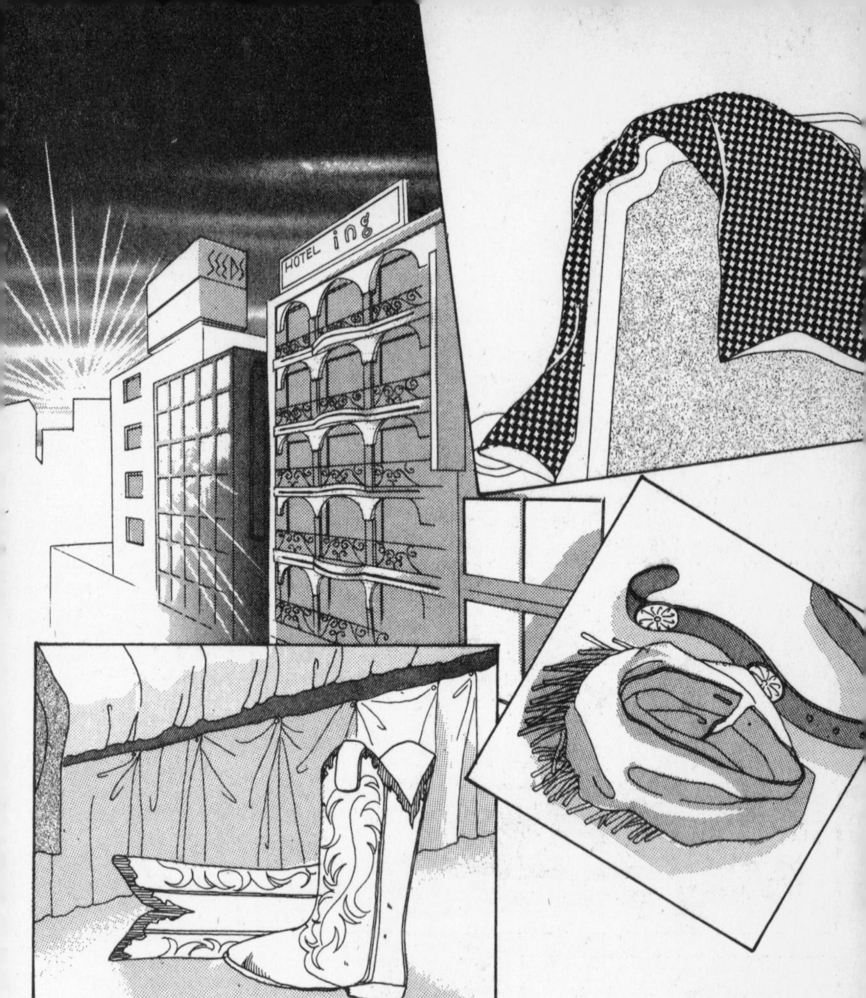
HOTEL ing
SEEDS

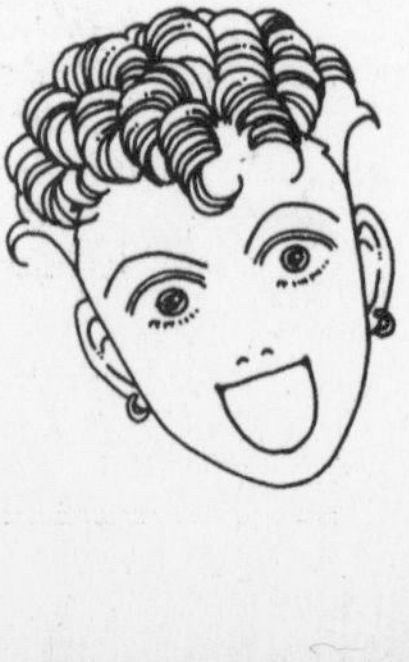

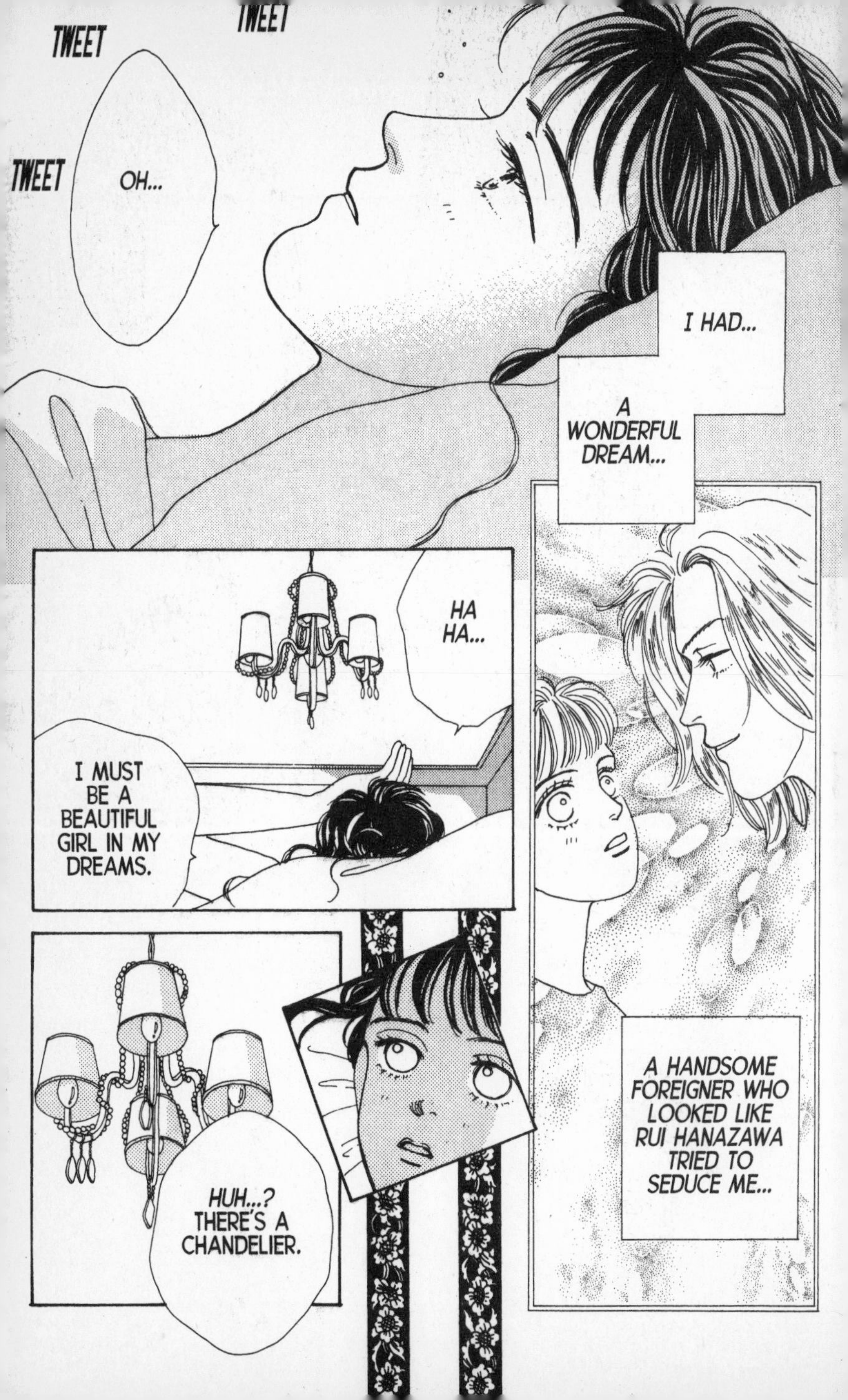
TWEET
TWEET
TWEET
OH...
I HAD...
A WONDERFUL DREAM...
A HANDSOME FOREIGNER WHO LOOKED LIKE RUI HANAZAWA TRIED TO SEDUCE ME...
HA HA...
I MUST BE A BEAUTIFUL GIRL IN MY DREAMS.
HUH...? THERE'S A CHANDELIER.

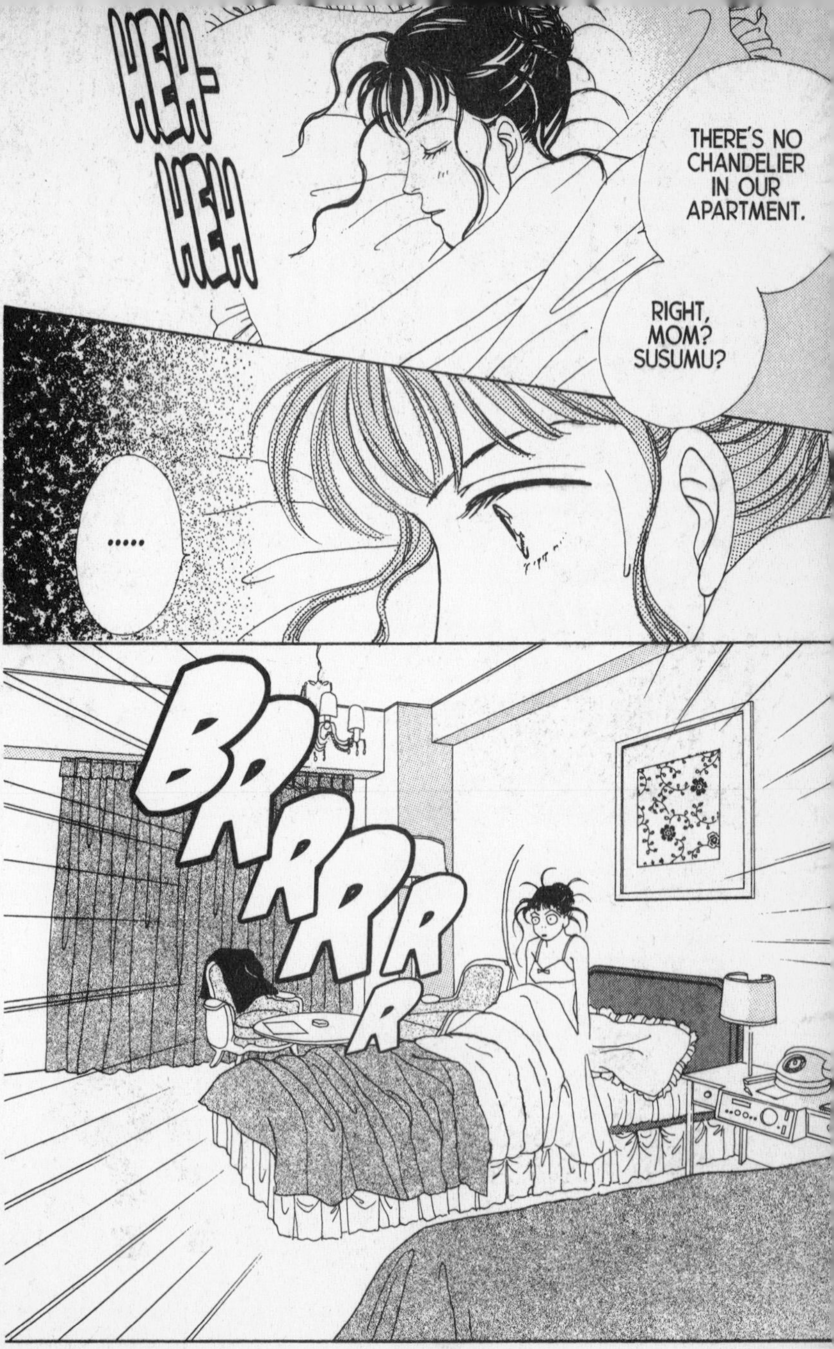
THERE'S NO CHANDELIER IN OUR APARTMENT.
RIGHT, MOM? SUSUMU?
HEA- HEA
.....
BRRRRR

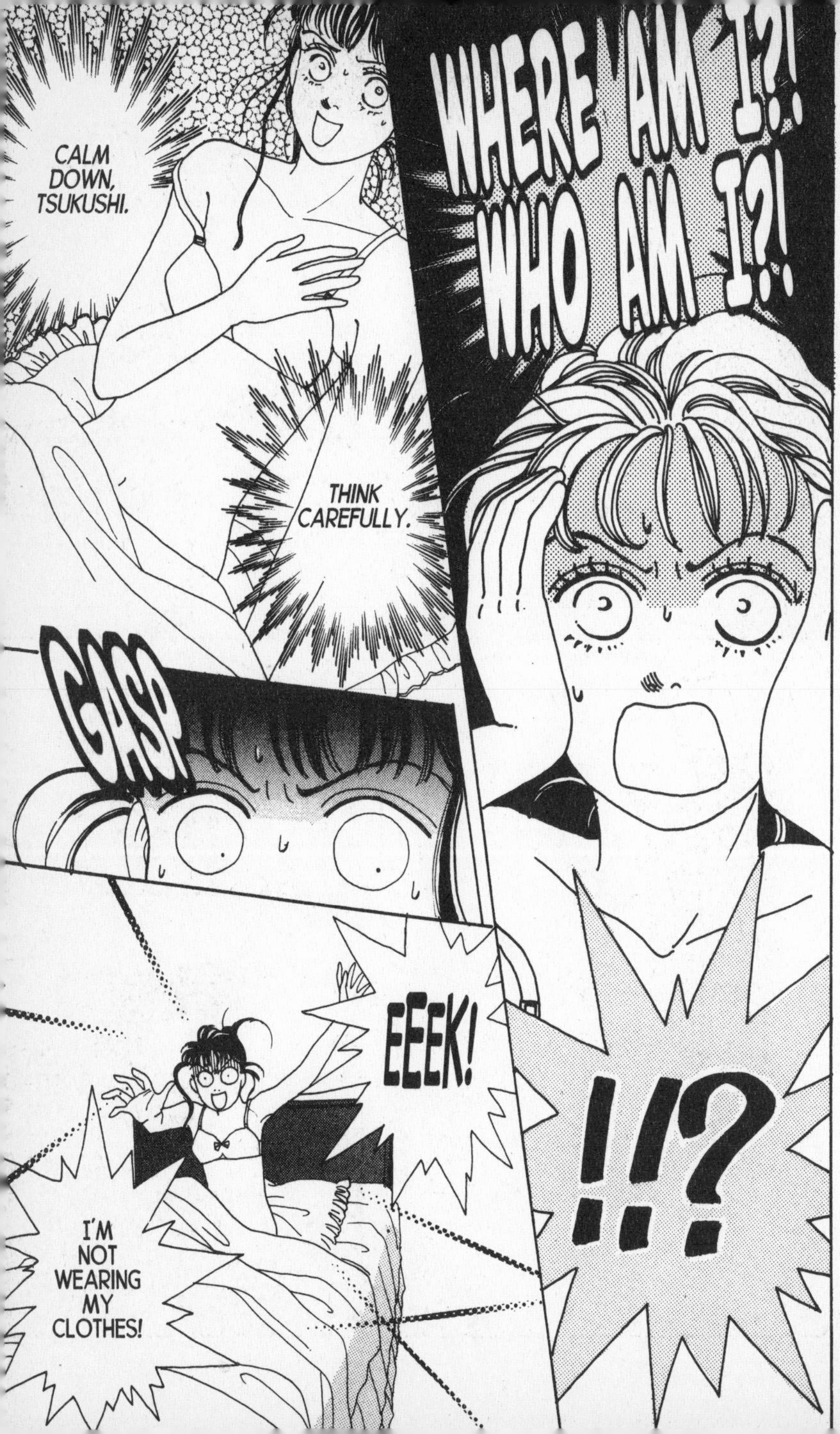
WHERE AM I?! WHO AM I?!
!!?
CALM DOWN, TSUKUSHI.
THINK CAREFULLY.
GASP
EEEK!
I'M NOT WEARING MY CLOTHES!

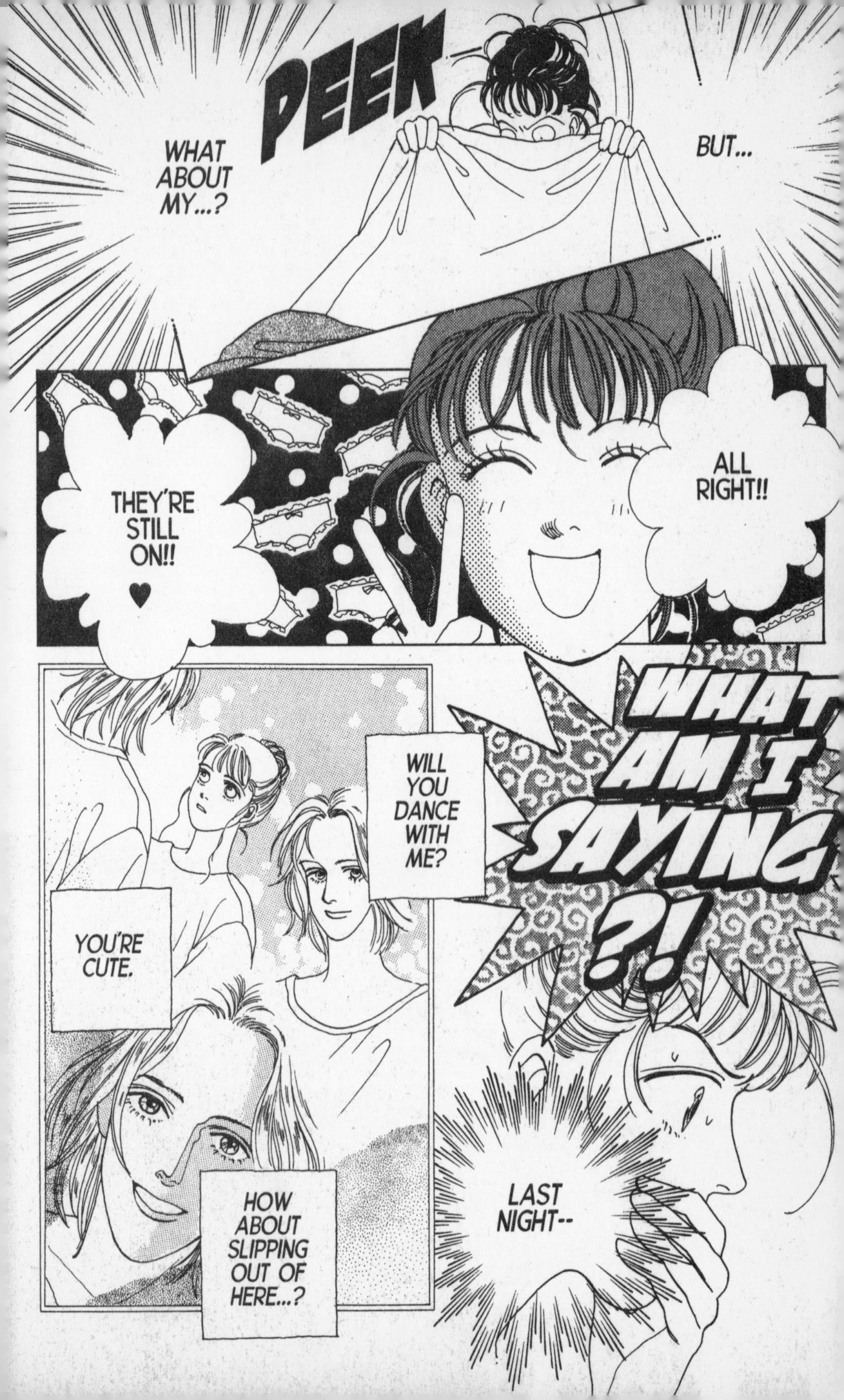
BUT...
PEEK
WHAT ABOUT MY...?
ALL RIGHT!!
THEY'RE STILL ON!! ♥
WHAT AM I SAYING ?!
LAST NIGHT--
WILL YOU DANCE WITH ME?
YOU'RE CUTE.
HOW ABOUT SLIPPING OUT OF HERE...?

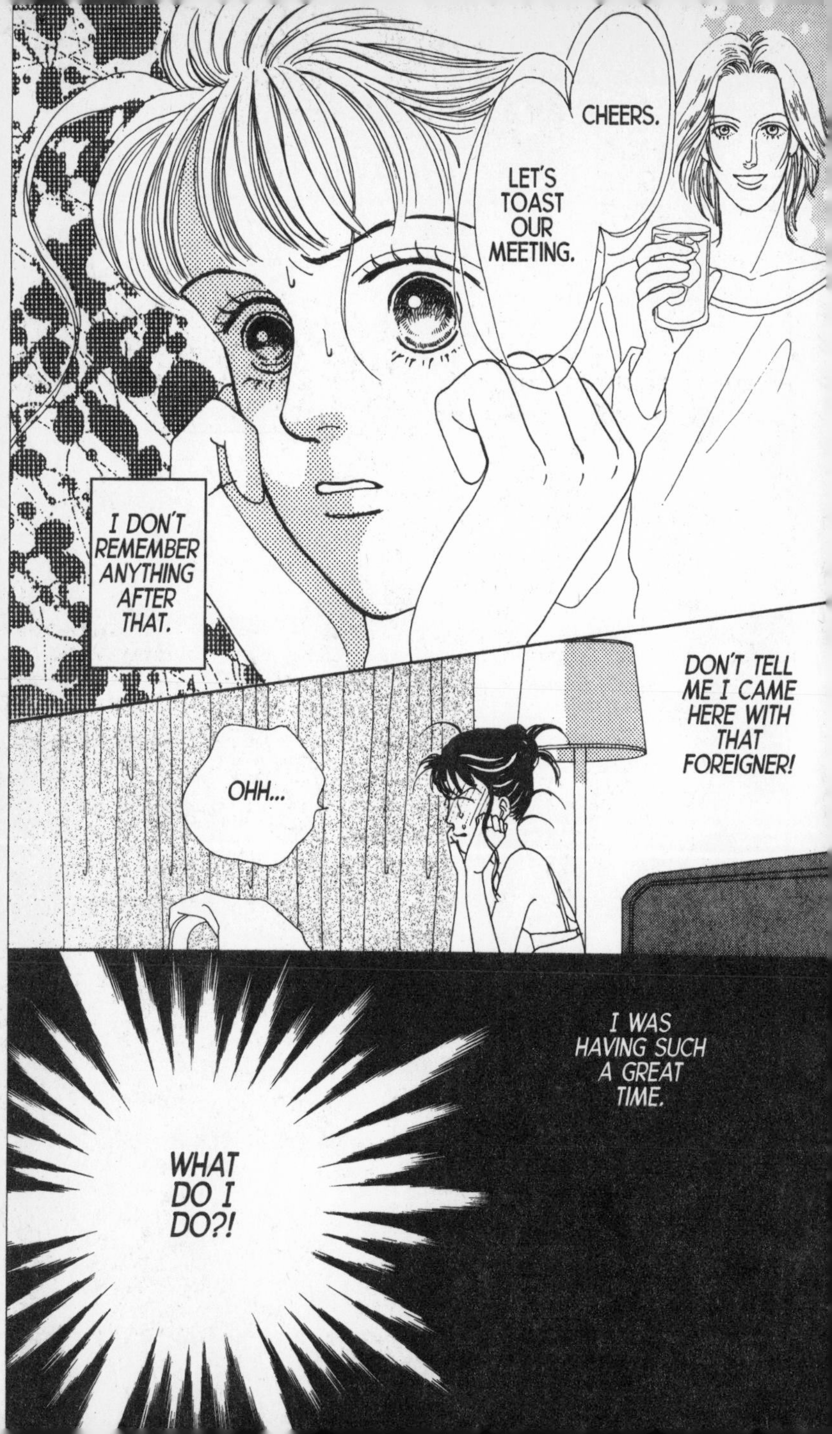
CHEERS.
LET'S TOAST OUR MEETING.
I DON'T REMEMBER ANYTHING AFTER THAT.
DON'T TELL ME I CAME HERE WITH THAT FOREIGNER!
OHH...
I WAS HAVING SUCH A GREAT TIME.
WHAT DO I DO?!

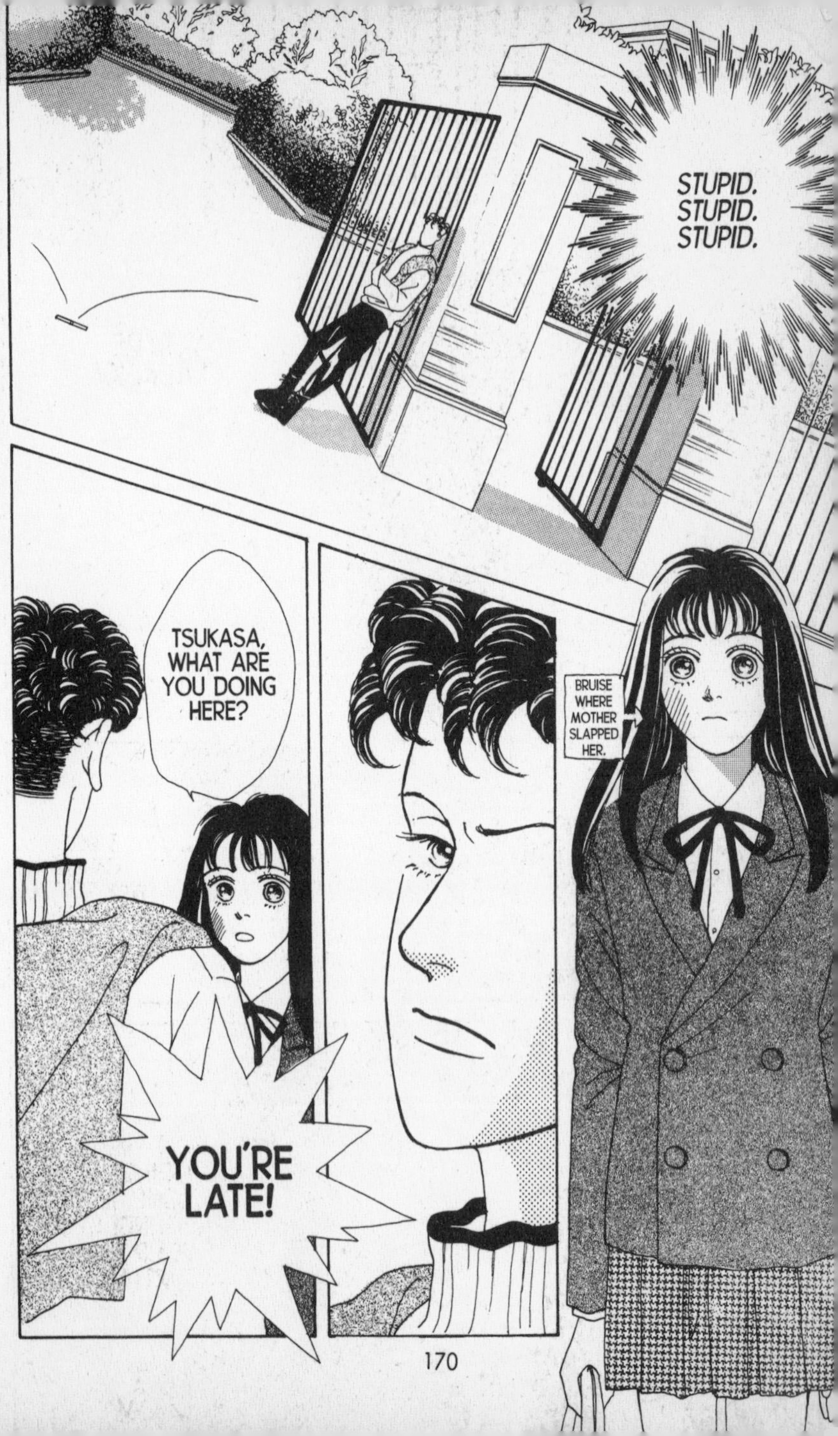
STUPID. STUPID. STUPID.
BRUISE WHERE MOTHER SLAPPED HER.
TSUKASA, WHAT ARE YOU DOING HERE?
YOU'RE LATE!

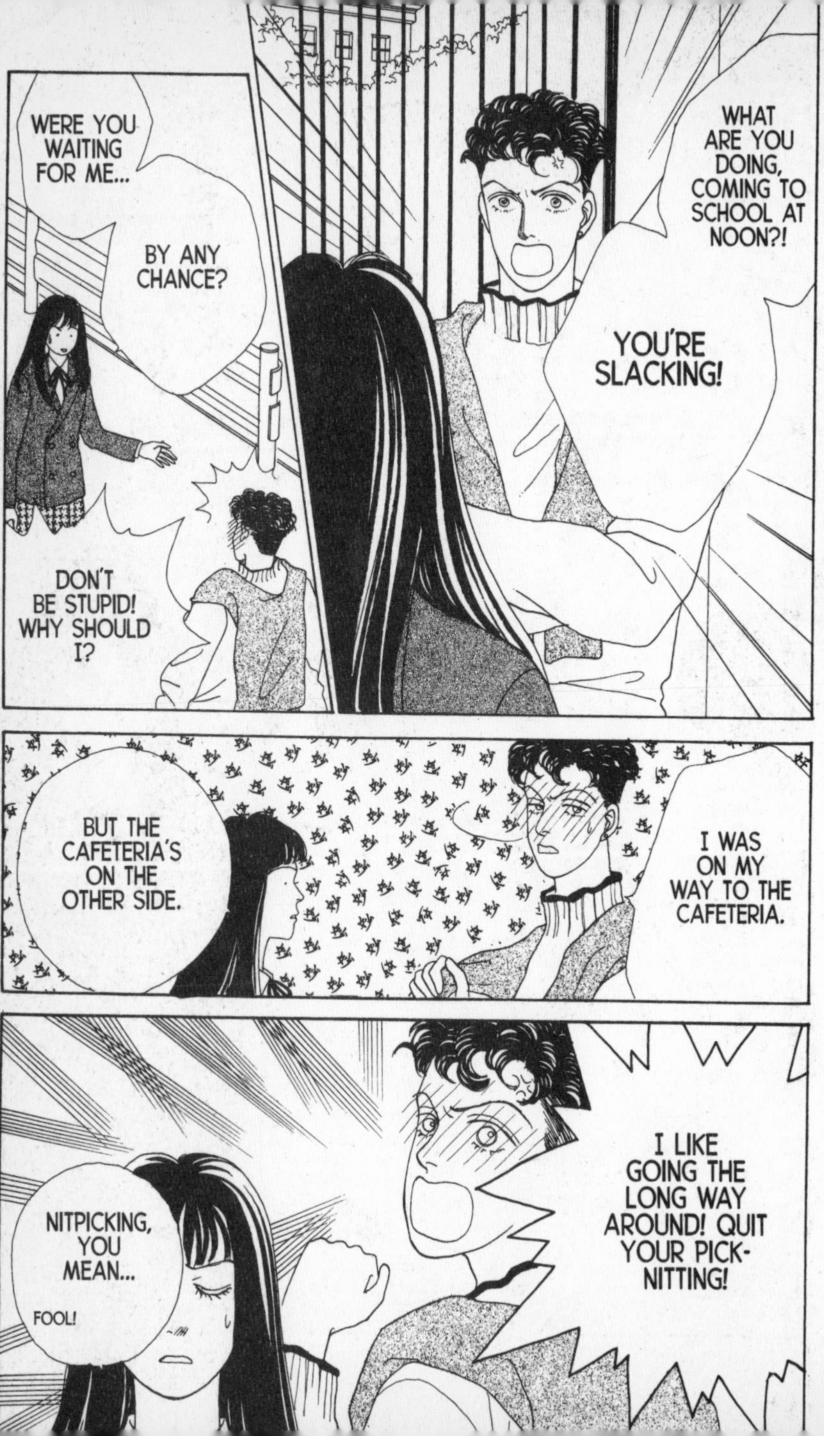
WHAT ARE YOU DOING, COMING TO SCHOOL AT NOON?!
YOU'RE SLACKING!
WERE YOU WAITING FOR ME... BY ANY CHANCE?
DON'T BE STUPID! WHY SHOULD I?
I WAS ON MY WAY TO THE CAFETERIA.
BUT THE CAFETERIA'S ON THE OTHER SIDE.
I LIKE GOING THE LONG WAY AROUND! QUIT YOUR PICK-NITTING!
NITPICKING, YOU MEAN...
FOOL!

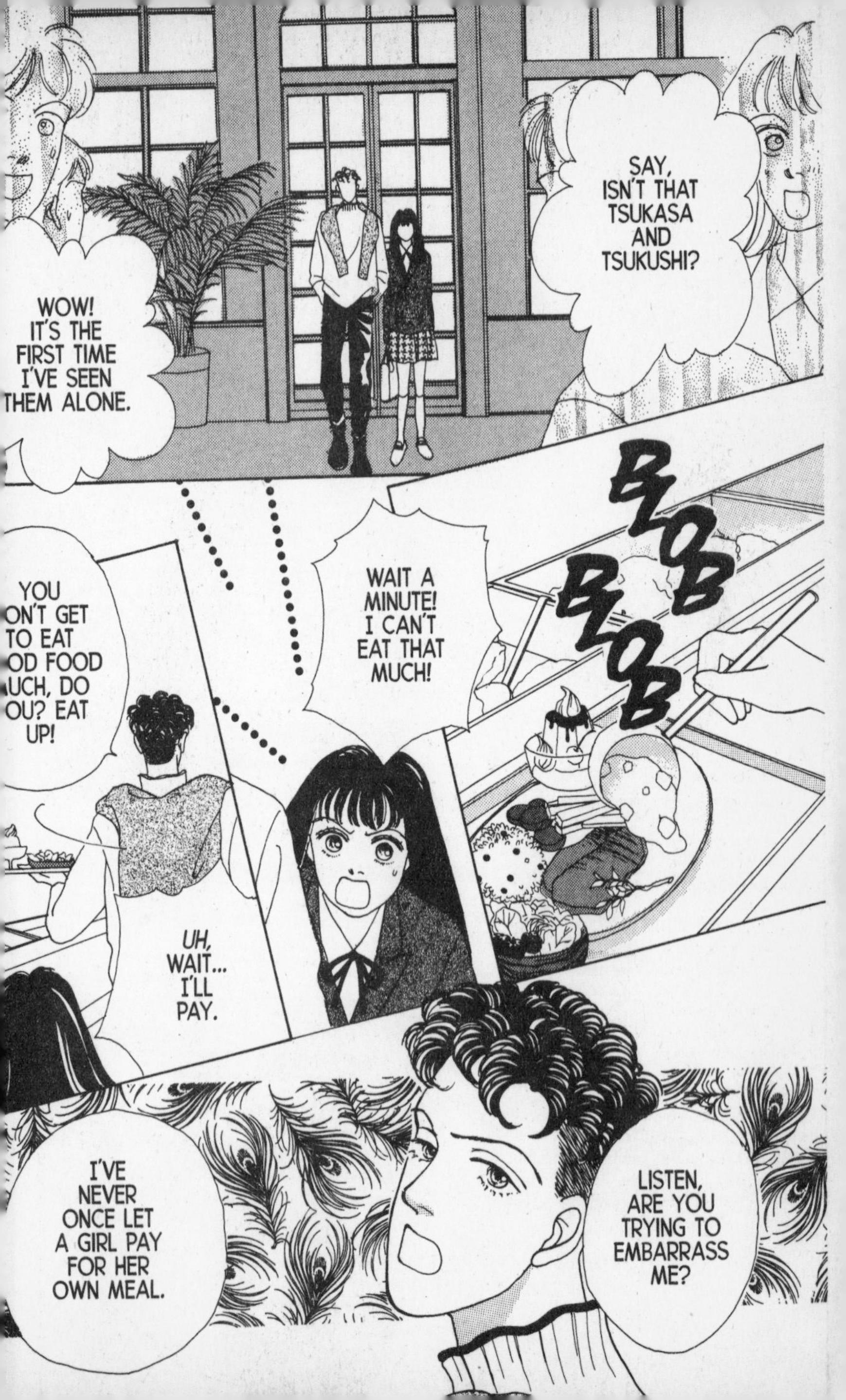
SAY, ISN'T THAT TSUKASA AND TSUKUSHI?
WOW! IT'S THE FIRST TIME I'VE SEEN THEM ALONE.
BLOB BLOB
WAIT A MINUTE! I CAN'T EAT THAT MUCH!
YOU ON'T GET TO EAT OD FOOD UCH, DO OU? EAT UP!
UH, WAIT... I'LL PAY.
LISTEN, ARE YOU TRYING TO EMBARRASS ME?
I'VE NEVER ONCE LET A GIRL PAY FOR HER OWN MEAL.

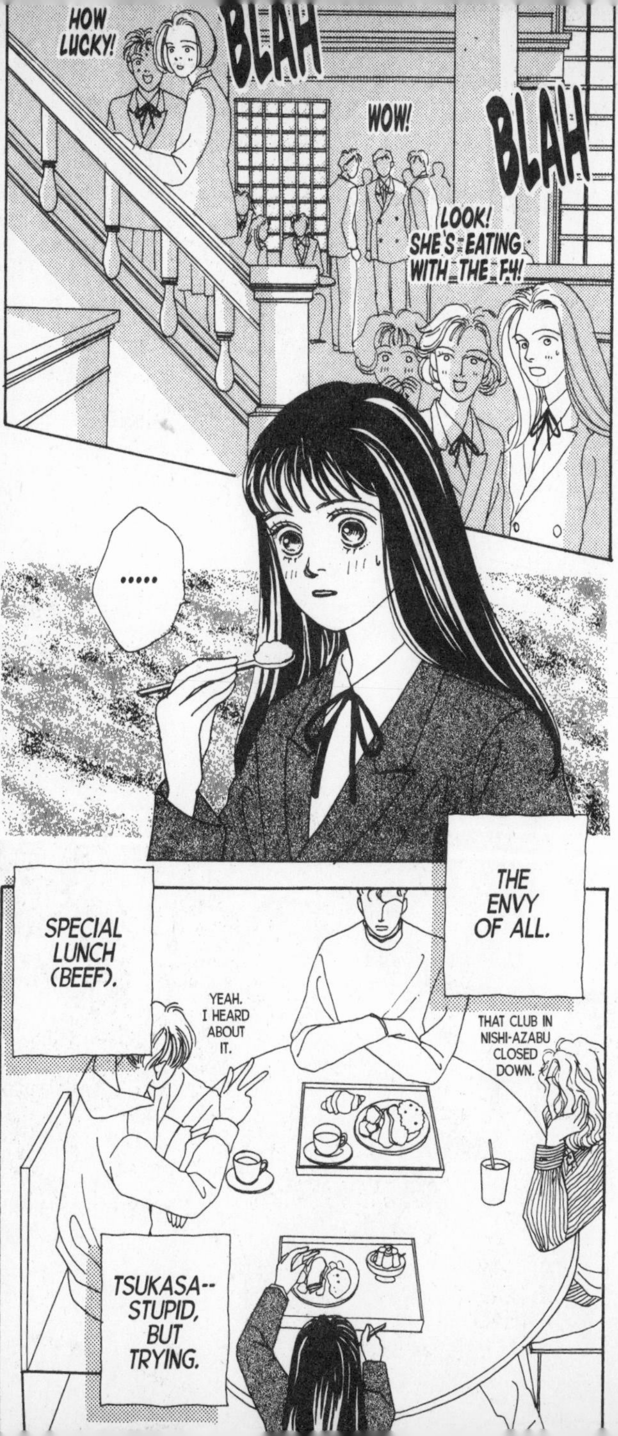
BLAH
LOOK! SHE'S EATING WITH THE F4!
WOW!
BLAH
HOW LUCKY!
......
THE ENVY OF ALL.
THAT CLUB IN NISHI-AZABU CLOSED DOWN.
YEAH. I HEARD ABOUT IT.
SPECIAL LUNCH (BEEF).
TSUKASA--STUPID, BUT TRYING.

13

On Fashion

I used to love black, too. Almost all my clothes were black NICOLE outfits.

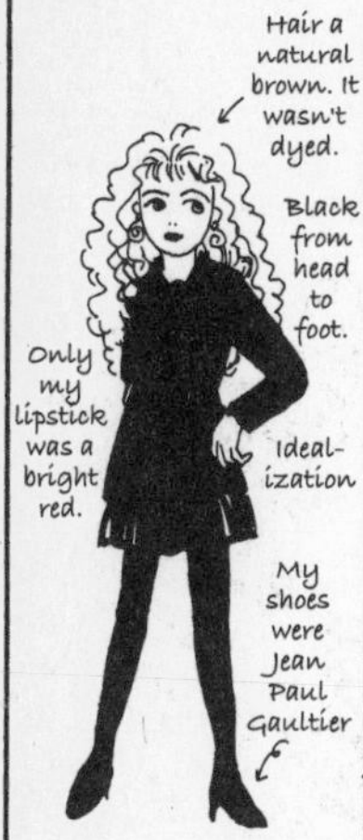
Hair a natural brown. It wasn't dyed.
Black from head to foot.
Only my lipstick was a bright red.
Idealization
My shoes were Jean Paul Gaultier

I had black, gray, and white--nothing but monotones--in my closet. Once, I suddenly wanted to wear pink, so I bought a pink Zucca sweater. Ever since then, the inside of my closet has been very colorful.

For some reason manga artists seem to love black. When I'd go out with a group of 5 or 6 manga artists we'd look like we belonged to some club. We'd all be wearing black with bright red lipstick and nail polish.

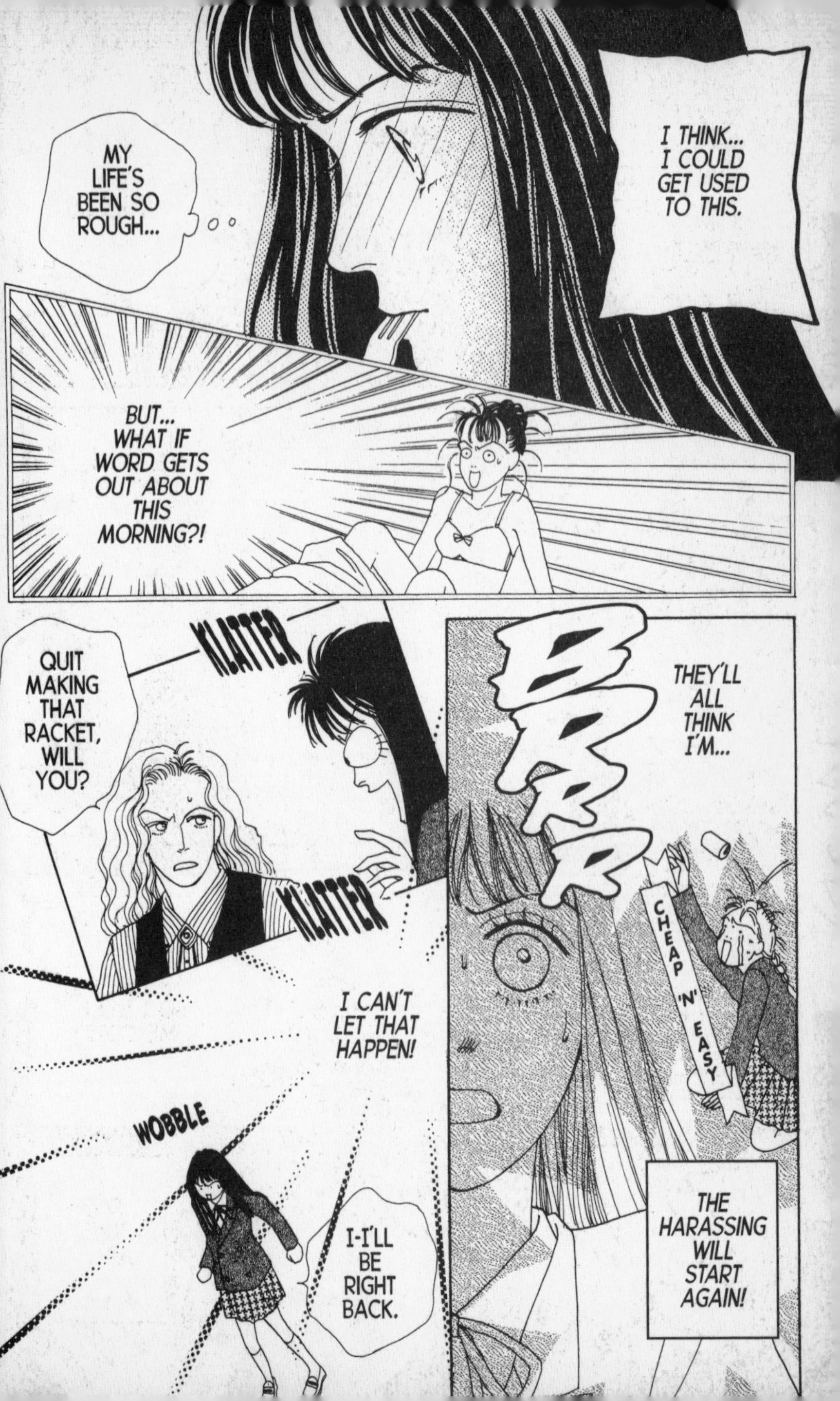
I THINK... I COULD GET USED TO THIS.
MY LIFE'S BEEN SO ROUGH...
BUT... WHAT IF WORD GETS OUT ABOUT THIS MORNING?!
THEY'LL ALL THINK I'M...
CHEAP 'N' EASY
THE HARASSING WILL START AGAIN!
KLATTER
QUIT MAKING THAT RACKET, WILL YOU?
KLATTER
I CAN'T LET THAT HAPPEN!
WOBBLE
I-I'LL BE RIGHT BACK.

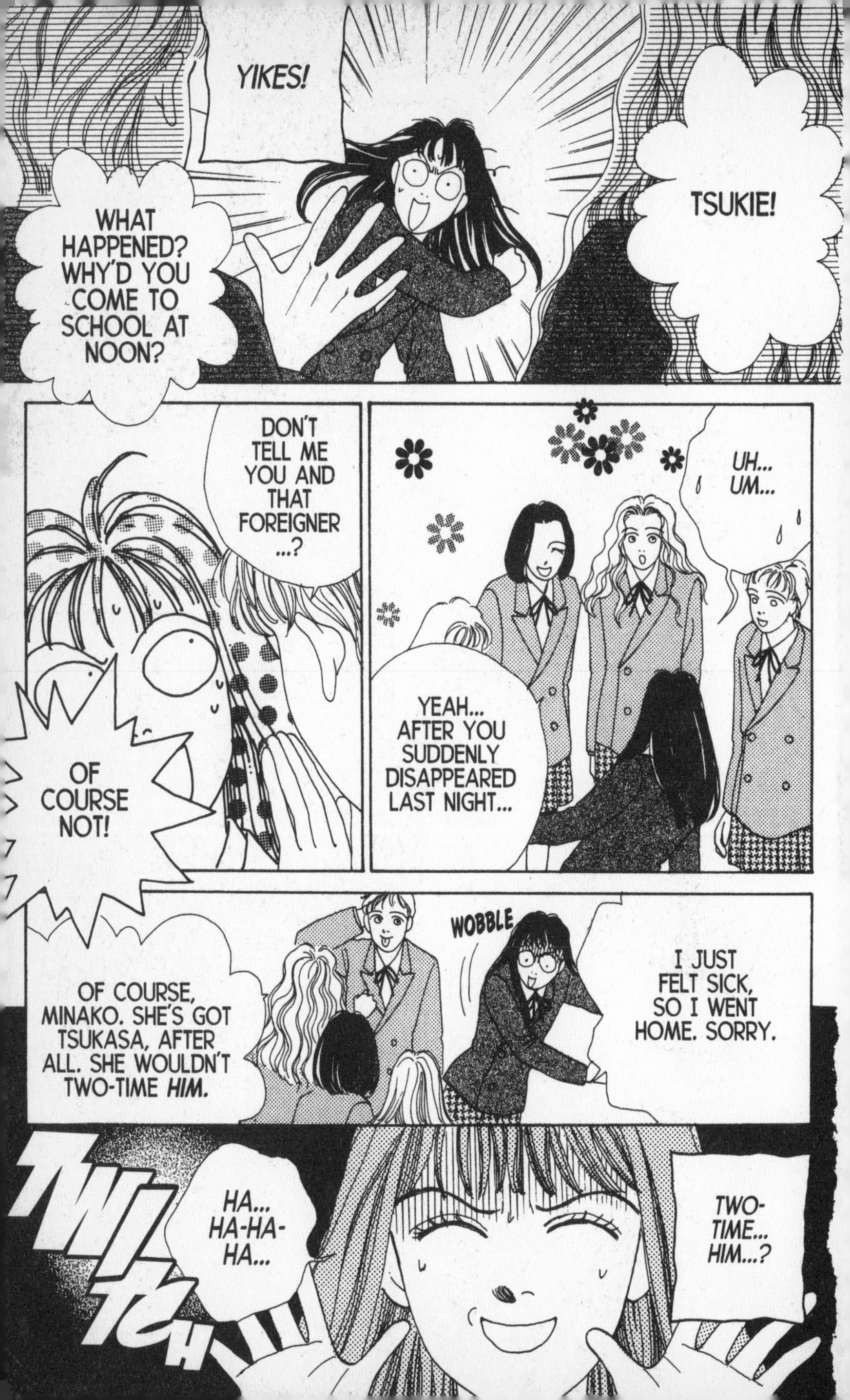
TSUKIE!
YIKES!
WHAT HAPPENED? WHY'D YOU COME TO SCHOOL AT NOON?
UH... UM...
YEAH... AFTER YOU SUDDENLY DISAPPEARED LAST NIGHT...
DON'T TELL ME YOU AND THAT FOREIGNER ...?
OF COURSE NOT!
I JUST FELT SICK, SO I WENT HOME. SORRY.
WOBBLE
OF COURSE, MINAKO. SHE'S GOT TSUKASA, AFTER ALL. SHE WOULDN'T TWO-TIME *HIM*.
TWO-TIME... HIM...?
HA... HA-HA-HA...
TWITCH

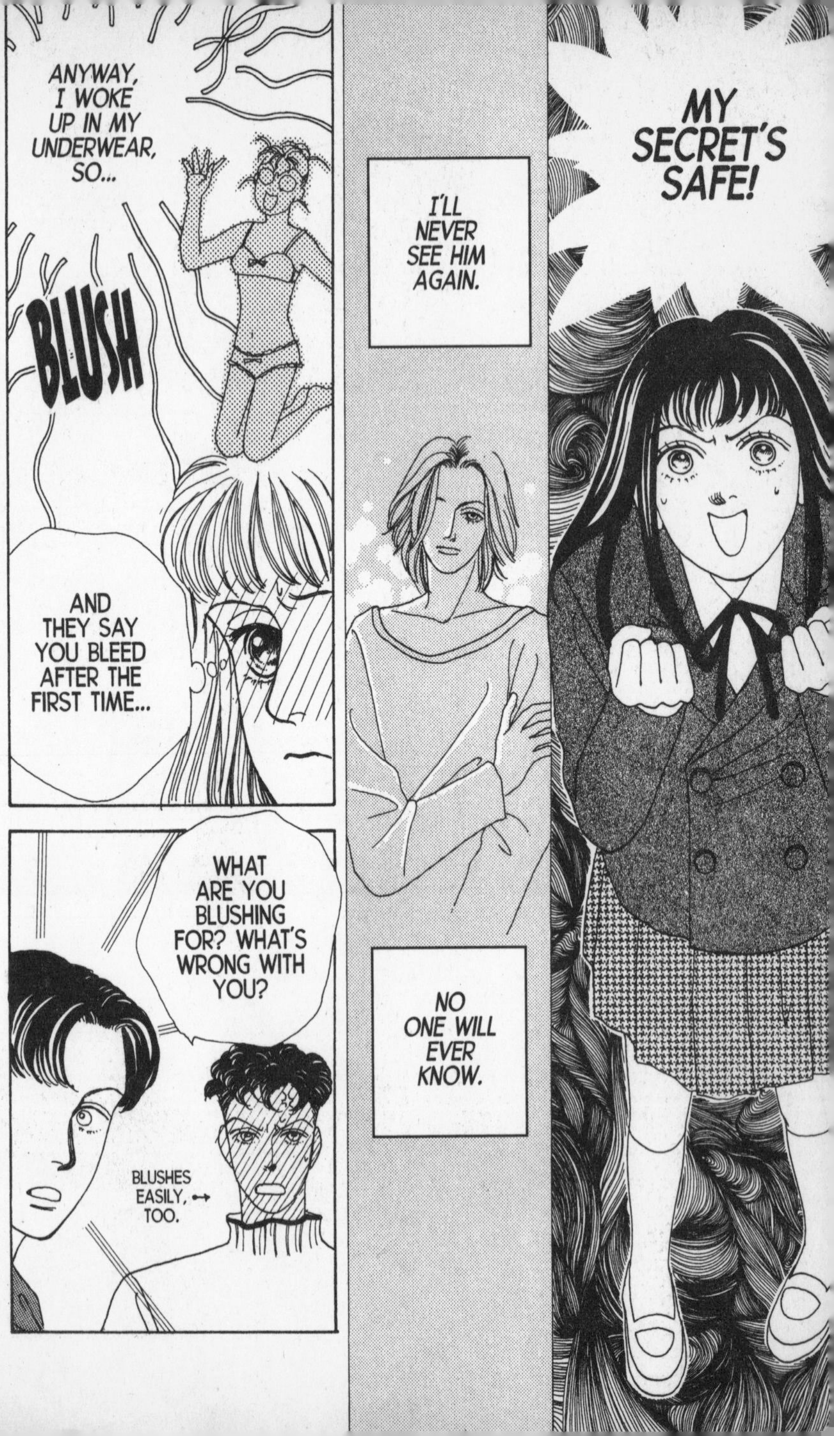
MY SECRET'S SAFE!
I'LL NEVER SEE HIM AGAIN.
NO ONE WILL EVER KNOW.
ANYWAY, I WOKE UP IN MY UNDERWEAR, SO...
BLUSH
AND THEY SAY YOU BLEED AFTER THE FIRST TIME...
WHAT ARE YOU BLUSHING FOR? WHAT'S WRONG WITH YOU?
BLUSHES EASILY, TOO.

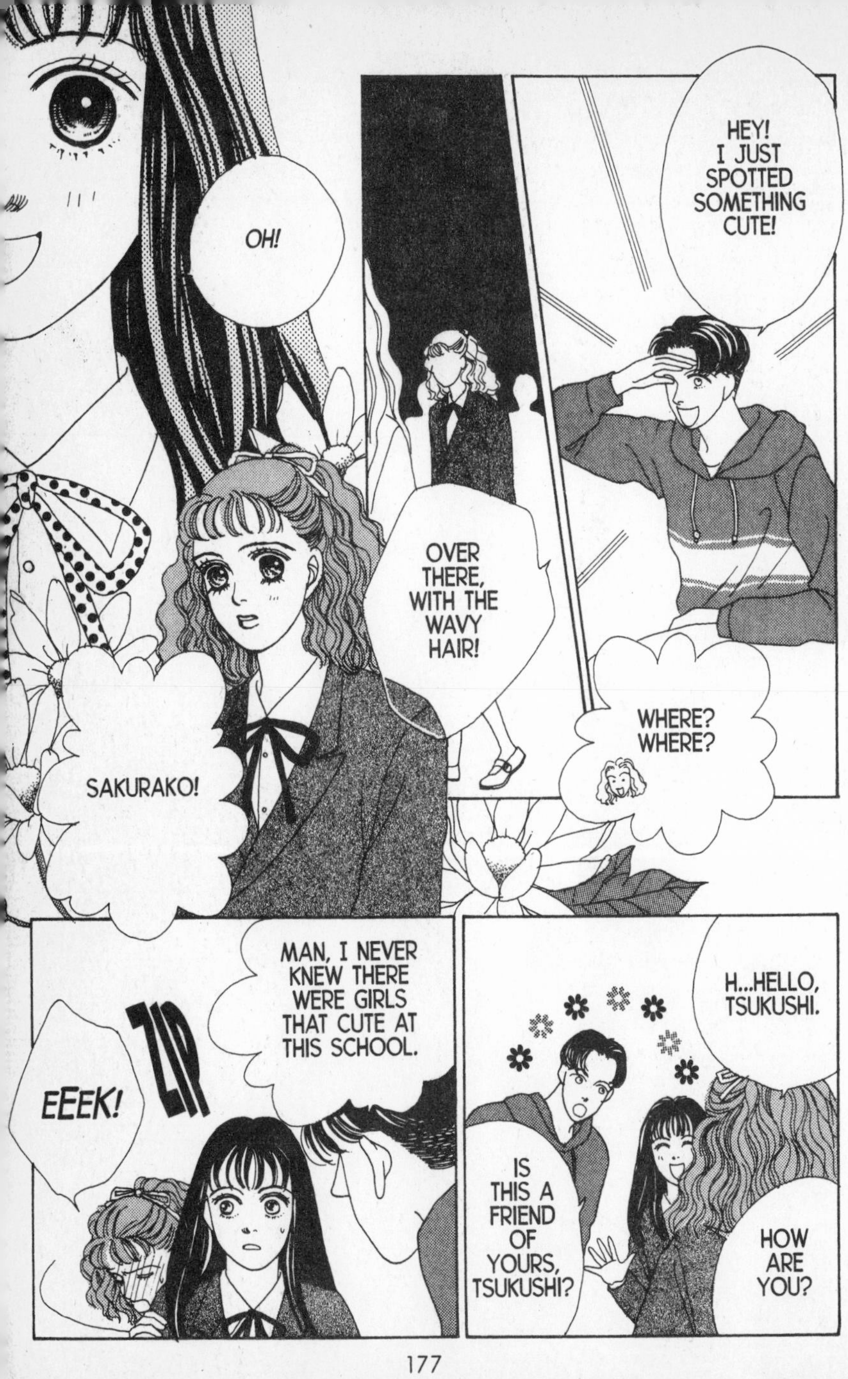
HEY! I JUST SPOTTED SOMETHING CUTE!
WHERE? WHERE?
OVER THERE, WITH THE WAVY HAIR!
OH!
SAKURAKO!
H...HELLO, TSUKUSHI.
HOW ARE YOU?
IS THIS A FRIEND OF YOURS, TSUKUSHI?
MAN, I NEVER KNEW THERE WERE GIRLS THAT CUTE AT THIS SCHOOL.
ZIP
EEEK!

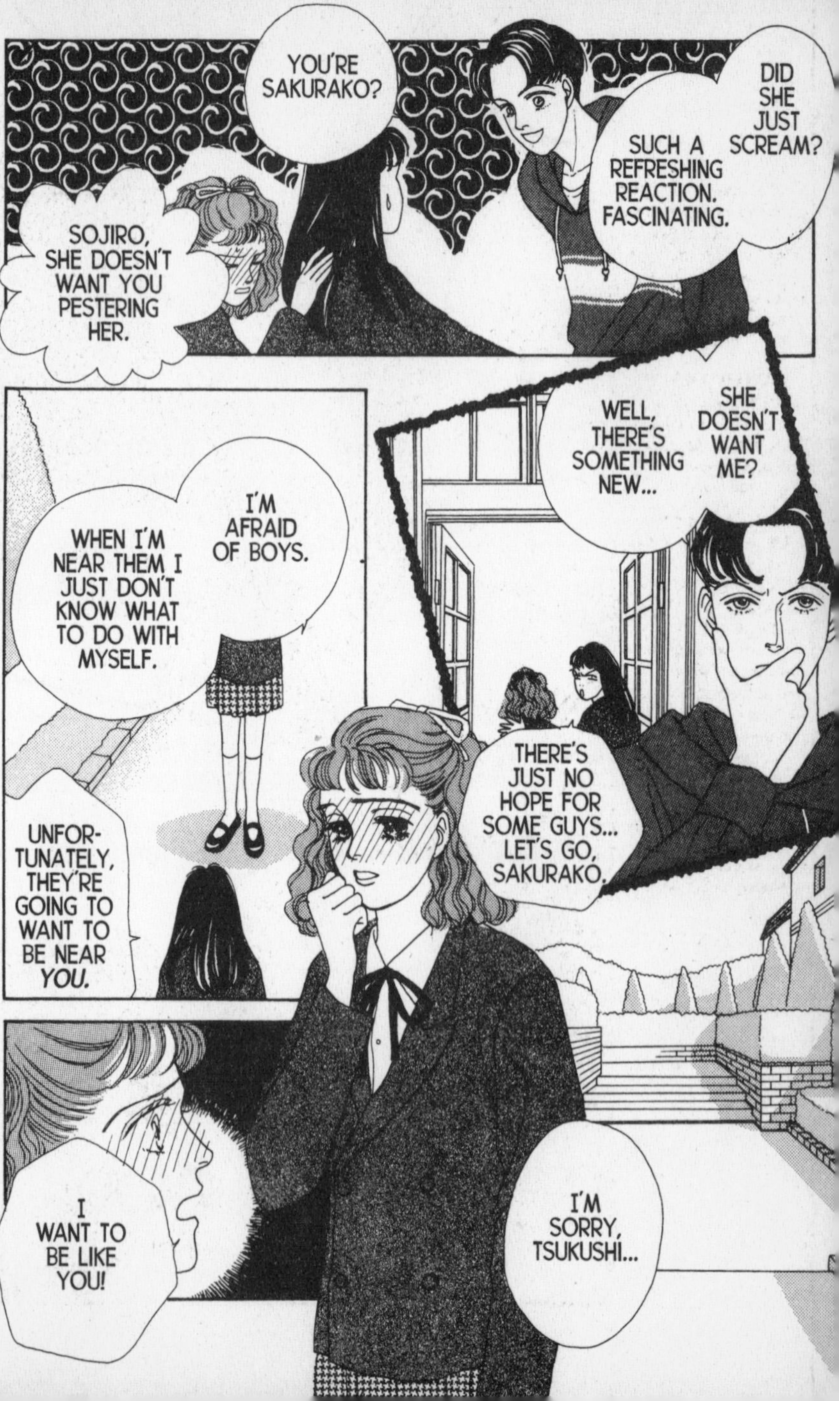
YOU'RE SAKURAKO?
DID SHE JUST SCREAM?
SUCH A REFRESHING REACTION. FASCINATING.
SOJIRO, SHE DOESN'T WANT YOU PESTERING HER.
SHE DOESN'T WANT ME?
WELL, THERE'S SOMETHING NEW...
THERE'S JUST NO HOPE FOR SOME GUYS... LET'S GO, SAKURAKO.
I'M AFRAID OF BOYS.
WHEN I'M NEAR THEM I JUST DON'T KNOW WHAT TO DO WITH MYSELF.
UNFORTUNATELY, THEY'RE GOING TO WANT TO BE NEAR *YOU.*
I'M SORRY, TSUKUSHI...
I WANT TO BE LIKE YOU!

This is the last of my little essays for this volume. It's getting difficult because I'm running out of things to write about. What'll I write about in Volume 5?

Thank you for reading everything I've written. I'll do my best to continue drawing as much as I can.

Lately, I've gotten a lot of letters from people who are battling illnesses, telling me that my manga cheers them up. It makes me happy to hear that. As a manga artist, it's always been my dream to be able to cheer others up. Please keep fighting. I'll be praying for you.

I'll see you in Volume 5. Good-bye!

Yoko Kamio

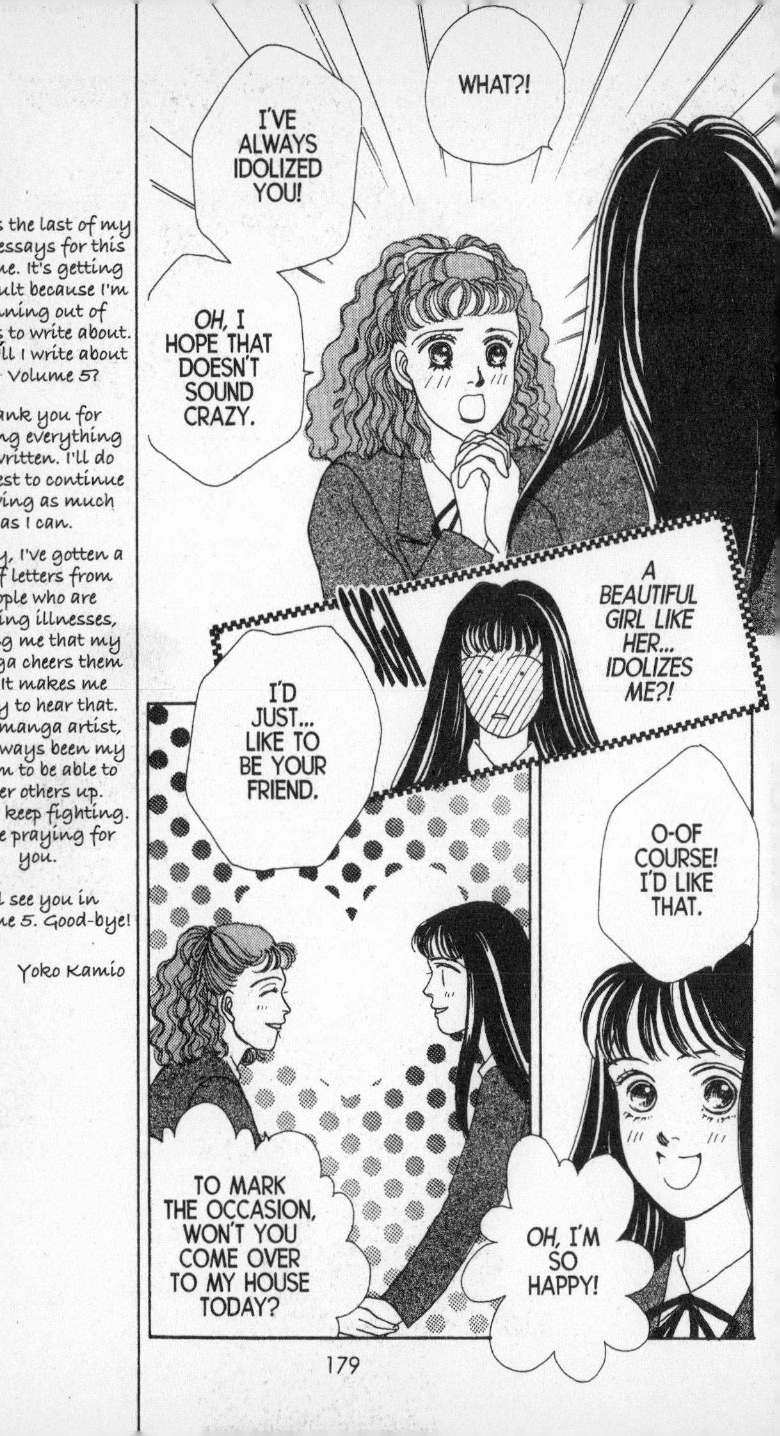
WHAT?!
I'VE ALWAYS IDOLIZED YOU!
OH, I HOPE THAT DOESN'T SOUND CRAZY.
A BEAUTIFUL GIRL LIKE HER... IDOLIZES ME?!
I'D JUST... LIKE TO BE YOUR FRIEND.
O-OF COURSE! I'D LIKE THAT.
OH, I'M SO HAPPY!
TO MARK THE OCCASION, WON'T YOU COME OVER TO MY HOUSE TODAY?

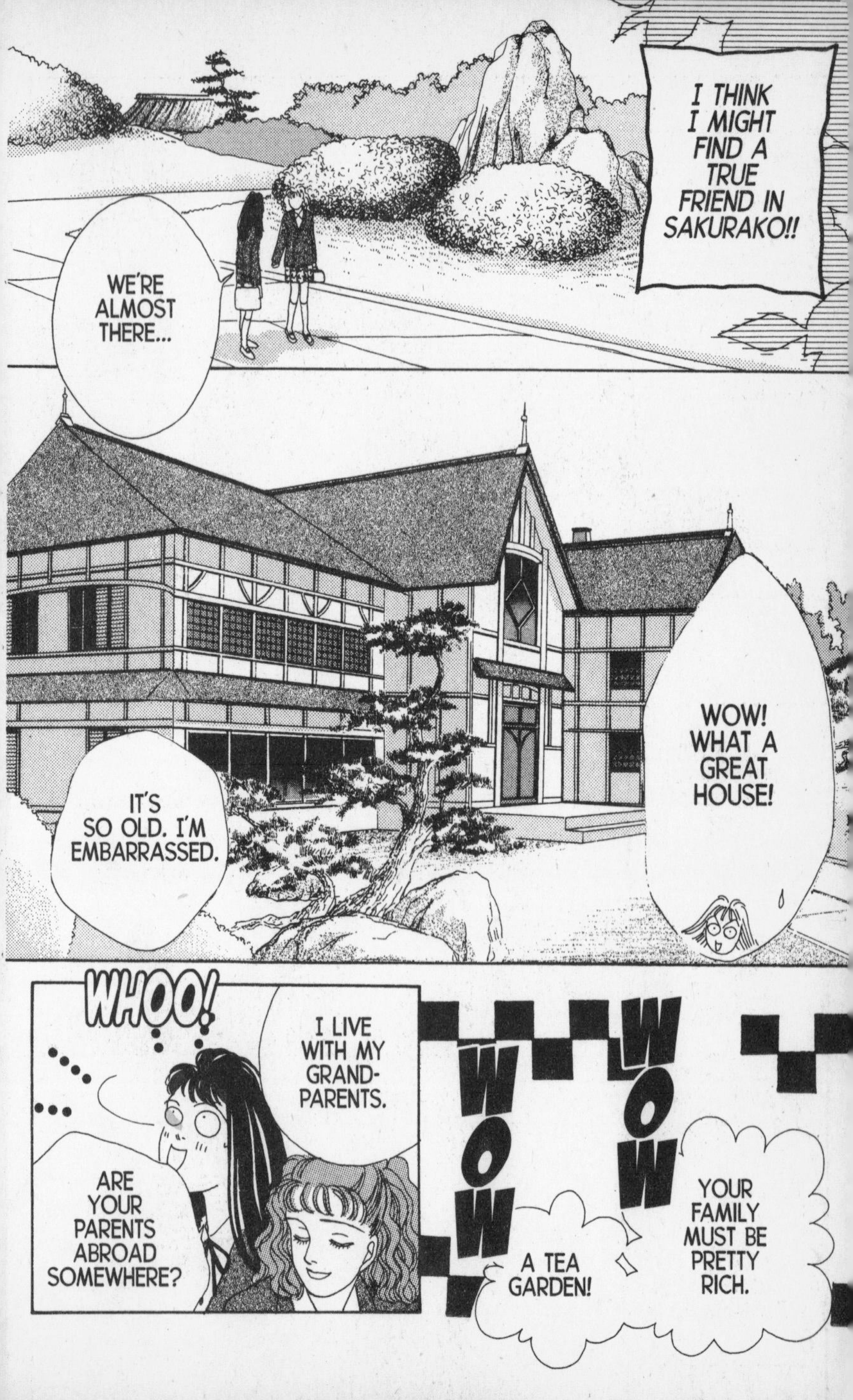
I THINK I MIGHT FIND A TRUE FRIEND IN SAKURAKO!!
WE'RE ALMOST THERE...
WOW! WHAT A GREAT HOUSE!
IT'S SO OLD. I'M EMBARRASSED.
WOW
WOW WOW
YOUR FAMILY MUST BE PRETTY RICH.
A TEA GARDEN!
WHOO!
I LIVE WITH MY GRAND-PARENTS.
ARE YOUR PARENTS ABROAD SOMEWHERE?

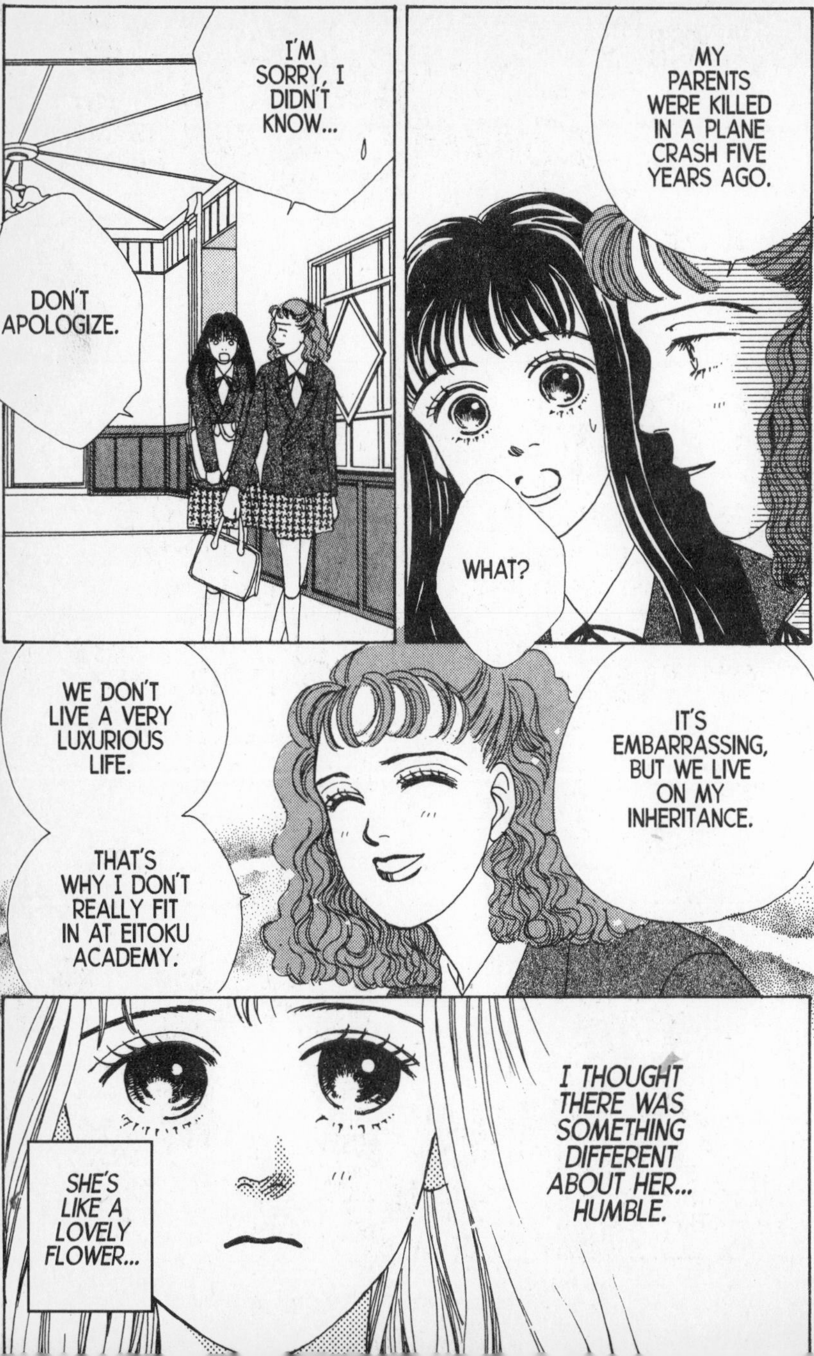
MY PARENTS WERE KILLED IN A PLANE CRASH FIVE YEARS AGO.
WHAT?
I'M SORRY, I DIDN'T KNOW...
DON'T APOLOGIZE.
IT'S EMBARRASSING, BUT WE LIVE ON MY INHERITANCE.
WE DON'T LIVE A VERY LUXURIOUS LIFE.
THAT'S WHY I DON'T REALLY FIT IN AT EITOKU ACADEMY.
I THOUGHT THERE WAS SOMETHING DIFFERENT ABOUT HER... HUMBLE.
SHE'S LIKE A LOVELY FLOWER...

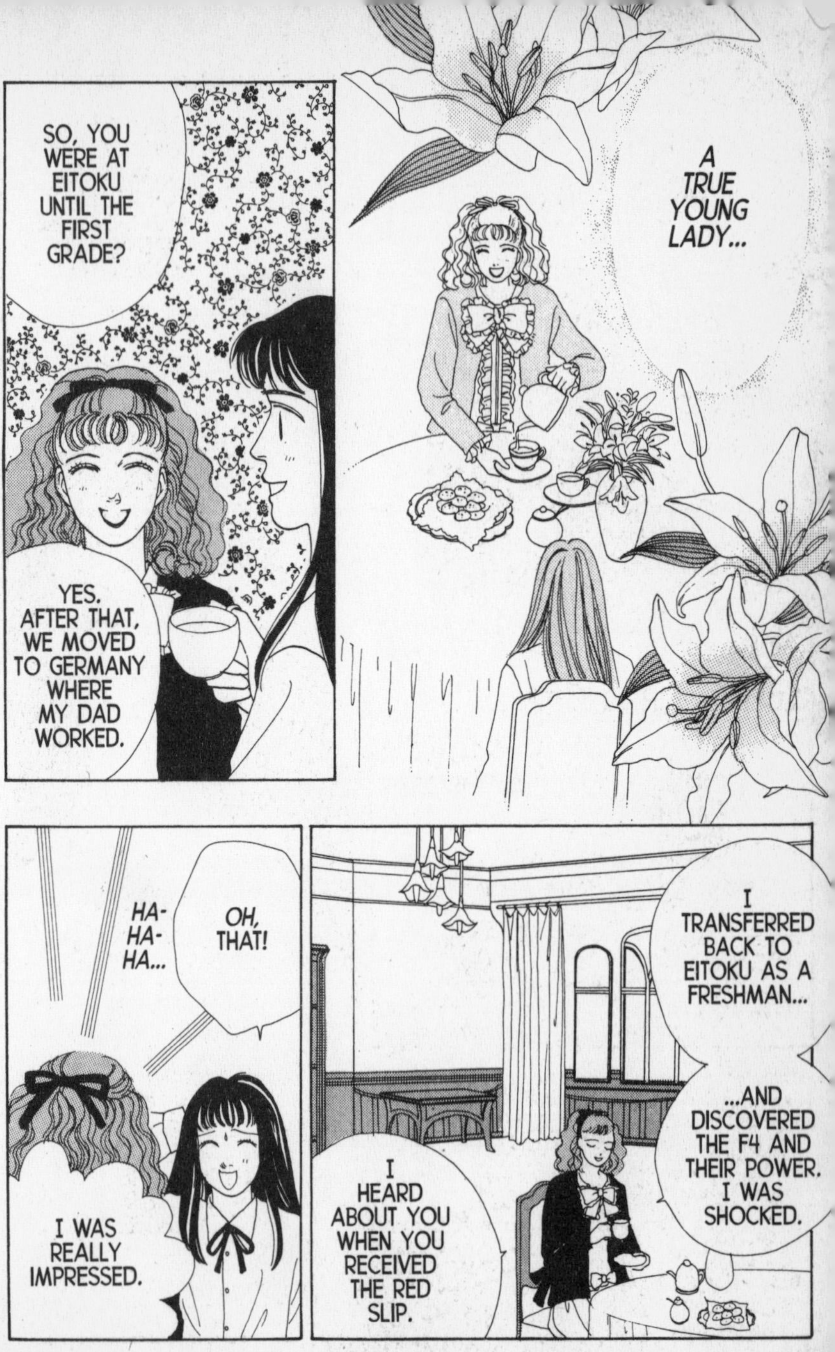
A TRUE YOUNG LADY...
SO, YOU WERE AT EITOKU UNTIL THE FIRST GRADE?
YES. AFTER THAT, WE MOVED TO GERMANY WHERE MY DAD WORKED.
I TRANSFERRED BACK TO EITOKU AS A FRESHMAN...
...AND DISCOVERED THE F4 AND THEIR POWER. I WAS SHOCKED.
I HEARD ABOUT YOU WHEN YOU RECEIVED THE RED SLIP.
OH, THAT!
HA-HA-HA...
I WAS REALLY IMPRESSED.

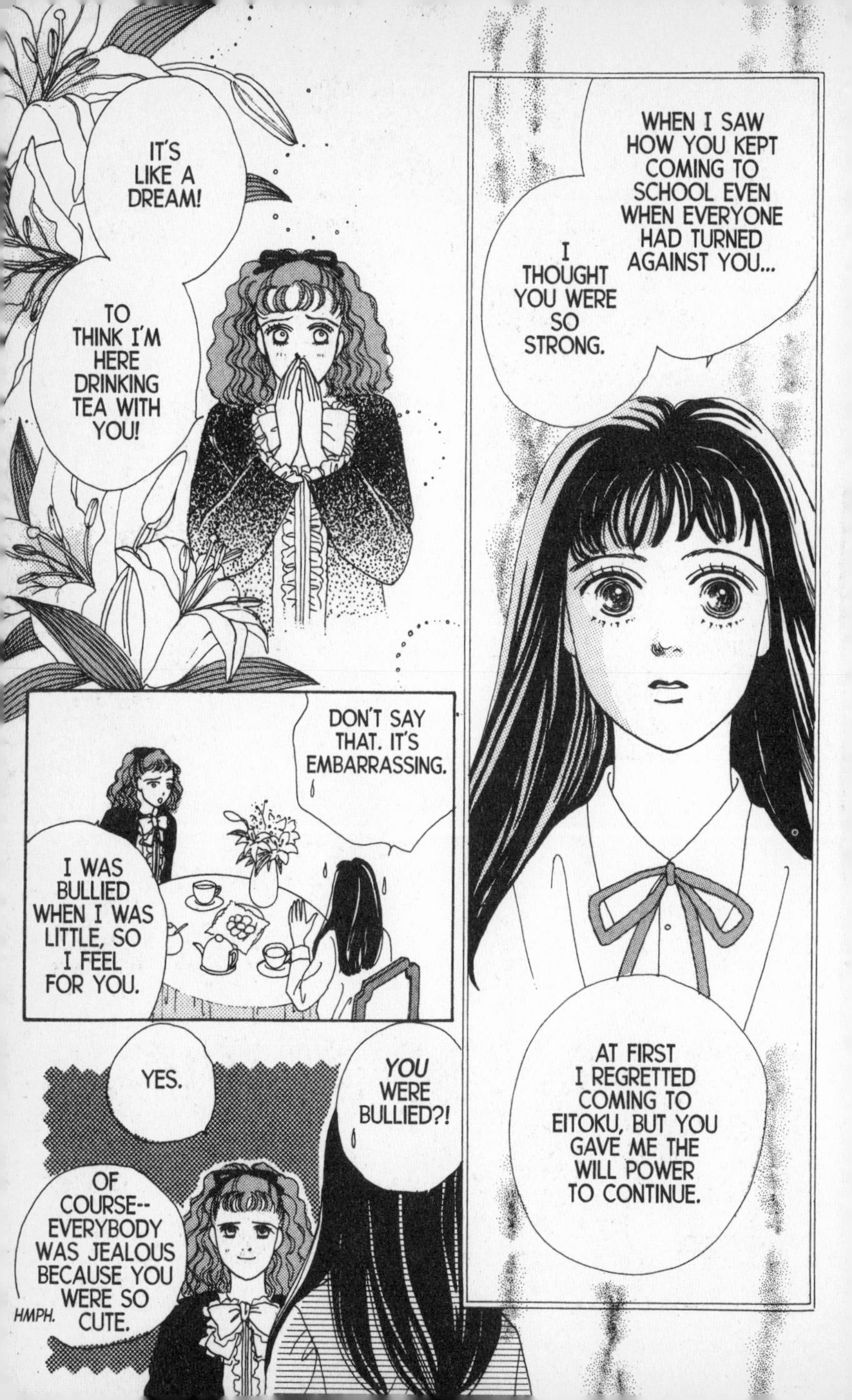
WHEN I SAW HOW YOU KEPT COMING TO SCHOOL EVEN WHEN EVERYONE HAD TURNED AGAINST YOU...
I THOUGHT YOU WERE SO STRONG.
AT FIRST I REGRETTED COMING TO EITOKU, BUT YOU GAVE ME THE WILL POWER TO CONTINUE.
IT'S LIKE A DREAM!
TO THINK I'M HERE DRINKING TEA WITH YOU!
DON'T SAY THAT. IT'S EMBARRASSING.
I WAS BULLIED WHEN I WAS LITTLE, SO I FEEL FOR YOU.
YOU WERE BULLIED?!
YES.
OF COURSE-- EVERYBODY WAS JEALOUS BECAUSE YOU WERE SO CUTE.
HMPH.

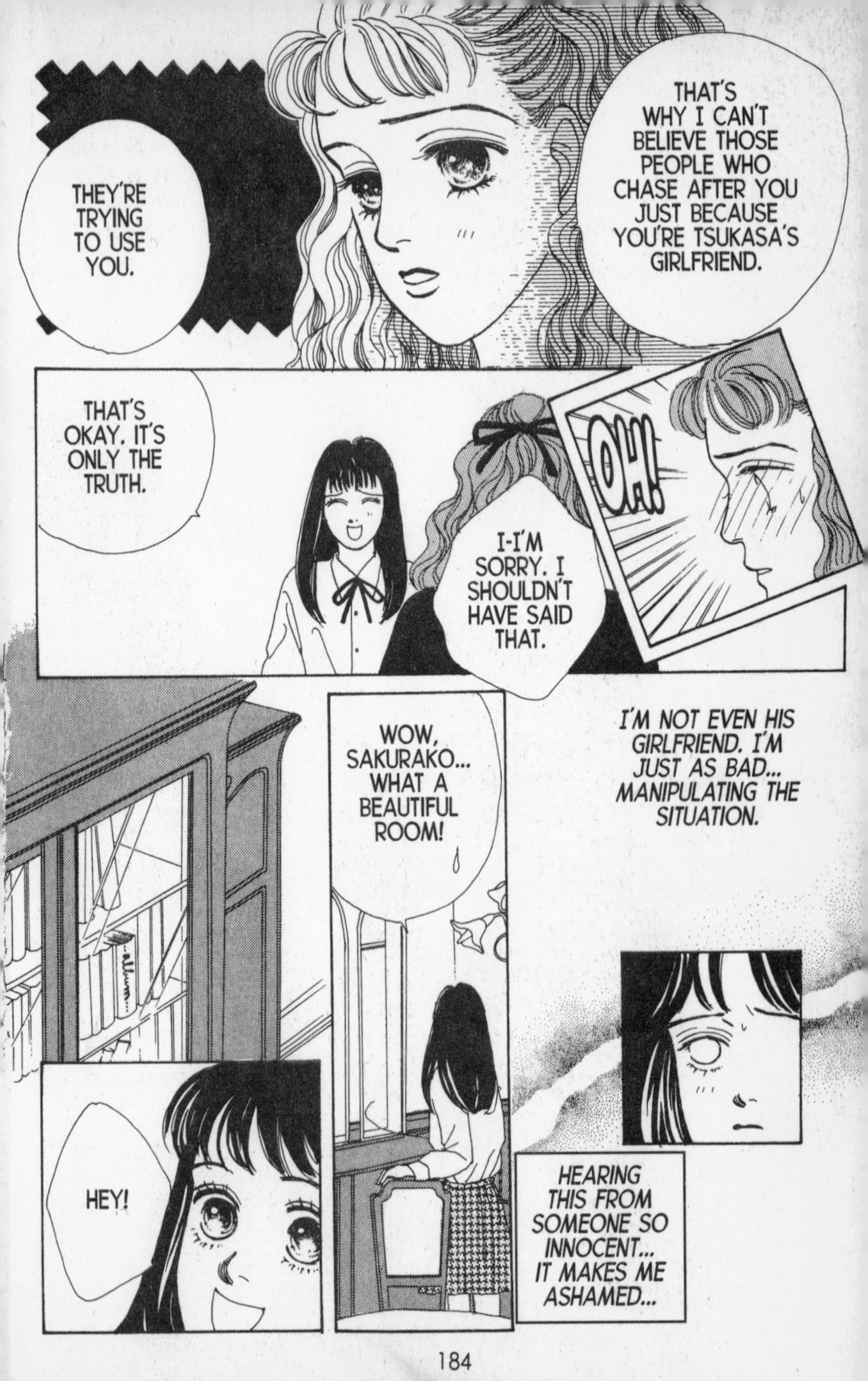

THAT'S WHY I CAN'T BELIEVE THOSE PEOPLE WHO CHASE AFTER YOU JUST BECAUSE YOU'RE TSUKASA'S GIRLFRIEND.
THEY'RE TRYING TO USE YOU.
OH!
I-I'M SORRY. I SHOULDN'T HAVE SAID THAT.
THAT'S OKAY. IT'S ONLY THE TRUTH.
I'M NOT EVEN HIS GIRLFRIEND. I'M JUST AS BAD... MANIPULATING THE SITUATION.
HEARING THIS FROM SOMEONE SO INNOCENT... IT MAKES ME ASHAMED...
WOW, SAKURAKO... WHAT A BEAUTIFUL ROOM!
HEY!

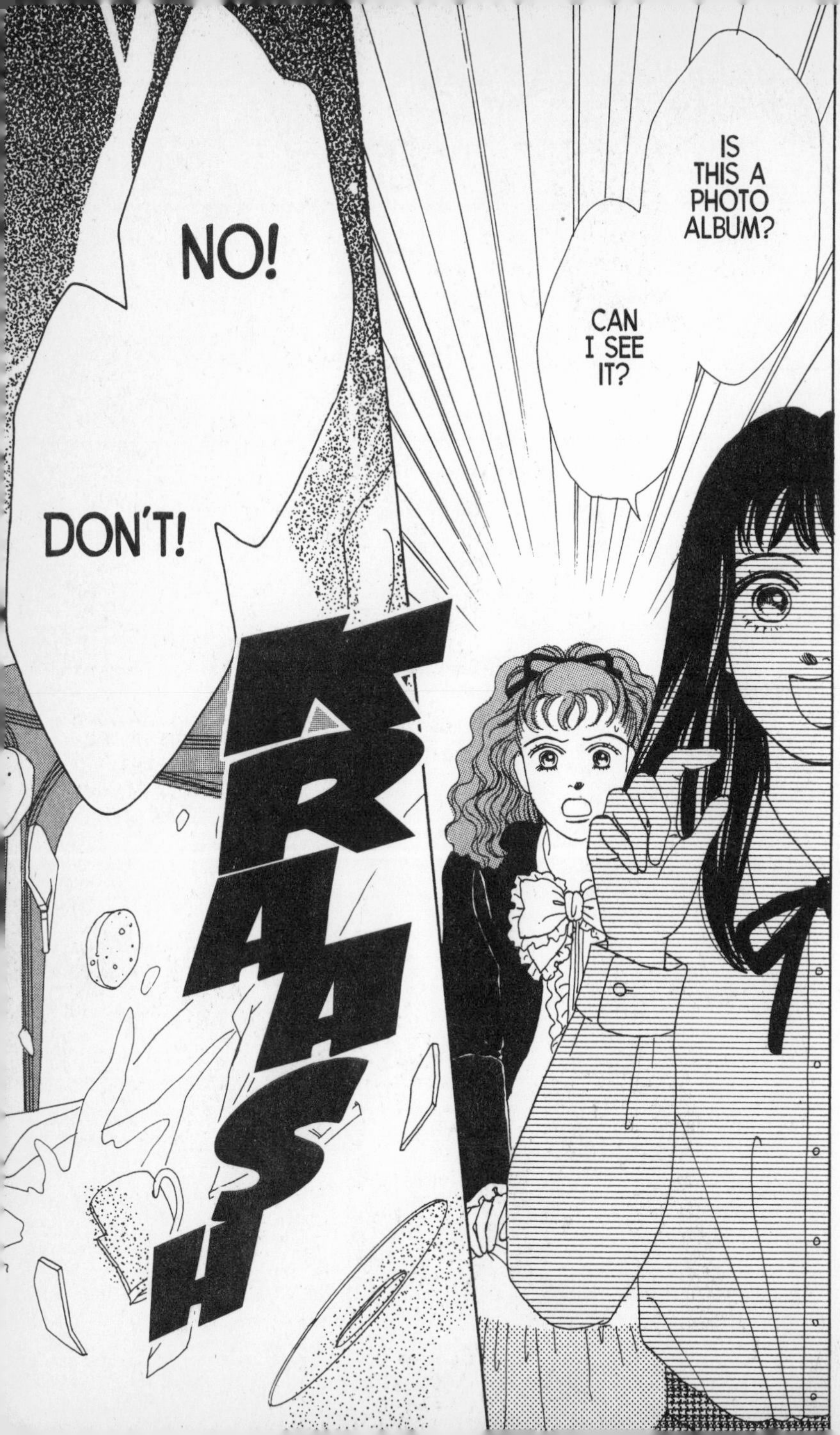
IS THIS A PHOTO ALBUM?
CAN I SEE IT?
NO!
DON'T!
KRAASH!

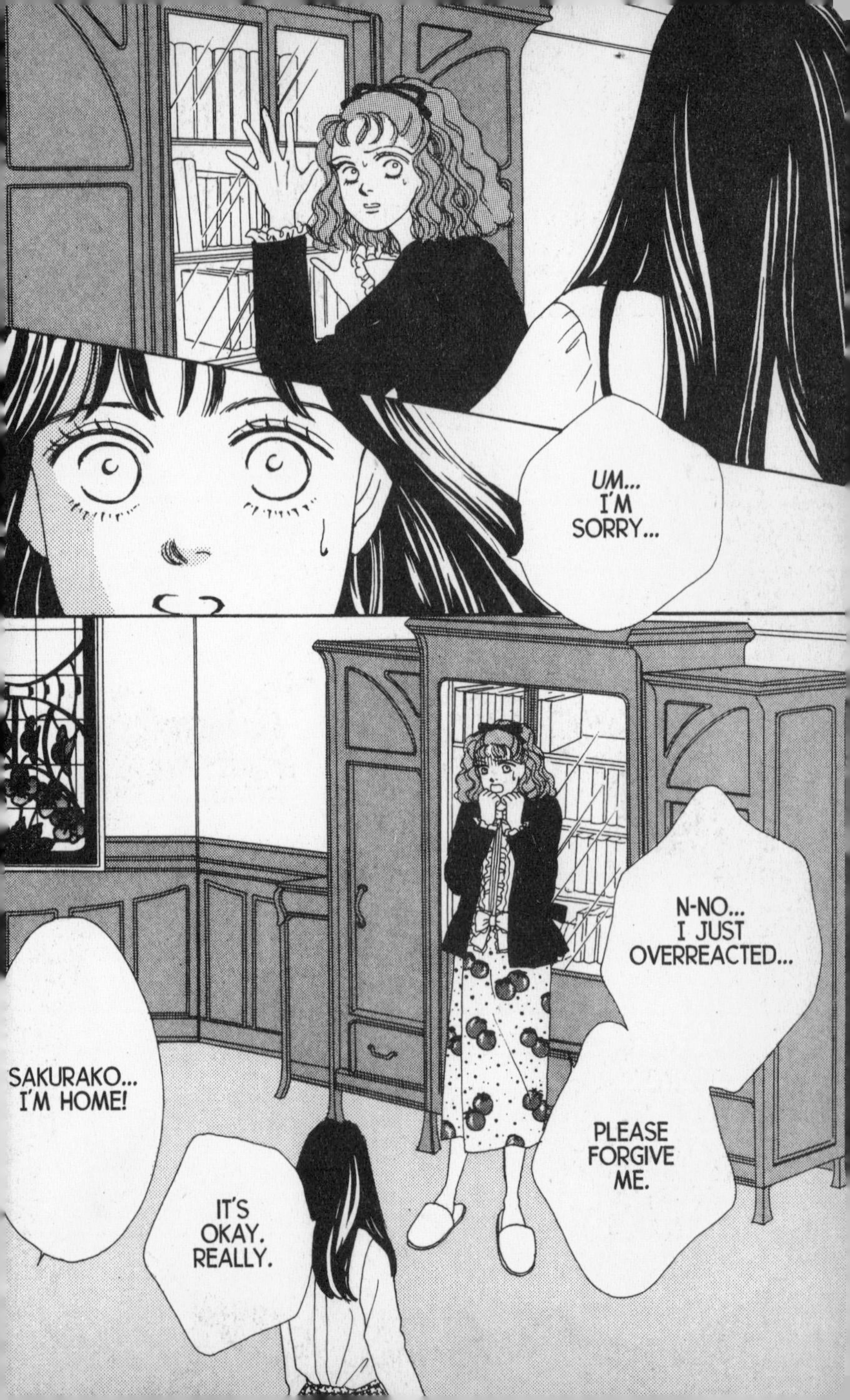
UM... I'M SORRY...
N-NO... I JUST OVERREACTED...
PLEASE FORGIVE ME.
IT'S OKAY. REALLY.
SAKURAKO... I'M HOME!

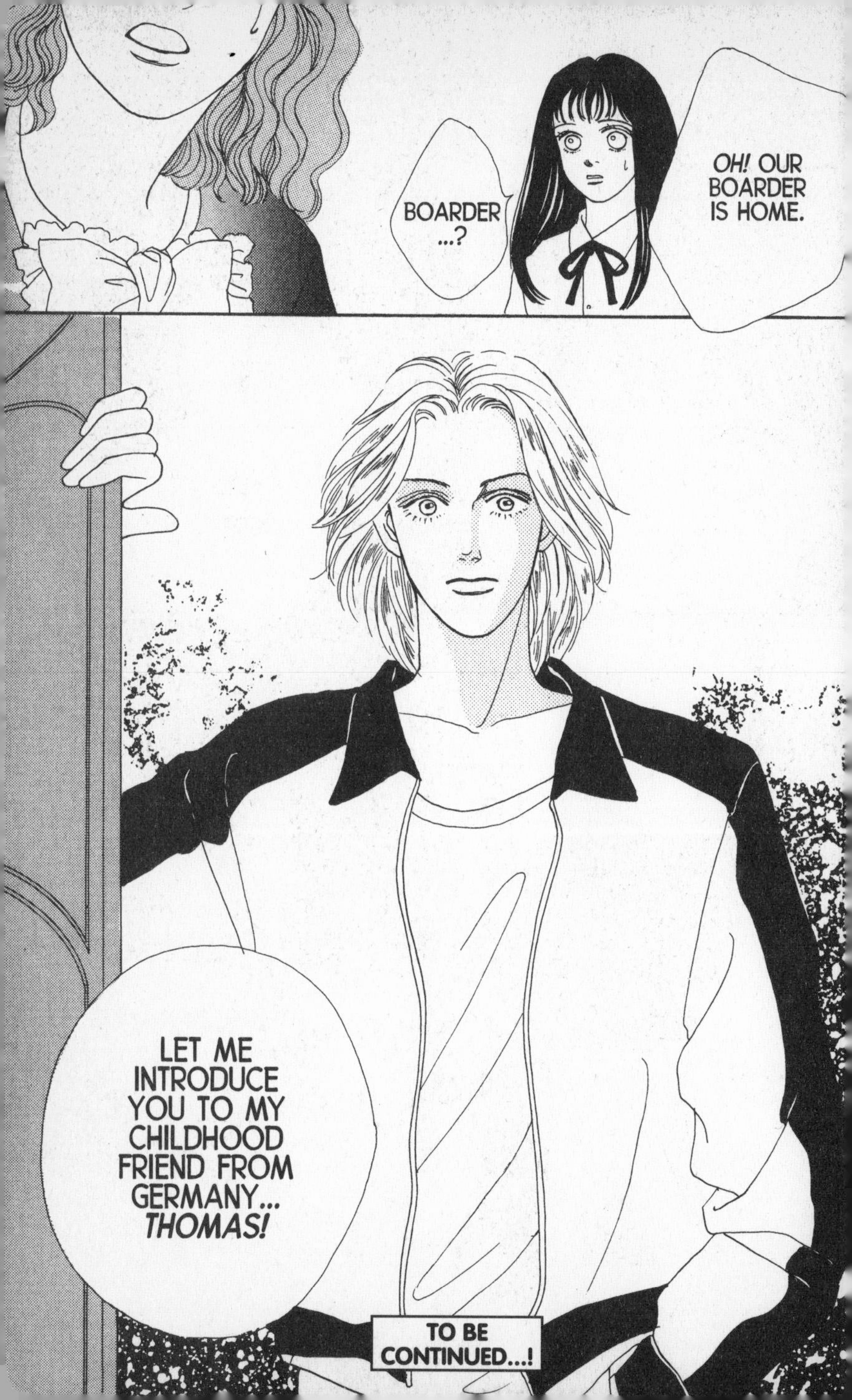
OH! OUR BOARDER IS HOME.
BOARDER ...?
LET ME INTRODUCE YOU TO MY CHILDHOOD FRIEND FROM GERMANY... *THOMAS!*
TO BE CONTINUED...!

EDITOR'S RECOMMENDATIONS

Hello, ***Hana Yori Danga*** fans I won't be gushing about my personal romantic life in my column this month. Now, you may be wondering why…well it's a secret! But, don't worry it isn't very exciting anyway. Hopefully I'll have something like that to share in the next volume.

Since Yoko Kamio mentioned her birthday in this volume I've been thinking about what we could do to celebrate it. Let's all rack our brains and see what we could come up with. Send in your ideas to:

Boys over Flowers
Birthday Bash
VIZ, LLC
P.O. Box 77010
San Francisco, CA 94107

If you enjoyed this volume of

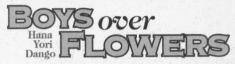

BOYS over FLOWERS
Hana Yori Dango

then here's some more manga you might be interested in.

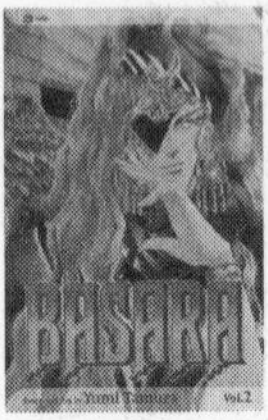
BASARA
Yumi Tamura
©1991Yumi Tamura/
Shogakukan, Inc.

BASARA

Yumi Tamura's BASARA is a post-apocalyptic fantasy/adventure series and was one of the most popular shôjo manga of the '90s in Japan. BASARA takes place in a very different setting than BOYS OVER FLOWERS, but it is similar at its core. They both feature a strong female fighting against an oppressive group. This is the story of how a young girl becomes "the child of destiny", seeking revenge for her dead twin brother. BASARA is heavier on the action and lighter on the humor than BOYS OVER FLOWERS.

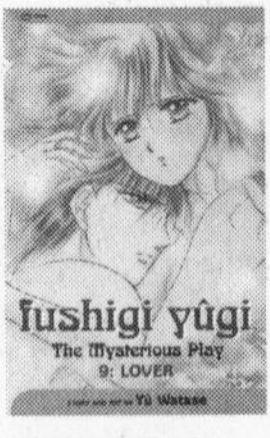
fushigi yûgi
The Mysterious Play
9: LOVER
Yû Watase
©1992 Yuu Watase/
Shogakukan, Inc.

FUSHIGI YÛGI

In Yû Watase's FUSHIGI YÛGI we follow the young girl, Miaka Yuki as she gets pulled into the world of a book, The Universe of the Four Gods. Within this book is a fictional, ancient Chinese world. In this world she becomes the priestess of the god Suzaku and must find all seven of her Celestial-Warrior protectors. This story is filled with romance and action with a dash of humor.

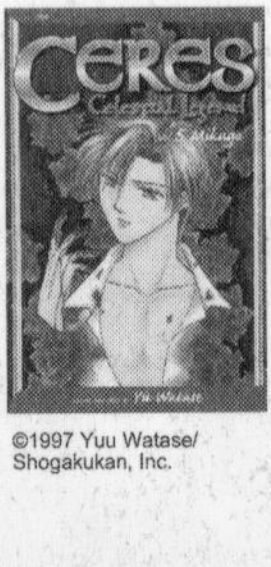
Ceres
Celestial Legend
©1997 Yuu Watase/
Shogakukan, Inc.

CERES: CESLESTIAL LEGEND

Also by Yû Watase, CERES: CESLESTIAL LEGEND is a somewhat darker than FUSHIGI YÛGI. It centers around a 16-year-old girl whose body houses a legendary power, and her family is determined to kill her in order to suppress it.

shôjo

AT THE HEART OF THE MATTER

- Banana Fish
- Basara
- Boys over Flowers
  ~ Hana Yori Dango*
- Ceres, Celestial Legend*
- Fushigi Yûgi
- Marionette Generation
- Please Save My Earth
- ◀ Revolutionary Girl Utena
- Wedding Peach
- X/1999

*Start Your Shôjo Graphic
Novel Collection Today!*

Also available on DVD from VIZ

www.viz.com

COMPLETE OUR SURVEY AND LET US KNOW WHAT YOU THINK!

☐ Please check here if you DO NOT wish to receive information or future offers from VIZ

Name: _____

Address: _____

City: _____ State: _____ Zip: _____

E-mail: _____

☐ Male ☐ Female Date of Birth (mm/dd/yyyy): ___/___/_____ (Under 13? Parental consent required)

What race/ethnicity do you consider yourself? (please check one)

☐ Asian/Pacific Islander   ☐ Black/African American   ☐ Hispanic/Latino

☐ Native American/Alaskan Native   ☐ White/Caucasian   ☐ Other: _____

What VIZ product did you purchase? (check all that apply and indicate title purchased)

☐ DVD/VHS _____

☐ Graphic Novel _____

☐ Magazines _____

☐ Merchandise _____

Reason for purchase: (check all that apply)

☐ Special offer   ☐ Favorite title   ☐ Gift

☐ Recommendation   ☐ Other _____

Where did you make your purchase? (please check one)

☐ Comic store   ☐ Bookstore   ☐ Mass/Grocery Store

☐ Newsstand   ☐ Video/Video Game Store ☐ Other: _____

☐ Online (site: _____)

What other VIZ properties have you purchased/own? _____

_____

How many anime and/or manga titles have you purchased in the last year? How many were VIZ titles? (please check one from each column)

ANIME	MANGA	VIZ
☐ None	☐ None	☐ None
☐ 1-4	☐ 1-4	☐ 1-4
☐ 5-10	☐ 5-10	☐ 5-10
☐ 11+	☐ 11+	☐ 11+

I find the pricing of VIZ products to be: (please check one)

☐ Cheap ☐ Reasonable ☐ Expensive

What genre of manga and anime would you like to see from VIZ? (please check two)

☐ Adventure ☐ Comic Strip ☐ Science Fiction ☐ Fighting

☐ Horror ☐ Romance ☐ Fantasy ☐ Sports

What do you think of VIZ's new look?

☐ Love It ☐ It's OK ☐ Hate It ☐ Didn't Notice ☐ No Opinion

Which do you prefer? (please check one)

☐ Reading right-to-left

☐ Reading left-to-right

Which do you prefer? (please check one)

☐ Sound effects in English

☐ Sound effects in Japanese with English captions

☐ Sound effects in Japanese only with a glossary at the back

THANK YOU! Please send the completed form to:

VIZ

NJW Research
42 Catharine St.
Poughkeepsie, NY 12601

All information provided will be used for internal purposes only. We promise not to sell or otherwise divulge your information.